Indigenous and Minority Placenames

Aboriginal History Incorporated
Aboriginal History Inc. is a part of the Australian Centre for Indigenous History, Research School of Social Sciences, The Australian National University, and gratefully acknowledges the support of the School of History and the National Centre for Indigenous Studies, The Australian National University. Aboriginal History Inc. is administered by an Editorial Board which is responsible for all unsigned material. Views and opinions expressed by the author are not necessarily shared by Board members.

Contacting Aboriginal History
All correspondence should be addressed to the Editors, Aboriginal History Inc., ACIH, School of History, RSSS, 9 Fellows Road (Coombs Building), Acton, ANU, 2601, or aboriginal.history@anu.edu.au.

WARNING: Readers are notified that this publication may contain names or images of deceased persons.

Indigenous and Minority Placenames

AUSTRALIAN AND INTERNATIONAL PERSPECTIVES

Edited by

Ian D. Clark, Luise Hercus and Laura Kostanski

PRESS

Published by ANU Press and Aboriginal History Inc.
The Australian National University
Acton ACT 2601, Australia
Email: anupress@anu.edu.au
This title is also available online at http://press.anu.edu.au

National Library of Australia Cataloguing-in-Publication entry

Author: Clark, Ian D., 1958- author.

Title: Indigenous and minority placenames :
Australian and international perspectives
Ian D. Clark, Luise Hercus and Laura Kostanski.

Series: Aboriginal history monograph;

ISBN: 9781925021622 (paperback) 9781925021639 (ebook)

Subjects: Names, Geographical--Aboriginal Australian.
Names, Geographical--Australia.

Other Authors/Contributors:
Hercus, Luise, author.
Kostanski, Laura, author.

Dewey Number: 919.4003

All rights reserved. No part of this publication may be reproduced, stored in a retrieval system or transmitted in any form or by any means, electronic, mechanical, photocopying or otherwise, without the prior permission of the publisher.

Cover design by Nic Welbourn and layout by ANU Press

This edition © 2014 ANU Press

Contents

Notes on Contributors vii

1. Introduction: Indigenous and Minority Placenames – Australian and International Perspectives 1
   Ian D. Clark, Luise Hercus, and Laura Kostanski

2. Comitative placenames in central NSW 11
   David Nash

3. The diminutive suffix *-dool* in placenames of central north NSW 39
   David Nash

4. Placenames as a guide to language distribution in the Upper Hunter, and the *landnám* problem in Australian toponomastics . 57
   Jim Wafer

5. Illuminating the cave names of Gundungurra country 83
   Jim Smith

6. Doing things with toponyms: the pragmatics of placenames in Western Arnhem Land 97
   Murray Garde

7. Locating Seven Rivers 123
   Fiona Powell

8. 'Many were killed from falling over the cliffs': The naming of Mount Wheeler, Central Queensland 147
   Jonathan Richards

9. Saltwater Placenames around Mer in the Torres Strait 163
   Nick Piper

10. Pinning down Kaurna names: Linguistic issues arising in the development of the Kaurna Place Names Database 187
    Rob Amery and Vincent (Jack) Kanya Buckskin

11. One name for one Place – but it is not always so 213
    Luise Hercus

12. Why did squatters in colonial Victoria use Indigenous placenames for their sheep stations? 225
    Fred (David) Cahir

13. Multiple Aboriginal placenames in western and central Victoria 239
    Ian D. Clark

14. Dissonance surrounding the Aboriginal origin of a selection of placenames in Victoria, Australia: Lessons in lexical ambiguity 251
    Ian D. Clark

15. Duel-Names: How toponyms (placenames) can represent hegemonic histories and alternative narratives 273
    Laura Kostanski

16. Water for country, words for water: Indigenous placenames of north-west Victoria and south-west New South Wales . . 293
    Edward Ryan

17. Obtuse anglers: The linguistics and ethnography of fishing ground names on Norfolk Island 305
    Joshua Nash

18. Sámi placenames, power relations and representation 325
    Kaisa Rautio Helander

19. Please adjust your bearings... 351
    Huia Pacey

20. Accommodating the Inuit majority: Traditional placenames in Nunavut today 365
    Lynn Peplinski

21. Khoisan indigenous toponymic identity in South Africa 381
    Peter E. Raper

Notes on Contributors

Dr Rob Amery, University of Adelaide

Rob Amery completed a PhD in 1998 at the University of Adelaide (published in August 2000) on Kaurna language reclamation. For the last 25 years he has worked closely with members of the Kaurna community to reclaim their language from historical materials and to develop the language for use in a range of contemporary contexts. In 2002, along with Kaurna Elders, he established Kaurna Warra Pintyanthi (KWP) through which he coordinates a research program into the Kaurna language, including placenames research, and facilitates the development of Kaurna language resources. Through KWP, Rob serves as consultant linguist to Kaurna programs in schools and various community projects and naming activity. In the 1980s he worked in a range of Aboriginal communities in Central Australia, the Top End and Kimberley regions. In 1993–94 he developed the innovative Australian Indigenous Languages Framework (AILF) for the teaching of Aboriginal languages in senior secondary studies.

Vincent (Jack) Kanya Buckskin, Kaurna Warra Pintyanthi, University of Adelaide

Vincent, or Jack, as he prefers to be called, is a Kaurna and Narrunga man. Jack began working on Kaurna language projects at the University of Adelaide including the Southern Kaurna Placenames, Kaurna in the Public Arena, Kaurna Learners' Guide and Kaurna Phonology projects. Jack began teaching Kaurna language at Warriparinga together with Rob Amery through the School of Languages in 2007. He has been the main teacher of Kaurna since then running three evening classes for adults as well as in schools during the day. Jack is a leading member of the Kaurna dance group called *Kuma Kaaru* and previously danced with *Taikurtinna* where he integrates Kaurna language into his performances. When not working and performing Jack likes to research and learn more about his culture and the history of his people. In July 2009 Jack was an invited participant at the 'Young, Gifted and BLAK' Aboriginal writers' workshop in Sydney with Alexis Wright. In 2011 he was recognised as SA Young Australian of the Year in recognition of his efforts. In 2013, *Buckskin*, an hour-long documentary profiling Jack's re-engagement with his language, was broadcast on ABC TV.

Dr David (Fred) Cahir, Federation University Australia

Fred Cahir is a senior lecturer in Indigenous Studies and the Australian History Higher Degree by Research program coordinator at Federation University Australia. His research interests include Victorian Aboriginal history and Aboriginal Ecological Knowledge in south-eastern Australia. His latest book publications are: *Black Gold: Aboriginal People on the Goldfields of Victoria 1850–1870* (Aboriginal History Inc. and ANU Press) and *The Aboriginal Story of Burke and Wills: Forgotten Narratives*, co-edited with Ian D. Clark.

Professor Ian D. Clark, Federation University Australia

Ian D. Clark is a Professor of Tourism in the Faculty of Business, at Federation University Australia. He completed his PhD in Aboriginal Historical Geography at Monash University in 1992. His areas of interest include Victorian Aboriginal history, Indigenous tourism, the history of tourism, and Victorian toponyms. He has been publishing in Victorian Aboriginal history since 1982. Recent works include I.D. Clark and D. Cahir (eds), *The Aboriginal Story of Burke and Wills: Forgotten Narratives* (CSIRO Publishing, Melbourne, 2013); and I.D. Clark, *'Prettily situated' at Mungallook: A History of the Goulburn River Aboriginal Protectorate Station at Murchison, Victoria, 1840–1853* (Ballarat Heritage Services Publishing, Ballarat, 2013).

Dr Murray Garde, The Australian National University

Murray Garde is a Research Fellow in the School of Culture, History and Language, at The Australian National University. His research interests have largely focused on the ethnography of communication in western and central-north Arnhem Land. Most of this work straddles the disciplines of anthropology and linguistics and is aimed at establishing long–term community-based projects that promote and maintain the use of endangered or minority languages, especially in Western Arnhem Land and on Pentecost Island in north-central Vanuatu. As a result he has paid attention to an eclectic range of cultural domains from kinship reference in everyday conversation, the language of myth and ritual, the language of traditional music (both song texts and metalinguistic aspects), concepts of health and the human body, the language of interaction with landscapes such as residence, land tenure, landscape burning, geomorphology, ecological zones, ethnobiology, rock art and toponymy. His present interests are community-based language maintenance programs, interpreting, translation and cultural site documentation in Kakadu National Park and the Arnhem Land Plateau. He is also involved in a vernacular literacy and language documentation project with speakers of the Sa language of southern Pentecost Island, Vanuatu.

Dr Kaisa Rautio Helander, Sámi allaskuvla, Sámi University College, Norway

Kaisa Rautio Helander is Associate Professor of Sámi and Finnish languages at Sámi allaskuvla | Sámi University College in Guovdageaidnu, Norway. She holds a PhD in Sámi language from the University of Oulu in Finland. Her doctoral thesis is a multi-disciplinary study of the history of official placename policy in Norway with regard to Indigenous toponymy. Among her current onomastic research interests are theoretical and methodological questions concerning the politics of naming, recognition of indigenous toponymy, colonial naming practices and contact-onomastics.

Dr Luise Hercus, The Australian National University

Dr. Luise Hercus (AM) was Reader in Sanskrit at The Australian National University and is now Visiting Fellow in the School of Literature, Languages and Linguistics. She has worked on Aboriginal languages and traditions for over 50 years, mainly in the Lake Eyre region.

Dr Laura Kostanski, Federation University Australia

Dr Laura Kostanski is the CEO and Director of Geonaming Solutions Pty Ltd. Her professional and research interests centre on developing robust geospatial, addressing and geographic naming policies and systems for government and private clients at national and international levels. She is a Churchill Fellow, an Adjunct Research Fellow at Federation University Australia, a Member of the Open Geospatial Consortium, a Director of the International Council of Onomastic Sciences, has been an Australian representative to the United

Nations Group of Experts on Geographic Names and recently was successful in collaborating to receive an Australian Research Council Linkage Grant. Laura has been Research Manager and Gazetteer Expert for the CSIRO Spatial Identifier Reference Framework (SIRF) program which examined methods for reengineering gazetteer development, maintenance and output processes with a key focus on Indonesia. In her previous role as Project Manager at the Office of Geographic Names Victoria (OGN Vic) she was involved in policy development, governance and stakeholder engagement in the spatial science domain and was involved in the development of the new *Guidelines for Geographic Names Victoria*. Laura is currently working on geonaming policy projects for the State Government of New South Wales and the Government of Abu Dhabi.

Dr David Nash, The Australian National University and Australian Institute of Aboriginal and Torres Strait Islander Studies

David Nash is an Honorary Visiting Fellow, School of Literature, Languages and Linguistics, The Australian National University (ANU) and Honorary Visitor, Australian Institute of Aboriginal and Torres Strait Islander Studies (AIATSIS). He grew up in central New South Wales, and graduated from ANU and MIT. In the 1980s and 1990s he was involved in a number of claims to traditional land in Australia, and in the mapping of sites in the country of the Warlpiri and their neighbours in central Australia. Over the last three decades he has published on Australian languages, including co-editing *Language in Native Title* (2002) and *Forty Years On: Ken Hale and Australian Languages* (2001).

Dr Joshua Nash, University of Adelaide

Joshua Nash is a visiting research fellow in linguistics at the University of Adelaide. He has conducted linguistic fieldwork on Norfolk Island since 2007. Joshua is the author of *Insular Toponymies* (John Benjamins, 2013).

Huia Pacey

Putauaki me Tapuwae o Uenuku nga maunga

Ko Tarawera me Hapuku nga awa

Ko Ngai Tahu me Tuwharetoa oku iwi.

Ko Huia ahau

Huia Pacey is an alumna of Lincoln University (New Zealand). She holds one of only two Masters of Indigenous Planning and Development degrees to have been conferred by that University. She has presented at a number of national and international conferences on placenames including a co-keynote presentation at the inaugural International Conference on Indigenous Place Names in Guovdageaidnu, Norway in 2010. Huia is an experienced cultural mapper and has worked with a number of New Zealand tribes mapping their sites of significance and recording their traditional placenames. Huia is currently the Chair of Te Kahui Manu Hokai (Maori GIS Association) and currently the Pouarahi (Maori Heritage Advisor) for the New Zealand Historic Places Trust Southern Region.

Lynn Peplinski, Inuit Heritage Trust, Nunavut

Lynn Peplinski, based in Iqaluit, Nunavut, has been researching traditional Inuit placenames with a view to getting them onto maps and bringing them to official status, since 1993. She has been with the Inuit Heritage Trust, a Nunavut Land Claims organisation whose mandate encompasses issues related to archaeology, heritage and placenames since 2001.

Nick Piper

Nick Piper is a postgraduate student at James Cook University. She has been involved with linguistic research in the eastern islands of Torres Strait since 1987. She compiled a grammar of Meriam Mir (Meryam Mir) for her MA (The Australian National University, 1989). From 2005 to 2008, she and Alo Tapim of Mer designed and delivered a Meriam language program through the Batchelor Institute of Indigenous Education. She produced the language report for Akiba on behalf of the Torres Strait Islanders of the Regional Seas Claim Group, and interpreted for a Meriam witness.

Dr Fiona Powell

Fiona Powell is a Canberra-based independent consultant anthropologist. Her doctoral research, conducted in the early 1970s, investigated developments in local and social organisation in south-east Cape York. Since 1995 she has worked as a consultant anthropologist and has prepared reports and provided advice on native title matters in Torres Strait, New South Wales, Queensland and Western Australia.

Professor Peter E. Raper, University of the Free State, South Africa

Peter Edmund Raper, Professor Extraordinary in Linguistics and Research Fellow, Department of Linguistics and Language Practice, University of the Free State, Bloemfontein, South Africa. Educated at the University of the Witwatersrand (PhD 1971), he is a member of the joint IGU Commission on Toponymy/ICA Working Group on Toponymy. He was head of the Onomastic Research Centre of the Human Sciences Research Council in Pretoria from 1970 to 1993. He was a member of the National Place Names Committee of South Africa from 1972 until 1999, and served as Chairman of this body from 1996 to 1999. He was President of the Names Society of Southern Africa from 1989 to 2006, and has served on the Editorial Board of the journal *Nomina Africana* since its inception in 1987. He has been a member of the American Name Society (ANS) since 1981, and serves on the Editorial Advisory Board of the journal *Names, a Journal of Onomastics*. He was South African delegate to the United Nations Group of Experts on Geographical Names (UNGEGN) from 1984 to 2002, and served as Chairman of the Group from 1991 to 2002. His publications include *Bushman (San) Influence on Zulu Place Names* (2013) and the *New Dictionary of Southern African Place Names*, of which the 4th edition, co-authored by Lucie A. Möller and L. Theodorus du Plessis, is at the press. He is currently researching Bushman (San) substructures of placenames in southern Africa.

Dr Jonathan Richards, University of Queensland

Jonathan Richards is an Adjunct Research Fellow, School of History, Philosophy, Religion and Classics, University of Queensland. He completed a Bachelor of Arts in Australian and Comparative Studies in 1995, and a Bachelor of Arts with Honours in 1997. After his doctoral thesis on Queensland's Native Police was accepted in 2005, he continued research into frontier policing and violence in Queensland, Indigenous and community history, and death in Queensland. He is currently engaged, with Professor Lyndall Ryan from the University of Newcastle, in an Australian Research Council funded investigation into frontier violence across Australia.

Edward J. Ryan, La Trobe University

Edward Ryan is a postgraduate student in the History Department of La Trobe University and is currently researching the history of the Wergaia and neighbouring peoples of north-west Victoria and south-west New South Wales. Besides placenames, his other research interests include landscape and environment change in the greater Mallee region. In a broader context he pursues similar research interests in Irish and Scottish Gaelic history, language and literature.

Dr Jim Smith

Jim Smith is a zoologist and independent researcher who works as a heritage and environmental consultant. He completed his doctoral research at Macquarie University, Department of Indigenous Studies. A special interest is the mapping of Aboriginal and non-Aboriginal cultural landscapes of the Blue Mountains.

Dr Jim Wafer, University of Newcastle

Jim Wafer is a retired anthropologist with a conjoint position at the University of Newcastle, and a member of the University's Endangered Languages Documentation, Theory and Application research group. His work with Aboriginal languages spans a period of almost 40 years, and he is co-author (with Amanda Lissarrague) of *A Handbook of Aboriginal Languages of NSW and the ACT* (Muurrbay, 2008).

1. Introduction: Indigenous and Minority Placenames – Australian and International Perspectives

Ian D. Clark
Federation University Australia

Luise Hercus
The Australian National University

Laura Kostanski
Federation University Australia

This book is the third volume in a series dedicated to Australian placenames. The earlier volumes are Koch and Hercus (eds) 2009, *Aboriginal Placenames: Naming and Re-Naming the Australian Landscape* (The Australian National University E Press and Aboriginal History), and Hercus, Hodges and Simpson (eds) 2002, *The Land is a Map: Placenames of Indigenous Origin in Australia* (Pandanus Books and Pacific Linguistics, Canberra). As in the earlier volumes, many of the papers in this volume originated as papers at a placenames conference, in this case one hosted by the University of Ballarat in 2007 that featured Australian and international speakers who spoke on aspects of Indigenous and minority toponyms. Added to these papers are three papers that are recipients of the Murray Chapman Award: Nash (Chapter 2) and Wafer (Chapter 4) won the award in 2011, and Nash (Chapter 3) in 2012. This award is sponsored by the Geographical Names Board of NSW. The papers have been arranged geographically, starting with New South Wales and ending with four international papers presented at the Ballarat conference.

The first collection of papers concerns New South Wales. The first paper by David Nash relates to comitative placenames in central NSW where he notes there is a concentration of placenames ending in *-dra*, *-drie*, *-dgery* and similar English spellings in central NSW. Historical investigation of these names reveals a subset with justifiable Wiradjuri etymologies, all involving the nominal Comitative ('with, having') suffix *-DHurray*. Similar placenames with less well known origins are also considered. The study reveals some patterns in the form of these placenames, including a previously unreported dependence of the form of the suffix on the final sound of the root word. The geographic distribution of the placenames is shown to match the extent of Wiradjuri country.

David Nash's second paper is on the diminutive suffix -*dool* in placenames of central north NSW where he has found there is a concentration of placenames ending in -*dool* (and -*dule*) in central northern NSW and adjacent Queensland, of which Angledool is probably the most widely known today. The study of over a dozen of these names shows they include the Gamilaraay and Yuwaalaraay nominal suffix -*DHuul*, with a definite or individuating meaning. The methodology of the study is to move from better known origins to inferred origins (and some speculation). General observations are made on the semantics of the stems, and of diminutives as toponyms. Another cluster of -*dool* placenames in the NSW Riverina is briefly discussed: there the syllable appears to be of disparate origins, and some -*dool* placenames are proposed to be a transplant (copied from central northern NSW).

Jim Wafer's paper is concerned with placenames as a guide to language distribution in the Upper Hunter, and the landnám problem in Australian toponomastics. The question of what language or languages were spoken in the Upper Hunter region of NSW is vexed. The NSW Aboriginal Languages Research and Resource Centre's current draft 'Map of NSW Aboriginal languages' leaves the Upper Hunter blank. In earlier attempts to identify the languages spoken in this region, from the coastal areas occupied by 'Awabakal' and 'Worimi' to the headwaters of the Hunter in the Great Dividing Range, Tindale filled the space with a language he called 'Geawegal', and the Central Mapping Authority ('CMA') of NSW and Horton followed suit. Brayshaw, on the other hand, analyses a number of historical documents that suggest a long-standing connection between speakers of 'Kamilaroi' and the upper Hunter, 'as far south as Wollombi Brook'. There seems to be little disagreement that the 'Kamilaroi' occupied the headwaters of the Hunter and the area around Murrurundi, close to the watershed. Further down the Hunter Valley, the literature often depicts the Kamilaroi as intruders. In relation specifically to the 'Geawegal', Fison and Howitt say that the latter 'were always in dread of war with the "Kamilaroi", who intruded down the heads of the Hunter across from Talbragar to the Munmurra waters, and even occasionally made raids as far as Jerry's Plains'. Wafer's paper attempts to throw some light on this matter, mainly through an analysis of placenames from the region, and then investigates some of the difficulties posed by landnám in the context of Aboriginal placenames. The term 'Geawegal' is investigated, since it has been given such prominence by Tindale and Horton and their scholarship remains the most influential record of Aboriginal language cartography.

Jim Smith's paper is concerned with the names of five caves in Gundungurra country which includes the catchments of the Wollondilly and Cox rivers. The caves are Jenolan, Womboyn, Tuglow, Colong, and Abercrombie. He analyses their etymology and their linguistic origins or etiology or 'the story behind the name'. He finds that Jenolan Caves and Colong Caves were named after nearby topographic features and are not the names of the localities to which they have been applied. He also discusses some of the meanings of the names in the sense of the mythological stories to which the names allude.

The next paper by Murray Garde concerns Western Arnhem Land in the Northern Territory. Garde notes that Australian Aboriginal cultures have dense systems of placenames, unsurprising given that they are used frequently in conversation and yet there has been little documentation of how placenames are used in interactions. In this paper he examines the pragmatics of placename use in everyday conversation in the Bininj Gunwok dialects of Western Arnhem Land. Gardes take an indexical approach to how placenames are used (and in certain contexts avoided) by the speaker in order to achieve a range of goals. These include recitation of placenames to create mental maps of walking routes, their use as deictics, personal expressions and their role in a certain kind of humorous language.

Fiona Powell's paper 'Locating Seven Rivers' is the first of two dealing with Queensland. Her paper describes the results of research about the Northern Cape York Peninsula (NCYP) placename 'Seven Rivers'. This placename occurs in the lexicons of English and NCYP Creole and in the NCYP ethno-historical, linguistic and genealogical records. It is also associated in these materials with places named 'Seven River', 'Severn River' and 'Seventh River'. Powell's initial research involved descendants of persons whose ancestors originated from places identified by these placenames. Powell established that there was no agreed view about whether these names referred to the same place or to different places, and her expanded investigation considers NCYP's wider toponymic history.

Jonathan Richards considers the naming of Mount Wheeler in central Queensland in the second contribution on Queensland. Many placenames in Queensland and Australia, at large, date from the frontier period. Some are ubiquitous but relatively harmless – for example, the many Rocky, Sandy and Stoney creeks – while other placenames are more sinister, including the various Murdering Creeks, Slaughterhouse Creeks, Skull Holes and Skeleton Creeks. These morbid names appear to refer to events that some Australians would rather forget, or deny ever happened. Richards further discusses a third group of names that commemorate pioneers, some of whom can also be connected with episodes of genocidal violence on the Australian frontier.

Nick Piper's paper is concerned with saltwater placenames around Mer in the Torres Strait. Specifically, the sources and meanings for saltwater placenames are examined based on the reefs and cays found around the Murray Islands (Mer, Dauar and Waier) in the eastern Torres Strait. These are named after ancestors, physical features such as shape, size, matter, location, wildlife or habitat, significant events. They can be conveyed literally or metaphorically. A singular feature of some saltwater placenames is their coincidence with a placename on land suggesting a close connection between land and sea. Comparisons with other Indigenous placename studies show remarkable similarities with a focus on the environment and its physical characteristics, connections to the flora and fauna, and mythological/ancestral associations. Furthermore, features from several categories are sometimes combined such as landscape and mythology. However, there are major differences with the mythological/ancestral names. While the Australian Aboriginal placenames evoke an event associated with the mythological being, the Meriam and Marquesan placenames are named overtly after the personal name of an ancestor.

South Australian toponymic issues are dealt with in the paper by Rob Amery and Vincent (Jack) Kanya Buckskin. They address some of the linguistic issues arising from the development of the Kaurna Placenames Database. They describe and analyse the linguistic issues arising in the course of developing a database of Kaurna placenames from the Adelaide Plains in South Australia. Kaurna people are in the process of reclaiming their identity and their language, a language that was considered to be 'extinct' by many or 'sleeping' by the people themselves. Kaurna people have expressed the view at Kaurna Warra Pintyandi (KWP) meetings that they wish to see Kaurna words spelt and pronounced correctly and they are keen to see that Aboriginal placenames in use on the Adelaide Plains conform to the sound patterns of the language. Consequently, names that appear to be of Indigenous origin are being sifted through – those that can be verified as Kaurna names are retained, others are discarded and some are translated into Kaurna or adapted into the Kaurna sound and spelling systems. The project is also attempting to pin down the meanings of Kaurna placenames. It can be shown that some etymologies previously recorded are fanciful, others verifiably false, while still others are highly questionable. In many cases we simply do not know. There are also difficulties in determining what a particular name relates to, or whether variants relate to the same word, or were in fact attempts to spell different though somewhat similar names. A set of principles for dealing with such uncertainty has been developed by KWP. Amery and Buckskin give many examples where these principles can be applied and other examples where they are still at a loss as to how we should deal with the names in question.

Luise Hercus's paper is entitled 'One name for one Place – but it is not always so'. She finds that Aboriginal placenames represent a very ancient layer of the vocabulary, just as placenames do in European traditions. Extensive work has been done on European river-names which, according to some scholars, are said to form the most ancient layer of the vocabulary, preceding the arrival of the Indo-Europeans. For a traditional Aboriginal person, as for the older Europeans, the geographical extent of their 'world' was much smaller than it is for people now in today's 'global village'. It was, however, infinitely more detailed and meaningful. Hercus looks at several aspects of Aboriginal placenames in the light of this: placenames may be old, but there is not an eternal relationship between a place and its name: there are cases of duplicates in name on the one hand, and dual naming on the other. Placenames are not immutable, there are cases where one can see new placenames evolve. Aboriginal placenames have special significance in the chronology of the creation of the landscape.

The final cluster of Australian papers is concerned with Victoria. Fred Cahir explores the question why did squatters in colonial Victoria use Indigenous placenames for their sheep stations? The archival records of many squatters in 19th century Victoria (formerly known as the Port Phillip District) often contain brief references to the processes involved in and decisions that led to the naming of their pastoral leases. This documentation in the official naming of a pastoral lease is unsurprising given that a squatter wishing to obtain a pastoral licence would have to register a legal document with the colonial government, stating the name of the run. What is perplexing is why a large number of pastoralists chose an Indigenous name. Most etymological discussions, in Australia at least, have largely centred on the placenames of towns, cities and geographical features such as rivers, mountains and lakes. The paper explores whether the same reasons Indigenous placenames were adopted in public spaces may also be applied to the private sphere of naming pastoral leases – the colonial desire to usurp placenames and their symbolism in 19th century frontier Australia.

Ian Clark discusses multiple Aboriginal placenames in western Victoria. In a recent paper on transparency versus opacity in Australian Aboriginal placenames, Michael Walsh noted that in 'Aboriginal Australia it is relatively common for a given place to have multiple names'. In providing an overview of multiple naming practices Walsh observed that he was unclear on how multiple naming operates and what its function is. Other than some case studies (such as, Schebeck on the Flinders Ranges, South Australia and Sutton on Cape York, Queensland) we are yet to gain a comprehensive picture of Aboriginal Australia. This paper builds on this discussion through a consideration of multiple naming in western Victoria using the results of research conducted by Clark and Heydon into Victorian Aboriginal placenames.

The second paper by Ian Clark is concerned with dissonance surrounding the Aboriginal origin of a selection of placenames in Victoria, Australia. In this paper Clark focuses on some 26 placenames for which there is dispute over their Aboriginal origin. These names are considered in some detail in an effort to resolve their lexical ambiguity to explain the reasons for the ambiguity and to find any patterns and causal factors. The merits of the claims and counter claims in each case are examined and an attempt made to categorise the assertion of Aboriginal etymology as either grounded in the historical evidence, or likely to be explained by folk etymology. The reasons for falsely attributing meanings include names based on structure or sound that may lack historical basis but have become accepted through common practice, or those names explained by false etymology that are unsupported by historical evidence or folk etymologies.

Laura Kostanski's paper is entitled 'Duel-Names: How toponyms can represent hegemonic histories and alternative narratives'. *Place identity* is stated to be a construct of emotional meaning through which societies assert social 'norms' and define cultural mores. Kostanski proposes that just as places assert hegemonic discourses, toponyms are powerful cultural tools utilised by societies to assist in defining social and cultural associations. Based on the available literature, place identity is formed through four key elements: history/memory, community, emotions and actions/events. Utilising data collected from residents near, or visitors familiar with, The Grampians (Gariwerd) National Park area in Victoria, Australia, (where the state government proposed in 1989–1990 to restore Indigenous names for the park and its various features) each of the four key elements is examined in an attempt to define whether they can form a new theory on toponymic identity. Kostanski asserts that those people who supported the restoration of Indigenous toponyms saw the potential for allocating counter-memories to the mainstream (colonially dominated) local histories, whilst opponents perceived the proposal to be an interference with the connections they made to local history. The paper concludes that toponymic identity can be defined as a construct through which people form links to history, allocate their memories and assert cultural ideologies.

Edward Ryan's paper entitled 'Water for country, words for water; Indigenous placenames of north-west Victoria and south-west New South Wales' discusses placenames of Indigenous origin of north-west Victoria and south-west New South Wales, continuing an exploration begun in his article 'Blown to Witewitekalk' in the book *The Land is a Map*. The question of the existence of placenames for areas of country rather than just specific localities is considered while 'regional' names and more specific placenames are examined in the light of their origin as sites of significance in creation stories, reflections of natural features or local flora. All featured placenames are considered in the light of the Aboriginal sources where identifiable and the relationships specific informants had to particular places across the region.

Moving on to Norfolk Island, Joshua Nash's paper is entitled 'Obtuse anglers: The linguistics and ethnography of fishing ground names on Norfolk Island'. The paper finds that fishing ground names provide an excellent example of place-creation being brought into existence by human necessity to name and remember. They are utilitarian placenames that are rarely mapped; they are easily forgotten and are some of the most ephemeral aspects of a people's toponymic inventory:

> It is not much use taking bearings if they are not accurately recorded for future reference. The human memory for such details is fickle and the eye is easily deceived. ... It is asking a lot to try to carry details of four points in the mind for each fishing point that may be worked. It is imperative that they be recorded, and it is a good idea to mark them on an Admiralty chart in similar manner [sic] to that used in our sketch. (Hardy 1974:227)

Nash's paper considers the historical and theoretical background of the toponymic role of fishing ground names. The relevance of fishing ground names to Norfolk toponymy and the Norf'k language is also outlined. A tagmemic analysis of Norf'k fishing ground forms offers reasons for the formal structure of these names. Finally a detailed analysis of a single fishing ground name is used to explore the role Norf'k fishing ground names hold in Norfolk toponymy as a whole and how fishing ground names can contribute at least in part to the writing of Norfolk's 'toponymic ethnography'.

The final cluster of papers is concerned with international perspectives into aspects of indigenous and minority placenames. In the first paper Kaisa Rautio Helander, considers power relations and representation in Sámi placenames. Language plays an important role in forming the social world and it is used to construct and shape social and political reality. According to Clark and Dear, 'language is studded with signs, icons or symbols, which may carry meanings in excess of the simple word being used'. Power relations are also institutionalised in language, at the same time as it functions as a means of social contact and communication. Language has the effect of including or excluding various groups and individuals according to their perception of the linguistically created 'reality'. As Taylor points out, 'it is language which enables us to draw boundaries, to pick some things out in contrast to others. Thus through language we formulate things, and thus come to have an articulated view of the world'.

The next paper from Huia Pacey is entitled 'Please adjust your bearings...' As an integral component of Māori culture, placenames are critical to maintaining identity and relationship to place. This paper will explore how 19th century survey programmes continue to affect contemporary identity relationships with place. It offers examples but looks beyond the historical narrative of a landscape where indigenous placenames were overlaid by early European explorers and colonists names – some of which are being re-commemorated by dual place naming. The purpose of the paper however, is to discuss a new placenaming phenomenon in New Zealand – where some land title appellations are changing to those of an imported survey system. This will mean some parcels of land will have three different names – the traditional, the historic and now the 'legal'. It is ironic when framed against the increase of dual placenames in New Zealand that names of land blocks attached to placenames commemorating ancestral connection may now be consigned to the 'other' alternative name. For a culture that relies on placenames as an integral part of identity – how will Māori preserve that relationship through future generations when their land blocks are named after and represented by a surveyors grid block?

Lynn Peplinski's paper concerns the Inuit languages in Canada. Canada is officially a bilingual nation with both English and French enjoying equal status even though only 23 per cent of the population considers French as their mother tongue and an overwhelming majority of Francophones (18.5 per cent) are concentrated in one province, the province of Quebec. Nunavut is a large territory of nearly 2 million km^2 comprising about one fifth of Canada's land mass. This large area has been home to Inuit and their predecessors for the past 4000 years. Today Nunavut boasts a population of about 27,000, 85 per cent of whom are Inuit, scattered in 23 communities. There are arguably two Inuit languages in Nunavut. Inuktitut is spoken in all but two communities, where Inuinnaqtun is spoken. Each community is made up of speakers of one or more language dialects depending upon where the family groups' ancestors lived prior to moving into established communities around 50 years ago. There can be many dialects present in one community, again depending on the land where individual families resided prior to moving into established settlements. Inuit Heritage Trust policy regarding naming features on maps aims to capture the most appropriate dialect for the place where possible. Thus, the dialects of descendants of family groups still closely tied to certain geographical areas will receive priority. Names for the same features in other dialects would appear in the legend of the map. This effort is also explicitly noted on the individual map sheets – an example of which Peplinski reproduces in this publication. The Inuit Heritage Trust has developed a theoretical model to address overlapping names for features between communities but it is as yet untested.

Moving to South Africa, Peter Raper considers Khoisan indigenous toponymic identity. The term Khoisan refers to the Khoikhoi ('Hottentot') and San ('Bushman'), and to the languages spoken by them. These people are the indigenous peoples of Southern Africa, and were the first to name features of the landscape. African peoples migrated southwards from Central Africa, followed by French, Dutch, British, German and other peoples from Europe and Asia. Each wave of migrants adopted existing placenames, adapting them phonologically and later orthographically, translating some names fully or partially, and bestowing new names in their own language. On the basis of lexical meanings of the names preserved in oral tradition or written records, and by syntactic and morphological analysis, African and European language names are shown in many cases to be adaptations, translations and folk-etymological interpretations of original Khoisan names. To demonstrate this, phonological processes and semantic comparisons are employed, and syntactic constructions of African language names compared with those of Khoisan ones. Lexical cognates are indicated and sound-shifts identified, many displaying click replacements, coalescence of vowel clusters, consonant and vowel adaptation, etc.

The focus of the Ballarat conference was current trends in toponymic research as they relate to Indigenous and minority placenames. The papers presented here provide us with insight into the quality of the research that is being undertaken here in Australia and in other countries such as Canada, Finland, South Africa, New Zealand, and Norway.

Reference

Hardy, W. 1974, *The Saltwater Angler,* Fifth edition, Murray, Sydney.

2. Comitative placenames in central NSW[1]

David Nash

The Australian National University and Australian Institute of Aboriginal and Torres Strait Islander Studies

1. Introduction

Jerilderie, Narrandera, Cootamundra, Gilgandra are placenames familiar beyond their districts in inland New South Wales (NSW), and the casual observer can notice dozens of placenames with similar endings *-dra, -drie, -dgery* (and other English spellings), all taken (correctly) to be of Indigenous origin. The places with these names are all in inland NSW, and not in adjacent Victoria (or elsewhere in Australia).

The common ending of these placenames reflect a particular ending in Wiradjuri, a widespread Indigenous language of inland NSW. Indeed the ending is also present in the name of the language, and has had dozens of variant spellings, notably Wiradhuri, and Waradgery (as in the commemorative names Waradgery County and Waradgery Shire centred on Hay). The ending (or suffix) involved indicates a meaning which in English is conveyed by a separate word such as 'with', 'having', 'accompanied by', and so on. The term Comitative or Proprietive has been used to designate a suffix with such meanings; here I use Comitative to denote the suffix. The modern Wiradjuri dictionary lists the suffix thus:

> *-dhuray* having, often used in place names applied to the name of an animal or vegetable, as in the following: Cootamundra (*gudhamang-dhuray* = having tortoise), Narrandera (*ngarrang-dhuray*, having frilled-lizard) Jerildery (*dyiril-dhuray*, having reeds) (R)[2] (Grant and Rudder 2010: 351)

This study looks into the etymology of placenames bearing the *-dhuray* suffix and shows that the evidence of these placenames can throw light on linguistic matters (such as on variation in morphology), on linguistic geography, and potentially on some aspects of culture.

---

1 This study overlaps with my presentation on the Wiradjuri Comitative suffix to the 11th Australian Languages Workshop, hosted by the University of Queensland at its Moreton Bay Research Station, Stradbroke Island, on 9-11 March 2012, and to the Parkes Wiradjuri Language Group on 13 March 2012. I am grateful to the participants, and subsequently to Ray Wood, for helpful comments. An earlier version of the data was included in Nash (1974), and Donaldson's (1984,1985) work on related topics has provided guidance.
2 (R) is a reference to the source Richards (1902–03).

2. Method

This study concentrates on the most securely documented instances of Comitative placenames: ones with a convincing combination of supporting information. I take as convincing the combination of two kinds of information from old sources (usually a source dating from the 19th century[3] when the Wiradjuri language was still widely known): (a) an attribution of meaning to the particular placename bearing the Comitative suffix, together with (b) a corroboration in the Wiradjuri lexicon of the implied stem. Thus we are considering the more securely documented placenames with an etymology based on older records ('testimony') and wordlist data. For these we can have 'greatest certainty about the meaning of a placename' (Koch 2009: 147–148).

The investigation began when I combed the historical sources on Wiradjuri, and on other sources which include placename origins for the general area including Wiradjuri country. I compiled a list of those placenames apparently bearing the Wiradjuri Comitative suffix (ones terminating in -*dra*, -*drie*, -*dgery* etc) and concentrated on those with supporting etymological information.

As a check whether I had overlooked relevant placenames, I used the Geographical Names Register (GNR) of NSW (Geographical Names Board 2011). All names with location west of Longitude 150°E were extracted from the GNR, as the 150°E meridian falls conveniently to the east of Wiradjuri country and excludes most of the NSW placenames on and east of the Great Dividing Range (which form the majority). This subset of NSW placenames was then sorted from the end of the word, thereby grouping spellings ending such as *dra*, *dry*, *drie*, *dgery*, *gerie*, and some in *dara*. For only a handful of the extracted placenames does the GNR provide any 'Meaning' information (and what does occur usually repeats information I had already found in an old source).

These potentially relevant placenames and the etymological information (where available) were combined into a spreadsheet along with attributes of location and feature type.[4] Along with the coordinates these placenames were transferred (via CSV format and GPSBabel+ software) to a KML file, and then displayed with software such as Google Maps, Google Earth, and QGIS.

---

3   The majority of the sources are lists published in the early 1900s in the journal *Science of Man* (SM). These lists are usually traceable to manuscript lists reproduced in Royal Anthropological Society of Australia (2004), comprising manuscript questionnaires on placenames returned in about 1899 from local Police and other officials.

4   The placenames in the spreadsheet can also be grouped into 'toponymic sets': placenames which involve the same base name (in the same spelling) in the one locality. Typically the places in such a set are differentiatied by feature type, and/or by various derivations of the base name (such as *Tenandra Creek, Tenandra Hill, Tenandra Plain, Tenandra Knob*). In this study, the toponymic sets were simplified by excluding names of the built environment, and prefering those of natural features and of intermediate types such as names of trignometrical stations (usually on a hill or mountain summit) or localities or cadastral divisions (parishes and counties).

2. Comitative placenames in central NSW

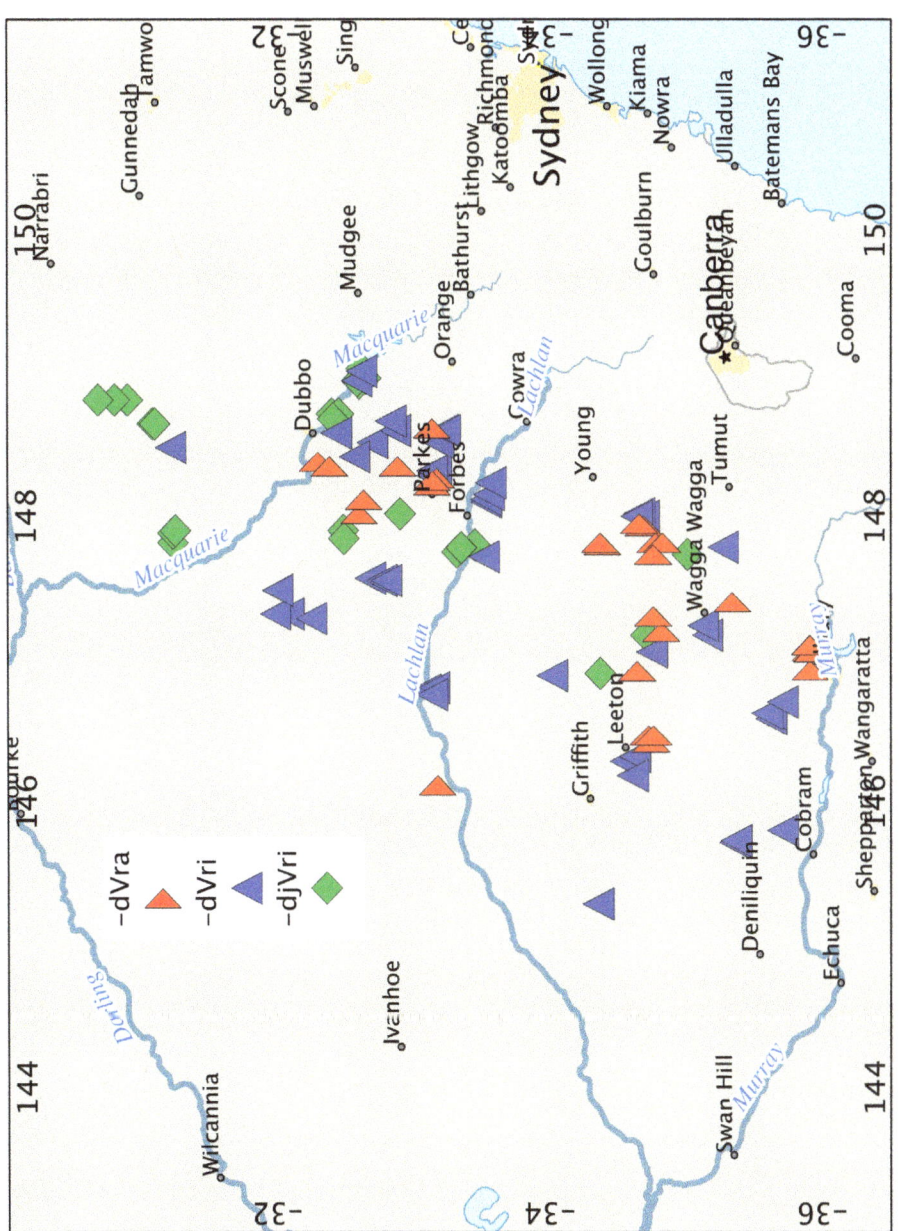

Map 1: Location of placenames with the Comitative suffix, from historical sources (table 1), Equirectangular projection.

Source: Made with QGIS and Natural Earth, free vector and raster map data from naturalearthdata.com.

13

3. Wiradjuri Comitative placenames

As can be seen in map 1, the placenames of this study form a north-south band across central NSW. The form of the ending falls into three main types, as indicated by the location symbol used on the map:

1. -dVra   *dera, dra*   Narrandera, Gilgandra, ...

2. -dVri   *dry, drie, darie, thery*   Jerilderie, Mulyandry, ...

3. -djVri   *dgery, gerie, gery, jerry*   Eumungerie, Coradgery, ...

The placenames shown in map 1 are listed in table 1 along with information on the etymology. The first four columns provide the coordinates (in decimal degrees), the placename, and its feature type. All this information has been copied from the GNR where possible, however a few extra placenames are included from other sources. The 'source' column in table 1 is where the placename is associated with a meaning in old (usually 19th century) records. The 'stem' and 'gloss' column provides the stem and its meaning (usually in Grant and Rudder's spelling or sometimes a similar spelling using cover symbols such as R for an indeterminate rhotic, or D for an indeterminate non-peripheral stop consonant).

Note that the first vowel of the Comitative suffix is the high vowel /u/, and so placenames ending like *dara* are unlikely candidates to involve the Comitative suffix. This fits with the lack of etymological information for any of the potential candidates (such as *Wattamondara*). Also, no placenames happen to be included whose spelling terminates like *djVra*, again because for none of the candidates (such as *Cookamidgera*) is there etymological information.

In table 2 are other placenames in the same general area which appear to involve the Comitative ending, with for each the Wiradjuri stem which appears best to match with the form of the placename. The placenames in Table 2, however, lack supporting testimony from older sources, and the association with the Wiradjuri stem is no more than a suggestion, one that may tested by further research. The placenames listed in Table 2 are shown on Map 2.

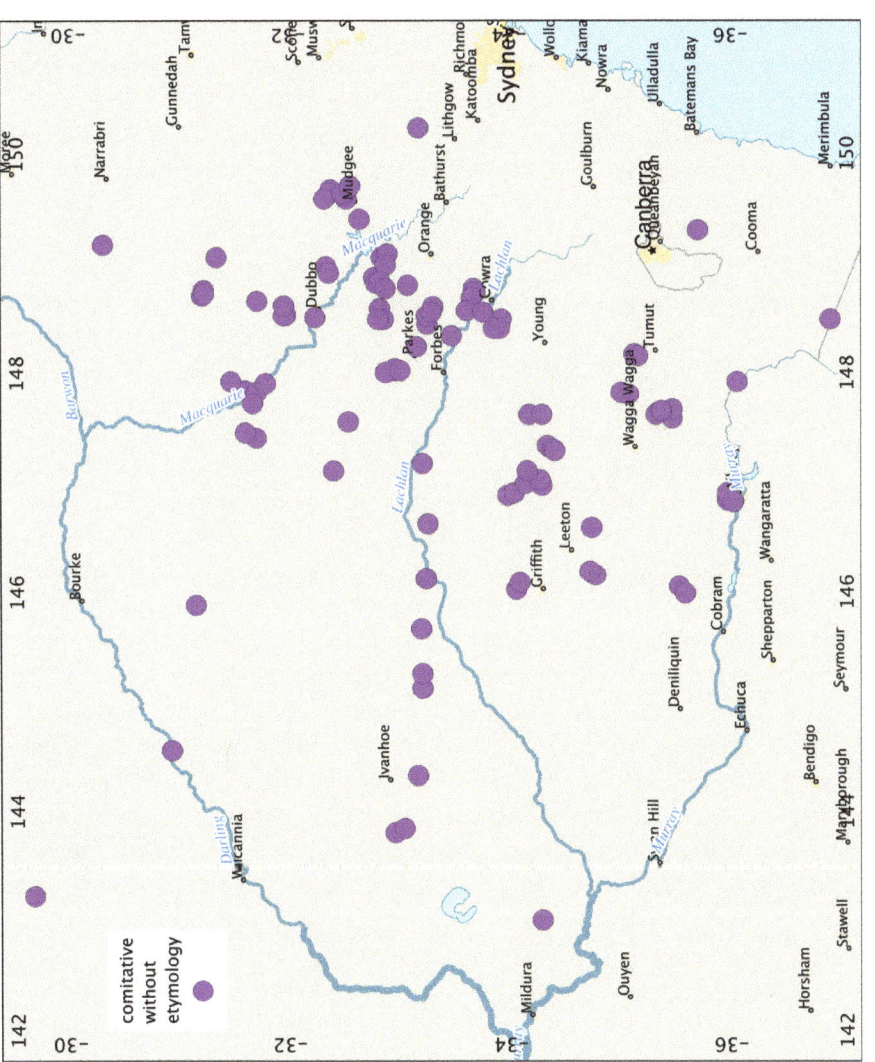

Map 2: Location of placenames possibly with the Comitative suffix, without historical corroboration (Table 2), Equirectangular projection.

Source: Made with QGIS and Natural Earth, free vector and raster map data from naturalearthdata.com.

4. Discussion

Now that we have assembled the fairly secure information in Table 1 (and Map 1), and the more speculative but nonetheless valuable information in Table 2 (and Map 2), we can make some generalisations about the geographic distribution of the Wiradjuri Comitative placenames, and about the form of the suffix, and about its meaning and that of words bearing the suffix.

4.1. Geographic distribution

The placenames with a fairly secure Wiradjuri etymology (those in Table 1 and on Map 1) are, unsurprisingly, within the territory of Wiradjuri. This can be seen more clearly on Map 3, on which the language areas have been marked by Bowern (2011) in accordance with Tindale's (1970) map and similar sources.

The only names not within the Wiradjuri area indicated on Map 3 are a couple of names (*Cajildry* etc, and *Gradgery*) within Ngiyampaa country not far northwest of Wiradjuri country, and *Teridgerie* in the north. Interestingly the GNR tells us that *Teridgerie Creek* has *Terembone Creek* as an alternate name, and previous names 'Myall Creek; Urawilkie or Terembong Creek Teridg; Urawilkie Creek'; among these *Terembone ~ Terembong* bears the Comitative suffix *-buwan* of the local language.

The names of Table 1 are noticeably absent from a strip along the east of Wiradjuri territory. The absence may be an accidental by-product of the adventitious ways in which Indigenous placenames made it onto colonial maps, or there may be some underlying causes discernible from the history of the early colonial period. One is that the colonists spreading westward from the Sydney region when first encountering Wiradjuri tended not to record Indigenous placenames, especially in the period before it was encouraged by the authorities (notably Macquarie and Mitchell). Another possibility is that Wiradjuri language is not involved in placenames in this eastern strip, and that the Wiradjuri spread eastward to occupy the strip when the original owning groups could not sustain their presence there (whether from disease, massacre, or forced relocation). Clearly this is a fraught topic, and I leave it for considered historical investigation.[5]

---

5   There is a parallel clustering of placenames ending in *bri*, such as *Narrabri, Boggabri, Collarenebri, Kenebri, Mickibri*. These derive from the Gamilaraay Yuwaalaraay suffix *-Baraay* (the reflex of *-baraay 'Comitative' pGY, Austin 1997: 33). Another parallel cluster is formed by placenames ending in *bone* (in English spelling), such as *Quambone, Girilambone, Galargambone, Buttabone*, exhibiting the Comitative suffix *-buwan* (as found in Ngiyaampa). These parallel placename endings are ripe for being analysed along similar lines.

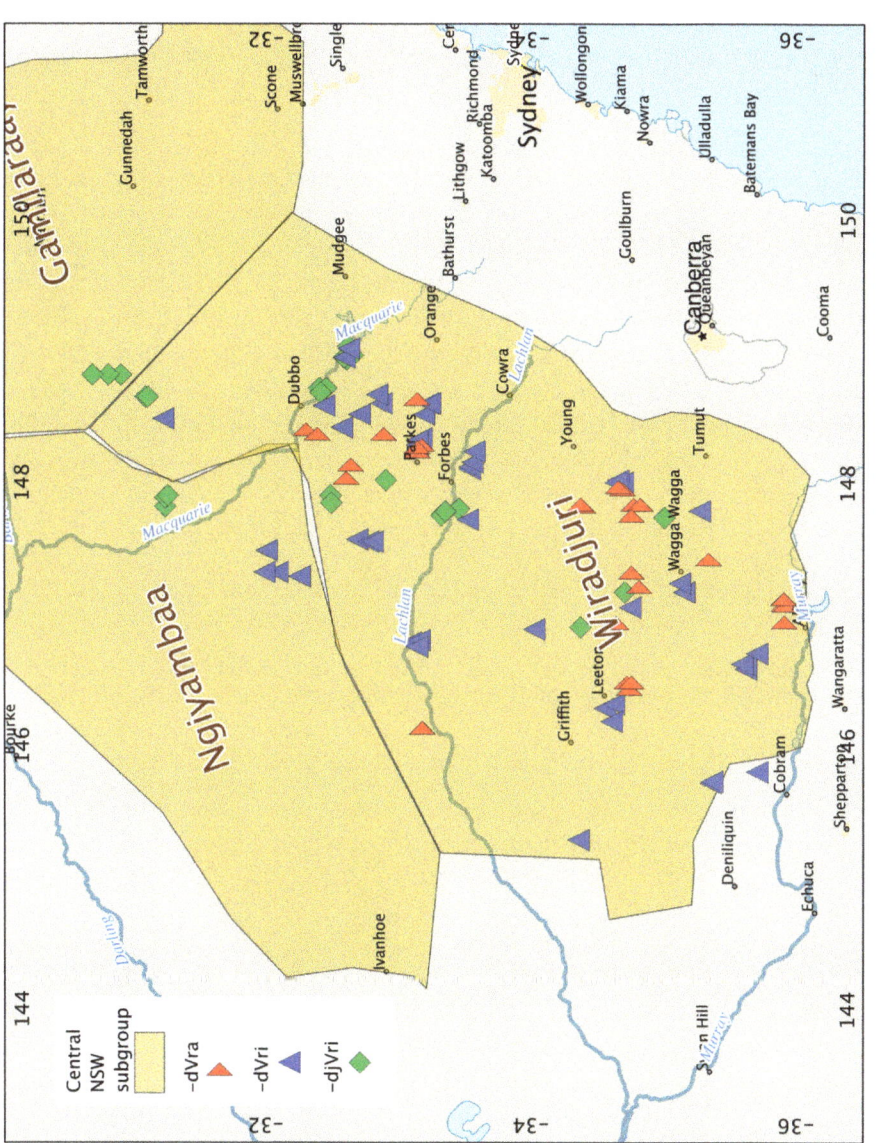

Map 3: Placenames of Table 1 overlain on language areas map (Bowen 2011). Equirectangular projection.

Source: Made with QGIS and Natural Earth, free vector and raster map data from naturalearthdata.com.

Turning to the placenames with speculative etymology involving the Wiradjuri Comitative, the names of Table 2, it is readily apparent that these (as on Map 2) are spread over a broader area. More so than on Maps 1 and 3, a number are located away from the focal cluster, and we can suspect these are not actually original Wiradjuri Comitative placenames. There are a couple of possible explanations for the existence of these outliers. One is that the placename shows a chance resemblance to a Wiradjuri word, but actually derives from its local language and does not exhibit the Wiradjuri Comitative ending. One possible example of this is Gindantherie Parish (about 35 km north of Lithgow).[6]

Another explanation for an apparent outlier is that it is a transplanted name, that is, one copied to another location in the colonial period or later. I have tried to minimise the effect of transplanted copy names in this study by the rule of thumb that names borne by natural or indigenous features are more likely to be original than names borne by an introduced feature (such as a street, house or small property). A copy name is noticeable when it is geographically out of place and spelled the same as a prior placename recorded within the focal cluster. A candidate example is Tarrabandra, a name applied to three separate Parishes; the ones in the far north-west and far south of the state may well have been copied, whereas the intermediate Parish is associated with a Rural Place (near Gundagai). We need to look for further historical evidence bearing on whether the outlier placenames were indeed transplanted.

Of course a transplanted name might be located well within traditional Wiradjuri country, and thus will not have an anomalous location. Similarly, some unanalysed placename may just show a chance resemblance to the Comitative ending. It has to be accepted that, given our incomplete record of the full Wiradjuri lexicon, and an absence of origin information for some placenames, there will be some placenames with unresolvable etymologies.

4.2. The Wiradjuri Comitative suffix

Grant and Rudder's Wiradjuri Dictionary (quoted in the Introduction) draws on the two previous published descriptions of Wiradjuri grammar. Both those descriptions date from the period 1838–40, at the Wellington Valley Mission, and were written independently of each other. Both arose from a missionary who was learning the language, namely J.W. Günther, and William Watson. (None of Watson's original analysis survives, and we know of it from his collaboration with the visiting philologist Horatio Hale.)

---

6   The name is borne also by a natural feature in the area, Gindantherie Pinnacle, for which the GNR records 'Named after the Parish in which it is situated.' This is an example counter to my rule of thumb: normally we would expect a Parish to be named after a natural feature rather than the reverse; however the natural feature name is of recent origin, and was 'Proposed 17th October 2006'.

The 19th century grammars describe the Comitative suffix, and transcribed it as follows:

-*durai* 'Conjunctive case' (Günther 1892)

-*dhurei*, -*dhurai* (Watson in Hale 1846)

-*durei* 'with, in company with' (Hale 1846: 492)[7]

Consistent with this, Austin (1997: 39) reconstructed *-*dhurraay* 'comitative' for the Ngiyampaa-Wiradjuri subgroup of Proto Central NSW (pCNSW), drawing also on Donaldson's (1980) grammar of Ngiyampaa, Wiradjuri's closest neighbour, and the only other language whose Comitative suffix can have the same form as Wiradjuri's:

-*DHuray* is occasionally substituted for -*buwan* by some Trida speakers. It does not appear to function differently from -*buwan* in any way, except that it is rarely used. (Donaldson 1980: 112).

In Ngiyampaa as in Wiradjuri, the suffix is the nominal Comitative, and "can often be conveniently glossed as 'having' or '(being) with'" (Donaldson 1980: 107). Note however there are next to no recorded placenames containing -*DHuray* in Ngiyampaa country (the exception is *Cajildry* etc on the Bogan River, mentioned in section 4.1 above). This would fit with Donaldson's (1980: 107) observation that the Ngiyampaa Comitative 'cannot mark forms whose reference is definite': placenames, like any proper name, are inherently definite.

The 19th century grammars of Wiradjuri described allomorphy in the nominal case endings of the Ergative and Locative, but mention no variation in the Comitative.[8] That is, they do not tell us about variation that is now readily seen in the recorded Wiradjuri placenames. Consider the placenames of types *dVra* and *dVri* on Map 1; both types have much the same spread across the Wiradjuri area. Notice though that almost all the placenames of types *dVra* and *dVri* in Table 1 have a *n* or *l* immediately preceding the suffix (as in *Narrandera, Jerilderie*, and so on), whereas in the *djVri* type a palatal nasal (in pronunciation) or vowel immediately precedes the suffix (as in *Eumungerie, Coradgery*). There is only one vowel-final stem (*dhulu* 'spear') represented in the *dVra* and *dVri* types in Table 1.

---

7   Hale (1846: 483-484) differed from 'the orthography of the missionaries' in 'the omission of unnecessary letters, such as double consonants, and the h, which is employed by them to denote sometimes a nasal and sometimes a dental pronunciation of the consonant which it accompanies' and it is clear from his notes that he observed a dental articulation of the stop beginning this suffix. Hale implies that the *r* is rolled or trilled (not the glide as in standard English). Hale also noted that the language basically had three vowels, and that e, o were variants of i, u respectively. Hence the three analysts effectively agree on the form and meaning of the suffix.

8   Richards (1902–03) does comment on variation between *dh* and *dj* (and *y*) variants, as witness the title of his articles.

The pattern can be described as an assimilation of the first consonant of the suffix, along these lines:

- *DH* → *d* immediately following *n* or *l*
- *DH* → *dj* immediately following a palatal consonant (*y*, *ny*)

Note that some of the *djVri* type are derived from a stem ending in *y*, such as *garay* in *Coradgery*, and the *y* drops out when the suffix is added. The general allomorphy pattern here accords with the pattern in Ngiyampaa, as detailed by Donaldson (1980).

4.3 Final vowel variation and doublets

There is variation evident also in the final vowel of the Comitative placenames. It seems that the *-DHuray* suffix can take two forms *-DHura* (the *dVra* type above) and *-DHuri* (the *dVri* and *djVri* types above). This variation was not described in the 19th century grammars of Wiradjuri. I have not detected any pattern to the final vowel variation, apart from a partial geographical component: most *dVra* type placenames on Map 1 (represented by a red pushpin) are in the southern half of the distribution. There are only two in the northern half: *Bulgandramine* and *Bindogandra*, and both of these are somewhat unusual: *Bulgandramine* is the only placename where the stem+Comitative is compounded with another noun, *barrgan+dura-mayin* 'boomerang+Comitative-man';[9] and *Bindogandra* has an alternate of *dVri* type, *Bindogandri*. On the other hand, several of the *dVra* type placenames with speculative etymologies (Table 2) are in the north, such as *Gilgandra, Gunnegaldra* and *Tenandra*.

It can be noted here that there are a few Comitative placenames recorded by Günther near his Wellington Valley Mission, and they include the only known placenames which retained the final diphthong of the Comitative. These are presented in Table 3. Two of these, *Dawindurai* ~ *Douwingerie* and *Yurugaidyurai*, are not listed in the GNR and there appears to be no other record of *Yurugaidyurai*. We might infer from this slim evidence that the pronunciation of the final *ay* diphthong changed to a simple vowel *a* or *i* during the 19th century.

Further on this variation, there are some pairs of similar placenames differing mainly in the final vowel of the ending (on the same stem), like the *Bindogandra / Bindogandri* pair already dicussed. Some of the pairs are quite distinct locations (such as *Geraldra / Gereldery / Jerilderie*, and *Willandra / Willanthry Willandry*), and some are a single location with variant forms of what we can presume is the one name (such as *Cootamundra / Cootamundry* and *Gunnegaldrie / Gunnegaldra*).

---

9   The final y of -*DHuray* also deletes before the suffix -*Da* in forming the instrumental suffix combination -*DHurada*; just as the final *y* of a stem (such as *garay* mentioned above, or *wiray* 'no' in the name *Wiradjuri*) deletes before -*DHuray*.

The others to be found in the tables are *Ulandra / Ulundry Yullundry*, and *Timaldra / Timaldrie*. (Another pair, not listed in the tables because of the lack of even a speculative etymology, is *Mundawaddra / Mundawaddery* in the Lockhart district.) The spread of these variant pairs counts against the north/south pattern discerned on Map 1, and we are left without a satisfactory explanation for the final variation.

4.4 Semantic pattern

Consideration of semantics can assist the assessment of the fragmentary etymological information. For the placenames with relatively secure etymology, in Table 1, we can see that the stem meanings are concrete entities: flora and fauna terms, some artefacts, and some topographic terms. This semantic range corresponds fairly well with the range seen across the speculative etymologies indicated in Table 2.

5. Conclusion

The study shows that placename evidence can provide linguistic information to supplement grammatical description, and can demonstrate the affiliation with country of a particular Indigenous language. The study of this one suffix used to form placenames in one language (Wiradjuri) has shown a logical pattern in variations in the form of the suffix. The geographic distribution of the placenames is shown to match, and thereby be a further expression of, the extent of Wiradjuri country.

Table 1. Toponyms in -*DHurray* with recorded source, in form types, each ordered alphabetically by stem.

Lat	Long	Placename	designation	source	stem	gloss
dVra						
-32.60	148.10	Bulgandramine	Rural place	DDB (Dubbo) AAJ 1.2,12; JJ Garnsey SM 3.6,98	barrgan[A]	boomerang (etc)
-32.63	148.20	Bulgandramine	Parish			
-33.13	148.30	Bindogundra	Rural Place		bindugan	mussel
-33.17	148.35	Bindogundra	Parish			
-33.13	148.33	Bindogundra Creek	Creek			
-33.13	148.70	Brymedura	Rural Place, Parish	SM 7.6,88 Manildra; Stutchbury 1852	?	'a mallee hen's nest'
-34.38	147.88	Geraldra	Parish		dyiRil	reeds
-34.37	147.90	Geraldra	Trig. Station			
-34.37	147.90	Geraldra Hill	Hill			
-35.33	147.48	Cajaldura Hill	Hill	JJ Baylis	gadyal	hollow
-33.15	148.25	Kamandra	Parish	'old woman' *Western Champion* 21/12/1916,22 http://nla.gov.au/nla.news-article112321812	ngamandhuray[B]	a marriageable woman
-34.81	147.28	Kindra	Trig. Station	JJ Baylis	giiN-	tree sp.
-34.75	147.38	Kindra Creek	River		-	
-34.65	148.03	Cootamundra	Locality	C Richards SM 5.11,181; Kutamundra 'river turtle' Howitt 1904:56[C]	guDamang	turtle
-34.63	147.00	Cootamundra	Parish			
-34.68	148.02	Cootamundra	Trig. Station			
-35.90	147.18	Mulyanjandera		JFH Mitchell p6 = SM 8.4,15 *Yan* is to go.	maliyaN	eaglehawk
-35.90	147.14	Mullanjandra	Trig. Station		maliyaN	eaglehawk

2. Comitative placenames in central NSW

Lat	Long	Placename	designation	source	stem	gloss
-35.90	147.18	Mullanjandra	Parish			
-35.92	147.13	Mullanjandra Creek	Creek			
-35.90	147.01	Mullengandra	Trig. Station		(malungaN?)[D]	
-35.92	147.13	Mullengandra	Locality, Ck			
-35.90	147.18	Mullengandra	Parish			
-34.72	146.55	Narrandera	Parish	C Richards SM 5.11,181; Nurrung-derry Woolrych 1890:68, Howitt 1904:56[c]	ngaRang	frill-necked lizard, 'prickly lizard'
-34.73	146.50	Narrandera	Trig. Station			
-34.75	146.55	Narrandera	Locality			
-33.18	146.20	Hyandra	Parish	'trees growing in locality now called Oak' RASA 2004:137 Euabalong	ngany (ngayiny?) Ngain(y) 'The "Forest" oak or "Belar" tree' (C Richards SM 5.10,165) (sc. *Casuarina cristata*)	oak tree, 'bull oak *Casuarina luehmannii*' (Grant & Rudder 2010)
-32.88	148.43	Hyandra	Parish			
-32.30	148.47	Hyandra	Rural Place			
-32.38	148.43	Hyandra Well	Spring			
-34.77	147.90	Ulandra	Parish		yulang	'a little shrub' (G in F 109)
-34.82	147.90	Ulandra	Trig. Station			
-34.75	147.82	Ulandra Creek	Creek			
dVri						
-35.62	146.60	Bulgandry	Rural Place	TL Richardson SM 2.11,212	bargan ~ balgang	boomerang
-35.62	146.63	Bulgandry	Trig. Station			
-35.59	146.64	Bulgandry	Parish			
-33.13	148.33	Bindogandri Creek	Creek		bindugan	mussel
-33.13	148.30	Bindogandri	Rural Place			
-33.17	148.35	Bindogandri	Parish			
-32.57	148.43	Dilladerry Spring	Spring	SM 7.4,43 Dubbo District	dhulu	spear (G in F 82)

Lat	Long	Placename	designation	source	stem	gloss
-33.23	148.62	Dulladerry Creek	Creek	A Dulhunty SM 3.2,32	dhulu	
-33.18	148.53	Delladerry	Ck		dhulu	
-35.27	147.80	Dellateroy Creek[E]	Creek		dhulu	
-32.70	148.53	Dilladerry	Rural Place		dhulu	
-32.43	148.60	Dilladery Creek	Creek			
-33.23	148.62	Dulladerry	Creek, Parish	'Dulladulladerry Ck' Stutchbury 1852	dhulu, dhuludhulu	big logs of wood (G in F 82)
-34.74	147.07	Dulah Dulah Derry Lagoon	Lagoon	RB Mackenzie SM 7.3,43	dhuludhulu	
-35.36	145.75	Jerilderie	Town	C Richards SM 5.11,181	dyiRil	reeds, reed spear
-35.70	145.82	Gereldery	Parish		dyiRil	
-35.35	145.73	Jerilderie	Trig. Station		dyiRil	
-31.98	147.33	Cajildry	HS	TL Richardson SM 2.9,155[166]	gadhal	smoke (cf gadjal 'hollow')
-32.00	147.50	Caddulddury			gadhal	
-32.08	147.33	Caduldary			gadhal	
-32.00	147.50	Cagildry		SM 7.6,90 Dandaloo	gadhal	
-32.25	147.30	Cajildry	Parish		gadhal	
-32.00	147.50	Cuddulduary			gadhal	
-34.55	146.30	Gogeldrie	Locality	JJ Baylis	gadyal	hollow
-34.62	146.33	Gogeldrie	Parish			
-32.68	147.58	Gobondery	Rural Place		guba(ng)	Cooba, native willow
-33.08	146.80	Coobothery	HS		guba(ng)	
-32.77	147.57	Gobondry	Parish		guba(ng)	
-32.80	147.57	Gobondry Mountains	Hill		guba(ng)	
-33.15	146.82	Goobothery	Parish		guba(ng)	

2. Comitative placenames in central NSW

Lat	Long	Placename	designation	source	stem	gloss
-33.13	146.77	Goobothery Ridge	Ridge	SM 7.6.88 Condobolin	guba(ng)	
-33.52	147.73	Gooburthery Hill	Hill		guba(ng)	
-34.68	148.02	Cootamundry	Trig. Station		gudhamang	turtle
-34.65	148.03	Cootamundry	Town			
-34.63	148.02	Cootamundry Creek	Creek			
-33.53	148.13	Mulyandry	Locality		maliyaN	eaglehawk
-33.53	148.12	Mulyandry	Parish			
-33.55	148.17	Mulyandry	Trig. Station			
-33.57	148.25	Mulyandry Creek	Creek			
-35.70	146.72	Walbundrie	Locality	JJ Baylis 'hurt in the hip'	wirbunba	lame (G in F 106)
-32.62	149.03	Waughgundrie		SM 7.6,89 Wellington	waagan	crow
-34.02	146.90	Wallandry Creek[F]	Creek	G in F 65	walang	stone
-35.15	147.18	Yarragundry	Trig. Station	JJ Baylis 'black lumps on gum trees'	yaRa-gaN-	white gum -?
-32.83	148.68	Yullundry	Locality	SM 7.6.90 Walgett	yulang	'a little shrub' (G in F 109)
-31.22	148.50	Ulundry	Parish		yulang	
-32.87	148.62	Yullundry	Trig. Station		yulang	
-35.12	147.25	Uranquintry	Parish, Town	JJ Baylis Yerongquinty 'plenty of rain', Reed 1969:143	yuRung	cloud, rain
-34.35	145.30	Uardry	Parish	JJ Baylis	yuwaR	yellow box tree
-34.60	146.20	Euwarderry Lagoon	Anabranch		yuwaR	

Indigenous and Minority Placenames

Lat	Long	Placename	designation	source	stem	gloss
dVrai						
-32.58	148.97	Dawindurai		G 1840 MS p341=97	dhawiny	stone axe
djVri						
-32.58	148.97	Balbudgerie		SM 7,6,89 Wellington	barrbay	rock wallaby
-34.70	147.18	Berry Jerry	Trig. Station	JJ Baylis AAJ 1,2,12	birri	white box tree, *E. albens*
-35.00	147.75	Wantabadgerie[G]	Parish	SM 7,6,89 Mudgee 'fighting'	bundi-nya	to fall
-35.07	147.70	Wantabadgery Lagoon	Lagoon			
-30.90	148.83	Teridgerie	Locality	Cain 1923:372 Tirridgeree 'rough bushes which grows in creeks'	daRi	old stumps of grass[H]
-30.80	148.89	Teridgerie	Parish		daRi	
-30.68	148.62	Teridgerie	Creek		daRi	
-32.58	148.97	Douwingerie		SM 7,6,89 Wellington	dhawiny	stone axe
-32.62	149.05	Galwadgerie Gully	Gully	SM 7,6,89 Wellington	galuwa	lizard
-32.65	148.98	Galwadgere	Parish		galuwa	
-32.90	148.03	Coradgery	Rural Place	SM 7,6,90 Peak Hill	garay	sand
-33.45	147.82	Corradgery Range	Ridge		garay	
-31.23	147.83	Gradgery	Rural Place		garay	sand
-33.32	147.77	Corridgery	Parish		garay	sand
-33.35	147.80	Corridgery	Trig. Station		garay	sand
-33.35	147.80	Corridgery Ridge	Ridge			
-31.23	147.90	Gradgery	Parish		garay	sand
-31.25	147.92	Gradgery	Trig. Station			
-32.40	148.73	Murrumbidgerie	Locality, Parish	'Murrumbidgere' Stuchbury 1852; E Gastelow SM 2.11,209	maRumbang	very good
-32.41	148.70	Murrumbidgerie Fall	Rapids			

2. Comitative placenames in central NSW

Lat	Long	Placename	designation	source	stem	gloss
-32.48	147.92	Mungery	Rural Place	DDB (Dubbo) AAJ 1.2,12; 'a place of native willow' (SM 2,11,211-3); 'sticky mud' (SM 3,6,98 7,4,58, 14.2,39), 'red ground' (SM 7.6,90 Peak Hill)	muny	swampy black soil; a kind of ground spider G in F 99
-32.49	147.86	Mungery	Trig. Station			
-31.10	148.67	Mungery	Parish			
-31.08	148.67	Mungery Creek	Creek			
-34.37	146.92	Yarranjerry Creek	Creek	G in F 108	yarrany	Acacia *homalophylla*

djVrai

Lat	Long	Placename	designation	source	stem	gloss
-32.60	148.95	Yurugaidyurai		G in F 109	yuRugay	thistle

Note A: The placename is glossed as 'blackfellow with a boomerang in his hand' (DDB (Dubbo) AAJ 1.2,12) Also Bulgandirramine dirra 'hand' RB Mackenzie SM 7.3,43; 'throwing boomerang from the hand' SM 7.4,58, corrected 'man with a shield' SM 7.5,77; 'where boomerangs are found' Peak Hill SM 7.6,90; Bulgandrammi from bulganderria-mine SM 14.2,39 (? from JJ Garnsey). The second stem is mayiN 'Aboriginal man'.

Note B: 'Ngamondurai—a marriageable woman' 'Ngamon—milk' (Günther 1892: 91).

Note C: Howitt (1904: 56) says this name applies to one of the sections (hordes) of the Wiradjuri 'perpetuated in the names of the places where these sections had their headquarters'.

Note D: The GNR gives Mullanjandra as the previous spelling of the four Mullengandra. Donaldson (1985: 77) proposed the etymology Maliyan-kaan-thurray 'with a small or young eaglehawk or eaglehawks'. The modern pronunciation of Mullengandra (with g pronounced [gɪ] might also allow the stem malungaN 'girl', as for Mullengudgery (Table).

Note E: The placename Dellateroy is included because of its similarity to Dilladerry, which in turn is sometimes given as an alternate of Dulladerry, and thus related to dhulu 'spear'. However, it is in a separate locality, has no related origin information itself, and is the only placename in this Table where the ending is spelled as a voiceless stop (t) rather than a voiced stop (d, dj, etc.).

Note F: Another possible placename with the stem walang is Wallanthery (a Locality and Parish at 33.35°S 145.83°E).

Note G: Charles Sturt first recorded this placename as Pondebadgery Plain (1829) (Reed 1969: 145), which form could be derived from the verb bundi-nya 'to fall', fighting with the meaning 'fighting'. However the connection with the 'fighting' meaning is by no means certain, as it is recorded in a Mudgee list, from a long way north of Wantabadgery; the Mudgee list may relate to Wantabudgery Creek (31.66°S 149.02°E) east of Gilgandra. Also J.J. Baylis recorded Wantabadgery 'getting wet', which lacks corroboration.

Note H: Darri 'old stumps of grass' (Günther 1892: 80) may be the same word as Dtha'ree 'pitted, excavated, hollow, casts' (C. Richards 1902: 166).

Table 2. Toponyms in -DHurray with no recorded source, in form types, each ordered alphabetically by suggested stem.

Lat	Long	Placename	designation	source	suggested stem	gloss
dVra						
-34.17	147.63	Boginderra	Parish		bagin	wound, sore; evil spirit
-34.28	147.63	Boginderra Hills	Hill			
-34.77	146.17	Banandra	Parish		baNang	flesh (not edible)
-34.72	146.20	Banandra State Forest	Forest			
-32.83	149.07	Boduldura Creek	Creek		buDul buDul	far off, high; bluish air at a distance
-32.88	149.10	Boduldura	Parish			
-32.77	148.88	Blathery Creek	Creek		biilaa	forest oak or belah *Casuarina cristata*
-33.3	148.60	Blathery	Rural Place	Stuchbury 1852		
-35.12	148.18	Tarrabandra	Parish		dhaRabaN	having many wives; to sit cross-legged
-29.67	143.24	Tarrabandra	Parish			
-35.15	148.17	Tarrabandra	Parish			
-36.90	148.50	Tarrabandra	Parish			
-35.97	146.85	Jindera	Trig. Station		dhin	meat, flesh; inner rind of wild pear
-35.97	146.88	Jindera	Locality			
-35.97	146.92	Jindera	Parish			
-36.02	146.83	Jindera Hills	Hill			
-36.05	147.93	Tintaldra	Locality		dhindDar	bald-headed
-31.60	147.85	Tenandra	Locality		dhinhang	foot
-35.07	147.82	Tenandra	Trig. Station			
-35.00	147.83	Tenandra	Parish			

2. Comitative placenames in central NSW

Lat	Long	Placename	designation	source	suggested stem	gloss
-31.47	147.93	Tenandra	Parish			
-31.22	148.77	Tenandra	Rural Place			
-33.67	148.78	Tenandra	Parish			
-32.33	148.98	Tenandra	Parish			
-32.95	148.03	Tenandra Creek	Creek			
-31.20	148.72	Tenandra Creek	Creek			
-33.68	148.75	Tenandra Creek	Creek			
-31.33	149.07	Tenandra Creek	Creek			
-31.22	148.73	Tenandra Hill	Hill			
-33.65	148.70	Tenandra Knob	Hill			
-32.95	148.05	Tenandra Plain	Plain			
-31.71	148.67	Gilgandra	Locality		gilgaay¹	gilgai, holes on ground
-31.70	147.83	Gunnegaldra	HS		guNigal	plain, valley
-33.20	148.62	Manildra	Locality	Minildra on Stuchbury 1852; cf. Nash 2010	?	?
-30.92	144.56	Wallandra	Parish		walang ?	stone ?
-33.19	145.68	Wallandra	Parish			
-34.28	143.02	Willandra Billabong	Billabong		?	?
-32.95	143.82	Willandra	Parish			
-33.03	143.85	Willandra Anabranch	Creek			
-33.16	144.34	Willandra	Parish			
-33.20	145.13	Willandra	Rural Place	'little waters, creek' E Sharpe SM 2.11,211		

Indigenous and Minority Placenames

Lat	Long	Placename	designation	source	suggested stem	gloss
-33.20	145.27	Willandra Creek (previously Billabong)	Creek			
-33.97	146.89	Willandra, previously Wallandra	Trig. Station			
-34.03	146.92	Willandra	Parish			
-32.23	148.52	Whylandra Creek, Willandra Creek, Woolandra Creek	Creek			
-32.37	149.68	Wyaldra	Trig. Station		wayal	kangaroo skin
-32.37	149.65	Wyaldra	Parish			
-32.32	149.60	Wyaldra Creek	Creek			
-32.36	148.93	Windora	Rural Place		wiing	wood, fire
-33.25	146.63	Yaddra	Rural Place	McCarthy (1963) in GNR	yaDal	to be too narrow
-32.53	147.57	Yethera	Rural Place		yaDal	to be too narrow
dVri						
-34.05	146.03	Ballandry	Trig. Station	JJ Baylis AAJ 1.2,12 'far away'	balang	head; Ballanda 'long ago; at the first; in the beginning' (G in F 70)
-34.08	146.10	Ballandry Tank	Tank			

2. Comitative placenames in central NSW

Lat	Long	Placename	designation	source	suggested stem	gloss
-32.40	147.12	Bumbaldry	Parish		? banbal[J]	the place where the native men meet first in the morning; a place of assembly (G)
-33.87	148.42	Bumbaldry	Locality			
-33.90	148.43	Bumbaldry	Village			
-33.92	148.50	Bumbaldry	Parish			
-33.90	148.42	Bumbaldry Creek	Creek			
-33.85	148.42	Bumbaldry Hills	Ridge			
-31.14	145.89	Tindayrey	Parish		dhin	meat, flesh
-35.70	149.32	Tinderry	Locality		dhin	meat, flesh
-32.87	149.00	Tinandry			dhinhang	foot
-32.82	148.85	Gerotherie	HS?		dyiru	kangaroo rat
-34.28	146.98	Kildary Creek	Creek		gil	urine
-34.13	147.00	Kildary	Rural Place			
-34.27	147.03	Kildary	Trig. Station			
-34.15	147.12	Kildary	Parish			
-33.17	150.25	Gindatherie	Parish		gindhaany	ringtail possum
-33.20	148.30	Cookemethery	out station	*Western Champion* 21/12/1916, 22 http://nla.gov.au/nla.news-article112321812; later Cookamidgera		
-32.87	148.78	Googodery Creek	Creek		gugu	water, cup
-32.63	149.42	Goondudery	Popl		gundhay	red stringybark tree
-33.23	146.13	Gooniguldry	Pond		guNigal	plain, valley
-31.67	147.73	Gunnegaldrie Tank	Tank		guNigal	
-33.23	146.13	Gunniguldrie	Hs		guNigal	
-32.87	148.02	Coogoorderoy	Ck		guugur	knee

31

Indigenous and Minority Placenames

Lat	Long	Placename	designation	source	suggested stem	gloss
-34.35	147.33	Quandary	Parish		guwaN^K	blood
-34.33	147.35	Quandary	Trig. Station			
-34.38	147.32	Quandary	Locality			
-34.40	147.32	Quandary Tank	Dam			
-35.47	147.60	Murraguldrie	Parish		?	
-35.47	147.68	Murraguldrie Creek	Ck			
-31.78	147.92	Wambandry	Hs			
-33.20	147.18	Willamundry Creek	Creek		wuluma	calf of leg
-32.52	149.60	Eurunderee	Locality		yuRun, yuRiin	Yoo' roon(y) 'a scab, a cicatrix' (Richards 1903:183), Yuren 'a scratch, scar, sore' (G in F 109)
-32.49	149.63	Eurundury	Trig. Station			
-32.48	149.65	Eurundury	Parish			
-32.55	149.72	Eurundury Creek	Creek			
djVra						
-33.20	148.30	Cookamidgera	Parish, Village	formerly Cookamethery (see above)		
-30.30	149.18	Gundidgera			gundyi	bark shelter; Goon' jee-gang, Goon' jee, Gon'ya 'house of Europeans not native huts or camps' cf. Goon'dthai 'stringey-bark tree' (Richards 1902–03:83)
-35.33	147.65	Keajura	Parish		giyal? giyan?	ashamed, stung, dug into, ground down; cf. Keadool (Nash, this volume); Gee' yan 'centipede; harlot' (Richards 1903:83)
-35.32	147.63	Keajura	Rural Place			
-35.37	147.67	Keajura Creek	Creek			
-35.37	147.67	Keajura or Six Mile Creek	Creek			

32

2. Comitative placenames in central NSW

Lat	Long	Placename	designation	source	suggested stem	gloss
djVri						
-32.82	148.60	Bolderogery	Parish	Balderodgery JJ Garnsey SM 3,6,98; Balduraidurai 'owl' (G in F);	baal(d)aRa-djuri 'spur-with'	a small plover[L]
-32.85	148.50	Balrudgery Creek	Creek			
-32.8	148.5	Braldugery	locality ?	Stuchbury 1852		
-34.73	146.60	Bundidjarie Hill	Hill	J.J. Baylis AAJ 1,2,12	bundi	club, cudgel
-35.53	146.07	Boreegerry	Trig. Station		burri	boree tree, weeping myall A. *pendula*
-33.60	148.58	Boridgery	locality ? www.bonzle.com; Boridgery Lane			
-33.75	148.57	Cocu'Jgery	Rural Place, Parish	'where the gum leaves lie in the lagoon, flavouring and staining the water' RASA 1 p286	gugu	water, cup
-33.47	148.35	Trajere[M]			?	cf. Teridgerie above
-31.70	147.42	Mullengudgery	Locality		maluŋgaN	young woman, female; a little girl (G), cf. Mullengandra above
-31.60	147.47	Mullengudgery	Parish		maluŋgaN	
-33.24	148.46	Mancagery	Locality		mandang	wood (G)
-33.24	148.53	Mancagery	Trig. Station			
-33.30	148.62	Mancagery	Parish			
-33.07	148.81	Mancagery Creek	Creek			
-33.28	148.57	Mancagery Ridge	Ridge			

Lat	Long	Placename	designation	source	suggested stem	gloss
-35.58	146.00	Algudgerie Creek	Creek		walgawalga	marks as on the trees near a native grave (G) [dendroglyphs]
-33.00	148.03	Weridgery	Parish		wirri	flat, level
-31.96	148.54	Eumungerie	Trig. Station		yumang	native willow, *A. stenophylla*
-31.95	148.53	Eumungerie	Parish			
-31.95	148.63	Eumungerie	Locality			

Note I: Carlgindra a long waterhole. 'So called because of the large natural waterhole in the Castlereagh at this point' (W.N. Thomas SM 7.4,58). The form and sense of gilgaay are both somewhat at variance with W.N. Thomas' record; and gilgaay has not been recorded with a final nasal. Donaldson's (1985: 77) etymology is kilkaanhthurray 'with a water-hole or gilgai'.

Note J: According the surveyor Woolrych (1890: 65), Bumbaldry was "A head station near the source of the Tyagong Creek. A water hole and great bathing place of the blacks. 'Bumbáld' indicates the jumping in of the gins or women, and darée (noise) — the noise made by their plunging into the water together." Some of Woolrych's other etymologies are rather fanciful, and the elements of this one are not corroborated, other than Bambinga 'to swim' (G).

Note K: Donaldson (1984: 32n26) proposed the derivation from 'blood', parallel to Quambone kuwaympuwan 'blood-having' in Ngiyampaa, and also repeated "a tradition, recorded by a local historian, that 'Quondary [as it was first spelt] ... is the aboriginal word for "place of the possum"'. The GNR also has 'place of the possum'. Donaldson found it difficult to corroborate a derivation from a 'possum' word.

Note L: If this placename contains the Comitative, it is internal (i.e. it is the word baal(dj)aRa-djuri 'spur-with' meaning 'plover'), whereas all the others here considered are formed with the Comitative externally. There is an alternative that the word is a partial reduplication not involving the Comitative, *baaldharradharra 'plover' pGY, 43 (Austin 1997), though this matches less well the form of the placenames.

Note M: Other spellings are Tragere (Stutchbury 1852) and Trajaree (Wellington District 1870 Runs of Crown Lands, Names of Lessees, and Rents. http://www.dcstechnical.com.au/Rusheen/1.0_People.htm).

Table 3: Comitative placenames recorded by Günther.

Günther placename	source	comment
Dawindurai	'present sheep station' (Günther 1840 MS, p. 341 = 97)	Douwingerie 'rocks from which stone tomahawks were made' (Wellington district, Science of Man 7.6(1904),89), from dhawiny 'axe, stone axe'
Gunnandurai	'a constellation of three stars seen in the eastern horizon soon after sunset' G 1839 MS6 p. 73	root possibly meaning 'yellow', cf. gunanggunang 'yellow ochre'
Murrumbìrraíduraí ~ Murrumbugirrí	Günther 1840 MS p. 343	cf. Murrumbidgerie in Table 1
Yurugaidyurai	'name of the mountain near my home' (Günther 1892:109)	Yurugai 'thistle' (Günther 1892:109)

References

Abbreviations in tables 1 and 2:

AAJ = *Australasian Anthropological Journal* (continued by SM)

G in F = Günther in Fraser: Günther 1892

GNR = Geographical Names Board 2011

R = Richards (1902–03)

RASA = Royal Anthropological Society of Australia

SM = *Science of man and journal of the Royal Anthropological Society of Australasia*

Some further details on sources are given at http://www.anu.edu.au/linguistics/nash/aust/wira/.

Austin, P. 1997, 'Proto central New South Wales phonology', in *Boundary Rider: Essays in Honour of Geoffrey O'Grady*, Darrell Tryon and Michael Walsh (eds), Pacific Linguistics C-136, Canberra: 21–49.

Baylis, J. J. 1900, Vocabulary of the Wiradjuri language, AIATSIS PMS 3887.

— 1927, *The Waradgery language (also spelled Wiradjuri or Wiradhuri)*, [J. Baylis], Euroa, [Vic.]. Reel CY 2549; Original held at Mitchell Library at MLAb 159/1.

Bowern, C. 2011, Centroid Coordinates for Australian Languages v2.0. Google Earth .kmz file, available from http://pamanyungan.sites.yale.edu/language-resources (accessed 7 July 2013).

Cain, M. J. 1923. 'Coonabarabran in the 'Sixties', *Royal Australian Historical Society — Journal and Proceedings* 8, supplement: 370–373. Reproduced in RASA 2004, roll 2, PDF, pp. 23–26.

Donaldson, T. 1980, 'Ngiyambaa, the Language of the Wangaaybuwan', *Cambridge Studies in Linguistics* 29, Cambridge University Press, Cambridge.

— 1984, 'What's in a name? An etymological view of land, language and social identification from central western New South Wales', *Aboriginal History* 8(1/2): 21–44.

— 1985, 'Hearing the first Australians', in *Seeing the First Australians*, Ian Donaldson and Tamsin Donaldson (eds), George Allen & Unwin, Sydney, London, Boston: 76–91.

Geographical Names Board 2011, Geographical Names Register (GNR) of NSW, Land and Property Information, New South Wales, http://www.gnb.nsw.gov.au/name_search (accessed 6 May 2012).

Geoscience Australia 2008, Gazetteer of Australia 2008 Release, searchable at http://www.ga.gov.au/map/names/ (accessed 6 May 2012). See also Gazetteer of Australia 2010 Release.

Grant, S. and J. Rudder 2010, *A New Wiradjuri Dictionary*, Restoration House, O'Connor, ACT.

Günther, Rev. J. W. (Jakob Wilhelm) 1838–40, Vocabulary of the Native/ Aboriginal Dialect ... spoken in the Wellington District &c &c &c; Unpublished manuscripts: 1838 MS Wirradurri, 1839 MS Wirradhurri (microfilm at AIATSIS Library), 1840 MS Wirradhurrei.

Günther, J.W. 1892, 'Grammar and vocabulary of the Aboriginal dialect called the Wirradhuri', Appendix D, in *An Australian language as spoken by the Awabakal* 're-arranged, condensed and edited with an appendix by John Fraser', Charles Potter, Govt. Printer, Sydney: 56–120. http://en.wikisource.org/wiki/Page:An_Australian_language_as_spoken_by_the_Awabakal.djvu/376 (accessed 8 July 2013).

Hale, H. 1846, 'The languages of Australia [including 'Wiradurei']', in *Ethnology and Philology*, Volume 6 of *Narrative of the U.S. Exploring Expedition during the years 1838, 1839, 1840, 1841, 1842, under the command of*

Charles Wilkes, U.S.N, C. Sherman, Philadelphia: 479–531. http://www.sil. si.edu/digitalcollections/usexex/navigation/ScientificText/usexex19_07b. cfm?start=502 (accessed 8 July 2013).

Howitt, A.W. 1904, *The Native Tribes of South-East Australia*, Macmillan and Company, London.

Koch, H. 2009, 'The methodology of reconstructing Indigenous placenames: Australian Capital Territory and south-eastern New South Wales', in *Aboriginal Placenames: Naming and Re-naming the Australian Landscape*, edited by Harold Koch and Luise Hercus (eds), Aboriginal History Monograph 19, ANU E Press and Aboriginal History Incorporated, Canberra: 115–171. http://epress.anu.edu.au?p=17331/ (accessed 6 May 2012).

McCarthy, F. D. 1963, *New South Wales Aboriginal Place Names and Euphonious Words, with their Meanings*, Australian Museum, Sydney.

Nash, D. 1974, 'The comitative affix in Wiradhuri', ANU Linguistics (Arts) term paper, copy held at AIAS Library, pMs 3688.

— 2010, 'A further note on Manildra', *Placenames Australia: Newsletter of the Australian National Placenames Survey*, December 2010: 6–7. http://www. anps.org.au/documents/Dec_2010.pdf (accessed 8 July 2013).

Reed, A.W. 1969, *Place-names of New South Wales: Their Origins and Meanings*, Reed, Halstead Press, Sydney.

Richards, C. 1902–03, 'Wirra'athooree. Wirrai'yarrai'. Wirrach'aree'. Wirra'jerree' (or, Aboriginal dialects)', *Science of Man* 5(5): 81–83 (G); 5(6): 98–102 (G,B); 5(7): 114–119 (B,G,W); 5(8): 133–138 (M,N,Ny); 5(9): 146–149 (Ng); 5(10): 165–168 (Ng,J,Dth); 5(11): 180–183 (Dth,Y); 5(12): 198–201 (Y,Gw,I,E).

Royal Anthropological Society of Australia (RASA) 2004, Royal Anthropological Society of Australia manuscripts dated 1900. 'anthropological society of aus roll 1', PDF file. CD-ROM, Geographic Names Board of NSW.

[Stutchbury, S.] 1852, [Geological map of area south of Dubbo to Lachlan River], State Library of New South Wales, Call No. Ca 85/35. http://acms.sl.nsw. gov.au/album/albumView.aspx?itemID=977102&acmsid=0 (accessed 8 July 2013).

Woolrych, F.B.W. 1890, 'Native names of some of the runs &c. in the Lachlan District', *Journal and Proceedings of the Royal Society of New South Wales* 24: 63–70. http://www.biodiversitylibrary.org/item/131299 (accessed 8 July 2013).

3. The diminutive suffix -*dool* in placenames of central north NSW[1]

David Nash

The Australian National University and Australian Institute of Aboriginal and Torres Strait Islander Studies

1. Introduction

Almost all the official Australian placenames ending in *dool* (as officially spelled) are in a region in central northern New South Wales (NSW) and adjacent Queensland; such as *Angledool* and over a dozen others. In the Riverina district of south-western NSW, in a separate language area, are about eight such toponyms, such as *Moombooldool*. This intriguing clustering invites investigation.

2. Method

The investigation was based on the 81,624 entries in the Geographical Names Register (GNR) of NSW (Geographical Names Board 2011). I also consulted the 36,165 entries in the Victorian placenames database, the Queensland register, and the *Gazetteer of Australia* (Geoscience Australia 2008).[2] The process would not have been feasible were these registers not available in bulk in digital form.

The NSW names were sorted from the end of the word, thereby grouping spellings ending in *dool*, and the few in *dule*, and one in *joole*. No other terminations were found which would rhyme with *ool* according to English spelling. The names were combined into a spreadsheet along with attributes of location and feature type and then were grouped into 'toponymic sets': placenames which involve

---

[1] An earlier version of this study was presented on 1 October 2005 as 'Little names: -*dool* in northern NSW' at the Australian Placenames of Indigenous Origin conference, hosted by the Australian National Placenames Survey at Geosciences Australia, Canberra, and I am grateful to the participants for comments, and subsequently to John Giacon and Maïa Ponsonnet, and Ray Wood. My interest in the topic was originally piqued in a conversation with Jack Waterford and the late Murray Chapman who unintentionally alerted me to the existence of Mercadool homestead in the Walgett district, which I then realised had to be the source for the same placename I had long known in the Parkes district.

[2] These and similar resources are conveniently linked from http://www.anps.org.au/resources.html maintained by Placenames Australia (Inc).

the same base name (in the same spelling) in the one locality. For example, in the Walgett LGA (Local Government Area) the Register has four placenames which I group into a single Yarraldool toponymic set:

Yarraldool parish

Yarraldool Bore bore

Yarraldool Ridge ridge

Yarraldool Sand Ridge ridge

Typically the places in such a set are differentiatied by feature type, and/or by various derivations of the base name. Further to this illustration, note that the *Gazetteer of Australia* (Geoscience Australia 2008) has two other placenames: both are of NSW homesteads in other localities, and so I do not add these into the above toponymic set:

Yarraldool 30°00'S 152°01'E

Yarraldool 29°08'S 150°29'E

This process arrived at a collection of basic placenames (and localities thereby named) which terminate in *dool* (or *dule, joole*). Along with the coordinates these placenames were transferred (via CSV format and GPSBabel+ software) to a KML file, and thereby displayed in Google Maps and QGIS.

3. Northern inland NSW

As can be seen in Map 1, the most notable cluster of placenames terminating in *dool* (or *dule*) is in central northern NSW and adjacent Queensland. The 50 or so placenames with this termination can be viewed on Map 1. The placenames in the northern cluster are gathered in Tables 1 and 2 along with information relevant to their etymology.

First we consider in Table 1 those *-dool* placenames for which we have an etymology based on older records ('testimony') and wordlist data, the placenames for which we can have 'greatest certainty about the meaning of a placename' (Koch 2009: 147–148). For the ten or so placenames in Table 1 there is an old source[3] which identifies the stem, and all these also involve *-dool* (or *-dule*) as a suffix. The suffix is readily identifiable in languages indigenous to the district, notably the closely related Yuwaalaraay and Yuwaalayaay (the name written *Euahlayi* by Mrs Langloh Parker 1905). This suffix attaches to nominals, is written *-dhuul* or *-djuul*

---

3 Notably Royal Anthropological Society of Australia (RASA) (2004) which comprises manuscript questionnaires on placenames returned in about 1899 from local Police and other officials.

in the orthography adopted for the language (or in the cover form -*DHuul* as in the *GYY Dictionary*) and carries a diminutive meaning, usually glossed '1. little, small (YR,YY,GR); 2. one (YR,YY)'. (Williams 1980; Ash et al. 2003: 68).[4]

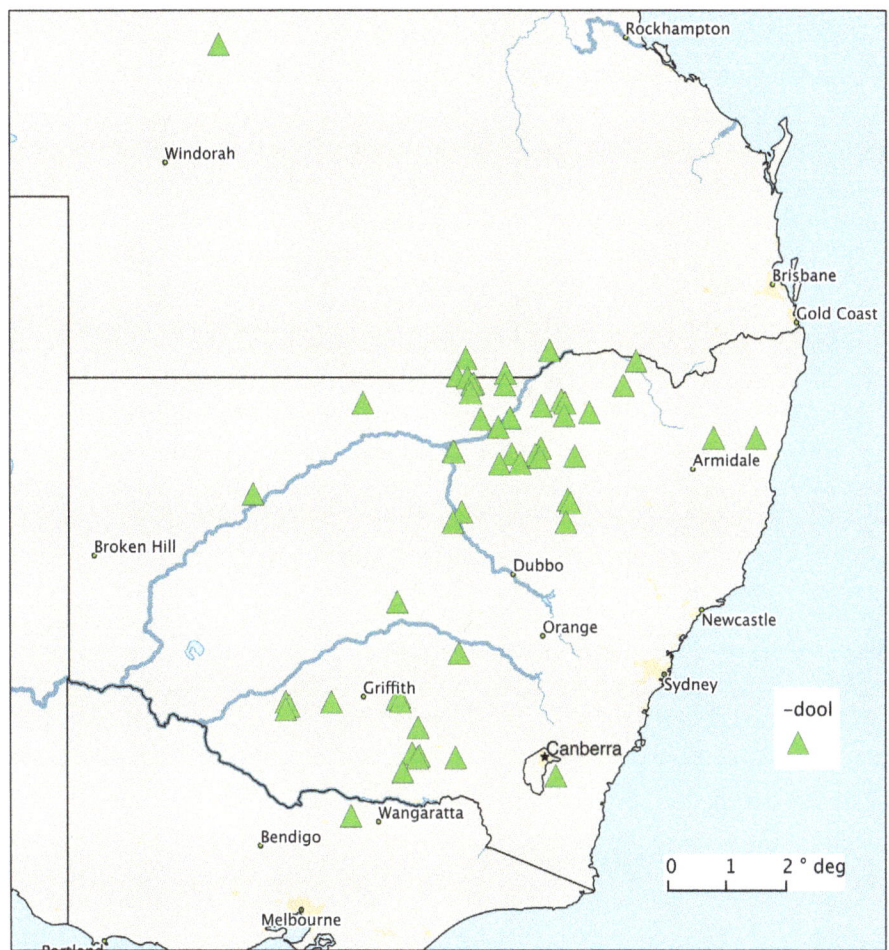

Map 1: Location of toponymic sets of placenames terminating in *dool* (or *dule*, *joole*) marked with green triangle.

Source: Made with QGIS and Natural Earth, free vector and raster map data from naturalearthdata.com.

Then in Table 2 are the remaining -*dool* placenames in the cluster in the same area, together with whatever stems in the *GYY Dictionary* can be matched with the form of the placename. The placenames in Table 2, however, lack

---

4   The abbreviation GYY is sometimes used to name the language comprising the closely related Gamilaraay (GR), Yuwaalaraay (YR) and Yuwaalayaay (YY) languages (Ash et al. 2003: 259).

supporting testimony from older sources. Note that the distribution of the *-dool* placename cluster approximates the territory of Yuwaalayaay (YY) and Yuwaalaraay (YR) as shown on the *GYY Dictionary* map (Ash et al. 2003: 2), and extending into the adjacent Gamilaraay area but noticeably absent from most of the eastern part of the Gamilaraay (GR) area (towards Inverell and Tamworth). I am not aware of what the reasons might be for this absence.

Next, consider the placenames on Map 1 located away from the focal cluster. First, the northernmost placename, the homestead Angledool in central Queensland has the hallmarks of being a transplanted copy name: it is a homestead rather than a natural or indigenous feature (or 19th century administrative area), and is spelled the same as the regionally well-known NSW village inside the focal cluster.

Some of the other outliers are most likely transplants. One such is the homestead name Mercadool west of Parkes: it is not recorded before 1900 (in a newspaper item), and has the same spelling as a well known 19th century pastoral property in northern NSW (see above) and of a racehorse of the period. Nor can the word be matched with a known word in the local Wiradjuri language. Another central NSW placename which may have been transplanted from the GYY area is that of the homesteads Eulendool and Eulandool,[5] as there is a Eulan parish in the Walgett LGA.[6]

I take the name of Bardool parish in north-eastern NSW (the easternmost location on Map 1) to be a chance resemblance of the final syllable of a disyllabic word: it is an isolated occurrence in a rather different language area. Similarly for the only other *dool* placename in other states: Coondool Pool (Western Australia).

4. Southern inland NSW

As can be further seen on Map 1, the Riverina district in southern inland NSW has virtually the only other placenames in Australia with the *dool* ending. The information on these is gathered in Table 3. About half have some fragmentary origin information. Little of the origin information can be matched with wordlist entries for Wiradjuri, the relevant language.

---

5   This name occurs on a homestead north-west of Condobolin, and also on a locality south of Dubbo not in the Geographical Names Register (Geographical Names Board 2011) nor the *Gazetteer of Australia* (Geoscience Australia 2008). Both of these locations are some distance south of the GYY area. However a possible Wiradjuri stem is *yulun* 'blackwattle tree' (Grant and Rudder 2010 from *Yoo'loon(y)* Richards 1902: 183), equivalent to *dhulan* (YR,YY)), and the owners of the Eulandool property south of Dubbo were told the name 'meant Wattle Clump' (pers. comm. 19 October 2011).

6   The stem cannot be readily matched with a known GYY stem, but compare *yulan* 'skin' *Science of Man* 1897 02 27 [GCN] (J. Steele pers. comm.), *yulang* 'skin' (Curr 3), corresponding to *yulay* (GYY) 'skin'. The placenames Ulan, and Ulandra (in the Junee area) may also be related, but there is no etymology recorded for these names.

A few of the placenames in Table 3 might have been copied from an original place the northern NSW cluster, notably the homesteads Burrandool and Yarraldool.

5. A chance syllable?

While seeking etymologies for the placenames in Tables 2 and 3, we need to allow for the possibility that final *dool* is just a syllable which chances to match the suffix morpheme *-DHuul*. To assess this we can consider the wider set of placenames, those which end in *ool*, and see what proportion of these are specifically *dool*.

Following the same method as described above, the NSW placenames were sorted from the end of the word, thereby grouping spellings ending in *ool*, and the few in *ule*. No other terminations were found which would rhyme with *ool* according to English spelling. All the names in *ool* and *ule* were combined into a spreadsheet along with attributes of location and feature type. Next, names that clearly involve English words were then excluded (e.g. names with *Wool*, *Pool* or *School*). Also the dozen or so placenames in north central NSW involving the topographic term *Warrambool* (Nash 2011) and similarly the dozen or so names with the term *Wakool* in the western Riverina, were set aside.

The locations of the remaining toponymic sets are displayed in Map 2. It is apparent on Map 2 that the green triangle *dool* markers are in the minority except in the north central NSW cluster (where they dominate). Note particularly that in the Riverina there are many more *ool* placenames than just the *dool* names, and so (in the absence of other evidence) the chances are higher there that a final *dool* is just a syllable not a morpheme and not a suffix in its own right. I conclude from the distribution shown in Map 2 that *dool* names predominate just where they are likely to involve the GYY suffix *-DHuul*, and elsewhere the placenames are likely to end in a meaningless syllable (i.e. not a morpheme) written *dool* (or else are a transplanted copy of a genuine *-dool* name from the GYY area).

Indigenous and Minority Placenames

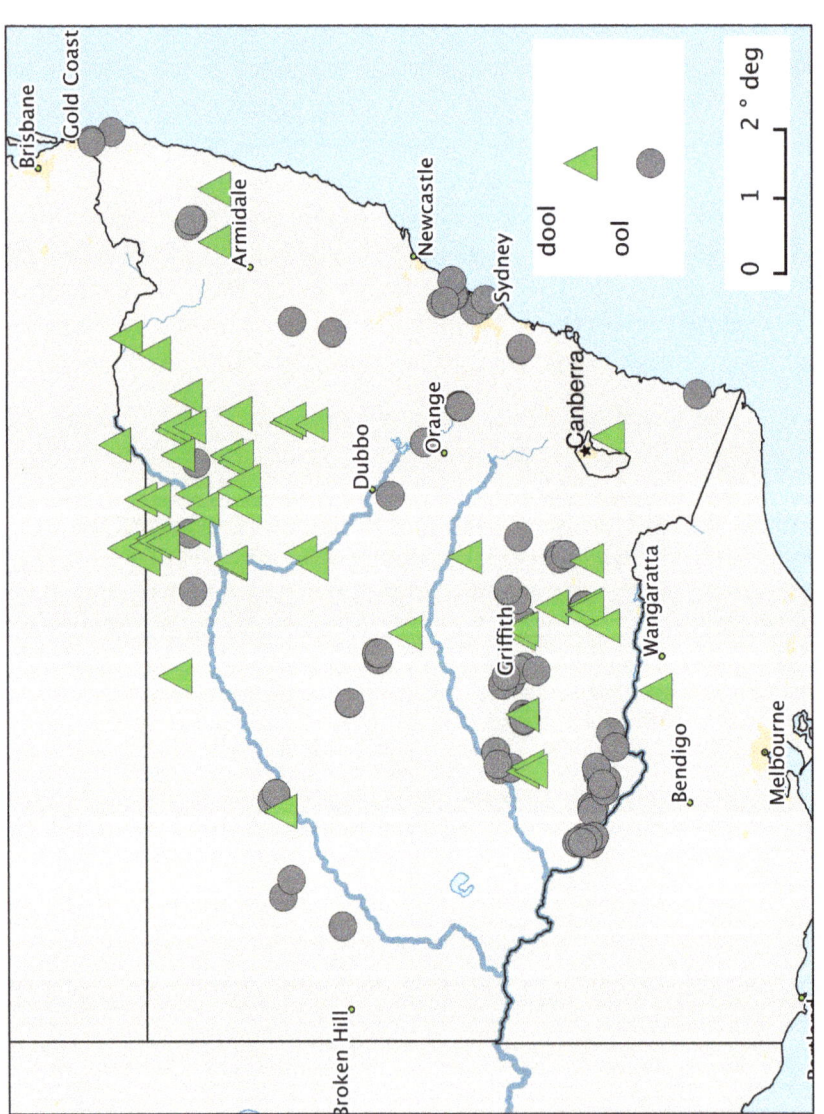

Map 2: Location of toponymic sets of placenames terminating in *ool* (or *ule*) marked with grey circle, along with *dool* (and *dule*) placenames of Map 1 with green triangle.

Source: Made with QGIS and Natural Earth, free vector and raster map data from naturalearthdata.com.

6. Semantic patterns

6.1 Stem types

Returning to the GYY placenames of northern inland NSW considered above, we can add some semantic considerations to help the assessment of the fragmentary etymological information. For the placenames with relatively secure etymology, in Table 1, we can see that the stem meanings are mostly concrete entities: two flora terms ('reeds' and 'swamp oak'), and two physical features ('cracks', 'stone') along possibly with 'rockhole' (as proposed in the note to *Mildool* above as an extended sense of 'eye'). The two non-concrete stems are attributes 'small' and 'blind, blunt', though possibly both denoting humans (or animals) ('child' and 'blind person').

These semantic ranges fit fairly well with the speculative etymologies indicated in Table 2: the possible GYY stems listed in Table 2 include flora terms (and also animals), a physical feature ('steep bank'), and human attributes.

6.2 Semantics of the 'Diminutive'

The *GYY Dictionary* glosses *-DHuul* as '1. little, small; 2. one' with the comment 'This suffix is attached to nouns, it has a wide range of meanings.'

The second sense is apparent where the suffix occurs in some GYY lexemes, such as Gamilaraay *dhiidjuul* 'piece of meat' from *dhii* 'meat' and Gamilaraay *gaaydjuul* 'small-little, just, one' based on *gaay* '1. small, little; 2. child'.[7] In other words, the so-called diminutive does not always carry the sense of 'little, small', but rather sometimes functions as a definitiser or individuator, related to its hypocoristic function and the formation of proper names. This extended function of the diminutive is not uncommon in languages around the world; see Dressler and Barbaresi's (1994: 116–169) wide-ranging discussion, and Jurafsky (1996: 555–556) on the Individuating or Partitive sense of the diminutive.

It is typical for a diminutive morpheme to have other senses as well as the two noted in the *GYY Dictionary*. It is common for the diminutive to be used affectively, so that the diminutive of X expresses an attitude to X, something like 'dear (little) X'. A couple of GYY lexemes possibly involve an affective component: *milanduul* (Y) 'alone, only one' (*milan* 'one'), and *marayrrdhuul* 'childless woman' from *marayrr* 'no, none', *-dhuul* 'one'. And in some languages the diminutive of a placename expresses that the place is familiar (Jurafsky 1996: 539 on Cantonese; Simpson 2001).

---

7   Recently an extra sense has been added for *gaaydjuul*: 'suffix/prefix' (Giacon 2006: 2), probably drawing on the homophonous stem *gaay* (YR,YY) '1. word; 2. message; 3. language; 4. story'.

From some of the glosses from old sources given in Table 1 we can see that the 'small' sense is not always present in GYY diminutives. For instance, when suffixed to a human attribute stem *-DHuul* means 'the one who is', possibly also with an affective component, such as *gaaynduul* 'baby' (Kiandool), and probably *mugadhuul* 'blind person' (Mookadool and possibly Murkadool). In the neighbouring language to the south-west, Ngiyampaa, '*-DHul* is a singular diminutive' and 'the 'littleness' of the diminutive is associated with emotional attachment' (Donaldson 1980: 100–102).[8]

It is thus likely that some of the *-dool* placenames do not involve the sense 'small' even where it might be plausible. Thus, when the diminutive is combined with a flora term such as 'reeds' or 'swamp oak', the sense could be better translated in English by the definite article; thus Drildool 'The Reeds', Mercadool 'The Oaks', Noongadool 'The Currajongs'. It is natural for a placename (as a proper name) to involve a sense of definiteness, and so it may well be that most *-dool* placenames are definites and do not involve literally smallness of size.

6.3 Diminutive placenames

Diminutives have not been reported in placenames elsewhere in Australia, at least, not in placenames in Australian Indigenous languages.

For Australian English Simpson (2001) has reported hypocoristic versions of Australian placenames, some of which (such as *Bundy* for *Bundaberg*) use the Australian English ending spelled *-y* or *-ie* which is a diminutive, among other functions. Another strand in Australian English hypocoristic placenames are formations with *The*, as in *The 'Gong* (Wollongong) (Simpson 2001). Thus there is a partial parallel in Australian English to my analysis of the *-dool* placenames in the Yuwaalayaay (and GYY) language.

Another formation which can be seen as another kind of placename diminutive is the pattern of English placenames modified with the adjective 'Little'. A placename *Little A* typically relates a location to another nearby location bearing the same base name *A*, as for instance the pair of locations Little Hartley and Hartley in the western Blue Mountains, or the Little Sandy Desert and Great Sandy Desert (in Western Australia). A related kind is represented by Little Austria in the Snowy Mountains, where the locality is named to echo a more famous distant locality with some perceived shared property. We could call this type an external diminutive; it is not uncommon in English placenames in Australia, but it is quite unusual (or perhaps nonexistent) in Australian placenames of Indigenous origin. There is no evidence that the external diminutive plays any

---

8   Note, however, there are no recorded placenames containing *-DHul* in the associated Wangaaybuwan country, unless one counts the Eulandool property north-west of Condobolin.

role in the -*dool* placenames of Yuwaalayaay and Yuwaalaraay. In central NSW there appear to be some external diminutive examples involving Nyrang[9] such as Boree Nyrang and Eurow Nyrang Mountain, but these placenames likely arose in the context of NSW Pidgin.

In contrast to the external diminutive is what could be termed the internal diminutive, of which some -*dool* placenames are exemplary. Thus the example above with the clearest known origin, *Mildool*, is '[[small rockhole] place]' rather than '[small [rockhole place]]'; the other, Yarraldool '[[small stone] place]', is also based on a physical feature stem. As an aside, note that English placenames with internal diminutive are also typically restricted to names derived from a feature type, such as Little Bay or Little River.

7. Conclusion

The recorded Australian placenames ending in *dool* are concentrated in the territory of the closely related Yuwaalayaay and Yuwaalaraay languages of central northern NSW and adjacent Queensland, and exhibit the nominal suffix -*DHuul* with definite, individuating or diminutive meaning in those languages. While this is an unusual derivation for placenames in Australian languages, there are some parallels in English. Another apparent cluster of *dool* placenames in the NSW Riverina are of disparate origin, and do not reflect a suffix of the local language there.

---

9   Nyrang is a spelling of the second of "Aboriginal colloquialisms such as 'cobbon' (big) and 'narrang' (small)" (Wesson 2001: 31), cf. Sydney Language *ngarang* 'small' Wafer and Lissarrague (2008: 623).

Table 1: Toponyms in -dool (or -dule) with recorded source in Yuwaalayaay and Yuwaalaraay area, ordered alphabetically.

Placename	Designation	State	possible GYY stem	meaning in source	source, comment
Burrawandool	parish	NSW	*barrawan* (YY) '1. golden bandicoot; 2. type of sedge'	Burrawarrendool 'Burrow [Berries?] in ground'	RASA 2004:70 Mogil Mogil
Drildool	locality, parish, hmsd	NSW	*dhariil* (GR) 'reed'	Drildool = Tareel-dool 'place of reeds' Tareeldool 'small reeds' Drildool 'Small water reeds'	RASA 2004:351, RASA 2004:354; Drildool = Dhariilduul (Ash et al. 2003:57)[A] RASA 2004:67
Gradule	locality, creek	QLD	*Garra-dhuul* 'cracks-DIM'; or *garaay dhuyul* 'sandhill'; *garra* (YR,YY,GR) 'cracks' (Ash et al. 2003:80)	cracks	Ash (2002) 'In Yuwaaliyaay, Sim (1998) mentions ... two other placenames: Garrabila, Garra-bilaa 'cracks-parallel' and Garradhuul, Garra-dhuul 'cracks-DIM'.'
Guraldool	not located		possibly *gurrulay* (YR,YY) 'river wattle' or *gurraay* (YR,YY) 'white cypress pine'	'Young box tree'	RASA 2004:66 Walgett
Kiandool	rsta	NSW	*gaaynduul* 'baby',[B] *gaayindjuul* 'small' (Austin & Nathan (1998)	Kindool 'small' Kiandool 'a baby'	RASA 2004:354 (Irish 1927)
Mercadool, Merkadool	hmsd	NSW	*murrgu* (YR,YY,GR) 'swamp oak, belah tree'	belah tree, oak trees (Merkadool Tank) (Irish 1927)	RASA 2004 Walgett
Mildool	hmsd, parish	NSW	*mil* (YR,YY,GR) 'eye'	rock with water in[C] 'Blackfellow's eye'	RASA 2004:66 Walgett RASA 2004:71 Angledool
Mirriadool	hmsd	NSW	*mirriyaa* (YR,YY) 'lignum (*Meuhlenbeckia cunninghamii*)	Mirradool 'Current bushes'	RASA 2004:70 Mogil Mogil[D]
Murkadool	parish	NSW	*muga* (YR,YY,GR) 'blind, blunt' or *muurrguu* (YR,YY) 'barking owl (*Ninox connivens*)'	Mookadool 'blind' or Murgudul 'abounding in the murgu, or night cuckoo' Ridley 1873:258	RASA 2004:354; or Murkadool may be a variant of Mercadool above
Noongadool	not located		*nhungga* (YR,YY) 'kurrajong tree'	'A quantity of currajong trees'	RASA 2004:66 Walgett

3. The diminutive suffix -dool in placenames of central north NSW

Placename	Designation	State	possible GYY stem	meaning in source	source, comment
Wambadule	parish	NSW	*wamba* (YR,YY,GR) '1. mad, crazy; 2. stupid, silly; 3. eccentric'	Wambadule 'Stupid fellow'	RASA 2004:67
Wergadool	not located	NSW	*barrgay* (YY) 'flowering lignum, lignum fuchsia (*Eremophila polyclada*)'	'Lignum bush'	RASA 2004:66 Walgett
Yarraldool	hmsd	NSW	*yarral* (YR,YY,GR) 'stone'	'Lot of stones' small stones Yarrandool 'A child picked up a little stone'[E]	RASA 2004:40 item 9; Yarralduul 'Location south of Burren Junction.' (Ash et al. 2003:152)[F]
Yarraldool	hmsd	NSW			see Yarraldool above and § 2

Note A: The dictionary entry also lists "**Dhariilaraay** (GR) *placename* Tarilarai. … Also Tareelaroi, east of Moree." (The Wiradjuri placename Jerilderie derives from a cognate stem with the same meaning.)

Note B: Compare *gaayŋgal* (GR) 'baby'. "Possibly originally a plural based on *gaay* (child, small) and -*gal* (many). Also found as *gaaynduul* which is probably a singular form." (Ash et al. 2003: 73). Another matching stem is *giiyan* (YY,GR) 'centipede' but this meaning is not supported by the 19th century source.

Note C: Parker (1905: 145) recorded the origin story (or etiology, Koch 2009: 117, 153) for this feature: "At Mildool is a scooped-out rock which Byamee made to catch and hold water; beside it he hollowed out a smaller stone, that his dog might have a drinking-place too. This recurrence of the mention of dogs in the legends touching Byamee looks as if blacks at all events believed dogs to have been in Australia as long as men." From this we can see that the placename focuses on the smaller rockhole at the site. (Note that in other Australian languages, the word meaning 'eye' can also in some contexts denote a point source of water.) The *GYY Dictionary* is less specific: "**Milduul** (YR,YY) *placename* Probably named because of marks in the rock or ground, that resemble eyes. Located between Angledool and Hebel in *Nhunggabarraa* territory. *Baayami* made a cave there for the warriors to rest and hunters camped there." (Ash et al. 2003: 111).

Note D: Mirriadool and Mirradool may not be the same place, because Mirriadool is about 100 km south-east of the Mogil Mogil district, and there is a discrepancy between the two kinds of plant ascribed.

Note E: The interpretation 'A child picked up a little stone' in the Pilliga district includes more than the literal meaning and suggests that a fragment of the origin story has been recorded here.

Note F: The dictionary entry also lists "**Yarralaraay** (GR) *placename* 'Yalaroi'. From *yarral* (stone) and -*araay* (with, having)"; RASA (2004:351,352, 354); RASA 2004:67 Pilliga.

Table 2. Toponyms in -*dool* (or -*dule*, -*joole*) in Yuwaalayaay and Yuwaalaraay area with no recorded source, ordered alphabetically.

Placename	designation	State	possible GYY stem	meaning	source, comment
Angledool	locality, hmsd	NSW	*nganggil* (YY) 'steep bank'	'Big bend in river'	RASA 2004:71 Angledool *Nerangledool* (Parker 1898:49, 53); Laves [1930] got the name as *Ngarangalduul* from a local woman, who didn't know what the name meant (I. Sim 2002 per J. Giacon p.c.); 'possibly a shortened form of Nerangledool' (R. Treweeke, p.c. 12/10/05)[G]
Ballandool	hmsd	QLD	*baluun* (YR,YY) '1. great egret (YR,YY); 2. Ballone (place and river) (YY).'[H]		
Berrieadool	locality	NSW			
Birreldool	hmsd	NSW			
Burrandool	hmsd	NSW	*barrabarruun* (YR,YY) 'quail'; *barran* (YR,YY,GR) 'boomerang'[I]		'Quail burrandool' Endacott 1925:16. Burrandoon, aboriginal Burran-dool—From name of tree growing there called Burran, and from which the aborigines make the Burran shield.' Greenway 1911:191 " cf. *barranbaa* (YR,YY)
Cudgildool	parish	NSW	*gagil-dhuul* 'unhappy; bad one, bad person'		cf. Gudgildool. 'Kuggildool nasty man or thing or place' Greenway 1911:191
Gudgildool	hmsd	NSW			cf. Cudgildool
Currindule	parish	NSW			cf. Grandool
Grandool[J]	parish	NSW	*girran* (YR,YY,GR) 'ashes'		cf. Currindule
Keadool	parish	NSW	*gii* '1. heart (YR,YY,GR); 2. gall bladder (YY); 3. bitter (YY); 4. blueberry (YY)'		

3. The diminutive suffix -dool in placenames of central north NSW

Placename	designation	State	possible GYY stem	meaning	source, comment
Keadool	hmsd	NSW			
Kynejoole	hmsd	QLD	*gayn* (YR,YY) 'scraper, fire rake'		
Menadool	hmsd, parish	NSW			
Narrandool	hmsd, parish	NSW	*nharran* (YY) 'skinny'ᴷ		
Ninedool	hmsd	NSW			
Pooloomoodool	hmsd	QLD	*bulumburr* (YR,YY) 'native tomato'		
Urandool	hmsd	QLD	*yuuraa* (YR,YY,GR) 'dogwood' (Ray Wood p.c.)		
Urandool	parish	NSW			
Widgeldool	hmsd	NSW			
Yarradool	hmsd	NSW			possibly a version of Yarraldool (above)

Note G: Note that "Angledool was previously known as New Angledool when it was established in the 1870s." (http://en.wikipedia.org/wiki/Angledool). The possibility that 'New Angledool' was a kind of anglicisation of *Nerangledool* needs further historical investigation.

Note H: This is my speculation; there are other similar stems; however this stem also occurs in another placename "**Baluunbilyan** (YR,YY) *placename* Bollonbillion. A waterhole at Angledool. From *baluur* (egret) and *bilyan* (waterhole), so 'Egret Waterhole.'"

Note I: I do not have origin information for either of the two Burrandool in the GYY area, and there is the possibility that it was chosen from '**Burrandool** Quail' in the widely available Curr (1888), Vol. 2, p.480-, vocabulary No. 131 Additional Words, from Cape River, Natal Downs Station (in northern Queensland), and this could be Endacott's (1925) source. A more straightforward GYY stem for Burrandool is *barran* 'boomerang' as in the placename Burren Junction (Ash et al. 2003: 35); this may be related to the the somewhat out of place entry Boorandool 'Country where Oak Timber grows' (RASA 2004: 43), in a list from Obley (south of Dubbo).

Note J: The GNB Register has two entries for Grandool parish both in County Clyde; they have almost the same coordinates, so I have taken them to be duplicates.

Note K: This speculation is based on Ash et al. (2003: 130), which entry also covers the placename Narran River. (The Wiradjuri placename Narranderra derives from Wiradjuri *nhaRang* 'lizard'.)

Table 3: Toponyms terminating in *dool* in southern NSW.

Placename	Designation	State	Meaning	Source
Bungadool	parish	NSW	Short Bungledool 'small or little woman'	(Endacott 1925: 15, RASA 2004: 353)
Burradool	hmsd	NSW		
Burrandool	hmsd	NSW		see Burrandool above
Carrathool	parish	NSW	Brolga **Cooradook** native companion Grus *rubicundus*	Carrathool 'native companion' (Irish 1927) Wesson (2001: 164) fauna Wiradjuri Language File
Carawandool, Currawandool	parish	NSW	Currathool 'Small pines'ʸ	(RASA 2004: 139 Carrathool area)
Cherridool	hmsd	NSW		
Leentool	hmsd	NSW		
Moombooldool	popl, parish	NSW	Moom, death	(Irish 1927)
Mumbledool	hmsd	NSW		
Toollendool	hmsd	NSW		
Tootool	village, parish	NSW	a bird, resembling a crow, now extinct; 'bird' (McCarthy 1963)	(Irish 1927)
Tootool	trig. station			
Wallandool	hmsd	NSW	Brown stone; 'a creek with deep holes'	(Endacott 1925: 53)
Wooloondool	hmsd, parish	NSW		
Yarraldool	hmsd	NSW		see Yarraldool above
Yundool	popl	VIC		

Note Y: For the stem compare Carawatha 'The place of pines'. This was the name of Murray Hut now known as Finley. (RASA 2004:363). There is a partial match with the GYY word *gurruay* '(white) cyprus pine', suggesting there may have been a similar Wiradjuri word.

References

Ash, A. 2002, 'Placenames in Yuwaalaraay, Yuwaalayaay and Gamilaraay of north-west New South Wales', in *The Land is a Map: Placenames of Indigenous Origin in Australia*, Luise Hercus, Flavia Hodges and Jane Simpson (eds), Pandanus Books for Pacific Linguistics, Canberra: 181–185.

Ash, A., J. Giacon and A. Lissarrague (eds) 2003, *Gamilaraay, Yuwaalaraay and Yuwaalayaay dictionary*, IAD Press, Alice Springs.

Austin, P. and D. Nathan 1998, Kamilaroi/Gamilaraay Web Dictionary. http://coombs.anu.edu.au/WWWVLPages/AborigPages/LANG/GAMDICT/GAMDICT.HTM (accessed 6 May 2012).

Donaldson, T. 1980, *Ngiyambaa, the Language of the Wangaaybuwan*, Cambridge Studies in Linguistics 29, Cambridge University Press, Cambridge.

Dressler, W. U. and L. M. Barbaresi 1994, *Morphopragmatics: Diminutives and Intensifiers in Italian, German, and other Languages*, Studies and Monographs 76, Walter de Gruyter, Berlin.

Endacott, S.J. 1925, *Australian Aboriginal Native Names, and their Meanings*, (2nd edn), Melbourne.

Geographical Names Board 2011, Geographical Names Register (GNR) of NSW, Land and Property Information, New South Wales: http://www.gnb.nsw.gov.au/name_search (accessed 6 May 2012).

Geoscience Australia 2008, Gazetteer of Australia 2008 Release. Searchable at http://www.ga.gov.au/map/names/ (accessed 6 May 2012). See also Gazetteer of Australia 2010 Release.

[Giacon, J.] 2006, Gaay Garay Dhadhin: new words. 3 pp. file. http://www.yuwaalaraay.org/documents/GaayGarayDhadhin.doc (accessed 24 September 2011).

Greenway, C.C. 1911, 'Kamilari tribe', *Science of Man* 12(10):191, 13(6):125.

Grant, S. and J. Rudder 2010, *A New Wiradjuri Dictionary*, Restoration House, O'Connor, ACT.

Irish, C.A. 1927, 'Names of railway stations in New South Wales. With their meaning and origin', *Royal Australian Historical Society* 13: 99–144. http://www.nswrail.net/library/station_names.php/ (accessed 6 May 2012).

Jurafsky, D. 1996, 'Universal tendencies in the semantics of the diminutive', *Language* 72(3): 533–578.

Koch, H. 2009, 'The methodology of reconstructing Indigenous placenames: Australian Capital Territory and south-eastern New South Wales', in *Aboriginal Placenames: Naming and Re-naming the Australian Landscape*, Harold Koch and Luise Hercus (eds), Aboriginal History Monograph 19, ANU E Press and Aboriginal History Incorporated, Canberra: 115–171. http://epress.anu.edu.au?p=17331/ (accessed 6 May 2012).

McCarthy, F. D. 1963, *New South Wales Aboriginal Place Names and Euphonious Words, with their Meanings*, Australian Museum, Sydney.

Nash, D. 2011, 'What's a Warrambool?', Posted on Endangered Languages & Cultures blog, 19 June 2011, 11:06 am, http://www.paradisec.org.au/blog/2011/06/what's-a-warrambool/ (accessed 6 May 2012).

Parker, K. L. 1898, *More Australian legendary Tales*, D. Nutt, London. http://www.archive.org/details/moreaustralianl00parkgoog (accessed 6 May 2012).

— 1905, *The Euahlayi Tribe. A Study of Aboriginal Life in Australia*, Archibald Constable and Company Ltd, London. http://books.google.com.au/books?id=vWU8Vu7enKwC (accessed 6 May 2012), http://www.gutenberg.org/ebooks/3819 (accessed 6 May 2012).

Richards, C. 1902, 'Wirra' Dthooree — Wirrai' Yarrai'. Wirrach' Aree' — Wirra' Jer-ree'', *Science of Man* 5(11): 180–183.

Ridley, W. 1873, 'Australian languages and traditions', *Journal of the Anthropological Institute of Great Britain and Ireland*, 2: 257–275. http://www.jstor.org/stable/2841174 (accessed 11 April 2014).

Royal Anthropological Society of Australia (RASA) 2004, Royal Anthropological Society of Australia manuscripts dated 1900, 'Anthropological Society of Aus roll 1', PDF file. CD-ROM, Geographic Names Board of NSW.

Simpson, J. 2001, 'Hypocoristics of place-names in Australian English', in *Varieties of English: Australian English*, Peter Collins and David Blair (eds), Benjamins, Amsterdam, Philadelphia: 89–112.

Wafer, J. and A. Lissarrague 2008, *A Handbook of Aboriginal Languages of New South Wales and the Australian Capital Territory*, Muurrbay Aboriginal Language and Culture Co-operative, Nambucca Heads.

Wesson, S. 2001, *Aboriginal Flora and Fauna Names of Victoria: As Extracted from Early Surveyors' Reports*, Victorian Aboriginal Corporation for Languages, Melbourne. http://www.vaclang.org.au/project-detail.aspx?ID=9 (accessed 6 May 2012) http://www.vaclang.org.au/admin%5Cfile%5Ccontent9%5Cc7%5Cff.pdf.

Williams, C.J. 1980, *A Grammar of Yuwaalaraay*, Pacific Linguistics B-74, Pacific Linguistics, ANU, Canberra.

4. Placenames as a guide to language distribution in the Upper Hunter, and the *landnám* problem in Australian toponomastics[1]

Jim Wafer
University of Newcastle

1. Introduction

The question of what language or languages was or were spoken in the Upper Hunter region of New South Wales (NSW) is vexed. The NSW Aboriginal Languages Research and Resource Centre's current draft 'Map of NSW Aboriginal languages'[2] leaves the Upper Hunter blank. In earlier attempts to identify the languages spoken in this region, from the coastal areas occupied by 'Awabakal' and 'Worimi' to the headwaters of the Hunter in the Great Dividing Range, Tindale (1974: 193 and map) filled the space with a language he called 'Geawegal', and the Central Mapping Authority ('CMA') of NSW (1987) and Horton (1996) followed suit.

Brayshaw, on the other hand, analyses a number of historical documents that suggest a long-standing connection between speakers of 'Kamilaroi' and the upper Hunter (1986: 38–42), 'as far south as Wollombi Brook'[3] (1986: 41). There seems to be little disagreement that the Kamilaroi occupied the headwaters of the Hunter (Tindale 1974: 194 and map) and the area around Murrurundi, close to the watershed. Further down the Hunter Valley, the literature often depicts the Kamilaroi as intruders. In relation specifically to the Geawegal, Fison and Howitt say that the latter 'were always in dread of war with the Kamilaroi, who intruded down the heads of the Hunter across from Talbragar[4] to the Munmurra waters,[5] and even occasionally made raids as far as Jerry's Plains'[6] (1880: 279).

---

1 I am indebted to Amanda Lissarrague, John Giacon, David Nash and Stephen Wye for helpful correspondence and conversations pertaining to this article.
2 http://ab-ed.boardofstudies.nsw.edu.au/bosImg_window.cfm?objectid=03540C9F-F074-1B07-416F6CDE53A110F7> (accessed 6 April 2014).
3 Which joins the Hunter just upstream from Singleton. Nonetheless, Brayshaw's map (1986: 39), probably following Tindale, allocates the Upper Hunter to speakers of Geawegal.
4 The Talbragar River rises in the Warung State Forest (between Murrurundi and Cassilis) and flows into the Macquarie River near Dubbo. (See http://www.gnb.nsw.gov.au/place_naming/placename_search/extract?id=TRlpXtsETR, accessed 6 April 2014.)
5 The Munmurra River is a tributary of the Goulburn that rises near Breeza Lookout and flows through Cassilis.
6 Between Denman and Singleton.

The present article attempts to throw some light on this matter, mainly through an analysis of placenames from the region, and then investigates some of the difficulties posed by *landnám*[7] in the context of Aboriginal placenames. But I begin with an investigation of the term 'Geawegal', since it has been given such prominence by the two scholars (Tindale and Horton) who have been most influential in determining the course of Aboriginal language cartography.

2. Geawegal

The use of 'Geawegal' as the name for a social and linguistic grouping originated with Fison and Howitt's account of 'The Geawe-gal Tribe' (Appendix G of their *Kamilaroi and Kurnai*, 1880: 279–284), based on information provided by G.W. Rusden.[8] This short study contains only six morphemes associated specifically with Geawegal. These include *geawe*, the word for 'no', from which the language derives its name.

The negligible size of this body of data makes the linguistic classification of Geawegal difficult. Tindale assumed that it was related to Worimi. He wrote as follows: 'Affiliated with the coastal Worimi. The grammar and vocabulary published by Hale (1845), following Threlkeld (1834), relates principally to this tribe. The ascription of it to Kamilaroi by Hale is an unexplained error' (Tindale 1974: 193).

Tindale mentions two dialect names here: 'Worimi' and 'Kamilaroi'. In a more contemporary orthography these would be 'Warrimay' and 'Gamilaraay'. Warrimay is a dialect of what I call the 'Lower North Coast' language (LNC), which includes as well the dialect known as 'Gringai' ('Guringay'). Gamilaraay is a dialect of what I call the 'Darling Tributaries' language (DT).

There is a third language that will be pertinent to the discussion here, namely, the Hunter River-Lake Macquarie language (HRLM). This is sometimes called 'Awabakal', although this name (invented by John Fraser 1892: v) is probably best reserved for the northern coastal dialect. The language includes other dialects as well, such as 'Wonnarua' ('Wanarruwa').

Tindale is correct that Hale's use of the name 'Kāmilarai' in reference to his published language material is a mistake, since it clearly pertains to the Hunter River-Lake Macquarie language. But he is wrong in his assumption that the

---

7 I shall consider the term in more detail at the appropriate point in this paper. Here, a simplified definition will have to suffice: 'the cultural adoption of a landscape by immigrants to an area'.
8 The material in Fison and Howitt's Appendix G summarises data about the Geawegal that are scattered throughout Howitt's later publication, *The Native Tribes of South-East Australia* (1904). Howitt's 1904 work adds nothing new.

linguistic work of Hale and Threlkeld refers to Geawegal, unless he is using this name as a general term for HRLM. This seems unlikely, given that he says the Geawegal are 'affiliated with the coastal Worimi'. In a similar vein, in his entry for 'Worimi', Tindale writes that 'Threlkeld's 1834 grammar is principally from the inland Geawegal with whom [the Worimi] were affiliated' (1974: 201).

Because of the influence of Tindale's work, it is worth untangling some of the strands of his argument. It is true that Horatio Hale visited Lancelot Threlkeld (in 1839), and, on the basis of his interpretation of Threlkeld's material, wrote a vocabulary and grammar that he called 'Kāmilarai' (Hale 1846: 482 and *passim*). As noted above, Tindale is right that such an ascription was an error on Hale's part. But I cannot find any reason why Tindale would attribute Hale's material (and the Threlkeld data on which it was based) to the 'inland Geawegal'.[9]

Threlkeld himself did not give any Indigenous name for the language he wrote about, but instead used the following formula (or variations of it): 'the language, as spoken by the Aborigines, in the vicinity of Hunter's River, Lake Macquarie *etc.*, New South Wales' (1834: iii). The only informant named (1834: ix) is M'Gill (Biraban), who is known to have been a native of the Lake Macquarie district. Threlkeld does mention that his own son had visited 'the higher districts of Hunter's River', but only in order to say that the language spoken there did not appear to be mutually intelligible with the (coastal) dialect of the language spoken by himself and, evidently, by his son (1834: x). So there is no evidence, linguistic or otherwise, to suggest that the language described in Threlkeld's work of 1834 does not pertain to the same variety he wrote about in his other works — that is, the dialect spoken at Lake Macquarie and the Lower Hunter — rather than to an inland variety (cf. Oppliger 1984: 1–3; Lissarrague 2006: 7–15).

Tindale's mention of the Threlkeld grammar under his entry for 'Worimi' suggests he believed that this grammar described the language spoken by the Worimi, or at least a closely related dialect — in other words, that HRLM and Worimi were dialects of the same language. Amanda Lissarrague and I have analysed in some detail the likely historical reasons for this error, and attempted to show that the Lower North Coast language (of which Worimi is a dialect) and HRLM are separate languages (Wafer and Lissarrague 2011: 149–150). For present purposes, it is sufficient to say that a comparison of the verb and pronoun paradigms of LNC and HRLM provides enough evidence to define them as distinct.

But is Geawegal related to either of these languages? Or is it perhaps, like Gamilaraay, a dialect of the Darling Tributaries language?

---

9   The only relevant source appears to be Enright, who says that 'the Geawegal was merely a horde, and a part of the Worimi tribe' (Enright 1932: 75). But this is not a reason to attribute the Threlkeld material to Geawegal.

Indigenous and Minority Placenames

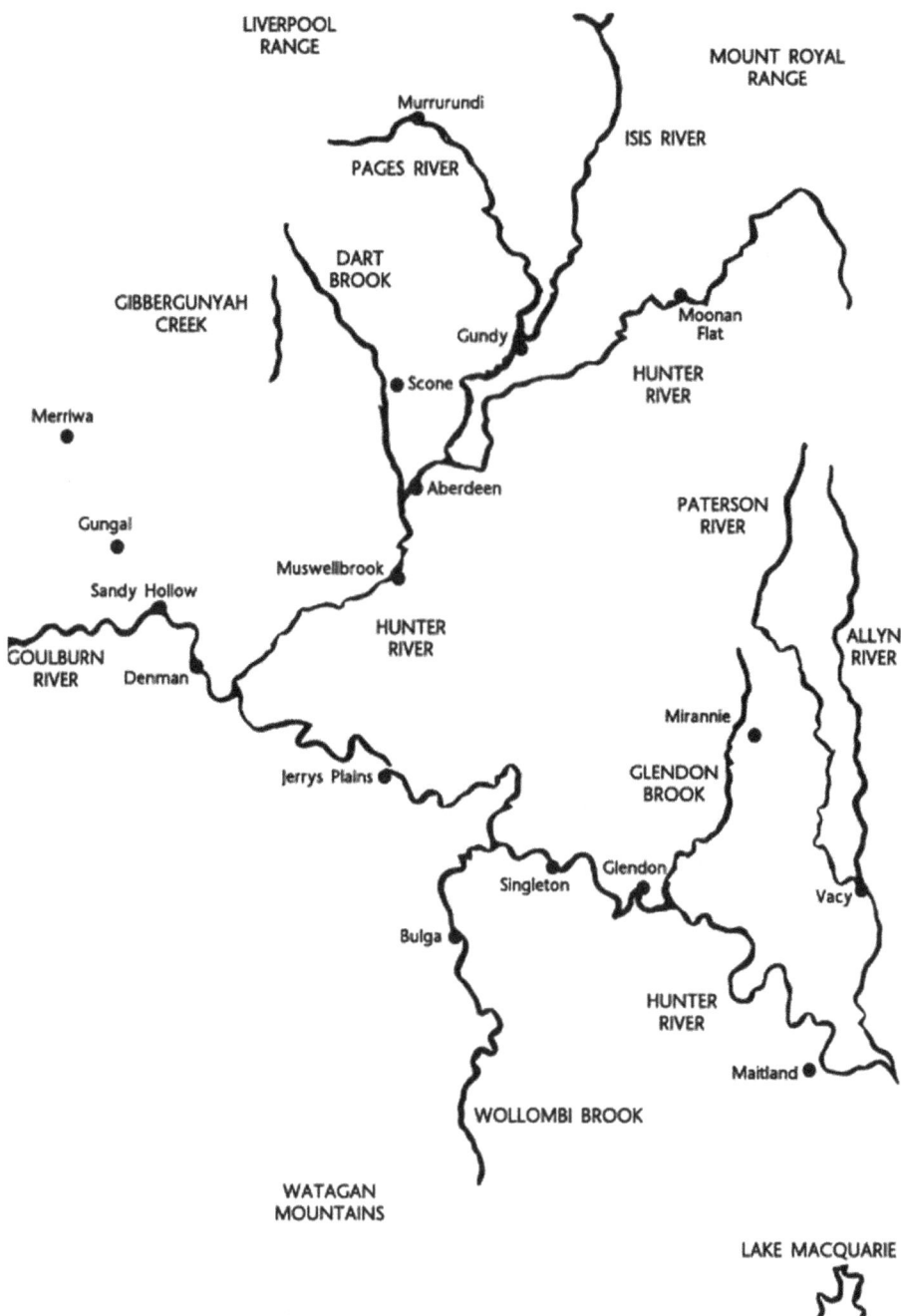

Map 1: Map of the Upper Hunter, with placenames mentioned in the text.

Source: The author.

As mentioned above, Fison and Howitt's account of 'The Geawe-gal Tribe' contains six morphemes from the Geawegal dialect. These include *geawe*, the word for 'no', from which the language derives its name. *Kayaway* is one of several alternative negative forms in HRLM (Lissarrague 2006: 98, 117), and is not used in LNC, where the common negative particle is *gurayn* (Lissarrague 2010: 238). Fison and Howitt mention two other items of vocabulary, namely *koradji*, 'wizard, medicine man' (1880: 281) and *murramai*, 'rock crystal' (1880: 283), both of which are also found in HRLM.[10] But the former has a cognate in Gamilaraay (*maarama*, 'stone'; see Ash, Giacon and Lissarrague 2003: 104) and the latter a cognate in LNC (*giraatji*, 'clever man'; see Lissarrague 2010: 229).

In addition, Fison and Howitt's informant, G.W. Rusden, used one Indigenous word, with a gloss, in the notes to his epic poem 'Moyarra'. This word he rendered as *barracun* and glossed as 'boomerang' (Rusden 1891: 51).[11] The same word occurs in both HRLM (*parrkan*, Lissarrague 2006: 131) and LNC (*barrgan*, Lissarrague 2010: 180).

Further, the dialect name 'Geawegal' (which I shall spell from here on as 'Kayawaykal') contains the derivational suffix *-kal*, which Lissarrague has described as the 'belonging' suffix in HRLM (2006: 62–63).[12] But this suffix also occurs in LNC.[13] According to Fison and Howitt (1880: 280), Kayawaykal had, in addition, words for the 'class divisions' Yippai (Yipay) and Kombo (Kampu).[14] Among the speakers of the HRLM dialects, the Wanarruwa also had these class divisions (Fawcett 1898: 180), technically known as 'sections', and the speakers of the eastern dialect ('Awabakal') did not. These names have cognates in the Darling Tributaries language (Howitt 1904: 104; Ash, Giacon and Lissarrague 2003: 10–12). The western dialect of LNC (Guringay) also used section names of this type (the 'Kamilaroi type'), but, according to Howitt, in a somewhat modified form (1904: 266–267).[15]

This is admittedly a very small body of language material on which to make a case. What we can say about it, in summary, is that all of the seven morphemes

---

10   Lissarrague has reconstructed these as *maRamay~maRama* (pers. comm.) and *kuratji* (2006: 120).
11   It is worth noting Fison and Howitt's observation that Rusden 'was identified with [the Geawegal 'tribe'], and spoke the language as a youth' (1880: 279).
12   As Lissarrague says, the name 'Kayawaykal' 'is composed of an HRLM word for "no", *kayaway*, and the belonging suffix *-kal*' (2006: 13).
13   In the orthography Lissarrague uses for LNC, this suffix is spelt as *-gal*. Its meaning is similar to that of *-kal* in HRLM, but in LNC Lissarrague glosses it as 'type [of person]' (2010: 47–48).
14   It is unclear why Rusden recorded only two names for the 'class divisions', where the neighbouring languages that use cognate terms have four. (There are usually four terms for males, and four corresponding terms for females.) Rusden himself admits that he could 'not recollect all their class divisions' (Fison and Howitt 1880: 280), so it seems more likely to be a result of the recorder's faulty memory than a reduction of the four 'section' terms to two.
15   'Most of the Gringai were named Kumbo, but there were some Ipai, Kubbi and Murri among them' (Howitt 1904: 266). Howitt goes on to observe what he regards as a 'complete breaking down of the old Kamilaroi system' among the Gringai (1904: 267).

that occur in Geawegal are found in at least some of the other dialects of HRLM. Moreover, while there are cognates in some of the surrounding non-HRLM languages, the cognate count is never higher than five out of seven items.[16] This suggests that, on the balance of probabilities, Kayawaykal was a dialect of HRLM, and not a dialect of one of the neighbouring languages, such as the LNC or the Darling Tributaries language.

3. Locating Geawegal

Because the corpus of linguistic data associated explicitly with Kayawaykal is so restricted, I have attempted to compensate for this lack by analysing sources which, while not specified as Kayawaykal, come from the area in which Kayawaykal was supposedly spoken. But the extent of this area is not unambiguous, since Fison and Howitt (the earliest source) and Tindale give different accounts.

According to Fison and Howitt, 'the territory claimed by them [the Kayawaykal] may be defined as being part of the valley of the Hunter River extending to each lateral watershed, and from twenty-five to thirty miles along the valley on each side of Glendon. [Glendon is a short distance south-east of Singleton.] These aborigines spoke the language of, and intermarried with, those of Maitland. Less frequently with those of the Patterson [sic] River, and rarely with those of Muswell Brook' (1880: 279).

This account is broadly contradicted by Tindale (1974: 193 and map), who provides this version of the location of the Kayawaykal: 'Northern tributaries of the Hunter River to Murrurundi; at Muswellbrook, Aberdeen, Scone, and Mount Royal Range'.[17] In other words, Tindale places the Kayawaykal quite a long distance further to the north-west than Fison and Howitt.

There are two manuscript documents that have the potential to adjudicate between these contradictory accounts. One pertains to a location reasonably close to that specified by Fison and Howitt, and another to a region well within the area specified by Tindale. The first of these (Anonymous ca 1845) is a wordlist collected at the Allyn River, which, at its closest point to Glendon (at its confluence with the Paterson River at Vacy) is roughly 40 km (25 miles) to the east. Lissarrague (2010: 12) treats the words in this list as belonging to the Lower North Coast language, and the available evidence supports this view

---

16   The cognate count appears to be five out of seven items in LNC, and three out of seven items in Gamilaraay.
17   See also the CMA (1987) map, the Horton map (1996), and Brayshaw's map (1986: 39).

(see Wafer and Lissarrague 2008: 165, 170). According to Miller (1985: 246, 256–257), the people of the Allyn River were the 'Gringai'; and these Guringay spoke a dialect of LNC.

The presence of LNC speakers at the Allyn is not fundamentally inconsistent with Fison and Howitt's claim that the land of the Kayawaykal extended 'to each lateral watershed [of the Hunter River], and from twenty-five to thirty miles along the valley on each side of Glendon' (1880: 279). If Glendon was at the centre of their territory, this probably means they also inhabited Glendon Brook, which flows from the southern foothills of the Mount Royal Range to join the Hunter just downstream from Glendon. In the direction of the opposite watershed, their domain could well have extended along Wollombi Brook, which rises in the Watagan Mountains and flows past Bulga, to join the Hunter upstream from Singleton.

It is worth noting in this regard that 'Bulga' is probably derived from the HRLM word *palkarr*, 'mountain'.[18] The name 'Watagan' is not so easy to analyse, but possibly includes the HRLM derivational suffix *-kan* (Lissarrague 2006: 65).[19] If the Kayawaykal inhabited the riverine margins of the Hunter and the tributaries converging on the region around Glendon, their range probably fell a fair way short of the Allyn. Thus the only evidence that contradicts the location given by Fison and Howitt is Tindale's account of Geawegal territory, which is centred on Scone.

4. The Scone list

It is for this reason that the second manuscript document, which pertains to Scone and its environs, merits a more extended treatment. The manuscript was a response to a survey carried out by the Anthropological Society of Australasia in 1899. A circular was sent to police stations throughout New South Wales, with a request for 'Native Names of places with their meanings'. Many of the responses were hasty and superficial, but some, including the return from Scone, included not just placenames that had been adopted by the settler culture, but a more

---

18 Lissarrague (2006: 130) reconstructs this word as *palkirr;* but it is *balgarr* in LNC (Lissarrague 2010: 175). Moreover, Miller (1887: 335) records the (Wanarruwa) expression *bulgargoba*, 'towards the south', which I interpret as *palkarr-kupa*, 'mountain' + genitive).
19 The morphemes *palkarr* and *-kan* also occur in LNC (albeit spelt differently). Nonetheless, I assume that the relevant placenames are derived from HRLM, since there is no evidence that the territory of LNC speakers extended this far west. In the direction of the opposite watershed, there is another placename of likely Indigenous origin that could have some relevance to the issues discussed in this paper, namely, 'Mirannie', which designates a locality close to the headwaters of Glendon Brook. But unfortunately there is no obvious way of analysing this word in any of the three languages discussed in this paper.

extensive list of vocabulary items as well. At least some, if not all, of these were probably Indigenous placenames, or at least place-descriptors, that were never incorporated into settler geography.

Here is the list, with its covering letter.[20]

>Anthropological Society of Australasia
>
>Police Station Scone
>
>16th Oct 1899
>
>Vide Anthropological Society's circular of the 15/8/99
>
>Senior Sergeant Coady begs leave to return attached list with the Aboriginal names of places etc, and their meanings[.] He has left manuscript lists with several of the oldest residents of this district, who are said to have a good knowledge of the aboriginal language, but some have not returned their lists, when they do so, he will forward them on.
>
>John Coady S.S.
>
>The Supt of Police
>
>West Maitland

---

20 My copy of this list comes from the version digitised by the Geographical Names Board of NSW and copied as PDF and TIFF files to CD. The contents of the CD are divided into five folders, corresponding to the rolls of the microfilm version. The Scone list is included in roll 1, and the frame numbers are 010328 and 010329 (the list itself) and 010330 (the covering letter). I have included it in the list of references under 'Coady'.

4. Placenames as a guide to language distribution in the Upper Hunter

Table 1: Scone wordlist transcribed from Coady (1899).

Name of Place [A]	*Meaning or reason it was given*	Possible etymology	Location
*Miketymulga Bibil	Tree struck by lightning White leaved box tree		
Moonbil (now Aberdeen)	Green head Ant	D *muwan*, 'greenhead ant' (A 117) + -*bil*, 'with a lot of' (A 38)	Aberdeen
Tamori	Pigeon ground	D *dhamarr*, 'bronzewing pigeon' (A 55) + -*araay*, 'with, having' (A 25)	
Dilgoor	Junction of Page & Hunter Rivers	? D *dhiil*, 'wilga'; 'tail' (A 61) + *guraarr*, 'long; tall' (A 97)	Junction of Pages River and Hunter River (short distance north-west of Aberdeen)
Goonindri	Water coming over Rocks	D *gungan*, 'water' (A 96) + -*baraay*, 'with, having' (A 33)	
Booloomin	Apple Tree	D *bulamin*, 'angophora (appletree)' (A 44)	
Booroobilla	Wild Turkey	?? D *burrgulbiyan*, 'turkey bush' (A 48)	
Downgimbie	Mussel ground	D *dhawun*, 'earth, ground' (A 59) + *giinbay*, 'small mussel' (A 188)	Muswellbrook? [B]
Boombil	Native Camping ground	D *bunbul*, 'meeting place' (A 46)	
Gillebri	Moonshine	D *gilay*, 'moon' (A 88) + -*baraay*, 'with, having' (A 33)	
Beroobri	Deep Water Hole	D *biruubaraay*, 'hollow' (A 42)	
Myoon Myooan	Red and Yellow Stones Natives used for Tattooing	?? D *maayama*, 'stone' (A 105)	
Goona Goona	Yellow stones for ditto	H *kunakuna*, 'stone... used for paint' (L06 119)	
Gullingoorar	Long Water Hole	D *gali*, 'water' (A 76) + *guraarr*, 'long' (A 97)	

Indigenous and Minority Placenames

Name of Place ᴬ	Meaning or reason it was given	Possible etymology	Location
*Miketymulga Bibil	Tree struck by lightning White leaved box tree		
Danboor	Clear Land, no water	D *dhawun*, 'earth, ground' (A 59) + ?? *bura*, 'bone' (A 47)	
Goombaban	Dusty soil	D *gumba*, 'flinty' (A 94) + *-baa*, 'place of' (A 25)	
Bragar	Sparrow Hawk	D *biyaagaarr*, 'brown falcon' (A 42)	
Goodangoodan	Hard substance	?? L *gurung*, 'solid' (L10 240)	
Kingimbon	Rocks	?? D *giin.gii*, 'froth' (A 87) Cf. Gingamboon (below)	
Yowri	Close to; Near	?? D *yawa*, 'to track' (A 152)	
Moonan	Difficult to accomplish	?? D *muurr*, 'blocked; blunt' (A 117)	Moonan Flat? (Upper Hunter)
Billar	Swamp Oak Trees	D *bilaarr*, 'swamp oak' (A 38)	
Naraman	A long way behind	? D *ngaarrima*, 'over there' (A 120)	
Woombrambilla	A flat stick with a hook used by Natives in Spear throwing	D *wamara*, 'spear thrower' (A 137) + ?? *burranbaa*, 'new' (A 48); H *wamarr*, 'woomera' (L06 140); L *wamarr*, 'woomera' (L10 268)	
Gooloorooeybri	Bull Frogs	?? D *yurayaa*, 'frog' (A 157) + *-baraay*, 'with, having' (A 33)	
Gingamboon	Hunter River	? D *giin.gii*, 'froth' (A 87) Cf. Kingimbon (above)	Hunter River
Bambill	Mistletoe	D *baan*, 'mistletoe' (A 26) + *-bil*, 'with a lot of' (A 38)	
Galliebarinda	Waterfall, Cascade	D *gali*, 'water' (A 76) + ? *barra*, 'to fly' (A 34); H *kali*, 'water' (L06 113)	
Gungalla	Rushes	H *kungka*, 'reed' (L06 119)	Gungal? (between Merriwa and Sandy Hollow)

4. Placenames as a guide to language distribution in the Upper Hunter

Name of Place [A]	Meaning or reason it was given	Possible etymology	Location
*Miketymulga Bibil	Tree struck by lightning White leaved box tree		
Yourooie	Kangaroo's Cave	?? D *gurru*, 'hole' (A 98)	
Marrawan	One hand	D *mara*, 'hand; finger' (A 108) + *-wan*, 'prominent (big)' (A 138) Cf. Murrurundi (below)	
Goolameran	Drooping Trees	D *gula*, 'fork in tree' (A 92) + ? *mirriraa*, 'lignum [shrub]' (A 113)	
Boogal	A Bush	? D *bugarru*, 'tree for storing poison sticks' (A 43)	
Mill	An Eye	D *mil*, 'eye' (A 110)	
Goolengdoogie	Spit Forehead	D *ngulu*, 'face; forehead; point [i.e. spit (in the geographical sense)]' + *dhugaay*, 'small' (A 65); H *ngulu*, 'forehead' (L06 128); L *ngulu*, 'forehead' (L10 261)	
Yeraan	High Wind	D ?? *yuru*, 'cloud' (A 157) + *-wan*, 'prominent (big)' (A 138)	
Goonabil	Covered with human excrement	D *guna*, 'faeces' (A 95) + *-bil*, 'with a lot of' (A 38)	[Cf. Coonamble]
Gooran	An Emu	? D *ganurran*, '[group of] emus' (A 79)	
Gooallie	Of ugly appearance	?? D *nguwalay*, 'here, (hereabouts)' (A 128)	
Doongoorwah	Rock running into the Water	D *dhawun*, 'ground' (A 59) + *guraarr*, 'long' (A 97)	
Youndayounda	A Sheet of Bark	?? D *yuundu*, 'stone axe, tomahawk' (A 158)	
Greenboon	Anything Green	English 'green' + ? D *buuwan*, 'black paint' (A 51)	

Indigenous and Minority Placenames

Name of Place [A]	Meaning or reason it was given	Possible etymology	Location
*Miketymulga Bibil	Tree struck by lightning White leaved box tree		
Boondool	A Shield	D *burriin*, 'shield' (A 48) + -*duul*, 'small' (A 68)	
Breeal	A Native Waddy for fighting	? D *bugu*, 'fighting club' (A 43)	
Marooan	Anything Good	H *marrung*, 'good' (L06 122); L *marrung*, 'good' (L10 248)	
Goolliar	White Gum Tree	H *kulay*, 'tree' (L06 118); ?? D *gulabaa*, 'coolabah' (A 92)	
Boonooboonoo	Kangaroo's camp	?? H *punu*, 'dust' (L06 135); ?? L *bunyu*, 'ashes; dust' (L10 193–94); ?? D *banuwa*, 'black soil' (A 33)	Boonoo Boonoo? (north of Tenterfield)
Youndoogeedan	Rock where blacks used to sharpen tomahawks	D *yuundu*, 'stone axe, tomahawk' (A158) + ? -*giirr*, 'like, similar to' (A 87)	
Woolbadoon	A little plain	H *wulu*, 'grass' (L06 143) + -*pa*, 'place of' (L06 129)	
Youan	A clear flat	H *ngarawan*, 'plain' (L06 156); L *ngarrawan*, 'plains' (L10 260)	
Billanbri	A Creek with rushes	?? L *bila*, 'river' (L10 183); D -*baraay*, 'with, having' (A 33)	
Woolamon	A high Cliff	?? L *wuruma*, 'wind' (L10 277)	
Walgooan	High wind	? L *biwal*, 'wind' (L10 187) + ? *guuwak* [~ *guuwang*], 'hard' (L10 241)	
Goorarman	A long sheet of water	? D *garragarraan*, 'straight river' (A 80)	
Yeerallah	A strong current	? D *yarrin*, 'water current' (A 152)	

4. Placenames as a guide to language distribution in the Upper Hunter

Name of Place ᴬ	Meaning or reason it was given	Possible etymology	Location
*Miketymulga Bibil	Tree struck by lightning White leaved box tree		
Yeroyan	A large cave in limestone Rock	? H *yiru*, 'water' (L06 146); ?? L *nguriyang*, 'ear' (L10 261)	
Gundeerari	Birds Feathers	D *gundiirr*, 'emu feather' (A 96) + *-araay*, 'with, having' (A 25)	
Woorwoor	Anything very large	L *wutu* [reduplicated], 'big' (L10 277)	
Berieel	Abounding with flaggy Rocks	?? L *birriwal*, 'big' (L10 186); ?? H *piriyal*, 'toes' (L06 133)	
Neemin	Kurrajong Tree	D *nhimin*, 'kurrajong tree' (A 130)	
Nirribingable	Swallows [sic] Nest	[??] + H *pilimalmal*, 'swallow' (L06 132)	
Goorawoon	Large Stones in the Water	D *guraarr*, 'tall' (A 97) + ? *-wan*, 'big' (A 138)	
Yallimbilla	Two men	D *ngali*, 'we two' (A 121) + *bulaarr*, 'two' (A 44); H *ngalin*, 'us two' (L06 40) + *pulawarr*, 'two' (cf. L06 134)	
Bunbibilla	An opossum cloak	?? D *baya*, clothes (A 36) + ? *-bil*, 'with a lot of' (A 38)	
Berginbah	A large Waterfall	? D *bagay*, 'creek; river' (A 30) + *-baa*, 'place of' (A 25)	
Geengullion	An elbow	D *dhiin*, 'elbow' (A 61) + ?? *galiya*, 'to climb' (A 77)	
Boolarie	Large lumps on Trees	D *buul*, 'tree knot' (A 50) + *-araay*, 'with, having' (A 25)	

Indigenous and Minority Placenames

Name of Place [A]	Meaning or reason it was given	Possible etymology	Location
*Miketymulga Bibil	Tree struck by lightning White leaved box tree		
Mallegal	A kind of timber or scrub	P 'mallee' ['eucalypts characteristically small and having several stems arising from a common base' D 139] + H -kal, 'pertaining to' (L06 62–63); + L -gal, 'type' (L10 47–48)	
Beerubri	An aperture in Trees	D biruu, 'hole' (A 42) + -baraay, 'with, having' (A 33)	
Goorangi	Red paint	? D guway, 'blood' (A 100) [hence guwaymbarra, 'red' (A 100)]	
Guyar	An opossum	D garrawirr, 'ringtail possum' (A 81)	
Bloombeen	A Green Parrot	D bulunbulun, 'mulga parrot; ringneck parrot' (A 45)	
Yawdool	A large hollow Stump	D ngadhul, 'hollow tree; stump' (A 120)	
Murrurundi	Five fingers	D mara, 'hand; finger' (A 108) + ?? -wan, 'prominent (big)' (A 138) [Cf. Marrawan (above)]	Murrurundi [C]
Bundadworndi	Kangaroo's playing	D bandaarr, 'grey kangaroo' (A 32) + ? wuu, 'to go into [an enclosed space]' (A 146); L bandaarr, 'wallaby' (L10 176) + ? wuuna, 'to leave' (L10 277); H pantarr, 'kangaroo' (L06 130)	
Bareemal	A large waterfall	?? L barray, 'earth' (L10 179) + ?? malu, 'thunder' (L10 246)	
Puen Buen	Small Stones	? H piwang, 'red tea-tree' (L06 134) ? D buuwan [reduplicated], 'black paint' (A 51)	Puen Buen (west of Aberdeen)

4. Placenames as a guide to language distribution in the Upper Hunter

Name of Place [A]	Meaning or reason it was given	Possible etymology	Location
*Miketymulga Bibil	Tree struck by lightning White leaved box tree		
Gibbagunyah	House built of Stone	P 'gibber-gunyah', ['a shallow cave used as a dwelling or for shelter'] (D 200)	Gibbergunyah Creek (west of Scone)
Womulguy	Bend in the River	? H *wampal*, 'beach' (L06 141) + ? *-kay*, 'characteristic of' (L06 116)	

Conventions followed in column 3

Reliability
No question mark: the etymology is convincing
? (one question mark): the etymology is plausible
?? (two question marks): the etymology is, at best, speculative
(The question marks – or their absence – may precede either or both parts of a word consisting of two morphemes.)

Language name abbreviations
D = Darling Tributaries language (Gamilaraay etc.)
H = Hunter River-Lake Macquarie language (sometimes called 'Awabakal'; includes Wanarruwa [Wonnaruah])
L = Lower North Coast language (Warrimay [Worimi], Guringay [Gringai] etc.)
P = Pidgin (which includes words borrowed from remote Aboriginal languages)

Source abbreviations
A = Ash, Giacon and Lissarrague 2003
D = Dixon, Ramson and Thomas 1990
L06 = Lissarrague 2006
L10 = Lissarrague 2010
(These abbreviations are followed by the relevant page number and placed in brackets.)

Glosses
The glosses follow as closely as possible those given in the sources; small emendations have been made in some cases for the sake of clarity and/or brevity.

Note A: The first two columns incorporate my transcription of the original list. The heading lines (here in italics) of these columns are type-printed on the original form. The two lines under the topmost heading are printed examples, not part of Coady's wordlist, which is hand-written. The two right-hand columns are, respectively, my interpretation of the etymologies, and the locations (where known. Some of these are speculative.) The conventions used in column 3 (the etymologies) are explained at the end of the list.

Note B: On the naming of Muswellbrook and the connection with mussels, see: http://www.muswellbrook.nsw.gov.au/About-Muswellbrook-Shire/History/Muswellbrook/Naming-muswellbrook.htm (accessed 14 September 2011).

Note C: According to McLellan (n.d.: 17), the Indigenous 'name for the area, Murrumdoorandi is now Murrurundi. The word particularly refers to the five rocks in the vicinity of the present town of which there are now four, a fifth having fallen since white men came into the area. Interpretation of the word is disputed, the favoured one is "the meeting place at the five fingers (rocks)".'

Source: Coady 1899.

Indigenous and Minority Placenames

5. Analysis of the Scone list

Even a cursory glance at the results of this tabulation indicates that the great majority of the words on the list pertain to a dialect of the Darling Tributaries language (which includes Gamilaraay). The figures are as follows: of the 78 items on the list, 60 (77 per cent) may be attributable to the Darling Tributaries language, and 38 of these (49 per cent of the total) are convincing; 12 (15 per cent) may be attributable to the Hunter River-Lake Macquarie language, and eight (10 per cent of the total) of these are convincing; six (8 per cent) may be attributable to the Lower North Coast language, but only one (1 per cent of the total) of these is convincing.[21]

Even if these figures are somewhat slippery (as a result, for example, of overlapping attributions where two or more languages use the same morpheme) the pattern is clear enough: the words on the list belong predominantly to the Darling Tributaries language. But what the list fails to provide is adequate information about the places these words were associated with, either as toponyms or simply as descriptors.

Certainly, the words were collated and transcribed at Scone, and a number of the recognisable names pertain to that region: Aberdeen; the junction of the Pages and Hunter Rivers (a short distance north-west of Aberdeen); possibly Moonan Flat, in the Upper Hunter; the Hunter River;[22] Murrurundi; John Bingle's property 'Puen Buen' (on Dart Brook, west of Scone, according to Gray 1966); Gibbergunyah Creek (west of Scone); and possibly Muswellbrook, although this one is questionable. If the 'Mussel ground' on the list referred to Muswellbrook, one might have expected the author to be specific about this.

What of the other placenames that may have some association with this list? Gungal (if the word 'Gungalla' can be linked to it) is a little remote from this region, lying about 40 km due west of Muswellbrook (between Merriwa and Denman). And Boonoo Boonoo lies north of Tenterfield, more than 400 km north of Scone, in the region where Marbal appears to have been spoken.[23]

---

21 These figures add up to 77, not 78, because I have attributed 'Gibbagunyah' to Pidgin. The word *giba* does occur in both Gamilaraay (Ash, Giacon and Lissarrague 2003: 85) and LNC (Lissarrague 2010: 226); but its use in the compound form 'Gibbagunyah' suggests a borrowing from Pidgin rather than from one of the source languages. In the case of 'Mallegal', on the other hand, I have attributed it to HRLM on the basis of the presence of the suffix -*kal*.
22 If 'Gingamboon' is indeed a name for the Hunter River, it seems likely that the river had different names at different points along its course. Wafer and Lissarrague (2008: 160, note 103) analyse four other names that have been attributed to it : 'Coquun', 'Myan', 'Coonanbarra' and 'Terrybong'.
23 See Wafer and Lissarrague (2008: 333). The 'Goonabil' on the Scone list is unlikely to refer to Coonamble (see Ash, Giacon and Lissarrague 2003: 95, 237), with which name it is undoubtedly cognate. Presumably the writer would have used the spelling 'Coonamble' if that is what he or she meant.

Whatever the reasons (and several could be adduced) for the appearance of these two (apparent) placenames in the list, if we treat them as anomalies this at least allows us to make a statistical comparison. Eight of the ten words that can be plausibly linked to places are associated with locations between Murrurundi and Muswellbrook; only two of the words are associated with places outside this region. If we apply the figure of 80 per cent to the items on the wordlist, this suggests that something like 62 of the words on the list refer to places in the Murrurundi to Muswellbrook region, or to vocabulary items that were used there.

We can take this procedure a step further by considering the language associations of the eight placenames in question. One of them (Gibbergunyah Creek) is derived from NSW Pidgin. The other seven can be linked to the Darling Tributaries language: three of them convincingly, three plausibly, and one speculatively.

This is not to say that there may not have been placenames derived from either HRLM or LNC in the region between Murrurundi and Muswellbrook. But the weight of evidence suggests clearly that the majority language used in this region at the time the Scone list was collected was a dialect of the Darling Tributaries language: possibly Gamilaraay, or at least a closely related dialect. For present purposes, I shall call it the 'Upper Hunter dialect'.

6. The language of the Upper Hunter

In other words, Tindale's assertion that the 'Geawegal' occupied this region appears much less convincing than the original information about their location given by Fison and Howitt. There is further support for the view that the Darling Tributaries language was spoken in this region in an article by Albert MacDonald concerning 'The Aborigines on the Page and the Isis', published in the *Journal of the Anthropological Institute* in 1878.

The Pages River is a tributary of the upper Hunter, flowing from the Liverpool Range, past Murrurundi and Gundy, to join the Hunter not far upstream from Aberdeen. The Isis River is a tributary of the Pages River, and the confluence is a short distance upstream from Gundy. MacDonald gives an account of a group who 'held their boras' at a spot 'near the junction of the Rivers Page and Isis ... not far from the town of Aberdeen' (1878: 255). He notes that this group spoke '"Kamilaroi," varying slightly from that of the Namoi and Barwon' (1878: 257). This is substantiated by the small samples of language material he gives. He calls the people of this place 'the Murri', and *mari* is the Gamilaraay word for 'man' or 'Aboriginal person' (Ash, Giacon and Lissarrague 2003: 109). He also gives a couple of other words, and a song. This material is quite clearly either Gamilaraay or a closely related dialect with numerous cognates,[24] and demonstrably not HRLM or LNC.

It is not clear how far down the Hunter Valley the country of these 'Murri' extended. But if they occupied the region between Murrurundi and Aberdeen, this would include the whole length of the Pages and Isis Rivers, and would also be consistent with my analysis of the toponymic data in the Scone wordlist.

There remains the question of whether the country in which the Upper Hunter dialect was spoken reached any further south than Aberdeen. The only placename on the Scone list that could provide any clues here is the one that is translated as 'Mussel ground' – and I have mentioned above that the link between this name and Muswellbrook is dubious. But I note in this connection that the title of a recent book about the Aboriginal history of Muswellbrook 'is drawn from the languages of the Kamilaroi and Wanaruah people who walked these lands' (Blyton, Heitmeyer and Maynard 2004: 2).

What this suggests is that Muswellbrook (just south of Aberdeen) may have been a transitional zone, or the southern limit of a transitional zone, between speakers of the Upper Hunter dialect and Wanarruwa (which is a dialect of HRLM). There is perhaps further confirmation of a meeting, perhaps even mixing, of languages in this region, or even further south, in the pen-name adopted by the same G.W. Rusden who provided the information for Fison and Howitt's account of the 'Geawegal'.

The name under which Rusden published the second edition of his epic poem on Aboriginal themes entitled 'Moyarra' (Rusden 1891) – and various other works – was 'Yittadairn'. As mentioned in an earlier note, 'Rusden was identified with it [the Geawegal 'tribe'], and spoke the language as a youth' (Fison and Howitt 1880: 279). But the components of this pseudonym could perhaps be analysed as *yitirr* (HRLM: 'name'; Lissarrague 2006: 146) + *dhayn* (DT: '(Aboriginal) man'; Ash, Giacon and Lissarrague 2003: 60). In other words, this *nom de plume* possibly has a mixed etymology.[25]

Brayshaw, in her foundational study of *Aborigines of the Hunter Valley* (1986) writes that 'the Wonaruah and the Geawegal and probably the Gringai in the central and upper Hunter were part of the "Kamilaroi nation"' (1986: 51). It is

---

24   John Giacon (pers. comm. 24 October 2006) observes as follows: 'there is a lot here that looks like Gamilaraay, so either it is Gamilaraay or a language with lots of cognates... The song looks as if it is about someone who is sick getting better – there are lots of Gamilaraay words, but I can't be all that sure about the overall meaning.'

25   The same may be true of the names of the various characters in 'Moyarra' (Koreungat, Moyarra, Muntookan, Myta, Warrawe), although they are hard to analyse, because of the absence of glosses. Nonetheless, they give strong hints of being a mixture of the three languages I have been dealing with in this paper. On Rusden, see Blainey and Lazarus (1976).

unclear how this conclusion has been arrived at, but it is probably based on the fact that the Wanarruwa, Kayawaykal and Guringay all used a section system in which the section names were cognate with those in Gamilaraay. This is certainly an indication of some kind of social relationship, which undoubtedly included intermarriage. But I suggest it is not sufficient to include Wanarruwa, Kayawaykal and Guringay as members of the Gamilaraay 'nation'. Linguistically, Wanarruwa, and – as I have tried to show – probably also Kayawaykal, belong with other dialects of the Hunter River-Lake Macquarie language, while Guringay belongs with the other dialects of the Lower North Coast language.

A discrepancy between linguistic affiliations and social affiliations is, of course, never out of the question, so I do not discount the possibility that the Wanarruwa, Kayawaykal and Guringay had a closer social relationship with the Gamilaraay than they had with speakers of dialects more closely related to their own. But this cross-cutting pattern of relationships is more an indication of the relative autonomy of local dialect groups, rather than evidence for their membership in some superordinate grouping such as a 'nation'.[26]

7. The *landnám* question

The only argument that could potentially save Tindale's attribution of the Upper Hunter region to 'Geawegal' would be one based on *landnám*. This would mean that the region had been inhabited originally by speakers of Kayawaykal, but the latter were succeeded at some point by speakers of the Upper Hunter dialect, who engaged in a process of renaming. In other words, one way of explaining the scattering of placenames on the Scone list that are possibly derived from HRLM would be as evidence of a prior linguistic stratum.

The term *landnám* comes from the mediaeval *Landnámabók*, 'The Book of the Settlement of Iceland'. Two Australian writers have glossed the expression as 'land-taking and land-naming' (Leer 1985: 11; Gilbert 1998: 16), and this captures the polysemous nature of the word *nám*.[27] Although it does not mean 'naming', but rather 'taking', this is not just 'taking' in a literal sense, but also in the sense of 'grasping with the mind'. In fact, one of its meanings is 'learning, study' (Zoëga 1910: 309–310).

---

26 There is a different aspect of this question that other researchers may wish to follow up, namely, whether the languages dealt with in this paper have some demonstrable relationship to the ecology of the region. There is a tantalising clue in the fact that the Upper Hunter is included in the Central Western Slopes (botanical) Subdivision, even though it lies to the east of the Great Dividing Range (Curran, Clark and Bruhl 2008: 385. See their bioregion map [fig. 1 on p. 383] for a clear visual representation). In other words, it appears that the vegetation, like the Darling Tributaries language, spills over the Range into the Upper Hunter.
27 My understanding is that *nám* is the nominative singular form of this (strong, neuter) noun, and *náma* the genitive plural. I am relying here on Zoëga's *A Concise Dictionary of Old Icelandic* (1910).

Indigenous and Minority Placenames

Image 1: G.W. Rusden dressed as 'Yittadairn'.[28]

Source: Pictures Collection, State Library of Victoria.

---

28 'Yittadairn' was, as mentioned above, the pen-name used by G.W. Rusden for some of his publications. This photograph on *carte-de-visite* mount is entitled 'G. W. Rusden as Yittadairn' in the catalogue of the State Library of Victoria (http://handle.slv.vic.gov.au/10381/111666, accessed 5 July 2013), from whose copy the version here is reproduced. The annotation in the catalogue of the Australian National Library quotes from the auction documentation: 'An extraordinary image of Rusden, the historian of Australia and New Zealand

Fick, Falk and Torp trace it to the proto-Germanic root **nem* (1909: 293), one of the glosses for which they list as *geistig aufnehmen* ('take in intellectually'). Campbell gives a sense of the semantic scope of *landnám* when he explains it as 'the method of acquisition of ... territory ... not by prosaic physical action, but poetically, by intelligence and the method of art' (1986: 34).

Typically, *landnám* entails two kinds of naming processes. One is the adoption of toponyms used by the previous inhabitants; the other is the introduction of new toponyms in the immigrants' own language, often derived from placenames used in their former place of residence.

Campbell implies that *landnám* is a cultural universal (giving as examples the myths of the Hebrews, the Vedic Aryans and the Navaho). But this is problematic in the context of Australia, since it is generally assumed that only non-Indigenous Australians engage in the practice. For Aboriginal people, 'since placenames are part of the Law (*yumi*) assigned by Dreamings (*mangaya, puwarraj*) to a specific place, mere human beings cannot lift those names up and drop them in other places' (McConvell 2002a: 52).

This apparent difference is perhaps merely a reflection of the different methods – and also time-scale – of *landnám* as practised by Indigenous and non-Indigenous Australians.[29] Presumably the first humans to arrive on these shores, whether they came in one or several waves, went through a process of 'land-taking and land-naming' as they spread throughout the continent; and the same process would no doubt have been necessitated by internal migrations resulting from the various climatic and geographical changes that the island has undergone since. So it would be surprising if *landnám* were not still practised, at least to some minor degree, in Aboriginal Australia – for example, in cases of succession to a particular tract of land (cf. McConvell 2004: 42). The fact that this is rationalised in terms of the ideology of 'the Dreaming' simply obscures the political processes involved.

---

dressed in an elaborate black fleshing costume, holding a boomerang and in a possum skin or Kangaroo rug' (http://nla.gov.au/nla.pic-vn4223009, accessed 17 September 2011). I have included a mention of this photograph in the list of references under the name of the photographers, 'Batchelder & Co.'.

29 Some good examples of the rather indiscriminate use by non-Indigenous Australians of Aboriginal placenames are provided by the Scone list itself. In recent times, one word (Galliebarinda) has been applied to a waterfall in the Otway Ranges, in Victoria, and another (Gillebri) to a property near St George, in Queensland. Other words on the list coincide with the names of a town (Bambill), a mountain (Moonbil), pastoral stations (Goonabil, Marooan, Woolamon, Neemin, Gungalla), a cattle company (Boogal), streets (Boombil, Billanbri, Walgooan), houses or homesteads (Bareemal, Marooan), a ship (Goorangi), a yacht (Moonbil), racehorses (Boogal, Goonabil, Moonbil) and a greyhound (Gibbergunyah). The spellings are identical to those on the Scone list except in the cases of 'Goorangi', which was a commonly used variant of the ship's correct name, 'Goorangai'; and of 'Gibbergunyah', which is in any case a Pidgin word with variable spellings. These usages come from various parts of Australia that have no obvious connection to the Upper Hunter. To thread a way through this labyrinth of possible borrowings is beyond the scope of the present paper.

Unfortunately, although there have been advances in what McConvell has called 'linguistic stratigraphy' in some parts of Australia (see e.g. McConvell 2002b, 2004), the Hunter does not yet fulfill the basic requirement of 'historical analysis on all or most of the languages in the region concerned' (McConvell 2002b: 262). In other words, it is too early to make any kind of case based on *landnám* for the area under consideration here. The mixture of languages reflected in the Scone list could, perhaps, be taken as an indication of an earlier process of *landnám*; but there are other, more plausible, explanations, too various to enumerate in any detail.[30] To conclude, the evidence, at this point in time, appears to demonstrate that the region attributed by Tindale to the 'Geawegal' was in fact occupied by speakers of a dialect – which I call the 'Upper Hunter dialect' – of the Darling Tributaries language.

References

Aboriginal Languages Research and Resource Centre n.d., 'Map of NSW Aboriginal languages': http://ab-ed.boardofstudies.nsw.edu.au/bosImg_window.cfm?objectid=03540C9F-F074-1B07-416F6CDE53A110F7 or alternatively http://www.tne.edu.au/~/media/images/website_images/Misc/NSWlanguagesmap.ashx (both accessed 6 April 2014).

Anonymous ca 1845, Vocabulary of the Allyn River Black's [sic] language, MS held by the Mitchell Library, State Library of NSW, Sydney (ML Aa52/1-3; CYReel 2355, frames 88–115).

Ash, A., J. Giacon and A. Lissarrague (eds) 2003, *Gamilaraay, Yuwaalaraay & Yuwaalayaay Dictionary*, IAD Press, Alice Springs.

Batchelder & Co. ca 1880, 'G. W. Rusden as Yittadairn', photograph on *carte-de-visite* mount, Batchelder & Co., Melbourne. Reproduced here from the copy held by the State Library of Victoria, which has made the image available online at http://handle.slv.vic.gov.au/10381/111666 (accessed 27 July 2013).

Blainey, A. and M. Lazarus 1976, 'Rusden, George William (1819–1903)', *Australian Dictionary of Biography*, National Centre of Biography, ANU: http://adb.anu.edu.au/biography/rusden-george-william-4523/text7405 (accessed 14 September 2011). First published in *Australian Dictionary of Biography*, vol. 6, Melbourne University Press, Melbourne.

Blyton, G., D. Heitmeyer and J. Maynard 2004, *Wannin Thanbarran: A History of Aboriginal and European Contact in Muswellbrook and the Upper Hunter*

---

30   It could, for example, be a result of what McConvell calls 'the normal process of contact and diffusion' (2002b: 263), possibly speeded up by forced displacement of Aboriginal people by the European colonisers.

Valley, Umulliko Centre for Indigenous Higher Education, University of Newcastle, and Muswellbrook Shire Council Aboriginal Reconciliation Committee, Muswellbrook.

Brayshaw, H. 1986, *Aborigines of the Hunter Valley: A Study of Colonial Records*, Scone & Upper Hunter Historical Society, Scone.

Campbell, J. 1985, *The Inner Reaches of Outer Space: Metaphor as Myth and as Religion*, A. van der Marck Editions, New York.

Central Mapping Authority, NSW Department of Lands ('CMA') 1987, 'Aboriginal New South Wales', Central Mapping Authority, Bathurst.

Coady, J. 1899, 'Scone' (return from Senior Sergeant John Coady, Police Station, Scone, of 16/10/1899), pp. 297–299, microfilm roll 1, frames 010328–010330). In 'Aboriginal names. "Collection of Native Names of places with their meanings."' Circular distributed to police stations in New South Wales, 16/8/1899, by the Anthropological Society of Australasia. Returns paginated and indexed. Microfilmed by W & F Pascoe Pty Ltd 1991, under the title 'Anthropological Society of Australia'. Roll 1 (of 5 rolls). Digital version made available by Geographical Names Board of NSW. CD Rom held by AIATSIS library at 910.3009944 GEO C-D. (Geographical Names Board of New South Wales [2003], 'Royal Anthropological Society of Australasia manuscripts dated 1900'. Microfilm has 476+456+949+449+1358 frames as reproduced in the 5 rolls on the CD.) Original documents now held by the Mitchell Library, State Library of NSW, Sydney. Catalogued under 'Royal Anthropological Society of Australasia – Records, 1885–1914, with additional material, 1921–1926, ca. 1991, and papers of Alan Carroll, 1886–1892' (MLMSS 7603). For further details see: http://acms.sl.nsw.gov.au/item/itemDetailPaged.aspx?itemID=421736 (accessed 16 September 2011). Scone list included in microfilm CY 4555, frames 1–495.

Curran, T. J., P. J. Clarke, and J. J. Bruhl 2008, 'A broad typology of dry rainforests on the western slopes of New South Wales', *Cunninghamia* 10(3): 381–405: http://www.une.edu.au/ers/staff-profile-doc-folders/peter-clarke/2008-curran-et-al-cunninghamia.pdf (accessed 5 July 2013)

Dixon, R.M.W., W.S. Ramson and Mandy Thomas 1990, *Australian Aboriginal Words in English: Their Origin and Meaning*, Oxford University Press, Melbourne.

Enright, W. J. 1932, 'The Kattang (Kutthung) or Worimi: an Aboriginal tribe', *Mankind* 1(4): 75–77.

Fawcett, J.W. 1898, 'Customs of the Wannah-Kuah [sic] tribe, and their dialect or vocabulary', *Science of Man* 1(8): 180–181.

Fick, A., H. Falk and A. Torp 1909, *Vergleichendes Wörterbuch der indogermanischen Sprachen, dritter Teil: Wortschatz der germanischen Spracheinheit*, Vandenhoeck & Rupprecht, Göttingen. Electronic version created by Sean Crist, 2003: http://www.ling.upenn.edu/~kurisuto/germanic/pgmc_torp_about.html (accessed 14 September 2011).

Fison, L. and A.W. Howitt 1880, *Kamilaroi and Kurnai*, George Robertson, Melbourne. (Appendix G: 'The Geawe-gal Tribe', pp. 279–284.)

Fraser, J. (ed.) 1892, *An Australian Language as Spoken by the Awabakal*, Charles Potter, Government Printer, Sydney.

Gilbert, H. 1998, *Sightlines: Race, Gender, and Nation in Contemporary Australian Theatre*, University of Michigan Press, Ann Arbor.

Gray, N. 1966, 'Bingle, John (1796–1882)', *Australian Dictionary of Biography*, National Centre of Biography, ANU: http://adb.anu.edu.au/biography/bingle-john-1780/text2001 (accessed 12 September 2011). First published in *Australian Dictionary of Biography*, vol. 1, Melbourne University Press, Melbourne.

Hale, H. E. 1846, 'Ethnography and philology', volume 6 of *United States Exploring Expedition, during the Years 1838, 1839, 1840, 1841, 1842, under the Command of Charles Wilkes, U. S. N.*, Lea and Blanchard, New York.

Horton, D. R. (comp.) 1996, 'Aboriginal Australia' (map produced to accompany David Horton (ed.), *Encyclopaedia of Aboriginal Australia*), Aboriginal Studies Press for the Australian Institute of Aboriginal and Torres Strait Islander Studies, Canberra.

Howitt, A.W. 1904, *The Native Tribes of South-East Australia*, Macmillan, London.

Leer, M. 1985, 'At the edge: geography and the imagination in the work of David Malouf', *Australian Literary Studies* 12(1): 3–21.

Lissarrague, A. 2006, *A Salvage Grammar and Wordlist of the Language from the Hunter River and Lake Macquarie*, Muurrbay, Nambucca Heads.

— 2010, *A Grammar and Dictionary of Gathang: The Language of the Birrbay, Guringay and Warrimay*, Muurrbay, Nambucca Heads.

MacDonald, A. C. 1878, 'The Aborigines on the Page and the Isis', *Journal of theAnthropological Institute of Great Britain and Ireland* 7: 255–258.

McConvell, P. 2002a, 'Changing places: European and Aboriginal styles', in *The Land is a Map: Placenames of Indigenous Origin in Australia*, Luise Hercus, Flavia Hodges and Jane Simpson (eds), Pandanus Books in association with Pacific Linguistics, Canberra: 50–61.

— 2002b, 'Linguistic stratigraphy and native title: the case of ethnonyms', in *Language in Native Title*, John Henderson and David Nash (eds), Aboriginal Studies Press, Canberra: 259–290.

— 2004, 'A short ride on a time machine: linguistics, cultural history and native title', in *Crossing Boundaries: Cultural, Legal, Historical and Practice Issues in Native Title*, Sandy Toussaint (ed.), Melbourne University Press, Carlton: 34–49.

McLellan, A.A. n.d., *Thomas Haydon of Bloomfield, Blandford*, Advocate Print, Quirindi.

Miller, J. 1985, *Koori, a Will to Win: The Heroic Resistance, Survival and Triumph of Black Australia*, Angus and Robertson, London.

Miller, R. 1887, 'No. 188: the Hunter River. The Wonnarua tribe and language', in *The Australian Race*, E.M. Curr (ed.), John Ferres, Government Printer, Melbourne: vol. 3 (of 4), pp. 352–359.

Muswellbrook Shire Council, n.d., 'The naming of our town as "Muswellbrook"', http://www.muswellbrook.nsw.gov.au/About-Muswellbrook-Shire/History/Muswellbrook/Naming-muswellbrook.htm (accessed 14 September 2011).

Oppliger, M. 1984, 'The phonology and morphology of Awabakal: a reconstitution from early written sources', BA (Hons) thesis, University of Sydney.

Rusden, G.W. (writing as 'Yittadairn') 1891, *Moyarra: An Australian Legend in Two Cantos*, E.A. Petherick & Co., London, Melbourne & Sydney.

Threlkeld, L. E. 1834, *An Australian Grammar*, Stephens and Stokes, Sydney.

Tindale, N. B. 1974, *Aboriginal Tribes of Australia*, University of California Press, Berkeley, and ANU Press, Canberra. (Includes map, 'Tribal boundaries in Aboriginal Australia'.)

Wafer, J., and A. Lissarrague 2008, *A Handbook of Aboriginal Languages of New South Wales and the Australian Capital Territory*, Muurrbay, Nambucca Heads.

— 2011, 'The Kuringgai puzzle: languages and dialects on the NSW Mid Coast', in *Indigenous Language and Social Identity: Papers in Honour of Michael Walsh*, Brett Baker, Ilana Mushin, Mark Harvey & Rod Gardner (eds), Pacific Linguistics, Canberra: 155–168.

Zoëga, G. T. 1910, *A Concise Dictionary of Old Icelandic*, Clarendon Press, Oxford.

5. Illuminating the cave names of Gundungurra country

Jim Smith

1. Introduction

Jenolan and Wombeyan are two of the most widely recognised Aboriginal placenames, while Tuglow and Colong are perhaps better known to bushwalkers and speleologists. These limestone cave complexes are in the country of the Gundungurra (also spelled Gandangara) speaking people.[1] Their territory, which included the catchments of the Wollondilly and Cox rivers and some adjacent areas west of the Great Dividing Range, has one of the richest concentrations of limestone caves in Australia. As well as the four main areas listed above there are many small, lesser-known karst areas. These places were very important to the local Aboriginal people. It is a common misconception that they were afraid to go into dark caves. Jeremiah Wilson, who was appointed the first caretaker of Jenolan Caves in 1867, was interviewed in 1896 and said:

> though he tried hard he could not ascertain the proper aboriginal name of the caves. He has never been able to induce an aboriginal to enter them, and does not believe the aboriginals knew of the interior Caves (Hoben 1896: 1247).

This was contradicted by the Gundungurra man Billy Lynch (c.1839–1913), who provided the Aboriginal name and also stated to the same interviewer:

> Mr Jerry Wilson is wrong in thinking the natives did not know or enter the Jenolan Caves. They penetrated them as far as the subterranean water, carrying in sick people to be bathed in this water, which they believed to have great curative powers (Hoben 1896: 1250).

A.L. Bennett obtained from another Gundungurra man, Werriberrie (William Russell, c.1835–1914), the legend of 'Old Gareem the God of sickness and health' who created the medicinal water (*morle-boc*) within limestone caves.[2] This was

---

[1] Although Tindale (1974: 193) recommended the spelling Gandangara, and this is used by most linguists today, the spelling Gundungurra is preferred by the current organisations representing the descendants of the speakers of this language.

[2] Camden grazier Alfred Leonard Bennett (1877–1942) recorded Gundungurra language and cultural information, mainly from William Russell, in the period c.1908–1914. His notes are privately held. They are unpaginated and nearly all undated. All references to Bennett in this paper are from these notes.

used in particular to cure skin diseases. Obviously these healing areas had placenames which were well known to Gundungurra people. Unfortunately, in nearly all cases, the names for these places on our maps are not the names used by the original inhabitants and the commonly accepted meanings of the placenames are incorrect.

Some of the placenames referred to in this article are connected with the Gundungurra 'Dreaming' (*gunyungalung*) story of Gurangatch and Mirragan (Mathews 1908: 203–206). Gurangatch, a type of 'rainbow serpent', was pursued by Mirragan, a 'quoll-man', from a waterhole near the junction of the Wollondilly and Wingecarribee rivers to Joolundo waterhole on the Duckmaloi River, 170 km away. Gurangatch tried to hide from Mirragan inside both Wombeyan and Jenolan Caves.

2. Jenolan

The Jenolan Caves were first known by the non-Aboriginal names of Binda Caves or Fish River Caves. These were examples of 'naming by proximity', as both the Binda property and Fish River were landmarks passed by travellers on their way to the caves but still at a significant distance from them. The official name of 'Jenolan Caves' was gazetted on 19 August 1884 at the suggestion of government surveyor William Cooper (Havard 1933: 31). It is regrettable that the real Aboriginal name for the Caves was not ascertained at the time. While Jenolan is a Gundungurra placename, it belongs to a mountain 13 km from the caves. Mount Jenolan is one of the placenames published on Thomas Mitchell's map of New South Wales (Mitchell 1834). The Parish of Jenolan was later named after this prominent feature within it. 'Jenolan Caves' is really only shorthand for 'the caves within the Parish of Jenolan'. Even though three versions of the true Gundungurra placename for the caves had been published by 1900 (Binomil, Binoomea, Benomera, see Table 1), so much promotional literature had disseminated the name of Jenolan nationally and internationally that no one wanted to change it.

For a brief period, before the name of Jenolan Caves came into common usage, the caves were known by another Gundungurra word. An English traveller (Roberts 1886: 578) was told by the Jenolan Caves guide Fred Wilson in 1885 that the caves were called 'Jelanda'. This is a version of the placename recorded by R.H. Mathews as 'Joolundoo', 'Dyoo-lundoo' and 'Dyulloondoo' (Mathews 1908: 206; Mathews undated 8006/5/10 and 8006/3/10: 20) and in a local newspaper as 'Jelleindore' (Anon. 1907). 'Joolundoo' is the name of the waterhole where the climactic scene of the Gurangatch and Mirragan legend takes place. Research by the author has established that this waterhole is in the lower Duckmaloi River, 14 km from Jenolan Caves (Smith 2008: 185–199). Fred

Wilson's conversation with his Aboriginal informant (or another non-Aboriginal intermediary) probably involved the usual type of misunderstanding where an Aboriginal word for one place was misapplied to another locality.

Table 1: Jenolan Caves.

Original spelling	Meaning	Reference
Binomil		Hoben 1896: 1250
Binoomea		Padley 1892: 4, Trickett 1899: 18
Benomera	'holes'	Anon. c.1899
Benomera	'holes in a hill'	Anon. 1900a: 80
Bin-noo-mur		Mathews 1908: 205
Benuma	'big hole in the ground'	Hanrahan 1909:1
Benumera	'hole in the hill'	Bennett c.1908–14

Source: The author.

Today, promotional and educational material about Jenolan Caves usually includes a reference to the original Aboriginal placename. However, it is nearly always published in Trickett's 1899 spelling of 'Binoomea'. The two vowels at the end are unlikely to reflect the Gundungurra sound of this word. This may be close to 'Binumirr' (Harold Koch, pers. comm. May 2013). The meanings attributed to it have the common theme of 'holes'. It is quite possible that there are other places in Gundungurra country where there were 'holes' in the landscape that were also called 'Binumirr'. One possibility appears on Mitchell's 1834 map. Mount Bannemir, near Hanworth Creek, is not in limestone country but may have some type of 'holes' in it. It would be interesting if the placename turns out to have 'predicted' the existence of a geological feature it has in common with the place we call Jenolan Caves.

3. The meaning of Jenolan

Visitors to Jenolan Caves are told by the guides, and in promotional literature, that Jenolan means 'high mountain'. This was first recorded by the Mines Department surveyor Oliver Trickett (1899: 18). As the caves are actually at the bottom of a deep valley, some tourists probably query this apparently contradictory 'meaning'. The non-Aboriginal person who asked his Gundungurra informant about the meaning of Jenolan (the name of the mountain distant from the caves) appears to have been given a descriptive, topographical or associative meaning. These have also been termed 'connotative' or 'affective' meanings (Amery 2002: 167). Popular books of mixed Aboriginal words from all over Australia, and the folklore of local community stories of placename meanings, contain many of these topographical and environmental descriptors. They have become established where there was mutual misunderstanding between Aboriginal people and early settlers about what was being asked with the question 'What is the meaning of [the local placename]?'. Aboriginal people realised that their white interrogators were not usually interested in the etymology of placenames and their cultural associations but were only looking for an English phrase to associate with the Aboriginal words. This occurred right across the continent, with a Western Australian researcher commenting:

> Part of the reason why these spurious etymologies arise is explicable if it is realised that 19th and 20th century recorders, because of their superficial understanding of Indigenous cultures and languages, often took attributes ascribed to a place by Indigenous informants as the derivation of its name (Gerritsen 2010: 1).

R.H. Mathews attempted to understand the etymology of Jenolan. One of his notebooks has this cryptic analysis: 'Jeno'lan, Jenno-wullan, caves (two feet or Bullen feet?)' (Mathews undated: 8006/3/7: 71). To decode this, it is useful to look at Bennett's records: *genna* or *geno* for 'foot' and *jenolan*, said to mean 'a man with a big foot'. The Gundungurra word for 'two' is *bulla* and the creator ancestors were called the *bullens*. In Gundungurra mythology the Bullen brothers created human beings during the *gunyungalung*, devised their initiation ceremonies and travelled the land destroying the many *gubbas* who preyed on people (Mathews 2003: 29–32). Mathews was apparently not able to distinguish whether *bulla* or *bullen* was incorporated into the four syllable version of Jenolan. In the Gundungurra language, where the second part of a compound word that begins with a *b* follows a vowel or dipthong, the *b* is changed to a *w*. The two words *jenno* and *bullen* cannot be combined as *jennobullen* and the combination was sounded as *jennowullan*.[3]

It is possible that, during the wanderings of the Bullen brothers, the landscape feature of Mount Jenolan was created. As their travels were extensive, there may be other places called 'Jennowullan' in Gundungurra country and, in fact, one other is known. Mount Genowlan (spelled 'Geenowlan' in some early records), near the Capertee Valley, is 78 km from Mount Jenolan.

4. Wombeyan

Wombeyan Caves are 'connected' to Jenolan Caves, as they are both major landmarks on the journey of Gurangatch and Mirragan during the *gunyunggalung*. Gurangatch reached Wombeyan by making a tunnel for himself.

---

[3] For other examples of this see the section on adjectives in Mathews 1901: 144.

On reaching the source of Jock's Creek, he burrowed under the range, coming up inside of Wam-bee-ang caves, which are called Whambeyan by the white people, being a corruption of the aboriginal name (Mathews 1908: 204).

Table 2: Wombeyan Caves.

Original spelling	Date of Publication	Meaning	Reference
Whambeyan	1862		Nurse 1982: 2
Wambian	1865		Nurse 1982: 2
Whombeyan	1868		Nurse 1982: 2
Wombeian	1868		Nurse 1982: 2
Wambiang and Wambeean			Mathews undated 8006/3/10: 18
Wam-bee-ang			Mathews 1908: 204
Wombeyang		'tunnel'	Bennett c.1908–14

Source: The author.

There are many early renderings of this placename (see Table 2). Bennett's spelling 'Wombeyang' may be closest, but should perhaps be spelled as 'Wombeeyang' to emphasise the long *ee* sound of the middle syllable. Only Bennett recorded a meaning. As it was obtained directly from his Gundungurra informant William Russell, the meaning of Wombeyan as 'tunnel' is probably authentic. Although all caves could be looked at as 'tunnels', it is possible that the Wombeyan Caves were named after their association with the tunnel created by Gurangatch. It is of interest that, even after more than one and a half centuries of speleological explorations of Wombeyan Caves, the tunnel connecting them with Jock's Creek has not yet been found. It may not actually exist, since Aboriginal mythology often used the device of underground travel to account for a 'Dreaming' being manifest at different locations (Harold Koch, pers. comm. May 2013).

There is the usual variety of incorrect 'meanings' published in popular 'Aboriginal words' books and tourist literature. These include 'caves in the hills' (Thorpe 1927: 15), 'gigantic kangaroo' (McCarthy 1959: 17) and 'grassy flats between two mountains' (Henderson 1985: 50).

Many of the individual caverns within the Wombeyan complex were given Gundungurra names by the first government appointed caretaker of the caves Charles Chalker (1845–1924). These were 'Wollondilly', 'Mulwaree', 'Guineacor', 'Bullio', 'Kooringa' and 'Miranda' caves. The first three are the names of local rivers and Bullio is a nearby locality. 'Kooringa' is a word of undocumented origin that could be a local placename.

Indigenous and Minority Placenames

'Miranda' is a commemorative name. Wombeyan Caves lie in the country of the Burra Burra clan of the Gundungurra speaking people (Smith 1992: 4–9). In the 1830s the leader of this clan was Murrandah (c.1788–1849). His breastplate, with the words 'Murrandah, Chief of the Burra Burra tribe' is in the Camden Museum. His name was anglicised to Miranda or Maranda. Charles Chalker's grandfather William Chalker (c.1775–1823) had lived in the district since 1821 and possibly knew Miranda personally.

5. Colong Caves

The naming of Colong Caves is another example of 'naming by proximity'. Two early names for the caves were Kowmung Caves and Bindook Caves, after the nearby Kowmung River and Bindook Highlands. The Aboriginal name for these caves does not appear to have been recorded.

Trickett wrote in his official report on the caves:

> I beg to suggest that they be called the Colong Caves after Mount Colong, a conspicuous landmark in the vicinity. The name is derived from the native word "Colung", signifying the home of the bandicoot (Trickett 1900: 211).

The scattered caves of the Colong Caves complex are all at least two kilometres from Mount Colong. Trickett's suggested meaning is not supported by several other independent sources (see Table 3) which confirm that Colong is the Gundungurra word for 'wombat'. Today, the first vowel of Colong is pronounced with a short *o* sound. However, those recorders who are known to have spoken directly to Gundungurra speakers, Mathews, Hoben, Feld and Bennett have renderings with either *u* or *oo*. It is of interest that descendants of the early pioneer families of the region and the older generation of bushwalkers often pronounce it as 'Coolong'. It is likely that Mathews' notebook (cited in Table 3) contains the most accurate rendering of the Gundungurra sound as *gulang* or *kulang*.

Unfortunately, the peak officially known as Mount Colong is incorrectly named. This confusion began in the 1830s with, for example, the 1833 *New South Wales Almanac* referring to 'Collong, which is a square-topped mountain visible from the Sydney Lighthouse' (reproduced in Anon. 1956). There are two mountains in this area, the tops of which are nearly four kilometres apart. Early settlers called the large northern one 'Big Rick' (today's Mount Colong, with the 'square top') and the smaller one to its south, which has a pointed top, 'Little Rick'. The official name of the latter today is Square Rock, a description of the shape of the cliffs around its base. The term 'rick' is a reference to the mountains' supposed resemblance to haystacks. A.L. Bennett made careful enquiries of his informant William Russell and recorded these names: Coolong for 'Little Rick' and the variants 'Gillingyang' and 'Gillinggang' for 'Big Rick'. Russell may have been annoyed by the white men's incorrect identification of the 'Big Rick' as Mount Coolong for he explained it as clearly as possible to Bennett on another occasion: 'Gillingang, Mtn Nth side of Mount Coolong' (Bennett, unpublished notes, c.1908–1914). Bennett's identification of this long-standing error was independently confirmed by Burragorang settler Martin Feld who recorded that 'Gill-in-gang' was the Gundungurra name for the peak 'now known as Mount Coolong'. Feld was the only person to record a 'meaning' for Gillingang suggesting, 'a high mountain, flat on top' (Feld 1900: 99). However, this is clearly a descriptive 'meaning'.

Table 3: Colong.

Original spelling	Meaning	Reference
Cullong		Barrett 1995: 15 (recorded 1827)
Collong		Mitchell 1834
Gulong	'wombat'	Hoben 1896: 1250
Colong 'pronounced Colung'	'wombat'	Anon. 1899: 2
Coolong	'wombat goes in'	Anon. 1900b: 95
Colung	'home of the bandicoot'	Trickett 1900: 211
Gulang and Gulung	'wombat'	Mathews undated 8006/3/10: 11, 14
Kaloong and Goolong	'wombat'	Bennett c.1908–14
Coolong	'valley of the native bears'	Battye 1977: 2

Source: The author.

6. Tuglow

Bennett recorded three separate references to this word.

1. 'tugga-going down low'.

2. 'Tuggaloe-a river going down a deep place or hole'.

3. 'Marrajung, the name of a place between Tugalo and Murrawone, the place of the hole'.

It is easy to identify 'Tuggaloe', the true three syllable version of Tuglow, as the Gundungurra name for what is now known as Horse Gully Creek (Central Mapping Authority 1982). The upper part of this creek, in wet weather, disappears underground into what are now known as the Horse Gully Sinkholes. 'Murrawone', 'the place of the hole' would, on first thought, appear to be the name for the main Tuglow Cave entrance. However, this entrance is only 200 metres away from the sinkholes, which does not leave much room for the other placename, 'Marrajung', between them. Although it does not appear on modern maps, Trickett's 1897 map of the Tuglow Caves area shows a locality, two kilometres south of the caves, called 'The Hole' (Cooper, Scott and Vaughan-Taylor, 1998: 25). Today's Tuglow Hole Creek is named after this 'hole' which is a striking natural depression or hollow in the ground (Peter Dykes, pers. comm. April 2012). Partial confirmation of this is provided by the proximity of this 'hole' to the 'Morong' locality (reflected in the current names Morong Creek and Morong Deep). It is quite feasible that 'Murrawone' (which probably sounded more like 'Murrawong') was corrupted to 'Morong'. Therefore Bennett's note 3 above is tentatively interpreted: 'Tuggaloe' was the Gundungurra name for the locality of Horse Gully Creek, including its sinkholes and cave entrances, and 'Murrawone' the name of 'the place of the hole' on Tuglow Hole Creek. It is not possible to exactly identify the location of 'Marrajung', a previously unrecorded placename, between 'Tuggaloe' and 'Murrawone'.

Gundungurra people were often named after the place where they were born (Russell 1914: 9). Placenames became people's names. William Russell told Bennett that the uncle who taught him the cultural stories, customs and placenames of his people was called Marrajung, because he was born at that place.

7. Abercrombie Caves

The creek flowing through Abercrombie Caves (shown on today's maps as Grove Creek) was known, at least as early as the 1840s, as Burrangilong Creek. This name was published in the *Sydney Morning Herald* on 25 April 1843 (Keck and Cubitt 1991: 18). When the artist Conrad Martens visited the caves in the following month he labelled his drawing of the main arch 'Burrangalong Cavern'. The cave complex was known for some years as the Burrangilong Caverns (also spelled 'Burrangylong' and 'Burran Galong'). It is likely that the Aboriginal name for Abercrombie Caves is close to 'Burrangylong'. Harold Koch (pers. comm. May 2013) has suggested the phonemic form of this name was *barrankalang*. The only published meaning for this word is 'bad tasting water' (Keck and Cubitt 1991: 51).

The name Abercrombie Caves was commonly used from the 1860s, as early visitors 'made the mistake of thinking that the creek flowing through the caves (Grove Creek) was the Abercrombie River' (Keck and Cubitt 1991: 7). The caves are five kilometres north of the Abercrombie River.

It is possible that analysis of the placename 'Burrangylong' could provide evidence of the language of the people whose country included Abercrombie

Caves. When the Gundungurra Tribal Council made its Native Title claim in 1997 (claim NC 97/7) they included Abercrombie Caves within their country. This was disputed by Wiradjuri claimants. The Burra Burra clan of the Gundungurra speaking people, according to one early account, ranged over the area 'from the Abercrombie to Taralga and Carrrabungla' (MacAlister 1907: 82). If Burrangylong could be shown by linguistic analysis to be either a Gundungurra or Wiradjuri word, that would strengthen the claim of one group of descendants to the Abercrombie area.

8. Discussion

Of the five cave complexes discussed in this article only one, Wombeyan Caves, is officially referred to by an Aboriginal placename that closely resembles the original Aboriginal usage. 'Jenolan' and 'Colong' are misplaced toponyms in their usage for cave names. The spellings 'Jenolan' and 'Tuglow' are missing a syllable. The well authenticated Aboriginal name 'Burrangylong' was replaced with the English name of a river five kilometres away.

A good case could be made that Abercrombie Caves would satisfy the New South Wales state government criteria for dual naming, to re-establish the early recognition of its Aboriginal name. However, it is likely that there would be very strong resistance in the tourism industry to changing the well-established landmark name of Jenolan Caves to its correct Aboriginal placename or even of adding a *g* to the end of 'Wombeyan'.

Bushwalkers are quite sensitive about any proposal to change the placenames associated in their minds with their personal journeys.[4] They would probably not support changing Mount Colong to 'Gillingyang', Square Rock to 'Coolung', Morong Falls to 'Murrawong' and Tuglow Caves to 'Tuggaloe' (or more linguistically exact versions of these placenames).

In the same way that Jenolan Caves and Colong Caves were named after previously named topographic features near them, probably hundreds of Aboriginal placenames across Australia are the names of nearby places rather than those of the localities to which they have been applied.

The small sample of Aboriginal placenames discussed in this article includes a significant percentage which is lacking syllables in their current usage such as 'Jennowulan', 'Tuggalow', and 'Murrawong'. There are probably many

---

4 The author published an article (Smith 2006: 1, 4–5) which suggested that some of the placenames of the prolific nomenclaturist Myles Dunphy (1891–1985) in the southern Blue Mountains should be re-evaluated. When this was reprinted in *The Bushwalker*, the magazine of the New South Wales Confederation of Bushwalking Clubs, subsequent issues carried letters expressing outrage from bushwalkers.

hundreds of officially recognised Aboriginal placenames across Australia which are shorter than those originally used by Aboriginal people. In New South Wales, the Surveyor General Thomas Mitchell issued instructions to his staff in 1829 to spell Aboriginal placenames 'with as few letters as possible' and to avoid 'unnecessary consonants and dipthongs' (Andrews 1992: 73). However, his surveyors were not encouraged to eliminate vowels. Therefore, Mitchell's policy should not have caused Aboriginal placenames to be written with missing syllables. They were lost because non-Aboriginal people did not listen carefully enough to the Aboriginal pronunciation, particularly to softly or quickly spoken syllables. Where early records of Aboriginal placenames contain more syllables than those in current usage, these should generally be hypothesised as being more accurate.[5]

When the full version of an Aboriginal placename is established there is a better chance of working out its etymology. In Gundungurra country some placenames appear to be general descriptions of topography. The same placename could therefore have been used in different localities. Just as there are at least two 'Jenolans' there could well be other 'Tuggaloes', 'Benomeras' and 'Wombeyans'.

Another layer of meaning associated with placenames is their 'etiology'. Koch (2009: 118) defines this as 'the story behind the name'. He points out that:

> In the long-settled areas of Australia, where the traditional languages have been poorly documented, we have very little hope of ever recovering the 'meaning' in the sense of the mythological story to which the name alludes (Koch 2009: 118).

Gundungurra descendants, and the settler communities which now live within their country, are fortunate that Mathews and Bennett did learn some of these mythological stories. The two Mount Jenolans may be connected with the travels of the creator ancestors the Bullens. Wombeyan Caves are likely to have been named after the 'tunnel' (real or imagined) created by a local variety of 'Rainbow Serpent' called Gurangatch. 'Binoomera's' meaning of 'holes' could also have a mythological connection. When the quoll ancestor Mirragan was hunting Gurangatch at Wombeyan and Jenolan Caves he poked his spear down into the underground caverns trying to capture him. These spear holes can still be seen at the caves today and are called potholes or dolines by non-Aboriginal people. It is possible that the word 'Binoomera' refers to these holes.

---

5   The following are some examples from Gundungurra country, sourced from the notebooks of Mathews and Bennett and early maps. The currently used placename is given first with the spellings from Gundungurra informants in brackets. Bimlow ('Bulla mullar'), Belloon Pass ('Belloonong'), Bullio ('Buli yoa'), Wingecarribbee River ('Winwingecarribbee'), Kanangra River ('Koo-nang-goor-wa'), Kanimbla Valley ('Kindingbula'), Marulan ('Murrawulan'), Mount Mouin ('Mee-oo-wun'), Duckmaloi ('Wan-dak-ma-lai').

We don't know the reason why the peak known as Little Rick or Square Rock is associated with the wombat. There is no recorded story explaining its origin and no resemblance between the shape of the mountain and a wombat. There may be a clue in one of the recorded meanings. A correspondent to *Science of Man* suggested that 'Coolong' meant 'wombat goes in' (Anon. 1900: 95). Perhaps during the *gunyungalung* a wombat ancestor did 'go in' the mountain. There is even a possibility, as Trickett (1900: 211) suggested, that the mountain was also 'the home of the bandicoot' in this lost story. Even apparently implausible placename meanings could contain a germ of truth relating to their etiology.

To conclude, it is hoped that analysis of the linguistic origins, etymology and distinctive features of Aboriginal placenames will be of assistance to those wishing to establish the original boundaries of language areas, such as Native Title claimants.

Acknowledgements

Thanks are due to Jim Barrett, Harold Koch and Luise Hercus for advice and to John Wylie for information on the cave systems and photos. Wilf Hilder (1934–2011), a former Counsellor of the Geographical Names Board (1967–1975), provided much information and stimulating discussions on nomenclature over the years.

References

Amery, R. 2002, 'Weeding out spurious etymologies: toponyms on the Adelaide Plains', in *The Land Is a Map: Placenames of Indigenous Origin in Australia*, Luise Hercus, Flavia Hodges and Jane Simpson (eds), Pandanus Books in association with Pacific Linguistics, Canberra: 165–180.

Andrews, A. 1992, *Major Mitchell's Map 1834*, Blubber Head Press, Hobart.

Anonymous undated [c.1899], [list of words headed 'Picton'] in Royal Anthropological Society of New South Wales papers, Mitchell Library, MSS, available on CD-ROM from Asia-Pacific Institute for Toponymy, Macquarie University.

— 1899, 'The Kowmung Caves', *The Mountaineer*, 5 May 1899.

— 1900a, 'Aboriginal names of places, etc., with their meanings', *Science of Man*, 21 June 1900: 80–82.

— 1900b, 'Aboriginal names of places, etc., with their meanings', *Science of Man*, 23 July 1900: 95–98.

— 1907, 'Duckmaloi', *Lithgow Mercury*, 26 July 1907.

— 1956, 'Burragorang', *The Waysider,* March 1956.

Barrett, J. 1995, *Life in the Burragorang*, self-published, Glenbrook.

Battye, R. 1977, *The Geology, History and Exploration of The Colong Caves*, self published, Sydney.

Bennett, A. L., undated [c.1908–1914], Notes on Gundungurra language and culture, unpublished manuscripts, private collection.

Central Mapping Authority 1982, [map] *Shooters Hill*, second edition, Department of Lands, Bathurst.

Cooper, I., M. Scott and K. Vaughan-Taylor 1998, *Tuglow Caves*, Sydney University Speleological Society, Sydney.

Dyson, H, R. Ellis and J. James (eds) 1982, *Wombeyan Caves,* Sydney Speleological Society, Sydney.

Feld, M. 1900, 'Myths of Burragorang Tribe', *Science of Man* 3(6): 99.

Gerritson, R. 2010, 'The meaning of Morawa', *Placenames Australia*, June 2010: 1, 3, 7.

Hanrahan, M. 1909, 'Aboriginal nomenclature', *Lithgow Mercury*, 28 June 1909.

Havard, W. 1933, *The Romance of Jenolan Caves*, Royal Australian Historical Society, Sydney.

Henderson, K. 1985, *The Wombeyan Experience*, Neptune Press, Geelong.

Hercus, L., F. Hodges and J. Simpson (eds) 2002, *The Land Is a Map: Placenames of Indigenous Origin in Australia*, Pandanus Books in association with Pacific Linguistics, Canberra.

Hoben, E.D. 1896, 'Round about the Mountains', *Sydney Mail,* 12 December 1896: 1246–1253.

Keck, K. and B. Cubitt 1991, *Abercrombie Caves, Cave Chronicles*, Abercrombie Caves Historical Research Group, Trunkey Creek.

Koch, H. 2009, 'The methodology of reconstructing Indigenous placenames. Australian Capital Territory and south-eastern New South Wales', in

Aboriginal Placenames: Naming and Re-naming the Australian Landscape, Harold Koch and Luise Hercus (eds), ANU E Press and Aboriginal History Inc., Canberra: 115–171.

Koch, H. and L. Hercus (eds) 2009, *Aboriginal Placenames: Naming and Re-naming the Australian Landscape*, ANU E Press and Aboriginal History Incorporated, Canberra.

MacAlister, C. 1907, *Old Pioneering Days in the Sunny South*, Charles MacAlister Book Production Committee, Goulburn.

Mathews, R. H. undated, Unpublished Notebooks, National Library of Australia, MS 8006.

— 1901, 'The Gundungurra language', *Proceedings of the American Philosophical Society* XL: 140–148.

— 1908, 'Some mythology of the Gundungurra Tribe, New South Wales', *Zeitschrift fur Ethnologie* 40: 203–206.

— 2003, *Some Mythology and Folklore of the Gundungurra Tribe* (edited by Jim Smith), Den Fenella Press, Wentworth Falls.

McCarthy, F. 1959, *New South Wales Aboriginal Place Names and Euphonious Words, with their Meanings*, Australian Museum, Sydney.

Mitchell, T. 1834, *Map of the Colony of New South Wales*, Engraved by John Carmichael, London.

Nurse, B. 1982, 'A History of the Wombeyan Caves Area', in *Wombeyan Caves*, H. Dyson, Ross Ellis and Julia James (eds), Sydney Speleological Society, Sydney: 1–12.

Padley, J. 1892, *Lithgow District Nomenclature*, Unpublished typescript, Mitchell Library, 981.5/P.

Roberts, J. H. 1886, *A World Tour*, The Author, Abergale.

Russell, W. 1914, *My Recollections*, Camden News, Camden.

Smith, J. 1992, *Aborigines of the Goulburn District*, Goulburn District Historical Society, Goulburn.

— 2006, 'Myles Dunphy and William Cuneo, two misguided nomenclaturists of the Blue Mountains', *PlacenamesAustralia*, March 2006: 1, 4–5. Reprinted in *TheBushwalker* 31(3), Winter 2006: 9–10.

— 2008, 'Gundungurra Country', PhD thesis, Department of Indigenous Studies, Macquarie University.

Thorpe, W. 1927, *List of New South Wales Aboriginal Place Names and Their Meanings*, Australian Museum, Sydney.

Tindale, N. 1974, *Aboriginal Tribes of Australia*, University of California Press, Berkeley.

Trickett, O. 1899, *Guide to the Jenolan Caves*, Government Printer, Sydney.

— 1900, 'Report on Colong Caves', in Annual Report of the Department of Mines for 1899, Votes and Proceedings of the Legislative Assembly, New South Wales: 211–212.

6. Doing things with toponyms: The pragmatics of placenames in Western Arnhem Land

Murray Garde

1. Introduction

As proper names, placenames do not, by convention, make their way into dictionaries of most languages, although lexicographers working on Australian languages might wish to disagree with this convention. Indeed Indigenous people themselves have insisted on occasion that placenames should play a significant role in dictionary making (Bowern 2009: 327; Aklif 1999). Relationships to land and place-based spirituality are central to Australian Aboriginal cultures and anyone who has had any exposure to an Australian language can testify to the saturation of placename reference in everyday conversation. The inclusion of placenames in dictionaries can be justified on many levels but a dictionary definition of a placename does not necessarily tell us much about how this special class of proper nouns might be used in everyday interaction in Australian languages. Uttering a placename indexes a particular location, but the reasons speakers might choose to do this are not limited to singling out a geographical site in the minds of their interlocutors. Because of the nature of relationships between placenames and the hierarchical structure of placename organisation in many Australian languages, speakers are always making choices about how to index a location.[1] Such choices tell us something about speaker intentions and the nature of the commitment a speaker has to the propositions expressed with the use of a particular toponym.

The purpose of this chapter is to explore how speakers of Bininj Gunwok dialects in Western Arnhem Land 'do things' with placenames, such as achieving particular interactional goals. Such interaction is presented so as to reveal something of the conception of toponymy in Western Arnhem Land. Analysing interaction ideally requires illustration with transcripts of natural speech and so this paper is organised around a number of such transcripts. I will look at five contexts of usage commencing with a discussion of place naming in

---

1 As others have pointed out (Morphy 1984: 26; Keen 1994: 104), it would not be totally accurate to describe Aboriginal land as bounded by a hierarchy of areas with clear cut boundaries. A better description would involve named sites as focal centres that have contextually determined expansions.

the Bininj Gunwok-speaking world and how the availability of choice widens the scope for pragmatic meaning. Following this, I examine how placenames are mentioned in relation to other placenames, especially in terms of mental maps made manifest by the recitation of placenames along traditional walking routes. Next, I examine the role placenames play as both personal referring expressions and reference to objects. Finally, I describe the practice of using placenames in a particular form of kinship-based joking and other kinds of light-hearted interaction.

2. The organisation of place naming in Bininj Gunwok

Bininj Gunwok, a member of the Gunwinyguan family of languages, is a collective name of convenience coined by linguists (e.g. Evans 2003) to designate a chain of dialects best known by the largest variety, Kunwinjku, as spoken at Gunbalanya in Western Arnhem Land. Neighbouring varieties are Gundjeihmi, spoken to the west in Kakadu National Park, Kuninjku, spoken in the Liverpool and Mann Rivers region south of Maningrida and Kune (also sometimes referred to as Mayali), spoken on a number of outstations in the Cadell River district south of Maningrida in central-north Arnhem Land (see image1).

The structure of Bininj Gunwok placenames is very similar to that described by Merlan (2001) for the neighbouring Gunwinyguan language of Jawoyn. Merlan describes the relationship between Jawoyn placenames and the places they designate as being 'non-arbitrary' (2001: 367), that is, toponyms project a meaning associated with a place, especially the dreaming or totemic identity of a place. Starting from these minimal points of reference, Jawoyn placenames can be 'expanded' (Merlan 2001: 367) to detail their economic, spiritual and cosmological signficance. To use a modern analogy pointed out to me by Peter Danaja, an Indigenous colleague who is a speaker of the Burarra language (coastal north-central Arnhem Land), 'our placenames are like hyperlinks on a computer – clicking on them opens up a story'. Merlan's description for Jawoyn also generally holds true for the semantics of Bininj Gunwok toponyms. Placename meanings extend along a continuum of semantic transparency. At one end of the continuum are maximally transparent forms such as those in (1)–(3):[2]

---

2 Abbreviations: 1- first person, 2- second person, 3- third person, a- augmented (plural), ABL ablative, COM comitative, DEM demonstrative, I- masculine noun class, II- feminine noun class, III- vegetal noun class, IMM immediate, INTERROG interrogative, IV- general noun class, LOC locative, m minimal (singular), NP non-past, ø- zero, P past, place.n.- placename, PP past perfective, prop.n.- proper noun, REDUP reduplication, REL relative, RR reflexive/reciprocal, SEQ sequential, ss.n- subsection name, ua- unit augmented (dual), lengthening is indicated by multiple colons ::::.

(1)   *Nabarrbinj Werrhmeng*
        na-barrbinj ø-werrhme-ng
        I-clan.name 3P-clear.ground-PP
        The man of Barrbinj patriclan cleared the ground (of vegetation).

(2)   *Kunj Kadjowkke*
        kunj ka-djowkke
        kangaroo 3NP-cross.overNP
        Kangaroo crosses over.

(3)   *Kabanibirliyingarrnghmang*
        Kabani-birli-yi-ngarrnghma-ng
        3ua-fire-com-negotiate.landscape-NP
        They (2) walked through the pass (whilst) holding fire.

The totally opaque end of the continuum is illustrated by the synchronically unanalysable examples in (4) and (5), although the placename Rarrekbaldeng (4) contains the formative verb theme *-deng,* which is a marker of a particular class of verbs in Bininj Gunwok. Following the common bipartite structure of many Bininj Gunwok placenames, this suggests a nominal subject *rarrek* and the verbal predicate *baldeng,* however these lexemes are unknown in modern Bininj Gunwok.

(4)   *Rarrekbaldeng*
        ?
        Place on the banks of the Mann River, near Kamarrkawarn outstation in the Kodwalewale estate.

(5)   *Dendenday*
        ?
        Place in the Kodwalewale estate.

Many other placenames have familiar or typical Bininj Gunwok morphology even though the semantics of at least some elements are impenetrable, as in (6).

(6)   *Anbarawanj Karri*
        An barawanj ka rri
        III-[unknown] 3mNP-stand
        Place of *an-barawanj* [an archaic plant name?]

The placename in (6) is an example of the common formula consisting of *X ka-rri* 'X it-stands' (or another stative verb such *-ni* 'sits' or *-yo* 'lies'). The morphology of the first segment of the binomial suggests a plant name, as the vast majority of plant names in Bininj Gunwok have a vegetal class prefix *(m)an-*. The meaning of the name *an-barawanj* is unknown and it assumed to be archaic. An absence of semantic transparency does not mean however, that there is no concomitant 'hyperlink' to an implicit cultural significance of such places.

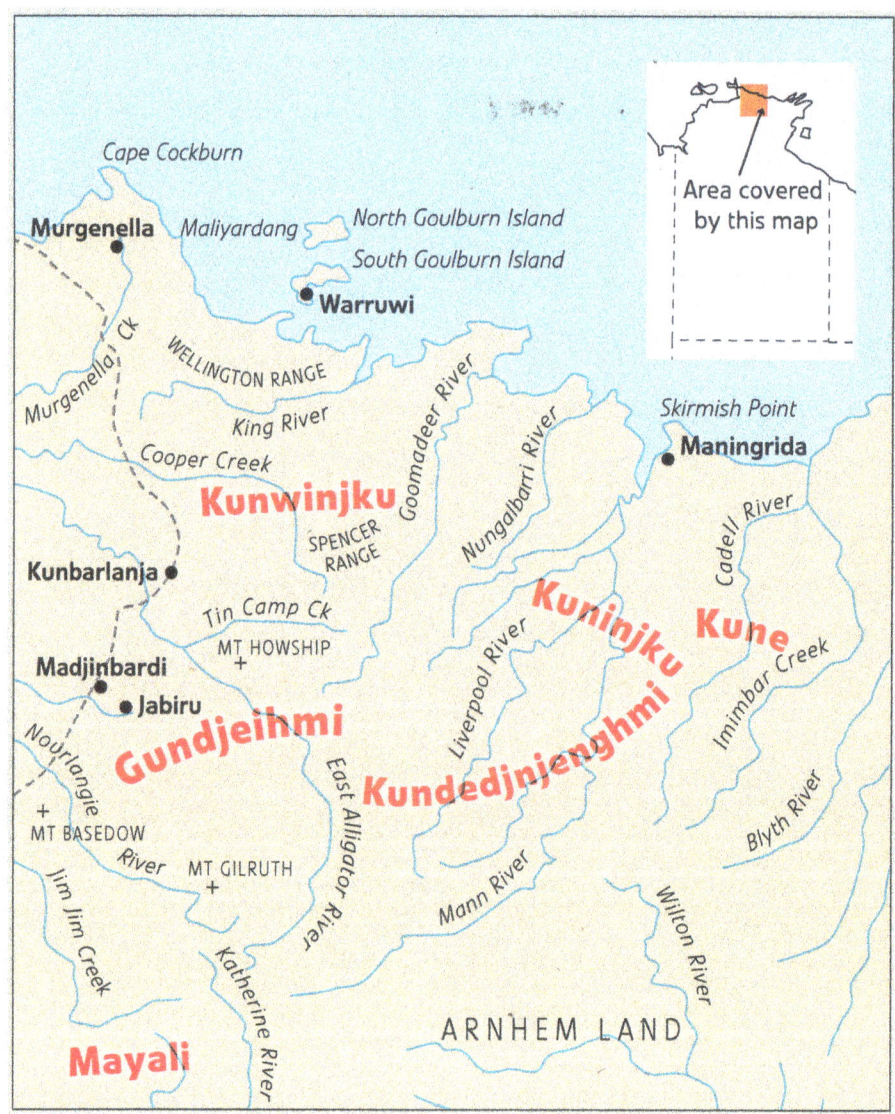

Map 1: Locations of Bininj Gunwok dialects in western Arnhem Land.

Source: Murray Garde.

On the other hand, Bininj Gunwok speakers do not always acknowledge links between placename meanings and an encoded cultural significance. Land, country and individual sites in certain general contexts are all referred to as *kun-bolk* in Bininj Gunwok where *kun-* is a general noun class prefix which includes words in the semantic domains of land, language, body parts and various abstract nouns. A more restrictive term *kun-red*, refers to any named location which is considered to be a site in a traditional repertoire of those places along walking routes or *Bininj man-bolh* 'Aboriginal roads'. *Kun-red* also refers to the concept of 'home, hearth – a place where people live'. When people 'shift camp' carrying all their possessions, they are said to be going *red-dorrengh*, 'camp/home-with', as opposed to just a day trip. Enquiries about the cultural significance of a placename, especially those which tend towards the transparent end of the semantic continuum, are sometimes met with a response along the lines of 'it's just a placename' or 'it's just a *kun-red* (traditional camping place)'. The transcript in (8) is an illustration of this when I once questioned the knowledgeable Kundedjnjenghmi elder Lofty Bardayal Nadjamerrek about the meaning of a placename *Dedjbang* which means *Vitex acuminata,* a tree with edible purple-black fruit:

(8)   MG: *Yi-bengkan Dedjbang, makka an-me an-dedjbang?*
        You know that place Dedjbang, is that [related to] the fruit tree Vitex acuminata?

        LBN: Kun-red!
        It's [just] a placename!

3. 'Big' and 'small' placenames

In (4) and (5) where there is no translation possible for such placenames, I have instead provided a lexical definition in relation to other placenames. In these examples the translation includes the term 'estate' which reflects the fact that certain placenames index areas that extend further from geographical focal points than others. Such regional placenames are called *kun-bolkngeybadjan* or *kun-bolkngeykimuk,* both meaning 'big placenames'. The opposite, *kun-bolkngeyyahwurd* 'small placenames' are lower order named sites within estates. Such 'big name' versus 'small name' distinctions and variations of these categories are found in other Australian languages (Keen 1994: 104; Bowern 2009). The choice of the English term 'estate' is intended to convey something about Bininj Gunwok land tenure, as all estates are owned by a particular *kun-mokurrkurr* 'patrifilial clan' or a 'company' of clans. All *kun-mokurrkurr* will have at least one *kun-bolkngeykimuk* estate name. Some clans are organised by separate lineages who share the same clan name but each lineage has their own exclusive *kun-bolkngeykimuk*.

This place-naming structure becomes relevant to pragmatic meaning when speakers make choices about how specific they wish to be, or for example when a speaker wishes to demonstrate their fine-grained knowledge of places by referring to a lesser known or rarely used *kun-bolkngeyyahwurd* 'small placename'. Choice of placename is also important when referring to the small remote outstation communities or 'homeland centres' which surround regional towns and settlements. In Western Arnhem Land, many outstations are referred to by their *kun-bolkngeykimuk* or 'big placenames' as such names are more widely known than the local 'small names'. Residents at these outstations in some cases will make use of a variety of designations for an outstation depending on who they are addressing. In-group usage (e.g. outstation residents) is more likely to be restricted to a small placename. In some cases some 'small names' are 'smaller' than others. An example is the outstation of Milmilngkan south of Maningrida which is owned by Kuninjku speaking people of the Kurulk *kun-mokurrkurr* or patriclan. The name Milmilngkan is not a Kurulk *kun-bolkngeykimuk* 'big/estate name'. Residents say that the outstation is actually located on a smaller site called Bulngandi and this is the name they use to refer to their outstation when addressing each other or residents from nearby outstations whom they consider close kin. In official contexts or interaction with out-groups (e.g. in contexts involving interaction with the local outstation resource centre), the outstation is always referred to as Milmilngkan. The Kurulk clan's estate name *Kidbulmaniyimarra* is rarely used and little known by others outside of the region.

Another large and well-established Kuninjku outstation south of Maningrida is Marrkolidjban. This outstation was established in the early 1970s and is located at a place referred to by the 'small name' of Manbodjub Kayo (literally '*Triodia* spinifex, it lies'). Whilst this seems to be common knowledge held by residents and neighbours, the outstation is never referred to by this small name and only ever as 'Marrkolidjban'. The community was established as an official outstation serviced by the government welfare settlement of Maningrida. However, the influential Kardbam clansman Peter Marralwanga is credited with establishing the outstation at a time when his own Kardbam patriclan was politically strong and numerous, and the land-owning Born patriclan was small and lacking in cohesion.[3] The Arnhem Land patrimoiety system dividing the world into either *duwa* or *yirridjdja* moieties also applies to land. Anbodjub Kayo is on Born clan land which is associated with the *duwa* moiety. Peter Marralwanga and his Kardbam clan were the opposite *yirridjdja* moiety. The politically incorrect arrangement involving a non-land owning group of the opposite

---

3   Peter Cooke, pers. comm.

6. Doing things with toponyms

moiety establishing and occupying a new outstation on someone else's country was also aided by the manipulation of placename conventions. It is common knowledge that the place designated by the name Marrkolidjban is actually an area of important wetland food resources located five kilometres to the east of the outstation at Manbodjub Kayo, and is on land belonging to the Marrirn clan, a neighbouring *yirridjdja* moiety clan. In 1999 when conducting cultural site surveys in the region, two senior long term residents of nearby Kumarrirnbang and Kurrukkurrh outstations, Peter Nabarlambarl (PN) and Timothy Nadjowh (TN) made the comments in (8):[4]

(8) PN: *Anbodjub Kayo, station there, Kunrak Kani, i gat Marrirn, Biliyedj.*

Anbodjub Kayo is [the name of] that outstation there [i.e. 'Marrkolidjban']. Kunrak Kani [an important sacred site about 200 metres from the outstation] belongs to the Marrirn clan, [where] Biliyedj [lives] [Biliyedj is a nickname of a senior long term resident at Marrkolidjban who is the eldest son of Peter Marralwanga].

TN: *That one Manbodjub Kayo ka-bolkngeyyo.*

The name of that place is Manbodjub Kayo.

PN: *Im not Marrkolidjban, that big plain you bin look there? That Marrkolidjban. Your brother ka-ni, well Anbodjub Kayo.*

That is not [really] Marrkolidjban; have you seen that big plain there [wetlands to the east]? That's Marrkolidjban. But where your brother lives, well that's Anbodjub Kayo.

A similar situation exists for the names used to refer to other outstations nearby. One of the *kun-bolkngeykimuk* or 'big names' for the Marrirn clan (bordering Marrkolidjban) is Kumarrirnbang (literally *ku-* locative prefix, *marrirn* 'proper name of a clan', *-bang* 'dangerous, sacred, restricted'). This is also the name used to refer to another large well-established outstation which similarly has a *kun-bolkngeyyahwurd* 'small placename' that is no longer used to refer to the location of the outstation. However, in contexts where precision is required (again, cultural site surveys to establish land ownership and clan affiliation registers), the 'small names' become relevant. The transcript in (9) details a discussion between myself and a senior placename expert Jimmy Kalarriya, which took place after a helicopter survey to record named sites near Kumarrinbang outstation.

(9) MG: *Kodjok, Kundjurrkamik karrimhdi?*

Kodjok [JK's subsection name], so we set out from Kundjurrkamik today?

---

4 These comments are a mixture of Kriol and Kunwinjku languages. Further, PN speaks a plateau dialect called Kundedjnjenghmi. In this variety, the vegetal noun class prefix which is *man-* in Kunwinjku, drops the initial nasal to become *an-*, thus accounting for the variation – Manbodjub Kayo (TN's version) and Anbodjub Kayo (PN's version).

JK: *Kukabo, dja karrkad Kuyahyay kure* station.
That's on the creek, but up higher on the bank is Kuyahyay, at the outstation.

MG: *Kure Kumarrirnbang Outstation?*
Is that at Kumarrirnbang outstation?

JK: *Yo.*
Yes.

MG: *Kuyahyay?*
[intonation suggesting – 'I don't know this place']

JK: *Kuyahyay. Kumarrirnbang ngarri-bolkngeybuni ku-bolkbadjan.*
We used the name 'Kumarrirnbang', the big estate name [to refer to the outstation at Kuyahyay].

MG: *Ku-bolkyaw?*
(So that is) a little place?

JK: *Ku-bolkyaw kure station ka-djaldi. Ku-kabo Kundjurrkamik kaddum Mandjabu Kalurlhdi. Kaddum anekke kaddum ngamed Dulkbordobom manekke manu yikurrmehkurrmeng djurra.*
The small name for the outstation still exists. On the creek [from the outstation] Kundjurrkamik is upstream and then Mandjabu Kalurlhdi [literally 'conical fish trap is swollen']. Upstream from there is Dulkbordobom, names which you recorded in your book.

Using a 'big placename' to refer to an outstation can in some contexts create confusion when such big names have also become designations for other focal sites in the 'estate'. An example of this involves the *kun-bolkngeykimuk* or 'big placename' of Kubumi, which was used to refer to an outstation on the Mann River established in the early 1980s by people of the Kulmarru clan. The *kun-bolkngeyyahwurd* or 'small placename' for the location of the outstation is Yikarrakkal. The focal place for Kubumi is a stretch of the Mann River where the river widens and white sandy banks are a popular camping place for people from the outstation, which is located only a kilometre upstream to the south. In the period of 1990 to 1997 when I lived at Yikarrakkal, movement between the outstation and the river camp was constant. With both the outstation and the river camp both being referred to by the name Kubumi, it became very difficult to disambiguate reference to these two places when speaking to people who did not live at Yikarrakkal. In 1990 the community decided to deal with this confusion by using the *kun-bolkngeyyahwurd* of Yikarrakkal for the outstation and the *kun-bolkngeykimuk* Kubumi, for the river camp. Kuninjku people in the

Mann River region will refer to the outstation as either Yikarrakkal or Kubumi depending on their assessment of shared knowledge with interlocutors. 'Big names' are more widely known outside of the local sphere of interaction.

4. Names for *djang* 'totemic sites'

Bininj Gunwok placenames do not index landscape features as is the case in English, e.g. Rose Hill, Alice Springs, Rabbit Flat. An exception, at least for an intangible cultural landscape feature, are names for totemic centres, most commonly translated in English as 'sacred sites'. Toponyms are said to be either the name of *kun-red* 'camping places/traditionally known sites', *kun-bolkngeykimuk* 'big placenames' or *djang* 'sacred sites/totemic sites'. Placenames that express something of a spiritual totemic force or 'dreaming' which is thought to inhere in a particular place are usually semantically quite explicit (as they are in Jawoyn, see Merlan 2001). Certain, but not all placenames associated with *djang* 'sacred sites/dreaming' are binomial of the form '*X Djang*' or '*X Kadjang(di)* (it-*djang*-stands)' where X refers to the totemic entity associated with the location:

(10)	*Bidjurru Djang*	'Whirlwind Dreaming'
(11)	*Dird Djang*	'Moon Dreaming'
(12)	*Wayarra Djang*	'Ghost Dreaming'
(13)	*Kodjdjorn Kadjangdi*	'Woodworm Dreaming'

Certain placenames can be referred to either by a placename, or the name of the *djang* which inheres in the site. On the upper Liverpool River is the outstation Kabulwarnamyo which has the literal sense expanded in (14):

(14) Kabulwarnamyo
Ka-bul-warnam-yo
3m-underground-be.horizontal-lie.NP

Kabulwarnamyo is a site within the Ankung Djang 'Honey Dreaming' estate. A complex of sites related to honey totems are all located within this estate belonging to the Mok clan. Large underground 'dreaming' honey hives are said to lie under the ground at key sites throughout the estate, as the name Kabulwarnamyo implies. Also located at Kabulwarnamyo is a *djang* for a species of wasp that preys on the larvae of native honey bees and known in some dialects of Bininj Gunwok as *norne*. The wasp is held in high regard by Aboriginal people as it is said to lead humans to hives where it will be rewarded with access to the bee larvae once the hive is broken open. The focus of the *norne djang* at Kabulwarnamyo is a particular *Syzygium suborbiculare* tree which, during species increase rituals, is struck with an axe in order to increase the abundance of both the wasps and honey. Since the establishment of Kabulwarnamyo outstation in 2002, most non-residents refer to the place by the name of the wasp totem *Norne,* whilst most residents use the placename Kabulwarnamyo. These preferences may be related to the relative ease of pronunciation (two syllables versus five) but there are also contexts where pragmatic meaning is relevant, as when some speakers who are in-group residents use the name Kabulwarnamyo with other residents, but use the name Norne with out-group or non-residents. Such evaluations of the mental states and knowledge of others are in this case influential in determining placename usage in interaction.

5. Connections of places to other places

Western Arnhem Land is, like the rest of Aboriginal Australia covered in a network of traditional walking routes which are still known by older *Bininj* ('Aboriginal people'), effectively in the form of mental maps (Hercus et al. 2002). As already mentioned, these routes are known as *Bininj man-bolh* 'Aboriginal roads' which are recalled by reciting placenames along a particular route. Not only do mental maps assist in navigation through what can be extremely confusing and dangerous physical environments, they also, as Levinson and Burenhult observe, allow speakers 'to linguistically "zoom in" and "zoom out" – to vary the granularity of place description' (2008: 139). Such 'zooming in' becomes extremely important when navigating throughout the dense stone country of the Arnhem Land plateau (see Image 1). A basic way to recite placenames is to list them in the order they are encountered, as in the following text by the Kundedjnjenghmi elder Jimmy Kalarriya. The text in (15) was made as part of a plan to conduct a low altitude helicopter route over the Kunburray estate (or 'big name') as part of a mapping exercise on the Liverpool River.

(15)   JK: ...*karri-durndeng kurih karri-djalyimiwon nane dubbeno:: Bibiddoy, Kudjarridjbolh, Bundjurrulk, Ngalkodjok Wokyirranj, Ngarrekorulk, Kunjberrinjbuk Wubarr, Kunjberrinjbuk Wubarr ka-yo kumekke, yiman mak Menedji kah-yo Mimburrng manu Wurrkeyele. And same way mak konda na-Durlmangkarr ka-yo. Ubarr.*

...we'll go back this way, we'll do it like this through the dense stone country that goes on and on: Bibiddoy, Kudjarridjbolh, Bundjurrulk, Ngalkodjok Wokyirranj, Ngarrekorulk, Kunjberrinjbuk, [which is] a Wubarr ceremony place, at Kunjberrinjbuk there is a Wubarr ceremony ground, in the same way that at Menedji in the Mimburrng region of the Wurrkeyele estate there is also a Wubarr ceremony ground. Well it's the same for this place here for the Durlmangkarr clan. An Ubarr ceremony.

In (15) Kalarriya recites the placenames along this route, until he arrives at a salient feature at the site Kunjberrinjbuk – an Ubarr ceremony ground (see Garde 2011). Here he 'zooms out' to compare the significance of this place with that in another location, a site Menedji (a 'small placename') within a larger region Mimburrng which in turn is located within the *kun-bolkngeykimuk* or 'big placename/estate' of Wurrkeyele.

Image 1. Dense sandstone country of the Arnhem Land Plateau.

Source: Murray Garde.

Another common strategy when reciting the places along a walking route is to use tail-head linkage of the form 'arrive at A, from A to B, from B to C, from C to D etc'. The example in (16) is again Jimmy Kalarriya reciting placenames along a river gorge as he explained to younger family members how to walk from places in the Kumarrirnbang estate to those in the Kunburray estate on the Liverpool River in the northern section of the Arnhem Land Plateau. This procedural discourse was produced in a didactic context – a cultural site survey, which apart from the mapping objective, was also organised as an excursion to facilitate intergenerational transfer of knowledge.

(16) 1. JK: *Ngalengman kabarrarnre:::, Kamanemdi, Kamanemdi*
2. *Yolngbuyken, Yolngbuyken Nadjabbarr, Nadjabbarr,*
3. *Kurrbbirnbaleng, Kurrbbirnbaleng kanjdjikanjdji ngalengman*
4. *Barrmo Kunburray kabalbarrarnbebme. Mani anbarrarn. mani*
5. *ngalengman anbarrarn mani yina kabale Kuwuluburrk mahni*
6. *karrbarda ... konda karrbarda mani anwandjad kabale*
7. *kabalbarrarnbebme Dobdobma Wurdib nuye kunu kantri...*

This gorge continues on and on... to Kamanemdi, Kamanemdi Yolngbuyken, Yolngbuyken Nadjabbarr, Nadjabbarr Kurrbbirnbaleng, Kurrbbirnbaleng downstream all the way to Barrmo where the gorge comes out in the Kunburray estate. This other gorge here [points], look here, it goes to Kuwuluburrk and the long yams here, yams on this little tributary here which continues, the gorge continues and arrives at Dobdobma there in Wurdib's [a man's name] country.

The clause chaining of the placenames in (16) consist of links in the 'chain' as discrete intonational units – 'from A to B' > 'from B to C' suggesting the procedural and linear nature of movement along a route. Further, the head-tail chaining reflects the process of arriving and then departing from a site as movement procedes along the walking route. Such tail-head chaining, typical of procedural texts (de Vries 2005), facilitates recall of each placename 'link' along points of this particular mental map. These kinds of recitations of spatial knowledge in Bininj Gunwok discourse are typically organised according to episodes characterised by a particular descriptive resolution. Descriptions of the route are laid out by reciting the order of *kun-bolkngeyyahwurd* 'small placename' in route segments. The speaker then typically zooms in to a single site to provide more fine-grained cultural, ecological or physiographic detail, as in the reference to the ceremonial associations of the sites Kunjberrinjbuk and Menedji in (15). In (16) Kalarriya 'zooms in' with comments on important resources at certain sites along the route. At Kuwuluburrk (line 5) yams are found and their association with *mani anwanjdjad* 'this creek/tributary' (line 6) which forms part of a watercourse valley or small gorge that is part of another route. Sets of 'small placenames' are ordered according to their estate and clan affiliations. The recitation in (16) involves listing places along a route in the Kunburray estate, a 'big name' or 'estate' owned by the Durlmangkarr clan.

Crossing over into the neighbouring estate is indicated by naming the first *kun-bolkngeyyahwurd* 'small placename' encountered (Dobdobma), and the personal name of the senior traditional owner (line 7). As well as establishing the social context of places, mentioning the name of the senior owner is another way of indexing the 'big placename', without actually mentioning it. Knowledge of this particular estate name – Kunukdi – is common ground to those present. This change in descriptive resolution illustrates the way fine-grained descriptions are then contextualised by 'zooming out' to a regional perspective.

Another type of site recitation along *Bininj man-bolh* 'Aboriginal roads' involves linear movement in relation to a landscape vector. Such recitation represents the relationship of placenames to landscape form. In the rock country and freshwater drainage systems of Western Arnhem Land, movement by humans in landscapes is indicated with spatial terms that involve travel by foot, either up or down in a drainage system. In (17) Bardayal Nadjamerrek preposes each placename along a water course with the locative adverb *kanjdji* 'down, downstream'.

(17) BN: ... Mongkebaldeng, **kanjdji** ngamed kukawadj, Kurrekbinj **kanjdji** ngaleh kaboyo anbokuyeng Mibudyibudyi, **kanjdji kabale** Midjandadj, **kanjdji** kare Wohwohkani, **kanjdji** kumekke Kolorrhyi.

Mongkebaldeng [a place], **downstream** to whatsit on the sand, Kurrekbinj, **downstream** the water is a long stretch of river [at] Mibudyibudyi, **it keeps going** downstream to Midjandadj, then downstream it goes to Wohwohkani, and **downstream** there to Kolorrhyi.

This type of recitation links each site to the next, but the relationships of one place to another are also linked to landscape. Frequent movement by foot along a route and the salient landscape features that distinguish one place from another (as in (17) – 'sandy place', 'long stretch of water') will have played their part in the development of the high linear density of placenames typical in parts of Western Arnhem Land. Obviously the choice of directional adverb in placename recitation, such as that in (17) and (18), is relative to the direction of movement along the watercourse – upstream or downstream.

(18) JK: *Andjerd kaddum-djam,* **kaddum** *Nawakka, kayawal mankuken, yam.*

Upstream [from Mokkorri] is Andjerd and **up further** is Nawakka, there are lots of long yams there.

JK: *Karrbarda Nawakka, bolk Wurrbbarn,* **kaddum** *kadjale Bamkorddji.*

Yams are at Nawakka, belonging to the Wurrbbarn clan and **upstream** it keeps going to Bamkorddji.

Returning to more immediate pragmatic meaning, the placename recitations in (16)–(18) were produced in didactic contexts, either for cultural site surveys or during an annual bush walk activity organised by Warddeken Ltd, an Indigenous land management company that administers an Indigenous Protected Area on the Arnhem Land Plateau. These 10-day excursions involve intergenerational knowledge transfer about places and *Bininj man-bolh* 'Aboriginal roads'. Elders such as Bardayal Nadjamerrek (deceased 2009) and Jimmy Kalarriya (deceased 2012) used placename recitation in these contexts to demonstrate their knowledge of placenames, walking routes and the resources associated with these places.

6. Placenames, personal names and other objects

As land, placenames and identity are so tightly interconnected in Aboriginal Australia, it is no surprise that there are possibilities for the development of metonymic reference, whereby both placenames and personal names are 'signs' (after Pierce 1955), which can in certain contexts refer to each other as 'objects'. That is, a person (or an object associated with them) can be referred to by a place linked to them in some way, either through clan identity or via primary residence. Alternatively, there are also examples of places being indexed by reference to their 'owners' as in (12), line 7. This kind of semiotic relationship between sign and object can be considered both 'indexical' and 'symbolic' in that for the former, there are contextual contiguities between a person and the place where they live, and for the latter, there are cultural conventions that imbue cosmological contiguities between people of a particular social category and places also classed within the same category.[5]

To illustrate the practice of placenames as personal referring expressions, the text in (19) is a conversation between myself (MG) and a visitor to my residence (AB) who had arrived to inform me of the death of a classificatory sibling.[6]

(19) 1. AB: *Yi-bekka-ng?*
            2m-hear-PP
            Have you heard?

       2. MG: *Na-wu njale?*
            I-REL INTERROG
            About what?

---

5   See also Enfield (2009) for a discussion of the relationships amongst signs, objects and interpretants in the Piercean schema.
6   Whilst critics might point out that this type of discourse illustrates how speakers of Bininj Gunwok use placenames when interacting with linguists/anthropologists, it is also worth pointing out that opportunities for recording such 'naturally occurring interaction' (i.e. death announcements) between native speakers are almost nil, and would pose serious ethical challenges. This transcript was constructed from field notes immediately after the event, not from an audio recording, for obvious reasons. Nevertheless, the identity and role of the participants in this particular speech event do not invalidate the point that placenames can also be used as substitutes for personal names in other contexts involving interaction between native speakers.

3. AB: *Bolk-warre-minj   ngune-danginj, Bulanj.*
    place-[become]bad-PP 2ua-siblings   ss.n.
    Something bad has happened [i.e. a death], your brother, Bulanj.

4. MG: *Na-ngale?*
    I-INTERROG
    Who?

5. AB: *Mankorlod*
    place.n.
    Mankorlod [a place].

Reference to recently deceased people by personal name is tabooed in Australian Aboriginal cultures and there are a number of strategies used to avoid this (see also Garde 2008a). The initial strategies used by speaker AB in (19), line 3 (a kin term and subsection) failed to establish the identity of the deceased person in my mind. After all, the subsection name *Bulanj* statistically represents one eighth of the male population and this death was totally unexpected. AB narrows the field of possible candidates in line 5 by using a placename, Mankorlod – both an estate name or *kun-bolkngeykimuk* and the name of an outstation community of some 12 residents (at that time), although the name could equally have referred to any male persons of *Bulanj* subsection who are members of the clan associated with the place Mankorlod.

Other cultural motivations for circumspect reference to people can also result in the use of placenames as personal referring expressions. As for the recently deceased, there is also a taboo on personal reference to certain categories of close affines as well as cross-sex siblings. Placenames can at times also operate as substitute referring expressions for people in such contexts. However, the close connection between places and the people who are associated with them can also mean that the use of placenames as personal referring expressions are subject to the same taboos. The conversation transcribed in (20), conducted in 1996, illustrates the co-presence of reference to both places and people who own them, as is also the case in (16). The speaker Bardayal Nadjamerrek was in a conversation with various family members and the rock art researcher George Chaloupka (thus the code switching between Bininj Gunwok and Kriol). The discussion focused on sites on the upper Liverpool River, especially religious sites associated with honey and bees. This particular segment of talk concerns Bardayal's Mok clan and the Ankung Djang 'Honey Dreaming' estate, as well as the land of their close neighbours, the Berdberd clan. In (20), line 2 (which is in Kriol), Bardayal initiates reference to a particular woman of the Berdberd clan. As this person happens to be a classificatory sister, uttering her name is subject to the cross-sex sibling name taboo and so she is introduced in terms of her kinship to another person ('Nabarade's mother', (20), line 2). A further complication is that the woman was named after her place of birth, Ngaldaddubbe, a site in Bardayal's Mok estate on the neighbouring Berdberd estate border.[7] The name *Ngaldaddubbe* literally means 'she with severed leg(s)' – *ngal* 'feminine noun class prefix' *dad* 'leg' *dubbe* 'terminates/blocked'. An 'expansion' of this placename involves reference to the local honey spirit being *Wakkewakken* who is depicted in artwork as a woman with no legs. The place is considered a *djang* 'totemic site' associated with *an-yalk* 'honey hives found in rock'. As Bardayal's intention is to discuss totemic honey sites such as this, he is faced with a dilemna of cultural protocol.

(20) 1. BN: *Konda-beh Kulnguki kaddum kunukka*
LOC-ABL prop.n. on.top IV.DEM
On this side is [the place] Kulnguki, upstream there.

2. BN: [Kriol] *You know that im mummy Nabarade, im got name there...*
Do you know Nabarade's mother, she has a name from that place [which]...

3. BN: *no matter, I call im might be Warnkulembakmeng*
even though I shouldn't, perhaps I'll refer to her [by a placename] Warnkulembakmeng.

4. GC: Aha.

5. BN: *im mummy; but my sister, ngal-Berdberd*
II-clan.n.
She is [Nabarade's] mother, but my sister of the Berdberd clan.

6. *barlmarded   ngadburrung Berdberd.*
sorry.for.swearing [my]sibling clan.n.
I shouldn't mention her, excuse me, my Berdberd clan sibling.

7. BN: *That, im ngal-Berdberd-ni, that Barade im mummy*
II-clan.n.-STAT   prop.n.
She was of Berdberd clan, and was Barade's mother,

8. BN: *yi-bengka-n that im maitbi imin born*
2-know-NP [Kriol...]

---

7 People in Western Arnhem Land are often named after their place of birth. For men, a place of birth is referred to as *ka-borndokdi* 'the spear thrower stands there' whilst for women the equivalent term is *ka-djadjdi* 'the digging stick stands there'.

you know, she was I think born

9. BN: *that girl long time Warnkulembakmeng*
                                              prop.n.
    that girl, a long time ago, Warnkulembakmeng.

10. BN: *Nga-yawoyh-durnde-ng nga-yawoyh-durnde-ng*
           1-again-return-NP   1-again-return-NP
    "I'll go back again, I'll go back again [to that place]"

11. BN: *ø-yime-ng Ngal-dad-dubbe*.
          3P-say-PP II-leg-cut.off
    she said, Ngaldaddubbe.

12. BN: *Kaluk bolk-balmarded,   ba-rrang-inj,*
          SEQ place-sorry.for.swearing 3P-stand-PP
    At that place whose name I can't say, she was born there,

13. BN: *ngadburrung, ...ngadburrung Berdberd.*
          sibling   sibling   clan.n.
    my sibling, my sibling from the Berdberd clan

14. BN: *nga-djal-kordidj-kordidjme-rr-en*
          1-just-REDUP-swear-RR-NP
    I am swearing at myself

15. BN: *tharran my sister*
          DEM[Kriol] ''
    that woman is my sister

16. BN: *imin born there, Ngaldaddubbe im name now.*
                               prop.n.
    She was born there, and that's her name, Ngaldaddubbe.

17. BN: *That Ngaldaddubbe now.*
              place/prop.n.
    Ngaldaddubbe, that's her now. But nevertheless, I'll say her name

18. BN: *But no matter, I call im my Ngaldaddubbe.*
                                place.n.
    I will call her name, my Ngaldaddubbe regardless.

19. BN: *I call him sister. I can't call him, might be.*
    I'll call the name of [my] sister. I'm not really supposed to say her name.

20. BN: *Ka-warre.   Bad   ka-mak, bonj   djang.*
        3-bad   but   3-good   finish sacred.site
    It's not good. But it's OK because we're talking about the sacred site.

21. BN: *Imin dai,*   *ba-yakminj ba-rrowe-ng.*
        [KRIOL code mixing]   3P-finishPP 3P-die-PP
    She died, she's finished.

22. BN: *That Ngaldaddubbe.*
    That Ngaldaddubbe.

Bardayal draws on a mental map of the 'honey dreaming' region and commences with the camping place Kulnguki. From Kulnguki, 'upstream there' *kaddum kunukka* (line 1) is the sacred site for rock honey Ngaldaddubbe which is also the name of Bardayal's classificatory sister. Initially he does not mention her name (and the place) because of the taboo, but refers to her by a nearby placename Warnkulembakmeng (line 3) which acts as a referential substitute for the purposes of this conversation. In this case, a placename which cannot be uttered is replaced by a neighbouring name. This is not a random solution as Warnkulembakmeng is also a significant site in the Ankung Djang 'honey dreaming' complex. The name is bimorphemic *warnkulem-bakmeng* 'warnkulem (?)- broken' and may also be associated with the broken or amputated legs of the female honey spirit being *Wakkewakken*. In lines 11 and 16–18 Bardayal says the name of the place and therefore his sister, but he is clearly not at ease with such reference and he excuses himself by calling the place *bolk-balmarded*, where *bolk* means 'place' and *balmarded* is an interjection that is most commonly used to express embarrassment when one hears a sibling subjected to joking relationship taunts and teasing, especially those of a sexual nature (see also Garde 2008b; Evans 1992). In this case, *bolk-balmarded* indexes a placename that encodes a sibling relationship to the speaker and that uttering this placename causes the speaker social embarrassment.

Placenames can be considered 'bad' in other ways. Embarrassing literal meanings may also result in *bolk-balmarded* reference as in (16), or the designation *ka-bolkngeywarre* 'the place with a bad name (literally: it-place-name-bad)'. There is a place Kubarledjawoy – a crossing on the Liverpool River along the Gunbalanya to Maningrida road. The name of this place literally means 'at the steamy vagina' and in certain contexts (especially those involving interaction between affinal kin), mention of the place is avoided and it is sometimes therefore referred to as *ka-bolkngeywarre* 'the place with the bad name'. Placenames can even be changed for this reason. In the late 1990s, Bardayal Nadjamerrek changed the name of a place on his Ankung Djang 'Honey Dreaming' estate. The place originally had two names:

(21)   *Wak Kabanikebngurlminarren*
        Wak kabani-keb-ngurlmi-na-rren
        crow 3ua-nose/face-dark-look-RR.NP
        The two crows look at each other's black faces.

(22)   *Wak Kakorddakan*
        wak ka-kord-da-kan
        crow 3m-shit-in.sun-take.NP
        Crow carries shit into the sun.

On expansion, the two names encode cultural meanings relating to the actions of two mythical crows. In one story they stand looking at each other's dark faces and in the other they carry bags of shit and place them in the hot sun. Image 2 is a photograph of Bardayal and his depiction of the two crow placenames. On one side of the painting the crows carry a bag of shit into the sun and on the other side the two crows look at each other's faces.

Such placenames were considered *ka-bolkngeywarre* 'bad placenames'. From the mid-1990s Bardayal was involved in a 'return to country' project that established an outstation and a land management program on his country at Kabulwarnamyo. He was involved in many years of intergenerational transfer of knowledge with younger *Bininj* who were encouraged to leave the town of Gunbalanya and find work in land management projects on his country. Wak Kabanikebngurlminarren (aka Wak Kakorddakan) was a popular camping place during the early days of this land management project, yet Bardayal always had reservations about referring to this place by these names. He therefore changed the name to Kulnguki (see his comment in text 23) but never explained the significance or origin of the new name, which is semantically unclear. It did however make the place easier to pronounce due to the marked reduction of syllables. Despite the change, knowledge about the original names and the association with crows persists through art works, including the rock art image at the site (see Image 3).

Image 2: Bardayal Nadjamerrek with this painting of 'two crows carry shit into the sun' and the rock art image at Kulnguki of 'two crows looking at each other's dark faces'.

Source: Murray Garde.

6. Doing things with toponyms

Image 3: The rock art image of two crows looking at each other at the site Wak Kabanikebngurlminarren.

Source: Murray Garde.

(23) *Arringarrnghmangi Nawalbirn rorrbono, kabono- here Kulnguki Wak Kakorddakan. Ngayi ngadjendjihmeng Kulnguki.*

We used to walk along the open and flat country at Nawalbirn, along the creek here at Kulnguki or Wak Kakorddakan, but I changed it [the name] to Kulnguki.

Changing placenames due to shifts in sensibilities or for other pragmatic purposes is not uncommon in other languages. Numerous street names in medieval London would now be considered vulgar (by some perhaps) had they not been bowdlerised. For example, Sherborne Lane was changed from the former Shiteburn Lane, meaning 'shit house' – a reference to the numerous public lavatories in the street (Partridge 2004). The idea of inviting family and visitors to your camp at 'Crows carrying bags of shit' has likewise prompted a name change.

Placenames in Bininj Gunwok may also be used to refer to other objects. The exchange in (24) occurred some weeks after the incident referred to in (19) and again there is reference to the place Mankorlod. In this conversation, however, the placename is used to refer to a motor vehicle belonging to the same recently deceased person referred to in (19).

(24)   Q: *Man-ngale ngurri-m-wam?*
          III-who   2a-hith-goPP
       Which one [*man-* class thing] did you come [in]?

       A: *Man-djare   ngarri-m-wam Mankorlod.*
          III-deceased.poss 1a-hith-goPP place.n.
       A deceased person's possession [of *man-* class] we came [in], [the one belonging to the person from] Mankorlod.

Motor vehicles are usually referred to either by a personal name of the owner or by some other characteristic such as the model and colour *Greiwan Doyorra* 'Grey one Toyota' or *Clark nuye Djudjukki* 'Clark's Suzuki'. The placename Mankorlod in (24) is a departure from this usual convention and so will be interpreted as a marked referring expression. The term *man-djare* means 'possessions of a deceased person' where the *man-* prefix on the interrogative suggests agreement with the class into which motor vehicles also fall.[8] This provides a contextualisation cue (Gumperz 1982) to the interpretation of the placename that follows – 'a *man-* class possession of a deceased person from place x'. The association of the recent death and the place of this person's residence facilitates unproblematic reference that respects local conventions of circumspection when referring to the recently deceased.

7. Placenames and joking

Placenames are also used in Bininj Gunwok as part of both formal joking relationship interaction (Garde 2008b) but also more incidental good-natured joking especially between youths who share a high degree of social familiarity. The usual strategy is to disparage a key site in the joking partner's clan estate. The partner may then retaliate with a similar jibe about a key site in the country of his adversary. The exchange in (25) is typical of this type of joking.

(25)   A   *Bulkay ka-bolk-banj*
           prop.n 3m-place-smell.bad
           Bulkay is a place that stinks.

       B   *Ku-wid,   kun-bolk-mak ku-mekke!*
           LOC-another IV-place-good LOC-DEM
           Not at that place, that is a good place.

---

8   Motor vehicles are classed in the *man-*vegetal class on the basis of the semantic extention of wooden things > canoes > vehicles of transport.

A similar exchange between two young men who are not in kinship-mediated joking relationship, but who frequently joke with each other based on their close social familiarity, is that in (26).

(26)	1	A	*Na-kkan ngalkordo ka-m-h-re!*
			I-DEM brolga 3-hith-IMM-go
			Here comes brolga!
	2	B	*Kandji wanjh na-kang Mankorlod!*
			jabiru SEQ I-from.place place.n
			It's the jabiru from Mankorlod!
	3	A	*Ku-wid, ngalkordo kure Kubumi ka-ngukde-ng*
			LOC-wrong.one brolga LOC place.n. 3-shits-NP
			No, not that place, it's brolga from Kubumi which shits
	4	A	*ku-bolk-kord-wern ka–bolk-warre-won.*
			LOC-place-faeces-much 3-place-bad-give.
			everywhere and makes a mess.
	5	A/B	[laughter]

Speaker A is a Kardbam clansman whose *kun-bolkngeykimuk* 'big placename' is Mankorlod (Cadell River tributary), whilst his joking partner is a Kulmarru clansman whose estate name or 'big place' is Kubumi (middle Mann River). The former is *duwa* moiety and the latter is *yirridjdja*. This is important because the two men use the names of birds associated with each other's moieties as part of the joke structure. Speaker A associates B with the brolga, a large *duwa* moiety bird whilst as a riposte, B lampoons the *yirridjdja* moiety Jabiru (or black-necked stork) 'from Mankorlod'. Again, reference to both people and and the places associated with them are frequently co-present and interchangeable, telling us something of the role of place in the conceptualisation of personhood.

8. Conclusion

Studies about placenames in Aboriginal Australia have typically grappled with systems and hierarchies of placename classification and their semantics – how languages organise reference to place and how to explain the origins and meanings of placenames. I have in this chapter explored these same topics as a point of departure and then moved on to illustrate how placenames are used in interaction. In addition to geographical sites, placenames in Bininj Gunwok can refer to both people and things and are also used in conversation to achieve interactive goals. The recitation of placenames in the order they appear along *Bininj man-bolh* 'Aboriginal walking routes' reflects their significance as part of mental maps. These maps afford the user and listener various advantages such as how to get from A to B, how to validate knowledge and prove ownership of places, and how to establish the relationships amongst places. Whilst the vast majority of placenames in Western Arnhem Land are usually immutable in form and often semantically archaic, names do get changed or modified. Cultural conventions may at times require the avoidance of certain placenames, whilst in other less weighty contexts there is a place for the use of placenames in humour and light-hearted interaction. Toponyms in Bininj Gunwok are more than just designations for places, but that should come as no surprise in cultures where the conceptual boundaries between places, people and things are fluid.

References

Aklif, G. 1999, *Ardiyooloon Bardi ngaanka: One Arm Point Bardi Dictionary*, Kimberley Language Resource Centre, Halls Creek, Western Australia.

Bowern, C. 2009, 'Naming Bardi places', in *Aboriginal Placenames: Naming and Renaming the Australian Landscape,* Harold Koch and Luise Hercus (eds), Aboriginal History Monograph 19, ANU E Press and Aboriginal History Inc., Canberra: 327–346.

Enfield, N.J. 2009, 'Relationship thinking and human pragmatics', *Journal of Pragmatics* 41: 60–78.

Evans, N. 1992, '"Wanjh! Bonj! Nja !": Sequential organization and social deixis in Mayali interjections', *Journal of Pragmatics* 18: 225–244.

— 2003, *Bininj Gun-wok: A Pan-dialectal Grammar of Mayali, Kunwinjku and Kune.* (2 volumes), Pacific Linguistics, Canberra.

Garde, M. 2008a, 'Person reference, proper names and circumspection in Bininj Kunwok conversation', in *Discourse and Grammar in Australian Languages,* Brett Baker and Ilana Mushin (eds), John Benjamins, Amsterdam: 203–232.

— 2008b, 'The pragmatics of rude jokes with Grandad: Joking relationships in Aboriginal Australia', *Anthropological Forum* 18(3): 235–253.

— 2011, 'The Forbidden Gaze: The 1948 Wubarr ceremony performed for The American-Australian Scientific Expedition to Arnhem Land', in *Exploring the Legacy of the 1948 Arnhem Land Expedition,* Martin Thomas and M. Neale (eds), National Museum of Australia, Canberra: 403–422.

Gumperz, J. 1982, *Discourse Strategies,* Cambridge University Press, Cambridge.

Hercus, L., F. Hodges and J. Simpson (eds) 2002, *The Land Is a Map: Placenames of Indigenous Origin in Australia,* Pandanus Books in association with Pacific Linguistics, Canberra.

Keen, I. 1994, *Knowledge and Secrecy in an Aboriginal Religion,* Oxford Studies in Social and Cultural Anthropology, Oxford University Press, Oxford.

Levinson, S. and N. Burenhult 2008, 'Language and landscape: a cross-linguistic perspective', *Language Sciences* 30: 135–150.

Merlan, F. 2001, 'Form and context in Jawoyn placenames', in *Forty Years on: Ken Hale and Australian Languages,* Jane Simpson, D. Nash, M. Laughren, P. Austin and B. Alpher (eds), Pacific Linguistics, Canberra: 367–384.

Morphy, H. 1984, *Journey to the Crocodile's Nest: An Accompanying Monograph to the Film Madarrpa Funeral at Gurka'wuy,* Australian Institute of Aboriginal Studies, Canberra.

Partridge, C. 2004, 'A street by any other name…', *The Observer,* http://www.guardian.co.uk/money/2004/apr/18/property.homebuying1 (accessed 20 March 2013).

Pierce, C. S. 1955, 'Logic as semiotic: the theory of signs', in *Philosophical Writings of Peirce,* Justus Buchler (ed.), Dover Publications, New York: 98–119.

Vries, L. de 2005, 'Towards a typology of tail-head linkage in Papuan languages', *Studies in Language* 29(2): 363–384.

7. Locating Seven Rivers

Fiona Powell

1. Introduction

In December 1890, while on patrol down the west coast of northern Cape York Peninsula (NCYP), accompanied by Senior-Constable Conroy and a few native troopers of the Thursday Island Water Police, Sub-Inspector Charles Savage visited 'the Seven Rivers'.[1] From this place, the party went south to the mouth of the Batavia (now Wenlock) River. There they met the chief or mamoose of the Seven Rivers tribe,[2] a man identified as Tongambulo (variations Tong-ham-blow,[3] Tongamblow[4] and Tong-am-bulo[5]) and also known as Charlie in one account.[6] At the time of this meeting, Sub-Inspector Savage was seeking another candidate for induction into government policies intended 'to civilize the Natives of Cape York Peninsula'.[7] The first NCYP Aboriginal person to have had this experience was Harry, also known as King Yarra-ham-quee, and described as the 'mamoose of the Jardine River'.[8] This man had been taken to Thursday Island earlier in the year:

> where he underwent a course of instruction and when he had sufficiently understood what was required of him was taken back and made king, his subjects and several visitors, Natives of Prince of Wales Island, being present.[9]

---

[1] 'Conciliating the Natives', *Torres Straits Pilot*, 6 December 1890, and published in *The Queenslander*, Saturday 27 December 1890: 1216 [hereafter 'Conciliating the Natives' *Torres Straits Pilot*].
[2] Savage, Charles 1891, Letter to the Honourable John Douglas, Government Resident Thursday Island, dated 11 February 1891, Queensland State Archives, Item D 143032, File - Reserve. Europeans used the term 'mamoose' to distinguish local headmen in Torres Strait island communities. The honorific was then bestowed on mainland local Aboriginal men of importance. It survives today as a surname, spelt variously as Mamoose, Mamus, Mamoos.
[3] Douglas, John Government Resident, Thursday Island, Letter to the Honourable The Chief Secretary, 16 February 1891 in Queensland State Archives, Item ID 143032, File - Reserve.
[4] Smith, George, 'Cruise of the S.S. "Vigilant" The Blacks of the Gulf Country', *The Brisbane Courier*, Tuesday 31 March 1891: 3.
[5] Report dated 31 July 1891 to the Home Secretary from The Honourable John Douglas, Government Resident, Thursday Island, in Queensland State Archives, Item ID 143032, File - Reserve. It is clear from this report that 'Tang-am-bulo' is Douglas's later rendering of the name of the man referred to in an earlier report as Tong-ham-blow and as the chief of the Seven Rivers tribe.
[6] 'Conciliating the Natives', *Torres Straits Pilot*.
[7] 'Conciliating the Natives', *Torres Straits Pilot*.
[8] 'Conciliating the Natives', *Torres Straits Pilot*.
[9] Savage, Charles 1891 Letter to The Honourable John Douglas, Government Resident Thursday Island dated 11 February 1891, in Queensland State Archives, Item ID 143032, File - Reserve.

Tongambulo accompanied Sub-Inspector Savage and his party to Thursday Island. One early account noted that he:

> cannot speak a word of English, nor had he been near a white man's abode until brought into our midst. One of his first impressions on rambling around the barracks was conveyed in the question he asked Kio[10] the interpreter: "Why white man could make the fowls stay about the house, when in his country they all flew away and could not be caught?" Kio explained as best he could to the mamoose that the white man possessed a magical power which was sufficient to tame anything; Charlie will probably realise this after he has spent two weeks here as the host of the Government. The rough edges of his savagery will be toned down a bit.[11]

The Chief of the Seven Rivers was also 'made King in the same manner as the Chief of the Jardine River had been,'[12] the Hon. John Douglas observing that:

> Tong-ham-blow, the chief of the Seven Rivers, is a very noticeable man. He is grey headed and has a most remarkable physiognomy. When he was brought to us here he knew nothing, of course, of the world or its inhabitants beyond the environment of the Seven Rivers, but during the three weeks he remained with us he made good use of his eyes and ears, and the impressions thus conveyed to him will doubtless be of use to us in our future communications with him.[13]

The placename 'Seven Rivers' occurs in the NCYP ethno-historical, linguistic and genealogical records and in both the English and the NCYP *Creole* toponymic lexicons. However, it has never been officially gazetted despite its continuing importance for those residents of Injinoo (formerly Cowal Creek)[14] whose ancestors originated from places named 'Seven Rivers', 'Seven River', 'Severn River' and 'Seventh River'.[15] Although in the records these placenames

---

10   This man's name is variously represented in the NCYP records as Keyo and Kaio. His role in the exploration and settlement of NCYP is the subject of the author's current research.
11   'Conciliating the Natives', *Torres Straits Pilot*.
12   'Conciliating the Natives', *Torres Straits Pilot*.
13   Douglas, John Government Resident, Thursday Island, Letter to the Honourable The Chief Secretary, 16 February 1891. Queensland Department of Lands Reserve File 91–14 Part 1, Mapoon Aboriginal Reserve, Transfer 1726/1, Box 167, Queensland State Archives.
14   The name of the community was changed by Governor in Council from Cowal Creek to Injinoo on 2 September 1989 (Queensland Place Names online search, retrieved http://www.nrm.qld.gov.au/property/placenames/details.php?id=16700).
15   The author first met Aboriginal people who originated from Seven Rivers in 1970 at Hope Vale, a Lutheran mission settlement north of Cooktown. They told her that as children, they had been removed from NCYP and sent to Cape Bedford mission, north of Cooktown and that during World War II, along with other Cape Bedford residents, they were sent to the Woorabinda Aboriginal Settlement, before resettlement at Hope Vale, which was established after the end of World War II. In 2003, the author met relatives of these people at Injinoo, and this meeting led to this research about NCYP placenames.

are associated with the coast north of Port Musgrave, there is not a settled view about whether they refer to the same place or to several places. This paper presents the results of my enquiries about this toponym.[16]

NCYP Creole, which is the first language of many Injinoo residents, has particular features that affect the pronunciation and hence the recording and subsequent interpretation of some placenames. For example, in NCYP Creole there is no phonemic/phonetic difference made between names such as 'McDonnell' and 'MacDonald', which are important family names and placenames in NCYP history. Neither does NCYP spoken Creole make a formal or overt marking of the difference in the grammatical category of number in nominals or noun phrases so that names like 'Seven Rivers' and 'Seven River', which are readily distinguished in spoken and written English, are: 'simply [sévanrìva] or similar. This has been true from the earliest contact period'.[17] Because NCYP spoken Creole does not distinguish between names such as 'Seven River' and 'Seven Rivers', one of the first tasks in analysing records about these placenames is to determine if such records refer to the same or to different places. This issue is particularly relevant for researchers who consider the NCYP linguistic, ethno-historical, genealogical and official records. Many of these records contain information elicited from NCYP Creole speakers. Contextual clues that might assist the interpretation of these records include the identity of the recorder and source, and the time and place when the record was created.

2. Seven Rivers

Although 'Seven Rivers' was not gazetted as an official placename, as shown in Maps 1 and 2, nineteenth century and early twentieth century maps of Cape York associate this placename with the coastal area north of Port Musgrave. The several river mouths that are passed when sailing between Thursday Island and Port Musgrave are a feature of this coast and it is likely that the placename 'Seven Rivers' originated during nineteenth century navigational surveys of the NCYP west coast. However, as shown by Maps 1 and 2, the early records differ with respect to location and extent of the area represented as 'Seven Rivers'.

---

16 I am indebted to many people for their valuable and generous assistance during the research and preparation of this article. In particular, I would like to express my thanks to the descendants of ancestral people associated with Seven Rivers, Seven River, Severn River and Seventh River and the MacDonnell telegraph station, to the late Mr Jack Callope, the late Dr Terry Crowley, Helen Harper, Professor Bruce Rigsby, Mr Bill Kitson, and Mr Geoff Wharton for their assistance with source materials; Professor Bruce Rigsby for his advice with respect to NPA Creole placenames; Dr Ben Smith and Dr Nicky Horsfall for their constructive comments on early drafts of this article, Dr Nicky Horsfall for her aerial photograph of the Skardon River, and Dr Luise Hercus for her persistent encouragement and advice with linguistic transcription.

17 Professor Bruce Rigsby, pers. comm. 19 March 2004. I am indebted to Professor Bruce Rigsby for his advice and information about NCYP creole. For further details about this language, see Crowley and Rigsby 1979: 153–208.

The earliest record found that shows this placename's location is a map attached to the 1891 Annual Report of the Government Resident of Thursday Island.[18] A copy of this map attached to an 1896 letter[19] from Archibald Meston to the Under Colonial Secretary is represented as Map 1.

The broken lines on this map mark several rivers that flow into the Gulf of Carpentaria and suggest the possibility that their representation is tentative. This map was made before the north-west coast and inland areas of the NCYP mainland had been comprehensively surveyed. It differs from contemporary maps, such as that represented below as Map 3, with respect to the location of some of the west coast rivers and the McDonnell telegraph station. This telegraph station was one of several transmitter stations that were constructed during 1886–1887 for the overland telegraph line which followed the route of the 1883 Bradford expedition and which linked Thursday Island with the mainland (Bradford 1962). The telegraph line opened on 25 August 1887 with transmitter stations positioned about 100–120 km apart at Musgrave, Coen, Mein, Moreton, McDonnell and Patterson. From Patterson a line was laid on the seabed to connect with Thursday Island. Later, the Patterson station was moved to Peak Point and renamed Cape York telegraph station. The McDonnell telegraph station began operating in 1887 and closed in 1929. The station comprised a substantial building with a large produce garden. Early NCYP maps, like those represented as Maps 1 and 2, locate the McDonnell telegraph station on the 'Skardon' headwaters. Map 1 represents this watercourse as the most southern of the rivers in the 'Seven Rivers' area. Map 1 also suggests that a watercourse (not named) that debouches into the sea just south of Crab Island might be the most northern of the rivers in the area asociated with the placename 'Seven Rivers'.

---

18 Attached to his annual report for 1891 is a map of northern Cape York Peninsula, which shows the placename 'Seven Rivers' along the west coast of the Peninsula. It also shows the McDonnell telegraph station on the headwaters of the 'Skardon' River (Douglas, John, 'Annual report of the Government Resident at Thursday Island', *Queensland Votes and Proceedings of the Legislative Assembly*, Volume 2, 1892: 1029-1035). I am indebted to Geoffrey Wharton for drawing my attention to this map and to Dr Nicky Horsfall for providing me with a copy. This same map is also contained in Appendix XXVI of the Minutes of Evidence taken before the 1908 Pearl-Shell and Beche-de-Mer Royal Commission (*Queensland Parliamentary Papers*, vol. 2, 1908, pp. 691–695).

19 Letter with map attached from A. Meston to the Under Colonel Secretary dated 14 March 1896, Queensland State Archives Item ID 847539 Series No 5253 Item Top Numbered 11535.

7. Locating Seven Rivers

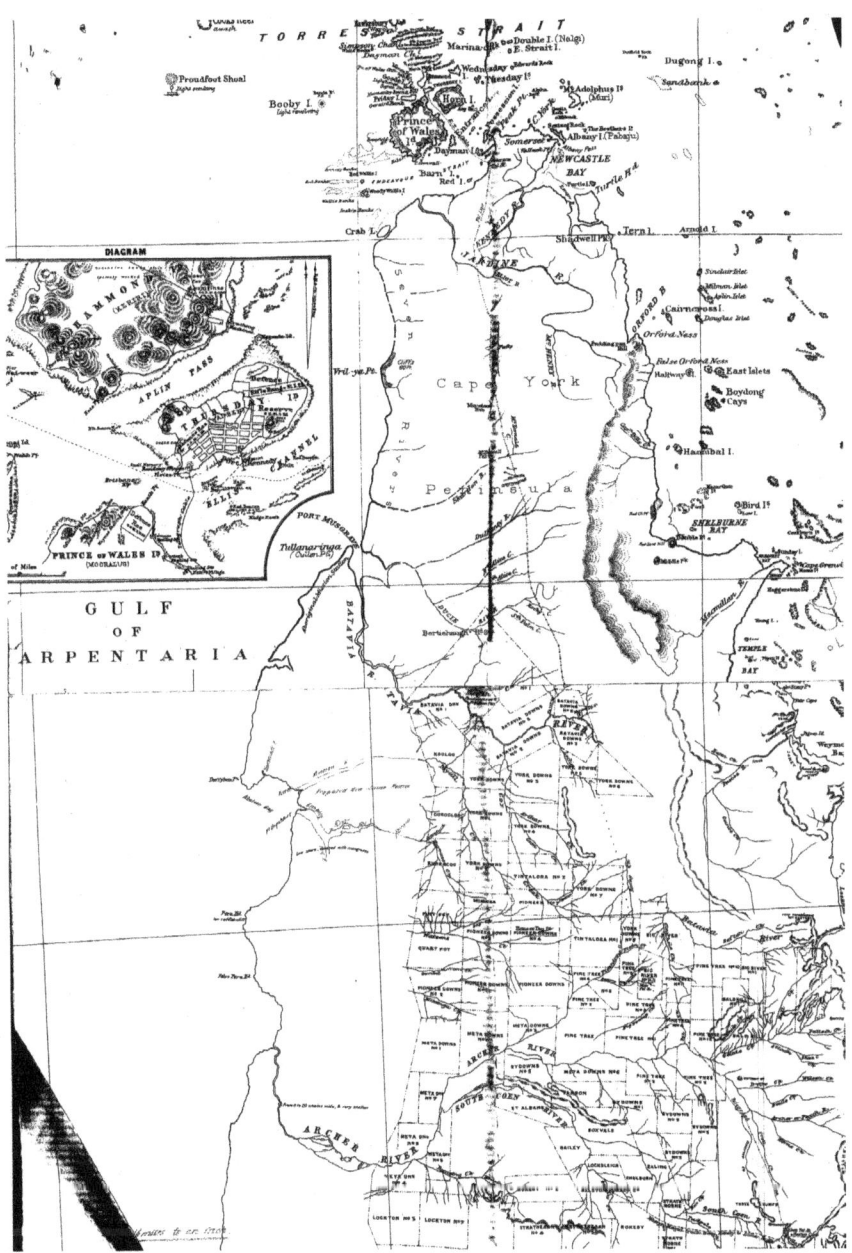

Map 1: An early map of Cape York.[20]

---

20 Map attached to Queensland State Archives Item ID 847539 Series No 5253 Item Top Numbered 11535.

The representation of 'Seven Rivers' in Map 1 corresponds approximately with the earliest written description found of the 'Seven Rivers' area as: 'that tract of country known as the 'Seven Rivers' – i.e., the coast district between the Jardine River and the Batavia' (Queensland Police Commissioner, W.E. Parry-Okeden 1898: 4). An account by Parry-Okeden's contemporary, the Aboriginal Protector Dr Walter Roth, provides a slightly different view. When describing the location of the 'Gamiti', one of several Aboriginal groups associated with the Port Musgrave region, Roth placed this group: 'on the north shore of Port Musgrave, i.e. between the Ducie R.[iver][21] and the Seven Rivers country' (Roth: 1900: 2; 1910: 96).[22] The assistant government geologist Clements F.V. Jackson who accompanied Roth on a 1902 visit to Mapoon, associated the placename 'Seven Rivers' with the coastal area on the northern side of Port Musgrave, noting that:

> The portion of the coast north of the Batavia River for about 60 miles [c.96.5 km] is known as the "Seven Rivers" district, and with the exception of Vrilya Point, which is the only prominent feature between Port Musgrave and the north-west corner of the peninsula, the whole of the land surface along the coast is characteristically low-lying and sandy (Jackson 1902: 7).

Other records clearly associate the river known today as the 'Skardon' with the placename 'Seven Rivers'. One early record mentions the 'Scarsden (or 7 Rivers) district' (Hardie and Robinson 1891)[23] and descriptions by others (Savage 1891; Douglas 1891) about the 'Seven Rivers' camp, establish its location near the coast and just south of the Skardon River.

My research found that the placename 'Seven Rivers' appeared in official records, at least until 1923,[24] although, as shown by Maps 1 and 2, its location varied.

Although Maps 1 and 2 represent a section of the west coast of NCYP as 'Seven Rivers', they differ with respect to the location and extent of this area. Map 1 represents the coastal region between Crab Island and the 'Skardon River'

---

21   The Government surveyor and geologist, R. Logan Jack considers that this river was first named 'Palm Creek' and then re-named the 'Ducie' by Frank Jardine during the construction of the Telegraph Line, in 1887 (Jack 1921: 319).
22   There is nothing in Roth's report to indicate that the term 'country' in this quotation is a reference to the notion of 'country' as this term is used today to signify Aboriginal traditional homelands or territory.
23   The Reverends Andrew Hardie and Samuel Robinson wrote to The Hon. The Premier of Queensland on 10 August 1891 that 'It has been accordingly decided that this district with Cullen Point as headquarters and a suitable reserve southward along the coast & eastward up the Batavia would be a suitable location for the Federal Assembly's Mission to the aborigines. From Cullen Point we can influence the Blacks of the Scarsden (or 7 Rivers) district (Queensland State Archives, Item ID 143032, File - Reserve, letter dated 10 August 1891). The contemporary spelling of this watercourse is 'Skardon'.
24   I am indebted to Mr Bill Kitson, formerly the Curator – Museum and Lands & Surveying, Department of Natural Resources, Queensland for this information. Mr Kitson kindly checked through the archival holding available to him and could not find the placename 'Seven Rivers' on maps printed after 1925.

7. Locating Seven Rivers

as 'Seven Rivers', while the later Map 2 associates this placename with a less extensive coastal area between just south of Vrilya Point northwards to a place opposite Crab Island. Both maps depict the McDonnell telegraph station in the headwaters of the 'Skardon', a location which is inconsistent with more recent maps such as represented in Map 3. A comparison of the early and contemporary maps of the west coast of NCYP show further changes in the representation of places named 'Seven Rivers, 'Skardon River' and the 'McDonnell telegraph station'.

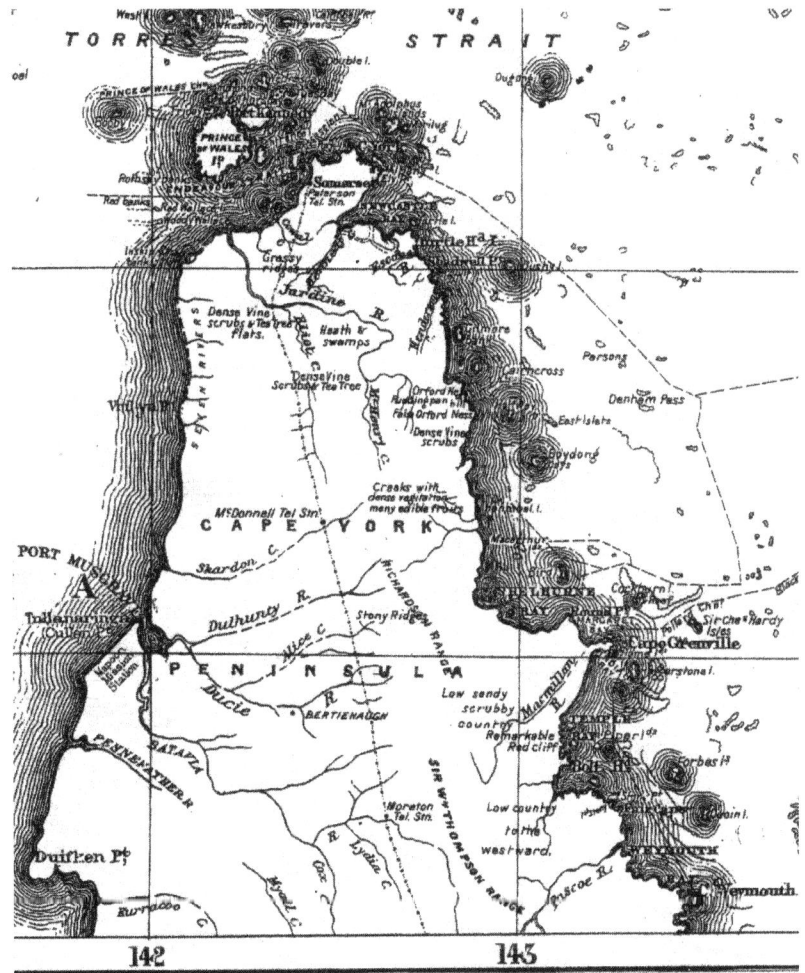

Map 2: Representation of a portion of a map of Cape York Peninsula, printed in 1924.[25]

---

25 Map 2 shows a portion of Sheet 6 of the 16 M Series 1 map sheets, printed in 1924 and based on the most recent surveys and information procurable constructed at the Surveyor General's Office, Brisbane, with additions and corrections to 1897, and used with the permission of the Department of Natural Resources and Mines, Queensland.

Indigenous and Minority Placenames

Map 3: Representation of a portion of a 2004 map of the west coast of NCYP.[26]

An inspection of Maps 1, 2 and 3 shows that the placename 'Seven Rivers' has disappeared from the more recent cartographical records, and that there are differences between the early and more recent maps in the location of places identified as the 'Skardon River' and the 'McDonnell telegraph station'. On contemporary maps such as the one shown as Map 3, the McDonnell telegraph

---

26 Map 3 represents a portion of the Jardine River Queensland NATMAP Sheet 1:250 000 scale prepared in 2004 by Geoscience Australia.

station is located near the confluence of McDonnell (formerly 'MacDonald'[27]) and Cockatoo creeks. The latter watercourse is a tributary of the 'Jackson River', which does not appear on the early maps.

2.1 'Seven Rivers' in NCYP linguistic and ethno-historical records

Notwithstanding its omission from contemporary maps of Cape York Peninsula, in the region's ethno-historical and linguistic records, 'Seven Rivers' is used to distinguish a portion of the coast north of Port Musgrave and Aboriginal people associated with this area. The linguist Terry Crowley, who conducted field research at Bamaga during 1975–76, described the Seven Rivers area as: 'the very narrow coastal stretch from the northern side of Port Musgrave as far as the Doughboy River and also the inland area of Crystal Creek and the middle Jardine River' and identified the seven watercourses associated with this area as the Jardine, Macdonald,[28] Skardon, Doughboy, Ducie, Jackson and Crystal (Crowley 1983: 310). However, Maureen Fuary and Shelley Greer (1993: 11) reported that the first river of the 'Seven Rivers' area is a small watercourse just south of the Jardine River that is known locally as 'No. 1 River'. Crowley associated the 'Seven Rivers' area with Uradhi[29] (Ankgamuthi) speakers and his 1983 map represents this region as extending from the northern shore of Port Musgrave to just north of the Jardine River (Crowley 1983: 306). The representation by Greer and Fuary (2008: 4, Map 1) of the area associated with the '7 Rivers People' shows a similar north-south extent. They describe the area associated with the '7 Rivers People' as:

> … the land on the west coast of the Peninsula from the Dulhunty River north to somewhere between the Jardine River and the location of the present settlement [Injinoo] (Greer and Fuary 2008: 6).

---

27 The map of the Hann Shire 1912-1919 names the creek near the site of the McDonnell telegraph station as 'Macdonald'. More recent maps name this creek 'McDonnell'.
28 This watercourse is not the same as the one named McDonnell (formerly Macdonald) Creek, which is near the site of the now defunct MacDonnell telegraph station.
29 Following Hale (1976), Crowley (1983) adopted the name *Uradhi* as a generic name for the several linguistic varieties associated with the NCYP region. Hale (1964: 252) noted one speaker used the term 'Uradhi' (meaning 'having ura' for 'this') as the name for his language, which was Hale considered was one "of several dialects of a single language spoken from the tip of Cape York Peninsula south to the Dalhunty [sic] R. on the west and Cape Grenville on the east."

2.2 Changes associated with the placename 'Skardon'

In NCYP records, 'Seven Rivers' (or one of its variants) is associated with a watercourse named the 'Skardon', a name that is also represented variously in the written records as Schardon,[30] Scardon,[31] and Scarsden[32] and in NCYP Creole sometimes as 'Scott'. According to R. Logan Jack (1921: 318)[33] the river now named the 'Dulhunty'[34] that joins the Ducie River, which debouches into Port Musgrave, was first named the 'Skardon' by the Jardine brothers Frank and Alexander during their 1865 overland trek from Carpentaria Downs to Somerset.[35] Later, they renamed this watercourse the 'Dulhunty'.[36] On early maps, such as those represented as Map 1 and Map 2, the 'Dulhunty' is clearly distinguished from the 'Skardon', which is shown to enter into the sea north of Port Musgrave. Maps 1 and 2 represent the McDonnell telegraph station in the Skardon headwaters. However, on contemporary maps, the site of the former McDonnell telegraph station is located in the headwaters of the 'Jackson River' which flows into the sea north of the watercourse now known as the 'Skardon'. Nowadays, this latter watercourse is sometimes referred to as the 'Last River' by Mapoon Mission residents because it is regarded as the last of the seven rivers passed by boats travelling from Thursday Island before they arrive at Mapoon.[37]

As Maps 1 and 2 show, the Jackson River is not represented in the early maps of the west coast of NCYP, which suggests that this part of the NCYP west coast was incompletely and/or incorrectly mapped, with the consequence that on these early maps 'Skardon' (or one of its variants) seems to have been used to refer to two quite separate watercourses. This conflation of the Skardon and

---

30 Douglas 1891 in Queensland State Archives, Item ID 143032, File - Reserve, letter dated 10 August 1891.
31 Woods 1891.
32 Spelling used in the letter by the Rev. Hardie to the Hon. Premier of Queensland dated 10 August 1891, about a visit to the Batavia River region. Queensland Department of Lands Reserve File 91–14 Part 1, Mapoon Aboriginal Reserve, Transfer 1726/1, Box 167, Queensland State Archives.
33 Robert Logan Jack was appointed Government Geologist for North Queensland in 1877 and for all of Queensland in 1879. During 1879–1880, he led a geological expedition that explored the eastern side of Cape York Peninsula from Cooktown to Somerset. His account of this trip and the explorations of others in Cape York Peninsula were published later in his *Northmost Australia* (Anon. 1922 Obituary: Robert Logan Jack).
34 Information from the Queensland Placenames On-line Data base. The database refers to 2 sources – *The Queenslander*, 10 February 1900, pp. 266–267; and F.J. Byerley, *Narrative of the overland expedition of the Messrs. Jardine from Rockhampton to Cape York*, Brisbane, 1867, p. 49.
35 The droving party left Carpentaria Downs in October 1864 and reached Somerset in early March, 1865. The route taken traversed the headwaters of some of the rivers flowing into Port Musgrave, including the Dulhunty River. The party had several violent encounters with Aboriginal groups along the way, the last being just north of the Batavia River (now named the Wenlock), and this was 'the last occasion on which the party was molested, their sable adversaries having, probably, at length learned that "they were worth better alone," and never again shewing themselves' (Byerley 1867: 48).
36 The river was renamed after Robert Dulhunty, a NSW pastoralist, whose sons were friends of the Jardine brothers. Information from the Queensland Placenames On-line Data base, which refers to *The Queenslander*, 10 February 1900: 266–267.
37 Geoffrey Wharton, pers. comm. 10 July 2003.

Jackson rivers and location of the McDonnell telegraph station on the Skardon River seems to have continued until at least 1940, as can be seen on maps made by Ursula McConnel (1939) and Norman Tindale (1940) of the territorial associations of various groups (termed 'tribes') in the Cape York region. This conflation should be taken into account when considering records based on information recorded from elderly NCYP Aboriginal people which sometimes associate 'McDonnell' or 'MacDonald' with the 'Skardon' and which refer to early placename locations that are no longer current.

2.3 Locations of places named 'Seven Rivers'

The earliest record found that provides details about the location of a specific place named 'Seven Rivers' is an 1885 report by Constable Percy Phillpotts of the Thursday Island Water Police. While on route from Thursday Island to the mouth of the Batavia (now Wenlock) River to return some Aboriginal men and boys rescued from bêche-de-mer recruiters, Phillpotts reported that he:

> dropped anchor at 8 pm, about a mile and half, off the entrance to a place known as the Seven Rivers, and distant about twenty-eight miles from the Batavia River.[38]

This distance – 28 miles – converts into either 45 km (when miles are read as land miles) or 51.8 km (when miles are read as nautical miles).[39] These calculations locate Phillpotts' 'Seven Rivers' near the mouth of the 'Jackson River'[40] of contemporary maps.

The next record found that mentions a specific place named 'Seven Rivers' is an 1891 report by Sub-Inspector Charles Savage which details his patrol down the Peninsula west coast to check on the welfare of the Jardine and Seven Rivers people, following the appointment by the Thursday Island government officials of their respective 'kings' or 'mamooses'. Charles Savage reported that:

> Permanent camps have been established at the Jardine River and Seven Rivers and large "Gunyas" have been built. Coco-nuts, sweet potatoes, pumpkin and watermelons have been planted and are growing well at the Jardine River. The matter now stands thus. The Natives at the Jardine and the Seven Rivers are aware that the Government takes an

---

38 Phillpotts, Percy 1885 Report for the Government Resident, Thursday Island, QSA COL/A444.
39 I have used these conversions, provided courtesy of the Department of Defence, Canberra: 1 nautical mile = 1.15625 miles; 1 nautical mile = 1.85 kilometres and 1 mile = 1.609 kilometres. I am indebted to Officers from Australian Surveying and Land Information Group [AUSLIG] associated with Geoscience Australia who provided advice about the distance in nautical and land miles and kilometres between the mouth of the Skardon and the northern shore of Port Musgrave, using contemporary maps.
40 According to R. Logan Jack, the Jackson River might be the Carpentier of the 1606 Dutch maps (Jack 1921: 318).

interest in them, is prepared to protect them when necessary from injustice and expects their assistance in punishing crimes committed by their tribes. They have been shown how to make houses of the bark and told that it is better for them to live in houses than to roam aimlessly about. They understand this completely but whether they will continue as well as they are going on now remains to be seen. I believe with constant supervision they will.[41]

Some months after submitting the above report, Sub-Inspector Savage accompanied an official party, which included the Thursday Island Resident, The Honourable John Douglas and two clergymen, to Port Musgrave to assess its suitability as a site for a mission for Aboriginal people. While on route, the party:

anchored that night off the Schardon River, which falls into the sea about twelve miles north of Port Musgrave and about ninety miles from Port Kennedy which we had left in the morning.[42]

As described in John Douglas' report, this watercourse is approximately 19.3–22.2 km from the northern point of the mouth of Port Musgrave.[43] This location, approximately 12 nautical miles north of Cullen Point (at the south head of Point Musgrave) establishes that the 'Schardon River' is the 'Skardon River' of contemporary maps. It is also clear that John Douglas' 1891 surveying party did not anchor near Phillpotts' 'Seven Rivers' (i.e. they did not anchor at the mouth of the river now known as the Jackson, which is approximately 36 km (c.22 miles) north of Port Musgrave). The official party visited: 'a native camp about two miles south of the Schardon, where we found about fifty natives of Tang-am-bulo's tribe'.[44] This description places the native camp about three kilometres south of the mouth of this river, posibly near a place identified by McKeown (1993) as 'Footprint Swamp'[45] near the headwaters of Namaleta Creek (once known locally as 'Mouth River'[46]), which flows into Port Musgrave. Another record (Smith 1891) mentions a native camp associated with 'Mamoose

---

41 Report from Sub-Inspector Charles Savage to the Hon. John Douglas, Government Resident, Thursday Island dated 11 February 1891.
42 Douglas, John, Report to The Honourable the Chief Secretary Re a visit to Batavia River with the Revd. A. Hardie & Revd. S. Robinson, dated 31 July 1891, Queensland State Archives, Item ID 143032, File - Reserve.
43 His 12 miles can be estimated as either 19.3 km or 22.2 km (depending on whether 12 miles is read as 12 land or nautical miles).
44 Douglas, John, Report to The Honourable the Chief Secretary Re a visit to Batavia River with the Revd A. Hardie & Revd S. Robinson, dated 31 July 1891, Queensland State Archives, Item ID 143032, File - Reserve. It is clear from this report that 'Tang-am-bulo' is Douglas's rendering of the name of the man referred to in an earlier report as Tong-ham-blow and as the chief of the Seven Rivers tribe.
45 This site was mapped by Dr Frank McKeown in 1993 (pers. comm. 10 January 2013 from Dr Nicky Horsfall who also has conducted research in this region).
46 The late Mr Jack Callope, who grew up at Mapoon Mission told me that in early mission times this was the name used for the watercourse that is now known as Namaleta Creek. Mr Callope referred to the people who lived in that area as the 'Seven River tribe' (notes made during an interview with Mr Jack Callope, 8 November 2004).

Tongamblow' and locates this place 'off one of the Seven Rivers' and 42 miles (c.67.6–77.8 km) south of Crab Island. From these two descriptions, it is clear that the Savage and Smith records refer to the same camp.

2.4 Alternative placenames: Seven River, Severn River and Seventh River

The NCYP records also mention the placenames 'Seven River' (Hey 1899;[47] Crowley 1975; Rigsby 1972), 'Severn River' (Shanahan 1897) and 'Seventh River'.[48] A 1908 record refers to a place identified as 'Seven River Lagoon'[49] but does not include enough information to determine its location.

The earliest mention of the placename 'Seven River' was found in a letter dated 4 August 1899 from the Reverend Nicolas Hey (missionary at Mapoon from 1891 to 1926) to R.H. Mathews, in which the Revd Hey notes that:

> The name of the tribe north of Batavia River between Seven River and towards MacDonald Telegraph Station is Gâmete (Hey 1899).

There is not sufficient information in this letter to determine either the location of Hey's 'Seven River' or whether this placename refers to a particular watercourse or to a camp known as 'Seven River'. A more recent record made in 1972 by Professor Bruce Rigsby clearly connects 'Seven River' with the 'Skardon River'. Rigsby (1972) recorded from a NCYP man named Larry MacDonald,[50] who was bilingual in the Uradhi (Atambaya) and NCYP Creole languages, the term *Eerrunyu* for the 'seven [th?] river' and that:

> Well they call that Seven River Langgus name *Eerrunyu* – you come this way between Seven River and Mapoon – well Whiteman he call Skardon – that river blo McDonnell, McDonnell River junction *Ithinmanyu*, call im *Ithinmanyu* – Langgus name – go up *Inbinh* – Langgus name *Inbinh*.[51]

It seems from this account that the Uradhi placenames *Ithinmanyu* and *Inbinh* could refer to places associated with the headwaters of the Jackson River, in the vicinity of the former McDonnell telegraph station. A transcription of a wordlist compiled by Terry Crowley (1975) from the same informant contains

---

47   Hey, Rev. Nicolas Letter to R.H. Mathews, dated 4 August 1899.
48   This placename occurs in records pertaining to an Aboriginal woman named Kitty.
49   This is recorded in the 1908 report by Constable Whelan.
50   Larry MacDonald was born about 1900 at 'MacDonnell', which may be a reference to the former MacDonnell telegraph station and/or the area where it was located. He died at Bamaga in 1981.
51   Transcription by Dr Helen Harper of an excerpt of side 2 of Field Tape number 72/30, recorded by Professor Bruce Rigsby. Helen Harper also made the following free standard English translation of this excerpt: 'Well the Language name for the seven[th?] river is Eerrunyu. If you come up this way between Seven River and Mapoon, white people call it Skardon River – the river from the McDonnell River junction. Its Language name is Ithinmanyu. Go up further, the Language name is Inbinh' (Harper 2003).

the terms *Ilunyung*? and *Atowiyangung*⁵² for 'Seven River' and Skardon River respectively.⁵³ The ? suggests some doubt about the term *Ilunyung*, but there is no further information available which explains this uncertainty. Crowley's recording of different Uradhi (Atampaya) names for 'Seven River' and 'Skardon River' suggests the possibility that the placenames elicited from Larry MacDonald may refer to different portions of watercourses distinguished by these names and/or to places associated with these watercourses.

2.5 Severn River

M.W. Shanahan's account of an 1896 expedition by a prospecting party that he led mentions the 'Severn River'. This expedition traversed the country from Patterson (the first site of the most northern of the Cape York telegraph stations) towards the Richardson Range.⁵⁴ Their guide and informant for the many Aboriginal placenames noted in Shanahan's account of the expedition was an Aboriginal man named Kio,⁵⁵ whose descendants now live at Injinoo. Kio was also a guide and interpreter for Sub-Inspector Savage and others during their exploratory forays along the NCYP west coast.⁵⁶ In the upper Ducie River area, Shanahan noted:

> ... great local excitement owing to the Severn River natives (who inhabit the western coast north of the mouth of the Batavia) having sent the Ducie boys a challenge to fight. The cause of the quarrel was an old one lying in abeyance since Charley, a brother of the Ducie mamoose, captured a Severn River gin.⁵⁷

The 'Batavia' mentioned by Shanahan is a reference to the watercourse known today as the Wenlock River. Shanahan's association of the 'Severn River natives' with the west coast north of the mouth of the Batavia is clearly a reference to the area that records made a few years earlier associated with the 'Seven Rivers' tribe, and his 'Severn River' is most probably a variant representation of the placename 'Seven Rivers' and/or 'Seven River'. The variant form 'Severn River' occurs in some later records. For example, an 1937 record mentions the

---

52 Another possible transcription of this term is *Atomyangung*.
53 Names reported in the transcript of Tape 14, A4137a and listed in the Atampaya (Uradhi) elicitation materials, Crowley Collection MS 1002, AIATSIS, Canberra. I am indebted to Dr Luise Hercus for advice about the transcription of these two words.
54 This account was published in serial form in *The Queenslander*. There is also a manuscript version, the original held at the John Oxley library.
55 Shanahan MS 1897: 19. Shanahan described him as a 'Red Island native [and] one of the mainland native police ... [and] one of the best trackers in the far North' (Shanahan MS 1897: 14–15).
56 In later records, Kio's name is represented as 'Kaio'. Kio assisted Sub-Inspector Savage in his west coast patrols and also helped the founding Mapoon missionaries during their first weeks at Port Musgrave.
57 Shanahan MS 1897: 39.

'McDonnell tribe' and the 'Severn and Jardine River men' at Cowal Creek[58] while an account of the settlement of Cape York Aboriginal people at Cowal Creek (now named Injinoo), states that:

> Twenty-five years ago, the remains of three powerful Cape York tribes – the Red Island, Severn River, and Cape York tribes – which had for generations been in an almost constant state of warfare, and had also been a menace to white settlers and travellers, decided to bury the hatchet.[59]

Mentions of the 'Severn River natives who inhabit the western coast north of the mouth of the Batavia' by Shanahan (1897: 39) and of the 'Severn River tribe' in the 1939 account are clearly references to the 'Seven Rivers' people, some of whom were encountered in 1891 by the Thursday Island Government Resident John Douglas and his party, at their camp just south of the present day Skardon River. During 2003–2010, I compiled additional information about these people from their descendants and the NCYP ethno-historical, linguistic and genealogical records that were available to me for my consideration.

2.6 Ethnonyms associated with the NCYP west coast

In the published records, the coastal area north from Port Musgrave to the Jardine River is associated not only with the Seven Rivers (var. Seven / Severn River) tribe or natives but also with the following ethnonyms:[60]

Ungpaygen, Ungcumtae and Oyn-Ohyunce (Savage 1892)

Umbaijan,[61] Yandaigan[62] (Meston n.d.); Yandigan (q), west of Cootung to Jardine River and Dolumthurra (w) 'Seven Rivers' (Meston 1896: 14)

Yadigan[63] (Shanahan 1897: 44)

Am–Komti, Ya-ra-kim (Parry-Okeden 1897: Appendix G)

Gâmete[64] (Hey 1899)

---

58 'Blacks Show Civic Spirit', The Sydney Morning Herald, Saturday 26 June 1937: 23.
59 *Walkabout*, 1 December 1939: 47. The author is not named but may be one of the anthropologists who conducted research at Cowal Creek and elsewhere in Cape York Peninsula in the 1930s (e.g. Ursula McConnel or R. Lauriston Sharp).
60 This list should be regarded as a list in progress, and as complete as known to me, at the time of writing.
61 Recorded on an unpublished sketch map, (Meston's Book of Pasted Notes: 77, OM64–17, John Oxley Library) and not included in Meston's 1896 list of Tribes Interviewed (see Meston 1896: 14).
62 According to Meston, the name derives from *Yanta* 'cave' and *daigan* 'inhabitant' (Map & Notes on Tribes of Cape York, Book of Pasted Notes: 77, Meston Collection, OM64–17 JOL).
63 This name used by Shanahan (1897: 44) for a "Cape York tribe" that "occupied the coast south of the Small River to south of the Jardine River, Vrilya Point."
64 Represented as Gametty by Matthews 1900:131.

Gamiti (Roth 1900)

Ngathokadi and Nggamadi (Lauriston Sharp 1939: 257; and Ngathokadi (Lauriston Sharp 1939: 265)[65] and An'Gamoti (Seven Rivers) / Nggamadi /Anggamudi (Lauriston Sharp 1933–34)[66]

Nggammatti (Thomson 1934: 219)[67]

Ngkamadyi / Nggamadi (McConnel 1939: 54, 60)[68]

Nggamadi (Tindale 1940 map;[69] 1974: 183)

Ankamuti (Tindale 1940: 154; 1974: 164)

Gamati (Rigsby 1972)

Gamuthi (Crowley 1981: 146)

Angkamuthi and Uradhi (Crowley 1983: 306, 310)

Uradi, Angkamuti (Nonie Sharp 1992: Map 2: 12)

Barranggu, Nggamati, Ankamuti (Davis 1993) and

Anggamudi (Horton 1994 Vol. 2: 50).

Crowley (1983: 310) has established that some of these names are variant representations of the name of a language distinguished as either Nggammadi (var. Gamati, Gâmete, Gametty, Ngkamadyi, Nggamadi, Ngammatti), which is a form used by the initial CV-dropping speakers south of Port Musgrave or as Angkamuthi (var. Ankamati / Angkamuthi / Angkamuti / Anggamudi / An'Gamoti). Other names in this list refer to entities that might not be equivalent. For example, depending on the context, Uradhi (var. Uradi) and Angkamuthi (var. Angkamuti, Anggamudi) are terms that may distinguish either a language or dialect or language-named group or language group.[70] Some of the names, such as Savage's Oyn-Ohyunce, Meston's 'Dolumthurra' and Davis' 'Barranggu',[71]

---

65 Sharp (1939: 265: note 14) states that his Ngathokadi are called Athokurra by Thomson (1934). McConnel (1939: 60) recorded Sharp's Ngathokadi as (Ng)uthukuti.
66 These names occur in Lauriston Sharp's unpublished field notes and genealogies that are held in the Lauriston Sharp Papers, #14-25-2618, Division of Rare and Manuscript Collections, Cornell University Library.
67 Thomson (1934: 219) describes the Nggammatti as "a tribe occupying a very large tract of country, extending from Port Musgrave to a little north of Vrilya Point."
68 According to McConnel (1939: 80): "The *Ngkamadyi*, Roth's *Gamiti* (Sharp: *Nggamadi*), occupied the coastland north of the Ducie River and south of the *Yumakundyi* of the Jardine River".
69 Tindale (1974: 183) states: "In the text of 1940 the heading Ngerikudi was in error associated with data for this tribe instead of Nggamadi. The map however, was correctly marked."
70 See for example, Sharp (1992: 12 ff); Crowley (1983: 308 ff).
71 This name appears on the 1993 Davis map of *Australia's Extant and Imputed Traditional Aboriginal Territories*. It might be a local name but unfortunately there is no further information about this name in the associated publication by Stephen Davis and J.R.V. Prescott's *Aboriginal Frontiers and Boundaries in Australia*.

have been recorded only once and are completely dissimilar to the other names reported for this region. The suffix 'thurra' in Meston's Dolumthurra – 'Seven Rivers' suggests that this might be the name of a local clan group[72] and his use of quotation marks for Seven Rivers suggests an acknowledgement that this is a local or unofficial placename.

Omitted from this list but of interest because of the time of its recording and its similarity to Hey's 'Gâmete' and Roth's 'Gamiti' is Meston's 'Gammatee', which he located 'east of Bertie Haugh'[73] (Meston 1896: 14), which is inland from the west coast. It is probable, however, that Meston's 'Gammatee' is a reference to the group represented as 'Gâmete' and 'Gamiti' by Hey and Roth respectively. The inconsistency between Hey and Roth on the one hand and Meston on the other in relation to the location of Gâmete (variation Gamiti, Gammatee) suggests that either their or Meston's placement of this group might be an error or that one of these observers may have recorded an outlier of this group or that the area inhabited by members of this group was more extensive than the narrow strip of the coast north of Port Musgrave that the early maps associate with the placename 'Seven Rivers'. The brief descriptions mentioned above suggest the probability of this last possibility, for they associate this group with an area that extends from the coast into the hinterland to include the Ducie River region and an area described as 'towards the McDonnell telegraph station'.

2.7 Seven Rivers in the genealogical records

The NCYP genealogical records include the names of persons reported born at 'Seven Rivers', 'Seven River' and 'Seventh River'. The records of one person report a birthplace by all these placenames, which clearly shows that, in this case, 'Seven Rivers' = 'Seven River' = 'Seventh River'.[74] The NCYP genealogical records mention persons with the surnames 'Seven Rivers', 'Seven River', 'Severin', 'River' and '7 River/s'. The use of placenames for surnames is common in Cape York Peninsula genealogies and signifies a close connection between bearer and place. However, my research found that these particular placenames as surnames have not survived because early NCYP naming practices precluded their bestowal on the children of parents so surnamed. Typically, in the early days, children took their father's (or, more rarely, their mother's) first name as their last name and spouses used their partners' first name as a surname.

Terry Crowley considers that 'some of the names in Davis's map are a bit linguistically incorrect. ...and my maps also have names attributed to areas that do not appear on Davis's map, and some of his names I do not recognise. I would not want to comment on the signfcance of these discrepancies' (Crowley 1995: 136).
72 Shanahan (1897: 45) notes that in Cape York languages, 'the termination "urra" – "durra", "murra," "gurra," – is the general verbal indication of present action'.
73 This was the name of Jardine's cattle property, the homestead of which was situated on the Ducie River.
74 These placenames occur in the records of one NCYP family. I am indebted to a member of this NCYP family for providing copies of these records and for permission to use this information for this article.

Thus, for example, the children of Peter Seven River (who is estimated born about 1860 or before) had the surname 'Peter' and the An'Gamoti (Seven Rivers) couple interviewed by the anthropologist, R. Lauriston Sharp in 1933, appear in his records as 'Jack Emley' and 'Emily Jack'. After the Second World War, mainstream Australian naming practices became widely adopted by NCYP people. However, by this time, there were no children born at Injinoo (then Cowal Creek) to persons having the surname 'Seven Rivers' (or one of its variations) so that Seven Rivers as a surname was discontinued and is found only in the historical records.

2.8 Lauriston Sharp's Seven Rivers people

R. Lauriston Sharp's research, undertaken at Cowal Creek during 1933–1934, directly associates the placenames 'Seven Rivers' and 'Seven River' with several of the ethnonyms listed above. Among Sharp's unpublished Cowal Creek genealogies are those for three persons named Frank Doyle, Jack Emley/Jack Sergeant and his wife, Emily Jack, all of whom are identified as An'Gamoti (Seven/7 Rivers).[75] Sharp (1939: 257) also used the form 'Nggamadi' as an alternative spelling for 'An'Gamoti'. Jack Emley died at Cowal Creek in 1942.[76] His death certificate reports that he was born at 'Seven River' around 1893 and was the son of Peter Seven River and Otemba/Wootinba Seven River. His wife, Emily Jack is reported born at 'Seven River' around 1891 and the daughter of Lily and Jimmy Woosup/Robson. Frank Doyle's records report that he was born around 1886 at McDonnell[77] and was the son of Jack Snake and his wife Mary. Descendants of Sharp's An'Gamoti (Seven Rivers) people reside at Injinoo (formerly known as Cowal Creek) and describe themselves as members of the Seven Rivers Angkamuthi people.

2.9 The Seven Rivers Skardon camp and the Seven Rivers People today

There has been no systematic search for traces of the former Seven Rivers camp that was located south of the Skardon River, where The Hon. John Douglas and his party landed in 1891 during their journey to Port Musgrave to select a site suitable for a mission to Aborigines. An archaeological survey conducted in 1993 noted scatters on the Skardon River bank.[78] A kaolin mine is now located

---

75   These are the Lauriston Sharp Cowal Creek genealogies numbered 5 (for Frank Doyle), 6 (for Jack Emley) and 7 (for Emily Jack) that are in the Lauriston Sharp Papers, #14-25-2618, Division of Rare and Manuscript Collections, Cornell University Library.
76   Information recorded on his death certificate. The informant for this certificate was his wife Emily.
77   This is a reference to the McDonnell telegraph station.
78   These were noted as lying on the southern shoreline of the Skardon River in 1993 during an archaeological survey for the Kaolin Mining and Processing Project. (See Yates and Quartermaine 1993: 19).

in the area south of the Skardon River. Aboriginal mining of kaolin (local name *ruah*) occured both prior to and after the establishment of the Mapoon Mission in 1891 and kaolin was used by Aboriginal people for body decoration, bush medicine for stomach and bowel complaints, and, in during the time of the Mapoon Mission (1891–1963), was mixed with water to make whitewash to whiten the internal walls of the mission's houses.[79]

Image 1: Aerial photograph of the Skardon River, showing its mouth and the kaolin mine barge landing.

In Seven Rivers Angkamuthi oral histories, their ancestors are described as 'walkabout people' whose movements over a large tract of NCYP were determined by seasonal changes, religious responsibilities, political issues and employment opportunities. These ancestors travelled between coastal camps to the Moreton and McDonnell telegraph stations and also regularly visited Mapoon Mission in its early years, where some attended school. However, with the exception of a few who were either removed by government authorities to Mapoon or who went there voluntarily, none became permanent residents of this Presbyterian mission. Instead, on the advice of an east coast man named Alick Whitesand,[80]

---
79 Dr Nicky Horsfall, pers. comm. 10 January 2013.
80 Alick Whitesand is recorded in the Register of Baptisms for St Michael and All Angels (the Anglican Church at Injinoo) as also named Alick Taitaia Onarwatanu and born about 1868 at Whitesand, a place on

they trekked north to settle at the place now known as Injinoo (previously named 'Cowal Creek' and once called 'Small River'). Whether several small family groups undertook this journey over a period of time or there was a mass relocation of all the Seven Rivers people is not recalled, although the available records suggest the latter possibility.[81] Nor do the Seven River Angkamuthi people at Injinoo recall the precise date when this relocation occurred. However, the genealogical records[82] and the 1939 *Walkabout* account suggest that it most probably happened during the period 1913–1914.

3. Conclusion

My inquiries have established that 'Seven Rivers' is a bilingual placename that is represented in the NCYP records also as 'Seven River' and 'Severn River'. In these records, this placename has several distinct but associated meanings, and has been and continues to be used by the Indigenous people of Cape York to distinguish:

- a substantial portion of the west coast of NCYP;
- specific places on the west coast of NCYP;
- a place of birth and/or origin of particular ancestors; and
- a contemporary Aboriginal group, whose members are descended from forebears associated with 'Seven Rivers'.

My research found that the placename 'Seven Rivers' probably originated during the early navigational surveys of NCYP and entered the lexicon of NCYP Aboriginal Creole speakers who do not make the singular v. plural distinction of native English speakers. Although the placename 'Seven Rivers' appears on early NCYP maps, it has not survived developments in the mapping of this region. These include the identification of the Jackson River, the re-mapping of the Skardon River, and the re-positioning of the former MacDonnell telegraph station from the Skardon River of the early maps to the headwaters of the Jackson River of the contemporary maps. Researchers investigating the signficance of place associations reported in NCYP genealogical, linguistic and ethno-historical records will need to take these cartographic changes into account as well as giving consideration to not only the time when records were created, but also to the role of NCYP Creole speakers in their creation.

---

the east coast of NCYP. He was the husband of a Seven Rivers Angkamuthi woman named Kitty. 'Whitesand' is most probably the place that the linguist, Terry Crowley (1983: 310) noted as 'the area known locally as "White Sands" (i.e. Double Point and nearby areas of Shelbourne Bay)'.

81 See the account recorded by Nonie Sharp from Snowy Woosup in Sharp 1992: 99–102.

82 An inspection of the available records found no records of births at 'Seven Rivers' after 1913–1914.

7. Locating Seven Rivers

Many people who are descended from ancestors regarded as originating from 'Seven Rivers' are known today by themselves and others as the Seven Rivers Angkamuthi. Although this placename no longer appears on contemporary maps, it is part of NCYP Aboriginal oral tradition and the above account of its location in the region's ethno-historical records may contribute to its restoration in NCYP's written history.

References

Anonymous 1912-1919, Map of Hann Shire 1912-1919, Queensland State Archives Item ID 629670, map 16M/SH5.N.D./C.

— 'Blacks Show Civic Spirit', The Sydney Morning Herald, Saturday 26 June 1937: 23

— 1922, 'Obituary: Robert Logan Jack, L.L.D., F.G.S., M.I.M.M.', The Geographical Journal 59(4): 318–319.

— 1937, Walkabout, 1 December 1939: 47.

Bradford, J. R. 1962, 'The Cape York Expedition of 1883', Journal of the Royal Historical Society of Queensland 6(4): 1014–1028.

Byerley, F.J. 1867, Narrative of the overland expedition of the Messrs. Jardine from Rockhampton to Cape York, Brisbane.

Crowley, T. 1975, Atampaya (Uradhi) elicitation, narratives and song words: transcription of tapes LA4137a-9a, LA4140a-b, 1. 48-131, MS 1002, Australian Institute of Aboriginal and Torres Strait Islander Studies, Canberra.

— 1981, 'The Mpakwithi dialect of Auguthimri', in *Handbook of Australian Languages*, R.M.W. Dixon and Barry J. Blake (eds), The Australian National University Press, Canberra, Volume 2: 146-194.

— 1983, 'Uradhi', in *Handbook of Australian Languages*, R.M.W. Dixon and Barry J. Blake (eds), The Australian National University Press, Canberra, volume 3: 306–428.

Crowley, T. and B. Rigsby 1979, 'Cape York Creole', in *Languages and their Status*, Timothy Shopen (ed.), Winthrop Publishers, Cambridge: 153–208.

Davis, S. 1993, *Australia's Extant and Imputed Traditional Aboriginal Territories* [map], Distributed by Melbourne University Press, Melbourne.

Davis, S. and J.R.V. Prescott 1992, *Aboriginal Frontiers and Boundariesin Australia*, Melbourne University Press, Melbourne.

Douglas, J. 1891, Report to The Honourable the Chief Secretary Re a visit to Batavia River with the Revd. A. Hardie & Revd. S. Robinson, 31 July 1891, Queensland State Archives, Item ID 143032, File - Reserve.

Douglas, J. 1892, 'Annual report of the Government Resident at Thursday Island', *Queensland Votes and Proceedings of the Legislative Assembly*, Volume 2: 1029-1035.

Fuary, M. and S. Greer, 1993, Preliminary Report on Families and People's Connections to Country for the Community of Injinoo, Cape York Peninsula. Prepared for the Injinoo Land Trust.

Greer, S. and M. Fuary 2008, 'Comunity consultation and collaborative research in Northern Cape York Peninsula – a retrospective', *Archaeological Heritage* 1(1): 5–15.

Hale, K. L. 1964, 'Classification of Northern Paman languages, Cape York Peninsula, Australia: a research report', *Oceanic Linguistics* 3(2): 248–265.

— 1976, 'Phonological developments in a Northern Paman language: Uradhi', in *Languages of Cape York*, Peter Sutton (ed.), Australian Institute of Aboriginal Studies, Canberra: 41–49.

Hardie, Revd. A. and the Revd. S. Robinson 1891, Letter to The Hon. the Premier of Queensland, dated 10 Aug 1891, Queensland State Archives, Item ID 143032, File - Reserve.

Harper, H. 2003, Transcription of Professor Rigsby's Field tapes numbers 72/14 and 72/20.

Hey, Reverend N. 1899, Letter to R.H. Mathews dated 4 August 1899 in the R.H. Mathews Papers, MS8006/1/2/5, National Library of Australia, Canberra.

Horton, D. (ed.) 1994, *The Encyclopaedia of Aboriginal Australia*, Australian Institute of Aboriginal and Torres Strait Islander Studies Press, Canberra.

Jack, R. L. 1921, *Northmost Australia*, 2 volumes, Simpkin, Marshall, Hamilton, Kerd & Co. Ltd, London.

Jackson, C.F.V. 1902, Report on a Visit to the West Coast of the Cape York Peninsula and some Islands of the Gulf of Carpentaria, Department of Mines, Brisbane.

Mathews, R.H. 1900, 'Marriage and descent among the Australian Aborigines. Appendix. Some tribes of Cape York Peninsula', *Journal and Proceedings of the Royal Society of New South Wales* 34: 131–135.

McConnel, U. 1939, 'Social organization of the tribes of Cape York Peninsula, North Queensland', *Oceania* 10(1): 54–72.

Meston, A. n.d., Map & Notes on Tribes of Cape York, Book of Pasted Notes, Meston Collection, OM64–17, John Oxley Library, Brisbane.

— 1896, *Report on the Aboriginals of Queensland*, Government Printer, Brisbane.

Parry-Okeden, W.E. 1897, *Report on the North Queensland Aborigines and the Native Police*, with Appendices, plus map. Government Printer, Brisbane.

— 1898, Condition of the Aborigines. Report of the Commissioner of Police on the Working of "The Aboriginals Protection and Restriction of the Sale of Opium Act, 1897". Report to the Under Secretary, Home Secretary's Department. Presented to both Houses of Parliament.

Phillpotts, Constable P. 1885, Report to the Government Resident, Thursday Island, dated 26 October 1885, Queensland State Archives, Item ID 847175 85/8632.

Rigsby, B. 1972, Aboriginal language: field books 1–8. Field book number 7. MS755, Australian Institute of Aboriginal and Torrest Strait Islander Studies, Canberra.

Roth, W.E. 1900, A report to the Under-Secretary, Home Dept. on the Aboriginals of the Pennefather (Coen) River district and other coastal tribes occupying the country between the Batavia & Embley Rivers. [visited by the Minister during his last trip] Cooktown 8 January 1900, MS346, Australian Institute of Aboriginal and Torrest Strait Islander Studies, Canberra.

— 1910, Social and Individual Nomenclature. North Queensland Ethnography Bulletin No 18, Records of the Australian Museum, 8 (1): 79 -106.

Savage, C. 1891, Letter dated 11th February 1891 to The Honourable John Douglas, Government Resident Thursday Island, Queensland State Archives, Item ID 143032, File - Reserve.

— 1892, *Report to the Commissioner of Police dated 21st May 1892*, Queensland State Archives, Item D 847435.

Shanahan, M.W. 1897, 'With the Cape York Prospecting Party: being an account of a trip from Cape York to the Carron Range, with various Peninsular sidelights', MS 1142, Australian Institute of Aboriginal and Torres Strait Islander Studies, Canberra.

Sharp, N. 1992, *Footprints Along the Cape York Sandbeaches*, Aboriginal Studies Press, Canberra.

Sharp, R. L., 1933-34 Cowal Creek genealogies numbers 2, 5, and 6 Kaurareg genealogies numbers 9 and 10, and document 43-B (Notes made during interview with Tommy Dodd at Cowal Creek, 16/11/1934) Lauriston Sharp Papers, #14-25-2618, Division of Rare and Manuscript Collections, Cornell University Library.

— 1939, 'Tribes and totemism in northeast Australia', *Oceania* 9(3): 254–275.

Smith, G. 1891, 'Cruise of the S.S. Vigilant. The Blacks of the Gulf Country', *The Brisbane Courier*, Tuesday 31 March 1891: 3.

Sutton, P. (ed.) 1995, *Country: Aboriginal Boundaries and Land Ownership in Australia*, Aboriginal History Inc., Canberra.

Thomson, D. F. 1934, 'Notes on a Hero Cult from the Gulf of Carpentaria, North Queensland', *Journal of the Royal Anthropological Institute* 64: 217–235.

Tindale, N. B. 1940, 'Results of the Harvard-Adelaide Universities Anthropological Expedition, 1938-1939, Distribution of Australian Aboriginal Tribes: A Field Survey', with one map Transactions of the Royal Society of South Australia, 64 (1): 140-231.

— 1974, *Aboriginal Tribes of Australia: Their Terrain, Environmental Controls, Distribution, Limits and Proper Names*, plus map, University of California Press, Berkeley, Los Angeles and London.

Whelan, D. 1908, Report of Acting Sergeant D. Whelan re lepers in Cape York Peninsula, Queensland State Archives, Item ID 847690, Correspondence, letter 09/81.

Woods, W. M. (Reverend) 1891, 'Cape York Peninsula Natives. A Cruise in the Albatross', *The Brisbane Courier*, Wednesday 10 June 1891: 7.

Yates, A. and G. Quartermaine 1993, 'A Report on an Archaeological Site Survey of the Skardon Kaolin Project, Cape York Peninsula, Queensland', Unpublished report prepared for Venture Exploration NL by Yates Heritage Consultants and Quartermaine Consultants.

8. 'Many were killed from falling over the cliffs':[1] The naming of Mount Wheeler, Central Queensland

Jonathan Richards
University of Queensland

1. Placenames

Many placenames in Queensland and Australia date from the frontier period. Names may arise from quite mundane circumstances, such as 'Dry Creek', 'Bullock Creek', etc. Some are ubiquitous, referring to relatively benign events and ideas – for example, the many Muddy, Rocky, Sandy and Stoney creeks – while other placenames are more suggestive of much more sinister affairs. The latter category includes places with frightening names: the various Murdering Creeks and Skull Holes, named after events that some people would apparently rather forget, or even better still, deny ever happened. A third group of names commemorate pioneers, some of whom are connected with episodes of genocidal violence on the Australian frontier. This paper concerns one of the latter.

Many people, especially Aboriginal Australians, are distressed by the continuing use of 'killing' placenames, terms and words which may remind them of the extensive violence that First Australians still experience today. Although European placenames replaced existing Aboriginal and Torres Strait Islander landmarks throughout Australia, not all the new names commemorate violence. However, many non-Indigenous Australians remain unaware of the connections and connotations of those that do. While some may claim ignorance of history as an excuse, Indigenous people could hardly be expected to casually ignore the frontier violence that gave us so many gruesome reminders of our past. However, their experiences are often ignored and their consultation is rarely sought in the persistent use of offensive placenames.

In Queensland, violence was perpetrated by two main groups: civilian 'vigilante' or 'black-hunting' parties, and an armed formation of Aboriginal men, the

---

1 The quote in the title is from a report held in the Queensland State Archives (QSA), Governor's Despatches, 16 December 1861, GOV/23, number 74 of 1861.

Native Police, led by Europeans and recruited at gunpoint, whose sole purpose was the elimination of Aboriginal resistance: police who were soldiers (Richards 2008a, 2008b, 2007).

The corps operated from 1848 to the beginning of the First World War as a regular branch of government, and was renowned for extreme violence and brutal sadism. Officially sanctioned frontier killings by the Native Police occurred throughout Queensland, including adjacent waters and offshore islands.

Further details on the history, impact and reputation of the Native Police can be found in the author's doctoral thesis '"A Question of Necessity": The Native Police in Queensland', and in *The Secret War: A True History of Queensland's Native Police*, or in several articles available in scholarly journals (see references). Offshore massacres are recorded on Fraser Island during the early 1850s, in the Whitsunday Islands (1878, see Richards 2008a: 147), as well as on islands off Cape York Peninsula and on a number of Torres Strait islands.

Placenames that commemorate violent episodes raise special questions. Should we, as a nation, continue to blithely use placenames known to be connected with frontier violence without showing consideration for the sensitivities of Indigenous people, particularly the direct descendants of massacre victims and survivors? While non-Indigenous Australians may claim ignorance as an excuse, if the names suggest violence and the places connected with them are associated with frontier killing, Aboriginal people will relate to them quite differently from others in the community.

Australia has a proud record of acknowledging those who died in the name of country, king or empire. If we are to take a different approach to historic names in the landscape, we could begin by commemorating Aboriginal deaths in defence of country and kin. Archival records show where many, but not all, of the inter-racial killings occurred in frontier Queensland. These sacrifices for `country' should be proudly and publicly acknowledged in the same way we honour other Australian war dead. Ignoring these deaths, and continuing to use offensive placenames, divides Australians into two discrete communities.

2. Landmarks of genocide in Queensland

Several Queensland placenames record the sites of police camps or barracks, while others incorporate the word `trooper'. We can assume that these usually refer to the Native Police because European police were nearly always located as `police stations', and the term `trooper' – in Queensland – refers exclusively to the Aboriginal members of the Native Police. Frontier explorers, pastoralists and police officers bestowed names on many features they `discovered'. Others are overtly racist, such as Nigger Creek, near Herberton on the Atherton Tableland. Indigenous requests have finally caused the use of this particular placename ('Nigger Creek') to be abandoned, but others persist.[2] Nine more 'Nigger Creeks' are still used, while other placenames feature derogatory terms such as 'Black Boy' and 'Black Gin'.[3]

The issue of racially contentious names continues to divide other Australian states and other settler societies, as well as Queensland.[4] Some may record the names of patrons, or of trivial episodes and family members, but others are not so benign. Placenames that commemorate and honour violence are not uncommon. For example, Murdering Point, near Innisfail, was named to record the killing of a small number of survivors from the *Maria* shipwreck by Aboriginal people in 1872. Despite the fact that many survivors were saved by Indigenous groups, the reprisals by Native Police, Royal Navy sailors and other Europeans were savage and widespread.

Probably one of the most alarming toponymic names in Queensland is 'The Leap', north of Mackay. This site is named for the plunge of an Aboriginal woman with a child, who chose suicide to avoid capture or killing by European vigilantes and Native Police. Several articles have been written about The Leap (Tareha 1986; Moore 1990).

The Mackay district, one of the most violent parts of the Queensland frontier, is conspicuous by an absence of records relating to frontier violence, yet this event is proudly acknowledged by a large sign outside the local hotel.

The earliest newspaper reference found thus far dates from 1894: 'Probably it derived its name from some tragic event in aboriginal history, or perhaps some incident of more modern date in which the white invader was concerned'.[5] According to historian Clive Moore, the story of The Leap's naming 'encapsulates Aboriginal-European relations around Mackay in the 1860s' (Moore 1990).

Noting the place's incorporation in work by author Thea Astley (1974) and literary historian Nicola Tareha (1986), Moore concludes '[t]here seems no doubt that a massacre occurred at The Leap in 1867' and 'the woman and probably others from her tribe were forced to jump' (Moore 1990: 68).

'Battle Hole', on the Barcoo River in western Queensland, records the killing of 'many Blacks' by local settlers and Acting Sub Inspector Thomas Williams' detachment of Native Police in the early 1870s. In 1872, Williams' activities

---

2 'Bid to change creek names', *Cairns Post*, 1 June 2002: 2.
3 'Placenames in the News', *Placenames Australia* (September 2003): 10.
4 See, for example, several articles on the renaming of the Grampian Mountains in Victoria – Davidson 1991; Birch 1996; Anonymous 1999–2000: 67–68.
5 'The Gin's Leap', *The Queenslander*, 10 November 1894: 888.

became the subject of a parliamentary inquiry.[6] He was suspended and later dismissed. A nearby site on the same watercourse records more violence, but the story of the Mailman's Gorge massacre remained largely unknown until Jane Black's *North Queensland Pioneers* was published in 1932. She stated:

> The blacks were very bad in the ranges around Aramac in the early days and the murder of a travelling jeweller and his wife and child caused reprisals. Harried by the police, the offending tribe took refuge in the country of a hostile tribe, and this precipitated wholesale tribal warfare. To this day it is said the mountain caves yield skeletons, the result of this tribal war. (Black 1932)

Although no records confirm this story, one 1865 account said the death of a shepherd or a government employee at Stainburn Downs station, north-west of Aramac, led to a revenge attack by squatters. Three Europeans are supposed to have tracked 30 Aborigines to a cave at Mailman's Gorge and shot them. Unfortunately further details of this particular clash have not been located to date.

According to one source, a site known as 'Skull Hole' or 'NP Hole' near Cloncurry, in Northwest Queensland, was a Native Police watering hole. Citing explorer JV Mulligan, this writer says 'these NP waterholes were called Skull Lagoons on account of the number of skulls and other human bones lying about' (de Havelland 1989: 169). The name of another watercourse, 'Skull Hole Creek' near Croydon, probably has similar origins. 'Skull Pocket', near Cairns, is reputed to be the site of a large-scale massacre, and the place where 'a whole case of skulls' was supposedly collected (Bottoms 2002: 149). One writer said he personally saw 16 skulls placed here on stumps and trees ('Coyyan' 1926).

There are eight Skeleton Creeks in Queensland, and it can be assumed that some if not all of these refer to the discovery of Aboriginal remains. One is situated close to Skull Pocket, and this particular 'Skeleton Creek' commemorates the discovery of human remains chained to a tree. Troopers led by Senior Constable Edmond Whelan, in command of the Mulgrave River Native Police camp from 1885 to 1889, are thought to have caused this 'lawful' death. Skull Creek near Nebo, in the Mackay area, was the site of a frontier killing in 1873. Although the name appears to be used from this time, there is little doubt that the killing of storekeeper Henry Maxwell, allegedly by Aboriginal people, resulted in revenge attacks by the Native Police and fellow colonists.

---

6 QSA, JUS/N36, inquest 64a of 1873; QSA, COL/A407, letter 8140 of 1884; *Queensland Police Gazette*, 1872: 108; *Queensland Parliamentary Votes and Proceedings*, 1884: 243, 269, 691–695.

3. Mount Wheeler

There are several problems in identifying massacre sites, besides official denial. Sometimes it is difficult to know where the killings occurred because the connections between a place and frontier violence are hidden, or obtuse. Some places throughout Queensland are named, apparently not after specific colonial events, but after individual pioneers with important connections to the local area. Yet, sometimes, in the case of 'settler' names, the individual involved is difficult to determine. One such example, the subject of this paper, is the naming of Mount Wheeler, a steep-sided volcanic plug located between Rockhampton and the coastal towns of Emu Park and Yeppoon in Central Queensland. Other similar peaks, including Mount Jim Crow and Pine Mountain, dot the surrounding flat landscape.

According to local historians, Mount Wheeler was first named 'Mount Cock's Comb' by Captain Cook in 1770 (Anonymous 1991: ix). The maritime inlet 'Broadsound' was one of Cook's names, as was the nearby Keppel Islands. However, Cook's *Endeavour* journal does not corroborate the peak's naming and nor do any other sources. The same writers claimed the mountain was allegedly renamed as 'Mount Wheeler' after 'an Inspector of Native Police who caught up with runaway Aborigines in the mountain foothills'. Who was this individual, and why should the use of his name for a landmark be significant? More importantly, what happened when Inspector Wheeler of the Native Police caught up with these 'runaway Aborigines'?

Frederick Wheeler, of Native Police fame, was a notorious character and more has been written about him than any other officer in the Native Police force. He has been described as 'cruel and merciless', 'the most callous and brutal officer', and called a 'sadist' (Rosser 1990: 93; MacMaster 1999: 68; Reid 2001: 7–8). His police staff file has not survived, but we can reconstruct his career through reports in the archives. There is no doubt, from this correspondence, that Wheeler was personally involved in the killing of Aboriginal people in southern and central Queensland, and probably also in parts of northern New South Wales.

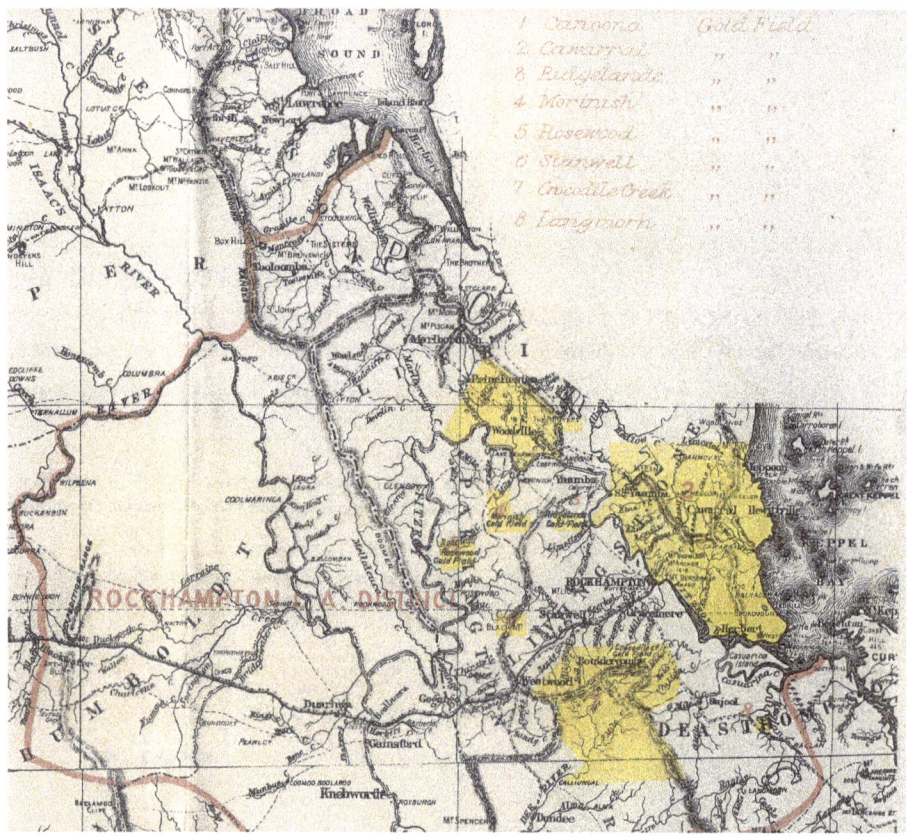

Map 1: Rockhampton district goldfields, showing Mt Wheeler between Cawarral and Yeppoon.

Source: Queensland Parliamentary Votes & Proceedings.

First appointed to the Native Police force in 1857 at the age of 27, Frederick Wheeler led a detachment known to have killed Aboriginal people near Brisbane during the early 1860s. Senior colonial officials exonerated Wheeler as a 'valuable and zealous officer', despite clear evidence of his part in the massacres, and promoted him.[7]

Mistakes about Wheeler's service in the Native Police have been incorporated into popular historical accounts. In 1941, an article, 'The Inspector Disappears', by 'Beachcomber' was published in Brisbane's *Sunday Mail Magazine*. Wheeler, claimed the writer, had 'been committing mass murder for almost twenty years' ('Beachcomber' 1941). According to the unnamed author of this piece, his flight from justice was probably assisted by his connections: 'Wheeler had many influential

---

7   QSA, JUS/N1, inquest 8 of 1860, JUS/N2, inquest 71 of 1860 and JUS/N3, inquest 1 of 1861.

friends, having married into a prominent squatter family'. 'Beachcomber' may have been a pen name for Brisbane journalist and historian Clem Lack, who devoted a chapter to Wheeler (titled 'Killer in Uniform') in his book *The Rifle and the Spear*. Wheeler's 'evil reputation', he said, became a 'byword among the colony's blacks and whites alike' (Lack and Stafford 1965: 124–136).

Recent work is no less blemish-free. For example, Ross Gibson's 2002 work *Seven Versions of an Australian Badland* describes Wheeler as 'a ghostly figure in the official records of Queensland', claiming 'there is little written evidence concerning him'. Gibson claims politicians 'worried that knowledge of his actions might spread beyond the frontier' if Wheeler was placed on trial and concludes he 'developed an ambiguous reputation in government circles' (Gibson 2002: 64).

Over the years, Wheeler's fate had been the subject of some speculation. As noted, his career ended at Clermont in 1876 when he was charged with the wilful murder of an Aboriginal prisoner.[8] Dismissed and released on bail, Wheeler absconded from the colony. Although his movements during the next six years remain a mystery, it is now known he died at Java, probably from disease, during 1882.[9]

4. Genocidal moments

The naming of Mount Wheeler therefore becomes an important marker of colonial genocide if the site is named after a particular individual known to have been connected with sanctioned frontier violence. This name becomes even more inappropriate if the individual being commemorated had successfully avoided trial for violence against Indigenous people. The mountain's naming could be seen, by some, as celebrating the illustrious career of a 'uniformed mass-murderer'.

The confusion over the origins of the name prompted a reader to ask Brisbane's *Courier Mail* whether the mountain was named after a miner, a gold commissioner or a police officer.[10] The newspaper asked several government departments for assistance, but no clear answer to the reader's query was found. My research on the Native Police has led to a greater knowledge and understanding about this force in Queensland history, and I was asked, specifically, does the name 'Mount Wheeler' commemorate a frontier police officer, a massacre, or something quite benign, such as an unsuccessful mining rush?

---

8   QSA, Supreme Court records, SCT/CG7/372.
9   Wheeler descendants, pers. comm.'
10 'Know your distric', *Courier Mail*, 29 October 2005: 36.

The question of Mount Wheeler's name raises some important issues because placenames vividly recalling frontier violence continue to re-impose pain and suffering on Indigenous people. Furthermore, if the site is connected with frontier killing, the violence, or 'lawful force', used by the Native Police force, and the force's place in the history of Queensland, becomes an important part of this investigation. Other questions soon emerge. How have local historians and writers spoken about this violence, and which versions of local history have they transmitted? How did different versions emerge?

'The Leap' is not the only place connected with the killing of First Australians by forcing them over precipices. Another story about Wheeler forcing Aboriginal people to jump from a cliff survives west of Rockhampton, not far from Mount Wheeler. According to local historian Marie Reid, the local settlers 'decided to organise all the force obtainable in the neighbourhood and declare war on the Aboriginals' after resistance increased during the mid-1860s.[11] Inspector Wheeler and his Native Police, she says, 'headed the white force, which numbered almost one hundred'. At dawn, the vigilantes attacked a camp. The Aboriginal people retreated, but 'the Native Police led the pursuit and mercilessly cut down men, women and children'. Many 'jumped into the lake at the base of the cliff'. Reid notes 'no confirmation' of this event has been found in records she searched but 'the oral tradition was strong enough to carry the story on to the end of the twentieth century'. According to Reid, a large number, possibly 300, were killed that day and 'the bones of the dead were still visible for at least thirty years'. Archival records of this event have not been found to date.

5. Frontier violence and Wheeler's career in Central Queensland

Comparing the recorded history of the mountain with the known details of Frederick Wheeler's police career is one way to investigate whether the mountain was actually named after him. He was stationed in Central Queensland twice. The first time, briefly in 1858, as a junior officer at 'The Fitzroy' (as Rockhampton was known in early years); and a second time when he returned to the area in 1866, taking charge of the Native Police operations in the Broadsound district, between St Lawrence and Marlborough.

There are graphic records of frontier violence in the district. Graziers had apparently been killing Aboriginal people in this area in retaliation for cattle spearing. An 1867 inspection report noted: 'The Blacks in the Broadsound district are still very troublesome on the cattle stations. They are continually

---

11   Reid 2001: 7 quoting *Rockhampton Bulletin*, 2 August 1899.

killing cattle and rushing large mobs from one run to another'.[12] One Broadsound station diary entry includes a chilling entry: 'Blacks been amongst the cattle – head for head', meaning one Aboriginal person had been shot for every head of cattle killed (McDonald 1988: 89).

Between 1866 and 1875, Frederick Wheeler's troopers patrolled from barracks at Marlborough, Stoodleigh and Waverley, all in the Broadsound area, north of Mount Wheeler. His 'district', centred on 'Barracks Creek' near Marlborough, covered all of Central Queensland, from the sea coast inland to the Mackenzie River.

Wheeler 'quietened' the 'Blacks' of his patrol district quickly and efficiently. In 1870, he was still stationed at Stoodleigh.[13] Records give us some idea of his tactics, and an insight into his personality. In January 1871, the *Rockhampton Bulletin* published a letter from 'A Lover of Justice', stating 'The blacks only stayed in Rockhampton to save their lives' because they were 'hunted back' by the Native Police if they went 50 miles from town. 'A Lover of Justice' claimed that 'an officer of the Native Police had recently boasted that he could shoot as many as he liked without interference'.[14] This was most likely Frederick Wheeler. According to one writer, his name 'inspired the aborigines with such a wholesome dread, that it was only necessary, when on any of their marauding expeditions, to say "Wheeler's coming" or "Here's Wheeler" and they would go yelling pell-mell into the bush'.[15]

There were further complaints from settlers about Wheeler's conduct towards Aboriginal people. In 1872, he was mildly 'censured' by the Commissioner of Police after an incident near Yaamba, north of Rockhampton, in which an Aboriginal prisoner allegedly 'threw himself from a horse, heavily chained and handcuffed as he was, into the river, with the intention of swimming to the other side and escaping'. 'Then', Wheeler wrote, 'after a few ineffectual struggles, he sank and was drowned'.[16]

In March 1876, while based at Mistake Creek near Clermont (inland from St Lawrence) he was reported to have whipped a young Aboriginal man to death. An inquest was held and credible European witnesses, including other police, gave evidence against him.[17] Charged with murder, he was committed for trial and dismissed from the Native Police in April. After a brief period in Rockhampton Gaol, two prominent graziers offered to provide him with sureties. Bail was granted in May by one of the colony's senior legal officers, Justice Lutwyche

---

12 Chief Inspector George Murray to the Commissioner of Police, 10 August 1867, QSA, A/36335, letter 123 of 1867.
13 *Queensland Blue Book*, 1870: 14–18.
14 *Rockhampton Bulletin*, 17 January 1871.
15 *The Queenslander*, 13 February 1875.
16 Wheeler to Colonial Secretary, 18 October 1872, QSA, COL/A170, number 1484 of 1872.
17 QSA, SCT/CG7/372.

of the Supreme Court, and approved by the colony's Attorney General, Samuel Griffith. The trial began at Rockhampton in October 1876, but Wheeler failed to appear, having absconded while on bail.[18] The Secretary of State for the Colonies wrote from London to the Queensland Governor, stating 'I very much regret that Wheeler should have escaped trial'.[19]

No warrant was ever issued for Wheeler's arrest, and two years later the Supreme Court was advised that no further charges would be laid against him.[20] Although Frederick Wheeler was technically free to return to Queensland, there is no evidence about his movements during the years between 1876 and 1882. All that is known is that he died at Java, probably from disease, in 1882 (Richards 2008a).

For many years, historical accounts of frontier violence in Queensland were more heavily influenced by hearsay and rumours than by rigorous research. Colourful and highly selective versions survived. For example, J.T.S. Bird's *The Early History of Rockhampton* published in 1904 has become an important reference source for family, local and regional history in Central Queensland.

Although some violent events are described, Bird does not mention a massacre at Mount Wheeler, or the well-documented killing of Aboriginal people at nearby Morinish in 1867 (Bird 1904: 102–103). Apart from a few isolated studies, the subject of frontier violence in Central Queensland has not been closely examined.

6. The naming of Mount Wheeler

According to a brief history of the goldfield published in the 'Annual Report of the Department of Mines for 1887', gold was found 'in the hollows of the spurs' of Mount Wheeler during 1868. 'It was here that one of the largest nuggets ever found in Queensland was discovered'. At first, the lode was rich but the ore soon 'petered out'.[21] The mountain became a popular lookout spot during the early twentieth century (Photograph 1921). As is often the case, sometimes an outsider can learn more about a district's myths than a local. Museum collector George Wilkins visited the Rockhampton district during the 1920s, writing afterwards about 'the sinister story in connection with the mountain and the man who named it' (Wilkins 1928: 111). According to Wilkins, the story of Mount Wheeler, 'as told to me', was 'probably an exaggeration':

---

18   QSA, CCT7/N32 and CCT7/N37; Alfred Davidson to Aborigines Protection Society, 9 October 1876, AJCP, M/2427.
19   QSA, GOV/11A, Despatch 310 of 1876.
20   QSA, CCT7/N34.
21   *Queensland Parliamentary Votes & Proceedings*, 1888.

> Years ago, a sergeant of the police, enthusiastic in his duty of quelling aboriginal disturbances, developed a blood lust and sought to carry on a wholesale slaughter in support of the theory that no matter how a good a black fellow may be, he is better dead. (Wilkins 1928: 112)

Saying 'two or three hundred' were supposed to have driven up the mountain side and over the sides, 'to be dashed to pieces on the rocks below', Wilkins dryly noted 'it is curious to notice that a hundred or so does not seem to matter in the estimate of number of victims in a tragedy'.

The steep cliffs and overhanging ledges were, he said, 'ominous from below and treacherous in approach from the top'. Wilkins further states that casual visitors might find 'apparently corroborative evidence' of the massacre story in what looked like a row of headstones 'standing upright on the border of a smooth, grass-covered mound at the foot of the cliff'.

> An active imagination might construct a scene where some black tracker or other sympathetic soul had crept to the scene of the slaughter to bury the dead and erect a rough headstone to their memory, but I am afraid that in the early days there was little sympathy with the natives, and that examples of Christian ethics in relation to them were rare. (Wilkins 1928: 112)

Rejecting the story of frontier killings, he said the 'headstones' were 'probably the side-posts on the claim of some itinerant prospector for gold' (Wilkins 1928: 112).

Was Wilkins' assessment of Mount Wheeler's naming correct? Although there is no evidence linking Frederick Wheeler with a cliff-top massacre of Aboriginal people in Central Queensland, one of his brother officers is connected with what may have been a very similar event. The path to this individual's record lies through an investigation of the other main candidate for Mount Wheeler's naming, frontier public servant John George Wheeler. According to the author of a 1950 article in the *Rockhampton Bulletin*, Mount Wheeler was really named after John Wheeler, Gold Commissioner at Peak Downs, and not Frederick.[22]

The coach road from Rockhampton to Peak Downs passed through Marlborough and Apis Creek north of the Fitzroy River, and John Wheeler probably travelled along the road many times. First appointed as the Clerk of Petty Sessions at Peak Downs in 1862, he was also appointed Sub Commissioner of Goldfields in 1863 and Sub-Inspector of Police in 1864.[23] John Wheeler visited many parts of the district in the course of his work. He probably climbed the mountain, and

---

22   Central Queensland Cutting Book, John Oxley Library, OM 91-58/2.
23   *Queensland Government Gazette*, 1862: 749; 1863: 829; 1864: 571.

the earliest reference found thus far to the mountain's name comes from this time ('The Gold Discovery near Rockhampton', *The Maitland Mercury & Hunter River General Advertiser*, 3 October 1863: 4).

In 1864, John Wheeler was appointed as Clerk of Petty Sessions at Princhester, north of Rockhampton.[24] He swapped his position at Peak Downs with William Cave, a former-Native Police officer, at Princhester.[25] Significantly, Cave was one of the officers in command of official reprisals after the killing of Horatio Wills' party of 19 Europeans at Cullin-la-Ringo station on the Nogoa River in October 1861. 'About thirty of the tribe of murderers are said to have fallen in the deadly struggle which ensued when the eleven English avengers stormed their camp'.[26] Letters between members of the Wills family mentioned reprisals: in November, Mrs Wills wrote to her sons about their father's death, saying 'Tom and the settlers around have well avenged his death before now'.[27]

Several Native Police detachments quickly converged on the district. One newspaper report claimed the troopers only stopped killing when they exhausted their ammunition.[28] According to official despatches from the Queensland Governor, Lieutenant William Cave and his troopers killed a number of Aboriginal people before the rest retreated to the top of a high hill. Towards sundown, the Native Police surprised them: 'Their loss was heavy and I consider that many were killed from falling over the cliffs'.[29] After two year's service in the Native Police, Cave left the Native Police and became the Clerk of Petty Sessions at Princhester in 1863, but was transferred to Peak Downs one year later.[30] It is possible that William Cave's exploits become confused in local memories with the careers of both Frederick and John Wheeler, which may explain the three versions of the peak's naming.

The archival evidence found thus far suggests that the mountain was most probably named after Gold Commissioner John Wheeler rather than after Police Inspector Frederick Wheeler. Since the Mount Wheeler gold rush took place in 1868, it would appear, therefore, that the mountain was named during the 1860s. Frederick Wheeler spent little time north of the Fitzroy River before 1866, so it is unlikely that the action of naming would have gone unrecorded

---

24   *Queensland Government Gazette*, 1864: 471.
25   *Queensland Government Gazette*, 1865: 1.
26   QSA, Governor's Despatches, GOV/23, number 74 of 1861.
27   Wills Manuscript, Central Queensland University, B9/1736.
28   *Sydney Morning Herald*, 11 December 1861.
29   QSA, Governor's Despatches, GOV/23, number 74 of 1861.
30   QSA, COL/A38, letter 506 of 1863; COL/A58, letters 2317 & 2443 of 1864.

by Bird and other local writers. On the other hand, John Wheeler worked in the area during the early 1860s and, as Gold Commissioner, inspected all newly found mining fields. His death in 1867 may have inspired the name.[31]

7. Conclusion

Placenames commemorating frontier times abound in settler-societies. Some are named after violent events that settlers would like to forget, but Indigenous people do not dismiss the past so easily. Furthermore, frontier violence is sometimes reiterated by the continuing use of 'racial' placenames. While some overtly contentious names have been dropped in recent years, others persist. Places and placenames known to be connected with frontier violence are, for Aboriginal and Torres Strait Islander people, confronting and distressing. If the truth about racial killings in frontier Queensland is acknowledged, their sacrifice for 'country' could be publicly commemorated rather than denied.

Although there is evidence in the records proving that the Native Police on at least one occasion forced Aboriginal people over a cliff, there is no account connecting this site with such an event. In addition, although there is adequate proof that Frederick Wheeler and troopers under his control killed Aboriginal men, women and children on a number of different occasions, there are no records to support the claim that he forced them to jump from cliffs. It would appear, on balance, that Mount Wheeler in Central Queensland is named after Gold Commissioner John George Wheeler. Renaming the mountain 'Mount John Wheeler' or 'Mount J.G. Wheeler' would prevent confusion. Massacres did happen at other places, but not here. How many more sites need similar investigation?

References

Anonymous 1991, 'Introduction', in *Livingstone: A History of the Shire of Livingstone, Brisbane*, Boolarong, Brisbane: ix.

—— 1999–2000, '"Nigger Creeks" are gone but there's still a lot of leftover racism on the maps of the United States', *The Journal of Blacks in Higher Education* 26, Winter: 67–68.

Astley, T. 1974, *A Kindness Cup*, Thomas Nelson, Melbourne.

---

31 Queensland Births, Deaths & Marriages; QSA, COL/Q4, letter 607 of 1867; *Queensland Government Gazette*, 1866: 39.

'Beachcomber' 1941, 'The inspector disappears', *Sunday Mail Magazine*, 8 June 1941.

Birch, T. 1996, '"A land so inviting and still without inhabitants": erasing Koori culture from (post) colonial landscapes', in *Text, Theory, Space: Land, Literature and History in South Africa and Australia*, Kate Darian-Smith, Liz Gunner and Sarah Nuttall (eds), Routledge, London.

Bird, J.T.S. 1904, *The Early History of Rockhampton*, Central Queensland Family History Association, Rockhampton.

Black, J. 1932, *Queensland Pioneers*, Queensland Country Women's Association, Townsville.

Bottoms, T. 2002, 'A history of Cairns', unpublished PhD thesis, Central Queensland University, Rockhampton: 149.

Central Queensland Cutting Book, John Oxley Library, OM 91–58/2.

'Coyyan' 1926, *Cairns Post Jubilee Supplement*, 1 November 1926: 19.

Davidson, J. 1991, 'Brambuk, capital of Gariwerd', *Australian Society* (December 1991).

de Havelland, D.W. 1989, *Gold and Ghosts Volume 4: Queensland Northern and Northwestern*, Hesperian Press, Perth: 169.

Gibson, R. 2002, *Seven Versions of an Australian Badland*, University of Queensland Press, Brisbane.

Lack, C. and H. Stafford 1965, *The Rifle and the Spear*, Fortitude Press, Brisbane.

McConnel Papers, John Oxley Library, OM 79.017/18.

McDonald, L. 1988, *Cattle Country*, Boolarong, Brisbane.

MacMaster, H. 1999, *Mostly Murder*, Central Queensland University Press, Rockhampton.

Moore, C. 1990, 'Blackgin's Leap: A window into Aboriginal-European relations in the Pioneer Valley, Queensland in the 1860s', *Aboriginal History* 14(1–2): 61–79.

Photograph 1921, 'View from Mt Wheeler near Rockhampton', *The Queenslander*, 1 January 1921: 24.

Queensland Blue Book, 1870: 14–18.

Queensland Government Gazette, 1862, 1863, 1864, 1865, 1866.

Queensland Parliamentary Votes and Proceedings, 1884, 1888.

Queensland Police Gazette, 1872: 108.

Reid, M. 2001, *Emerald: A Place of Importance*, Emerald Shire Council, Emerald.

Richards, J. 2007, 'Frederick Wheeler and the Sandgate Native Police Camp', *The Royal Historical Society of Queensland Journal* 20: 107–122.

—— 2008a, *The Secret War: A True History of Queensland's Native Police*, University of Queensland Press, Brisbane.

—— 2008b, 'The Native Police of Queensland', *History Compass* 6(4): 1024–1036.

Rosser, B. 1990, *Up Rode the Troopers*, University of Queensland Press, Brisbane.

Tareha, N. 1986, *The Legend of the Leap*, James Cook University, Townsville.

Wilkins, Captain Sir G.H. 1928, *Undiscovered Australia*, Ernest Benn Ltd, London.

Wills Manuscript, Central Queensland University, B9/1736.

9. Saltwater Placenames around Mer in the Torres Strait

Nick Piper

1. Introduction

This paper explores the names and meanings given for some of the reefs and cays (small low-lying islands) around Mer, Dauar and Waier (known as the Murray Islands) in the Torres Strait.[1] Such placenames 'tell us something not only about the structure and content of the physical environment itself but also how people perceive, conceptualize, classify and utilize that environment' (Thornton 1997: 209). They therefore 'intersect three fundamental domains of cultural analysis: language, thought and the environment' (1997: 209). The aims of this paper are to bring to light naming patterns for places around Mer. It is hoped that such a focus on saltwater placenames will prompt other researchers to document this knowledge as a potential resource for sea claims.[2]

The paper is organised as follows: the first section looks at different sources for placenames in other parts of the world. The second section introduces the reader to the Torres Strait region and its languages, in particular the languages of the eastern islands. The third section focuses on the names for saltwater places around Mer, their lexical source, grammatical structure and in some cases, the choice of language.

2. Sources for placenames

In North America, interest in Indigenous placenames was raised by an American anthropologist, Franz Boas, who worked with Inuits around Baffin Island (Thornton 1997: 211). Since 2000, a large project has aimed at further documenting Inuit placenames, specifically those of the Sikusilarmiut (Henshaw

---

[1] My thanks to the following people for their comments and suggestions: Dana Chahal, Penny Johnson, Rachel Nordlinger, Colin Scott, Anna Shnukal, Jane Simpson and Felix Ameka. I also thank the two reviewers for their insightful comments. My gratitude to Garrick Hitchcock for helping me with the maps. A special thanks to the Mer community, in particular Usiam and Atai Wailu, both now deceased, as well as Alo and Terry Tapim, Simeon and Adimabo Noah, Mabigi Tabo, Dalton Cowley and Palen Passi.

[2] For example, the case of Leo Akiba and George Mye on behalf of the Torres Strait Islanders of the Regional Seas Claim Area and the State of Queensland and others, filed in the Federal Court of Australia in November 2001 and determined by the High Court on 7 August 2013.

2006). This study, based on 420 placenames, found that people's discussions about places revolved around a number of recurrent themes listed below (i)–(vii) (2006: 56). Furthermore, the researchers found that certain themes, such as topography, were more common than others, such as harvesting activities. On this basis, they constructed a typology of salient features for Sikusilarmiut people when talking about place:

(i) topographic features such as mountains, cliffs and peninsulas;

(ii) descriptive features based on animals, plants, and animal behaviour;

(iii) climate sensitive features such as seasonal camping areas, sea ice, ocean currents, snow conditions, temperature conditions and wind direction, animal migrations and nesting areas;

(iv) metaphorical features based on animals or humans or mythical associations;

(v) historic events;

(vi) travel routes and camp sites;

(vii) harvesting activities such as hunting, processing and caching areas.

The typology identifies themes or features most commonly associated with places. The environment dominates through its landscape, plants, animals, seasonal accessibility and associated mythology.[3]

In the Marquesas Islands in French Polynesia, a study on landscape terms shows an overlap between the themes associated with Sikusilarmiut places and the categories used for naming Marquesan places (Cablitz 2008: 209):

(i) topographic features such as *Tepapa* 'the lava rock';

(ii) descriptive features of plants or animals such as *Fafa'ua* 'manta ray';

(iii) metaphorical features such as body part terms as in *Te'uma* 'the breast';

(iv) mythological figures such as *Teohootupa* 'the cape of Tupa';

(v) objects or things such as *Ke'atu'ipopoi* 'poipoi (*Citrifolia morinda*) pounder' or *Popomā'* 'fermented breadfruit ball'.

Placenames can also combine several semantic categories. For example, *Matafenua* 'land's end' means literally: eye land, combining a topographical feature with a body part. Grammatically, the placenames can be a single noun,

---

3   Only one mythological example is provided. A place called *Iqsauti*, literally 'side of a face', which evokes a story about an illicit love affair.

a complex noun phrase such as '*Otopuhi* 'moray's hole' (literally: inside moray) or a descriptive phrase which can be expanded to include events or states such as *Tutaekena* 'Kena defecates'.

Australian Indigenous naming patterns vary across the country depending on the society and environment (Hercus and Simpson 2002: 2). In their introduction, Hercus and Simpson (2002: 19) provide a summary of common semantic categories found for central and southern placenames (exemplified with Warumungu, a language spoken in Central Australia):

(i) topographic names which describe the land and/or environment such as *Karlukarlu* 'boulders';

(ii) incidents or events connected to a mythological figure or Ancestral Being such as *Karnkka* 'moon' or *Ngurru pakinyi* '(someone) pierced a nose';

(iii) names which evoke a mythological figure and a descriptive feature at the same time. The names may be literal such as *Kijjiparraji*, 'white ghostgums', where ancestral Mungamunga women turned into white ghostgums, or metaphorical such as *Parakujjurr* 'two body entrances', which marks the place of two rockholes.

While these naming patterns may be common for Australia, they are not universal. Some of the variations include placenames which overtly name an ancestor such as the Ngalakgan place *Ganjarri* 'bonefish' (Baker 2002: 109) or those which can have a generic topographic term included such as the Wik places W*ayingk Thiikanen* 'Wayingk Island' and *Merrek Ngamp* 'Merrek River' (Sutton 2002: 82) or the Yir-Yorront name for a land-tract *Larr-Low+Pannan* 'Crying place' with the noun *larr* 'place' (Alpher 2002: 134).

In terms of their grammatical structure, Australian Indigenous placenames can be a simple noun or complex noun phrase (such as the examples given above), a verb or verb phrase or headless relative clause. Thus, the Arabana people call Mount Arthur, *Pakalta* 'he is digging for someone else', and the site of a water bore, *Wabma tharkarnayangu* '(where) the Snakes stood up' (Hercus and Simpson 2002: 20).

In summary, common semantic features for naming places emerge: environmental such as topography, plants, animals and mythology. These features may be expressed literally or metaphorically. In terms of their grammatical structure, placenames may be expressed by single words, complex phrases or clauses. Some of these patterns and structures are also found with saltwater placenames in Meriam, a language of the Torres Strait (sections 5 to 11).

3. Torres Strait

The Torres Strait is the stretch of water between Australia and Papua New Guinea (see Map 1). It is dotted with over 100 islands, 15 of which are permanently inhabited. To the east of the Strait lies the Coral Sea and to the west, the Arafura Sea. The waters have countless coral reefs which abound in natural resources. Torres Strait Islanders' lives revolve around the sea and they rely on it for their daily diet, or at least to supplement it. They catch fish on the foreshore using lines or nets, forage at low tide or travel by dinghy to fish, dive and hunt sea creatures such as turtle or dugong. Their life at sea is celebrated through their songs and dances. Their identity is connected to the sea and this is evidenced by their marine totems which are, amongst others, dolphins, whales, turtles and fish.

Linguistically, the Torres Strait is at the intersection of two large language regions, Papuan and Australian. The eastern islands language is related to Papuan languages from the Eastern Trans-Fly River family (Alpher et al. 2008: 15). The western and central Islands language and its dialects are related to Australian Pama-Nyungan languages (2008: 28).

4. Meriam language

The original language spoken in the eastern Torres Strait is Meriam or Meriam Mir (MM), literally 'Meriam language'. Like many Papuan languages, it is a verb final language (S-O-V) with agglutinating morphology. Nominals are casemarked to show their syntactic role and there is a regular process of nominal compounding, typically in a modifier-head relationship. Verbs cross-reference core arguments of the sentence and carry information for person, number, tense and mood. Number distinctions are singular, dual, paucal and plural, which are marked syntactically and through verb root forms. Although Meriam was originally spoken throughout the eastern islands, nowadays, the majority speak the regional creole, Torres Strait Creole (TSC) as their first language.

Topographical marine terms are often given in the creole rather than in Meriam. Sandbars or cays are called *sanba* (TSC) rather than *wésor*[4] (MM), literally 'sand back'; small sunken reefs are referred to as *spot* (TSC) 'small sunken reef' rather than *kep* (MM), literally 'seed, spot, small sunken reef'; a lagoon is usually called *lagun* (TSC) rather than *keper* 'a pool', *siridsirid* (MM) 'a shallow lagoon' or *ubir* (MM) 'a deep lagoon' and channels are called *pasis* (TSC) rather than *kes*

---

4   I am using Meriam orthography with the addition of accents. Stress is contrastive although typically, the second syllable is stressed. When the pattern diverges from this, the stressed syllable is overtly marked with an accent.

(MM) 'channel' or *karem* (MM) 'deep sea or deep channel'. However, Eastern Islanders tend to talk about their reefs as *nor (*MM) rather than *rip* (TSC) 'reef' so that the Barrier Reef is called *Baria* or *Op Nor* (MM).

5. Meriam saltwater placenames

This study is based on the saltwater placenames around Mer, Dauar and Waier (see Maps 2 and 3).[5] The following categories are sources for naming: i) descriptive, ii) ancestral, iii) narrative and iv) miscellaneous for those placenames of unknown origin (see List of placenames). Most places are named after the personal name of an ancestor. The next largest group of places are named after a physical or descriptive feature such as the marine or bird life, habitat, physical properties or location. Only a few places are named after an event. In addition, there are placenames associated with several semantic categories as their name is a combination of a descriptive feature and ancestral name, or the ancestral name itself is descriptive. Furthermore, some places have alternate names that relate to a different semantic category.

6. Descriptive names

Reefs can have descriptive names drawn from one or more of the following features:

- marine life and habitat
- bird life and habitat
- physical properties such as size, shape or matter
- relative location/direction

While most descriptive names are given with a literal meaning, those which describe the shape of a reef are given metaphorically.

6.1 Marine life and habitat

There are reefs named after fish. *Bologor Kep* (*kep* 'small sunken reef') is named after the sawfish and *Pakor* reef is named after the red bass fish.[6] Two personal ancestral names, *Au Siar* and *Kebi Siar*, mean literally 'Big Cod' and 'Little Cod'

---

[5] Variations between places on the map and my own references are due to different spelling and some places referred to in my paper are not marked on the map.
[6] There is one reef which has the public name of a type of fish but it is a permutation of an ancestor's name. It is kept secret because it marks the spot where the ancestor was killed by sorcery. In this instance, the name is not associated with the prevalence of a fish but used because of a taboo placed on the real name.

(see section 7 for a discussion on ancestral names). There is one reef, *Adud Nor*, named literally: Bad Reef because it had no fish. Although the reef now has coral and hence fish, it has retained its original name.⁷ There are surprisingly few reefs named after fish considering Meriam people's extensive knowledge and dependence on marine resources. This may be that good fishing spots are regarded as private information and thus kept secret from other fishermen. Alternatively, it may be that fish are not so localised.⁸

Reefs are also named after other marine creatures. Thus, *Nazir Bed* is the name of a reef based on *nazir* (MM) 'trochus shell' and *bed* (TSC) 'bed or layer'.⁹ The use of a TSC word suggests a newly coined name. It was probably renamed in the early 20th century when the Torres Strait had a thriving trochus shell industry and these were collected for making buttons.¹⁰ According to one Meriam, it was made into a communal area in his father's time and profits from the shell sales were pooled for the benefit of the whole community.¹¹

While the previous placenames are based on marine life, they can also be named after habitat. There is a point on one of the reefs called *Wazar* which is possibly related to the Meriam word *zar* 'the place where fish go to hide and rest' (it also refers to a type of garden plot) and is found in the Meriam idiom: *lar waikwereder taba zarge* 'The fish stay in their place'.¹²

6.2. Bird life and habitat

Reefs are also named after bird life. *Serar* reef is named after the tern (MM). *Tolitoli Nor* (*nor* 'reef') is named after the sandpiper, *toli* (MM). Birds' habitat can also be a source for naming. Raine Island, which is south of Mer and known to Meriam people through their sea travels, is called *Ebur bub werwer kaur*, literally: 'bird chest eggs island', because birds go there to nest and keep their eggs warm by covering them with their chests.¹³

6.3. Physical properties or relative location/direction

The physical dimension of the reef can be incorporated into its name. Adjectives such as *au* 'big' and *kebi* 'little' indicate the reef's relative size: *Au Meiri* and

---

7   Atai Wailu, pers. comm.
8   I am grateful to an anonymous reviewer for suggesting this second possibility.
9   I am assuming that the word has been borrowed from TSC rather than English although there may have been a local English at the time.
10 No-one can recall its former name.
11 Alo Tapim, pers. comm.
12 Alo Tapim, pers. comm.
13 Colin Scott (email 19 October 2009) was also given the alternate names: *Eburira Ged* 'bird-poss place', *Sub Kaur* 'foreign island' and *Maizab Kaur* which is also the name for Bramble Cay near Erub.

Kebi Meiri (*Meiri* – personal name of ancestor), *Au Siar* and *Kebi Siar* (*Siar* – personal name of ancestor), *Au Karmeri* and *Kebi Karmeri* (*Karmeri* – personal name of ancestor), *Au Bomi Nor* and *Kebi Bomi Nor* (*bomi* – from TSC *bomi* 'bommie or bombora').[14]

The relative location of a place can also be a source for naming. Two reefs called by the personal names of ancestors, *Madir* and *Marirar*, have alternative names identifying their relative location. *Madir* is also known as *Mer Au Nor*, literally: Mer Big Reef, because it is closer to Mer, and *Marirar* is also known as *Sanba Au Nor*, literally: Sanba (TSC) Big Reef, because it is closer to the sandbar, *Kérged*.

The name for the Barrier Reef itself, *Op Nor*, provides information about its direction and spatial orientation. *Op*, which is the personal name of an ancestor, also means front, face, upper or outside. Thus, *Op Nor* is the reef that faces directly into the southeasterly wind *sager*, an important wind in the Torres Strait.[15]

Placenames can also incorporate the names of objects which resemble the shape of the reef. In some instances, they are part of the name whilst in others, they are the name for the reef itself. As such, it is not a literal use of the name but a metaphorical use drawn from the similarity between object and reef. For example, the long, narrow shape of a handle is extended in meaning to refer to the shape of a reef: *Giau+lit* (*Giau* – personal name of an ancestor+handle), *Wabi+lit* (personal name of ancestor+handle) and possibly, *Tu+lit* (Tu – unknown origin+handle).

Other objects which are a source for placenames, include the leaves, roots and seeds of plants. For example, *Ap* is a reef named after the Macaranga shrub because its leaves are similar in shape to the outline of the reef. Other reefs named after plants are: *Sim Kep*, named after the hibiscus tree, and *Girwai*, named after the wild yam because it is round with roots growing away similar to that reef. *Sirib*[16] reef may also be related to the vine bearing the same name. The generic term for a small sunken reef *kep* is related to the word for a seed and hence, metaphorically extended in meaning to include small, sunken reefs.

Body parts can be a source for reefs' names because of their shape. The reef *Pokopoko* is named after the top of the turtle's intestines: *pokopoko teibur* because it twists around like a turtle's intestines. The reef *Ped*, which is the personal name of an ancestor, means literally 'bald'. Its appearance is similar to a bald man's patch as it has an outer circle and a solid coral mass in its centre. It is not named this way because of scarce resources.

---

14 My thanks to Anna Shnukal for pointing out its source.
15 Alo Tapim (pers. comm.)
16 My thanks to Anna Shnukal for pointing out the correct pronunciation.

6.4. Ecology or topography

Reefs are also named after their geological matter. Thus, the reef *Bur* is named after the MM word for saltwater mud from the adjective *burbur*, and *Akesakes* reef derives its name from the verb *dikes* meaning 'break into pieces' as the reef is large chunks of cracked and broken coral. Another reef *Zor*[17] means literally pumice stone. The reef *Wewe Mebgor*, shortened to *Mebgor*, is formed with the adjective *wewe* meaning 'sandy' and *Mebgor*, the personal name of an ancestor. A stretch of the Barrier Reef called *Garargarar Op Nor* is derived from the noun *garar* meaning 'raised rocky platform'.

Generic topographic features may also co-occur with a placename. In some cases, it has become an integral part of the name and in other cases, it is optional. For example, the Barrier reef is always called *Op Nor* and omission of the word *nor* yields a different meaning:

(1) **Ka nabakiamulu Op Norem.**
I'm going to the Barrier Reef.
ka   na-bakiamu-lu   Opnor-em [A]
1.SG.S   FUT.1-go-FUT.1.SG   Place-ALL

(2) **Ka nabakiamulu opem.**
I'm going to the front.

Note A: The following conventions are used for glossing in all examples: SG: singular; PL: plural; 1: first person; 3: third person; S: subject; PERF: perfective; FUT: future; INTR: intransiviser; NOM: nominaliser; O: accusative case; LOC: locative case; ALL: allative case.

In other instances, the topographic feature does not have to be overt, which suggests that it is not part of the placename. For example, when talking about the reef *Wad*, named after the personal name of an ancestor, the speaker can say:

(3) **Ka nabakiamulu Wadem/Wad norem.**
I'm going to Wad reef.
ka   nabakiamulu
1.SG.S   FUT.1-go-FUT.1SG
Wadem/Wad norem.
Place-ALL/Place reef-ALL

A topographic feature may also be used to identify a specific place within a place. For example, the reef *Eur*, named after an ancestor, has a passage through it called *Eur Kes* 'Eur passage'. A topographic feature may also be used to disambiguate between two places. The small reef close to the landsite *Ed* is usually called *Ed Kep* to disambiguate it from the landsite with that name.

---

17   It may actually be a stretch of reef.

7. Ancestral names

The most common source for the names of reefs are ancestors; that is, the places are named after the personal name of an ancestor, not what the ancestor did in that place. This contrasts with Australian Aboriginal placenames where the name generally evokes an incident or event associated with the Ancestral Being.

Around half of these personal ancestral names in Meriam have no literal meaning or the meanings have been lost. These include: *Aum, Asmet, Birig, Eur, Gaidan, Giau, Karas, Karmeri, Keud, Madir, Marirar, Meme, Mer, Merad, Neiri, Or, Sagore, Sarek, Seu, Simu* or *Smu, Soswared, Tobag,* and *Wad*.

A few of these personal ancestral names combine with a meaningful word. (These have already been discussed). They include: *Giau+lit* (Giau+handle), *Au/Kebi Meiri* (big/little Meiri),[18] *Tu+lit* (Tu+handle) and *Wabi+lit* (Wabi+handle). There is another ancestral placename, *Seutam,* which is derived from the ancestral name, *Seu,* and the word for the branch of a tree: *tam*. The ancestors, *Seu* and *Seutam,* were in a mother-daughter relationship. The use of the word 'branch' in the daughter's name signals through metaphor the relationship between parent and offspring.

Other ancestral placenames also have a literal meaning (some of which have already been discussed in earlier sections):

Girigiri 'bird of paradise'

Kérged 'ovary+place'?

Koki 'northwest wind'

Op 'front, face, upper or outside'

Ped 'bald'

Sam Karem 'cassowary'

Seibri 'crocodile',

Sepgiz 'earth+root'

Serar 'tern'

Siar 'cod'

---

18   These reefs are sometimes called in TSC Big Mary and Little Mary but Meriam speakers say that the ancestral name is *Meiri*.

Wai 'sprouting coconut'[19]

Wewe Mebgor 'sandy moon+saltwater?' (*gor* an earlier form of *gur* 'saltwater'?) or from 'sandy moon+slope'.[20]

There is a myth which details how reefs to the north of Mer came to be named:[21] There were ten brothers and one sister. While the brothers were building fences to stop thieves from entering, their sister, *Kérged*, would visit her girlfriends and speak ill of her brothers. When the eldest brother, *Limaranda*, heard about it, he got very angry. As Meriam law forbids gossip, he ordered his brothers to kill her and her girlfriends. The brothers took the girls and threw them into the water. These are the reefs named after the girlfriends: *Op*, *Aum*, *Kebi Meiri* and *Au Meiri*, *Birig*, *Or*, *Wabilit*, *Giaulit*, *Tulit*, *Garboi*, *Merad*, *Au Siar* and *Kebi Siar*, *Koki* and *Wad*. The brothers were too upset to throw their sister into the water so *Beizam*, the eldest in the group, took her and laid her down on the sandcay, *Kérged*. When *Limaranda* saw their actions, he banished his brothers from the island. The following reefs are named after them: *Marirar*, *Meme*, *Sarek*, *Gaidan*, *Madir*, *Karas* and *Ped*. Their physical proximity replicates the blood ties of the ancestral brothers.

8. Narrative names

There are a few reefs whose names evoke an incident, mishap or event that occurred at the place and as such, they can be categorised as narrative. These are not restricted to ancestral events and in fact, seem to indicate relatively recent origin given that some of the names are in TSC, which only arose in the late 1800's (Shnukal 1988: 5). The main protagonist(s) or an object associated with the event may be the source for the name.

For example, the reef *Ped* is also known as *Muma Kep*,[22] the name of the dinghy that nearly sank when it was overloaded with trochus shells. Similarly, *Digi Kep* (TSC) is named after a dinghy which sank at the place. *Nazir Bed* may also belong to this category with a name shift occuring when people started collecting trochus shell for payment.

In some cases, the person or people involved with the event have become the name for the place. For example, *Mesnare Nor* (TSC) was coined after the first

---

19   Ricardo Idagi, pers. comm.
20   Anna Shnukal (pers.comm.).
21   The story was told by Usiam Wailu to Colin Scott in English in August 2001 and told to me in Meriam in September 2006.
22   I have not investigated the use of alternate names in discourse or whether there are differences in register. This awaits further study.

missionaries spent a night there on their way to Erub (Darnley Island) in July 1871.[23] *Napolan Kep* is named after the man who was killed in that spot by sorcery when a shark ate him.[24] *Bologor Kep* is also known as *Zozi Spot* because a man called George/Zozi (TSC) was diving for trochus and mistook a bird for a big shark so swam back at full speed to his dinghy!

The coexistence of several names for reefs and/or the replacement of names with another name demonstrates the ongoing relationship between the people and their waters; that is, Meriam people continue to travel, hunt, dive and fish in these waters. When significant events occur, they are recounted back to family on Mer. The association of the person or thing to the place becomes the name for the place itself.

9. Miscellaneous names

There are a number of placenames whose origins are unknown. People cannot remember the reasons or circumstances for such names. Some possible lexical sources for the more opaque names have been provided:

Arbori Kep – possibly derived from the nominalised form of the verb: *darborik* 'to aim and miss' or *barbor* 'to stand out or be prominently visible'[25]

Au/Kebi Dudum 'big/little speed'

Bau Kep – possibly from the word *bau* 'seat' because of its shape or from a personal name

Dingi New Pas (TSC) 'Dinghy New Patch' – an alternative name to *Sepgiz*, the personal name of an ancestor

Wamkem – derived from the reduced form of *bisiwam* 'a type of grass skirt' and *kem* 'with'[26]

Werer 'Hunger' – possibly coined when someone became stranded and hungry or to identify it as hazardous and 'hungry' for dinghies[27]

Zer Kep 'banana skin' – possibly based on its shape or from resource depletion and stemming from the idiom: *No kaba zer eme abi* (literally: just banana skin hang fell) 'I have passed on all that I know'.

---

23   No-one can remember its former name.
24   Usiam Wailu (pers. comm.)
25   Alo Tapim (pers. comm.), has heard the place called Arborarbor Kep.
26   Alo Tapim (pers. comm.), believes it is associated with the women from Dauar island.
27   This was suggested by Jane Simpson (pers. comm.).

10. Coreferential names

There are a few reefs whose names coincide with the names of landsites or fishtraps. In some cases, these reefs are a short distance from the landsite bearing that name. It is conceivable that the name designates an area which includes both land and sea, or that the name for the landsite is extended seaward to include the reef. Thus, the reef *Karmeri* is a short distance from the site on Dauar island with that name. Likewise, *Ed Kep* is a small, sunken reef close to the landsite *Ed* on Mer.

There are, however, other reefs which are distant from the landsite or fishtrap with which it shares its name. For example, *Birig* reef is far from the landsite with that name and *Giau* reef is also some distance from the fishtrap with the same name. In such instances, one cannot argue that the shared name is based on proximal distance. Nonetheless, these places must be connected in some way. When Meriam people were asked about these, they could not provide an explanation. Whatever the connections, these have been forgotten.

There are, of course, examples of water sites in other areas which share a name and these may be some distance apart. Consider the two billabongs in the Roper River region in northern Australia called *Yawurlwarda*; one is near Roper Bar and the other, near Ngukurr (Baker 2002: 127). There are also two lakes, which are ecologically linked,[28] near Cape Keerweer on Cape York Peninsula called by the Wik people *Uthuk Eelen* or *Weenem Eelen* 'Small Milky Way' or 'Small Lawyer Cane' and *Uthuk Aweyn* or *Weenem Aweyn* 'Big Milky Way' or 'Big Lawyer Cane' (Sutton 2002: 79). While the above examples are freshwater sites, there are also saltwater sites sharing a name. For example, the Bardi people in Western Australia call several reefs *Mardaj* (Bowern 2009: 323). However, these examples all involve billabongs, lakes or reefs sharing a name with other billabongs, lakes or reefs whereas the Meriam reefs *Birig* and *Giau* share their name with a landsite and fishtrap.

Since these Meriam places are named after ancestors, it is reasonable to conclude that the ancestors were involved in some kind of incident at each place, both on land and at sea. Scott and Mulrennan in their discussion about land tenure on Erub island, a neighbouring island closely connected to the Meriam people, found that the same creation myths connect outlying reefs and cays to the home island (1999: 155). The Meriam coreferential names for places on land and at sea suggest a similar case.

---

28   Peter Sutton (pers. comm.)

11. Grammatical structure

Meriam placenames are grammatically nouns, nominal compounds or complex phrases.

They can be a common noun such as *Bur* 'Saltwater Mud', a personal name such as *Karas* or a nominalised verb such as *Akesakes*. These nouns can take nominal inflections. For example, in the following sentence, the placenames are suffixed with the locative inflection:

(4) **Ka nabakiamulu nazir atakrem Burge/Karasge/Akesakesge.**
I'm going to pick up trochus shell from Bur/Karas/Akesakes reefs.

ka	na-bakiamu-lu	nazir
1.SG.S	FUT.1-go-FUT.1SG	trochus.O
a-etaker-em	Bur/Karas/Akesakes-ge	
NOM-pick.up-ALL	Place-LOC	

Unlike Australian Aboriginal languages, there are no inflected verbs, verb phrases or headless relative clauses as placenames. Any verb which is part of a placename in Meriam, will be in a nominalised form. This is formed by dropping the first syllable in the verb and adding the prefix *a-*. For example, the reef *Akesakes* is derived from the nominalised form of the verb *dikes*.

Placenames can also be formed with a common noun or personal name plus a limited set of generic topographic terms (*wésor* 'sandcay or sandbar' is never used with placenames). Examples of compounds are: *Sim Kep* 'hibiscus+small.sunken.reef' or *Gaidan Pasis* 'ancestral name+passage (TSC)' or *Op Nor* 'ancestral name/front/face+reef.'

The grammatical structure of placenames with generic topographic terms varies. There are examples of placenames where the topographic feature has become incorporated into the name. For example, *Aum Kep* is a compound of an ancestral name and topographic term which is inflected as a single syntactic phrase:

(5) **Nar baitri Aum Kepge.**
The boat sank at Aum Kep.

nar	ba-iter-i	Aum+kep-ge
boat.S	INTR-immerse-PERF	Place-LOC

However, there are also examples where it is ambiguous as to whether the generic topographic term is part of the placename. For example, the reef *Akesakes* is inflected with or without the generic topographic feature:

(6) **Nar baitri Akesakesge.**

>   The boat sank at the reef Akesakes.
>   nar   ba-iter-i   Akesakes-ge
>   boat.S   INTR-immerse-PERF   Place-LOC

(7) **Wi emetu tabakomerti Akesakes Norlam.**
>   They've returned from Akesakes reef.
>   wi   emetu   ta-ba-akomeret-i
>   3PL.S   finish   TO-PL.S-return-PERF
>   Akesakes + nor-lam
>   Place + reef-ABL

Further work is needed to determine their precise grammatical status.

Placenames can be adjectival phrases formed with a modifier and head noun. Two examples were given earlier: *Adud Nor* 'bad reef' and *Au/Kebi Siar* 'big/little cod/personal name.' As there is a regular process for deriving modifiers from other parts of speech through reduplication, other adjectival phrases for placenames would include *Tolitoli Nor* 'tern+tern(adj) reef' and *Akesakes Nor* 'Broken up reef'. It may be that some of the common nouns used as placenames are reduced adjectival phrases.

Other types of complex nominal phrases for placenames are modifications of the grammatical types outlined above. Thus, there are placenames which are modified compounds: *Garargarar Op Nor* 'raised rocky platform(adj)+[front/personal name+reef]' or *Au/Kebi Bomi Nor* 'big/little(adj)+[bomi (TSC)+reef]', or there are complex phrases which are compounds with an embedded adjectival phrase: *Dingi New Pas* 'dinghy(TSC)+[new(adj from Eng)+patch(TSC)].' Similarly, the alternative names for *Madir* and *Marirar* are compounds with embedded adjectival phrases: *Mer Au Nor* 'Mer+[big+reef]' or *Sanba Au Nor* 'sandbar(TSC)+[big+reef].'

The Meriam placename for Raine Island: *Ebur bub werwer kaur*, can either be analysed as a string of associative phrases with an embedded adjectival phrase:

bird-chest-[egg(adj)+island], or as a single associative phrase formed with a whole-part type compound and an embedded adjectival phrase: [bird+chest]-[egg(adj)+island].

12. Conclusion

This study has focussed on the linguistic content and semantic classification of Meriam saltwater placenames. Sources for semantic categories are ancestral, descriptive or physical and narrative. Taking into account alternative names and multiple associations with categories, the most common sources are ancestral (62 per cent) and descriptive (55 per cent). The overall high proportion from these semantic domains reflects the very personal relationship that Meriam people have with their environment; these reefs are not only an integral part of their physical environment through travel, hunting and fishing but also a link to their ancestral past.

Comparisons with other Indigenous placename studies show remarkable similarities with a focus on the environment and its physical characteristics, connections to the flora and fauna, and mythological/ancestral associations. Furthermore, features from several categories are sometimes combined, such as landscape and mythology. However, there are major differences with the mythological/ancestral names. While the Australian Aboriginal placenames evoke an event associated with the mythological being, the Meriam and Marquesan placenames are named overtly after the personal name of an ancestor.

An interesting feature of some Meriam saltwater placenames is their shared name with a landsite or fishtrap. In some instances, the proximity of the two sites accounts for the same placename being used. In other cases, where these are distant, a possible explanation could be that the same ancestor was involved in events at both sites. It may also be suggestive of a close connection between land and sea in Meriam culture as put forth by Scott and Mulrennan (1999: 153).

Whether or not the same naming patterns can be found across the Torres Strait remains an open question. Maritime places listed in the statements from the two Erub claimants for the sea claim, George Mye and William (Bully) Saylor (September 2007) suggest similar patterns. However, it is essential that indigenous people's knowledge and information about their places be fully documented for future generations. The urgency of this task has been brought home to me by the death of two dear friends and contributors for this study, Atai and Usiam Wailu.

Map 1: Torres Strait.

Source: Torres Strait Island Regional Council.

9. Saltwater Placenames around Mer in the Torres Strait

Map 2: Outer reefs for Mer, Dauar and Waier.

Source: Courtesy of Atai Wailu, Native Title Office, Torres Strait Regional Authority, 2008.

Indigenous and Minority Placenames

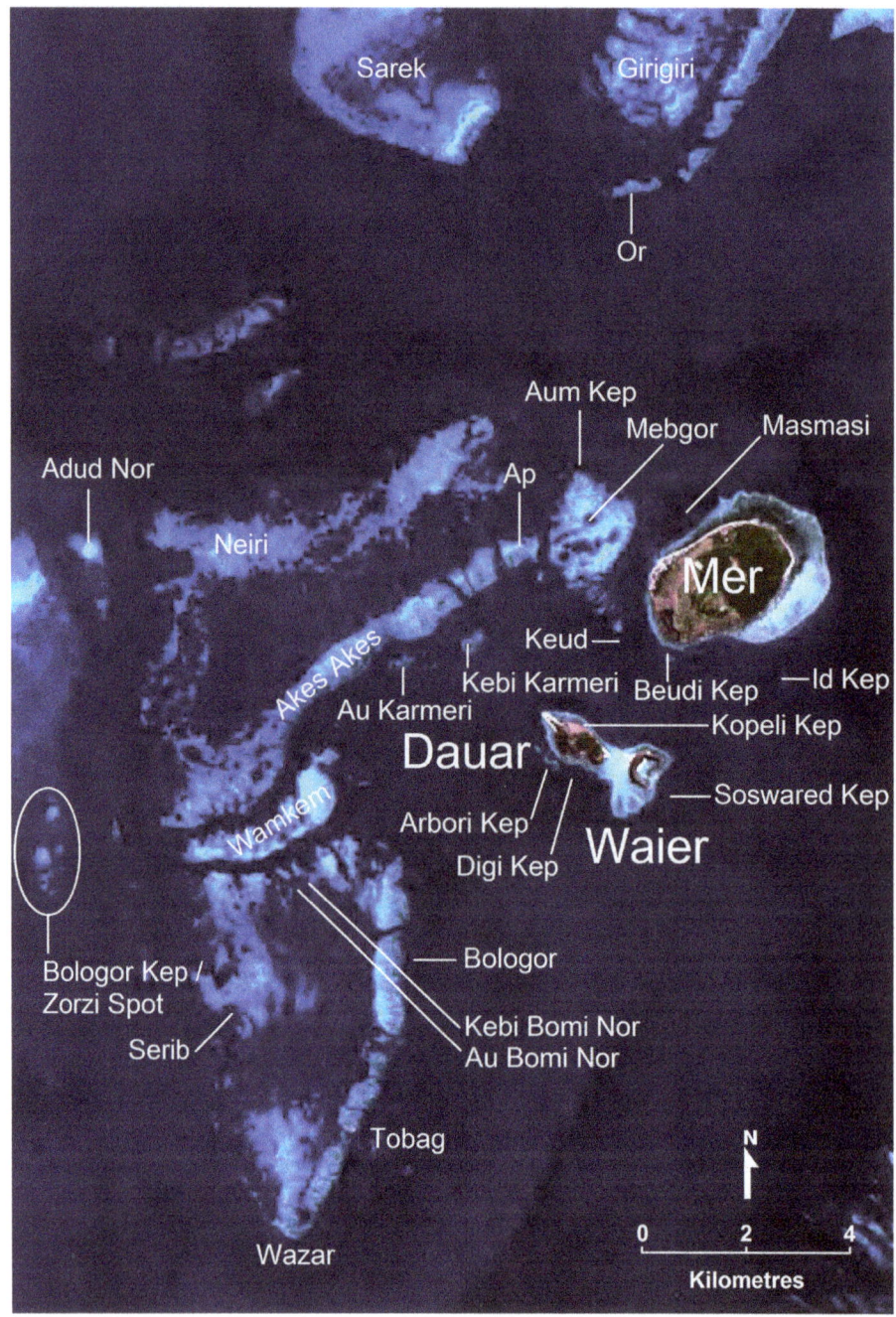

Map 3: Inner reefs for Mer, Dauar and Waier.

Source: Courtesy of Atai Wailu, Native Title Office, Torres Strait Regional Authority, 2008.

List of Placenames and Meanings

nor	reef
kep	small, sunken reef
pasis	passage (TSC)
kes	passage

To the north of Mer:

Asmet Kep	Ancestral name; also known as Asmed Kep
Bau Kep	Unknown origin; possibly from the proper name Bau or the noun meaning 'seat'?
Birig	Ancestral name
Gaidan	Ancestral name
Gaidan Pasis	Ancestral name
Garboi	Ancestral name (not on map)
Giau	Ancestral name; also known as Giawei, Gawei or Giawi
Giaulit	Ancestral/Descriptive name; literally: Giau + handle; also known
Girigiri	Ancestral/Descriptive name; as Giaulet literally: bird of paradise
Karas	Ancestral name
Kérged	Ancestral/Descriptive name; literally: ovary + place?
Madir	Ancestral/Descriptive name; also known as Mer Au Nor literally: Mer big reef
Marirar	Ancestral/Descriptive name; also known as Sanba Au Nor literally: 'sandbar' (TSC) big reef; also known as Marir
Meiri (Au/Kebi)	Ancestral/Descriptive name; literally: big/little Meiri
Mesnare Nor	Narrative name; literally: missionary reef; so called because the missionaries spent their first night there on their way to Erub
Nazir Bed	Historical/Descriptive name; literally: trochus shell and bed (TSC)
Or	Ancestral name
Ped	Ancestral/Descriptive/Narrative name; literally: bald; also known as Muma(r) kep
Sarek	Ancestral name
Seibri	Ancestral/Descriptive name; literally: crocodile
Sepgiz	Ancestral/Descriptive name; literally: earth + root; also known as Dingi New Pas literally: dinghy new 'patch' (TSC)
Seu	Ancestral name
Seutam	Ancestral/Descriptive name; literally: Seu + branch

Siar (Au/Kebi)	Ancestral /Descriptive name; literally: big/little cod
Simu	Ancestral name; also known as Smu
Wabilit	Ancestral/Descriptive name; literally: Wabi + handle; also known as Wabilet
Wad	Ancestral name
Zor	Descriptive name; literally: pumice stone

Close to Mer, Dauar and Waier:

Akesakes	Descriptive name; from the nominalised form of dikes 'broken into pieces'
Ap	Descriptive name; literally: Macaranga shrub
Arbori Kep	Unknown origin; from the nominalised form of darborik 'throw' or darbor 'prominent'?
Aum Kep	Ancestral name; also the name for the cloud that hangs directly above Mer
Beudu Kep	?
Digi Kep	Narrative name; also known as Dingi Kep; named after a dinghy which sank there
Gebar	? (not on map)
Id Kep	Unknown origin; also known as Ed Kep; the same name as the adjacent land site
Karmeri (Au/Kebi)	Ancestral/Descriptive name; literally: big/little Karmeri
Keud	Ancestral name
Kopoli Kep	Descriptive/Narrative name; literally: sea perch; also related to a secret event
Lager Kep	Descriptive name; literally: vine (not on map)
Masmasi Kep	?
Mebgor	Ancestral/Descriptive name; also known as Wewe Mebgor literally: sandy moon + saltwater? or sandy moon + slope
Sagore	Ancestral name
Soswared Kep	Ancestral name

To the southwest of Mer:

Adud Nor	Descriptive name; literally: bad reef (not on map)
Neiri	Ancestral name
Pokopoko	Descriptive name; literally: turtle's intestines
Sam Karem	Ancestral name; literally: cassowary deep channel (not on map)

To the east of Mer:

Op Nor	Ancestral/Descriptive name; literally: front/face/upper/outside

9. Saltwater Placenames around Mer in the Torres Strait

To the south of Mer:

Bologor Kep (Au/Kebi) Descriptive/Narrative name; literally: big/little sawfish; also	known as Zozi (George) spot because George mistook a diving bird for a shark
Bomi Nor (Au/Kebi)	Unknown origin/Descriptive name; literally: big/little bombora?
Bur	Descriptive name; literally: saltwater mud
Dudum (Au/Kebi)	Unknown origin/Descriptive name; literally: big/little speed
Eur (Kes)	Ancestral name
Garargarar Op Nor	Descriptive name; literally: raised rocky platform front reef; a raised rocky area used by birds for rest and nesting
Girwai	Descriptive name; literally: wild yam
Lim	Unknown origin; literally: sun (not on map)
Mer Kep	Ancestral name
Napolan Kep	Narrative name; name of someone killed by sorcery
Pakor	Descriptive name; literally: red bass (not on map)
Serar	Descriptive name; literally: tern
Sirib	Descriptve name; literally: a type of vine
Sim Kep	Ancestral/Descriptive name; literally: hibiscus tree
Tobag	Ancestral name
Tolitoli Nor	Descriptive name; literally: sandpipers; also a landsite
Tulit	Unknown origin/Descriptive; literally: Tu-handle (not on map)
Unui Ubi	? (not on map)
Wai	Ancestral/Descriptive name; literally: sprouting coconut
Wamkem	Unknown origin; related to bisiwam 'type of grass skirt'?; literally: grass skirt-with; connected to an incident with the Dauar women?
Wazar	Descriptive name; related to the modern MM word zar 'the place where the fish go to hide'
Zer Kep	Unknown origin; literally: banana skin

Not listed on the map and precise location unknown:

Edgor	?
Koki	Ancestral name; literally: northwest wind
Meme (Nor)	Ancestral name; also known as Meimei Nor
Werer	Unknown origin; literally: hunger

References

Alpher, B. 2002, 'The archaism and linguistic connections of some Yir-Yoront tract-names', in *The Land is a Map: Placenames of Indigenous Origin in Australia*, L. Hercus, F. Hodges and J. Simpson (eds), Pandanus Books in association with Pacific Linguistics, Canberra: 131–139.

Alpher, B., G. O'Grady and C. Bowern 2008, 'Western Torres Strait language classification and development', in *Morphology and Language History: In Honour of Harold Koch*, C. Bowern, B. Evans and L. Miceli (eds), Benjamins, Amsterdam/Philadelphia: 15–30.

Baker, B. 2002, '"I'm going to where her brisket is": placenames in the Roper', in *The Land is a Map: Placenames of Indigenous Origin in Australia*, L. Hercus, F. Hodges and J. Simpson (eds), Pandanus Books in association with Pacific Linguistics, Canberra: 103–129.

Bowern, C. 2009, 'Naming Bardi places', in *Aboriginal Placenames: Naming and Re-naming the Australian Landscape*, L. Hercus and H. Koch (eds), ANU E Press and Aboriginal History Inc., Canberra: 327–346.

Cablitz, G. 2008, 'When "what" is "where": a linguistic analysis of landscape terms, place names and body part terms in Marquesan (Oceanic, French Polynesia)', in *Language and Landscape: A Cross-linguistic Perspective*, N. Burenhult and S. Levinson (eds), Language Sciences 30: 200–226.

Henshaw, A. 2006, 'Pausing along the journey: learning landscapes, environmental change and toponymy amongst the Sikusilarmiut', *Arctic Anthropology* 43(1): 52–66.

Hercus, L. and J. Simpson 2002, 'Indigenous placenames: an introduction', in *The Land is a Map: Placenames of Indigenous Origin in Australia*, L. Hercus, F. Hodges and J. Simpson (eds), Pandanus Books in association with Pacific Linguistics, Canberra: 1–23.

Mye, G. 'Witness Statement', in *Leo Akiba and George Mye on behalf of the Torres Strait Islanders of the Regional Seas Claim Area and the State of Queensland and others*, Federal Court of Australia November 2001.

Saylor, W.H. 'Witness Statement', in *Leo Akiba and George Mye on behalf of the Torres Strait Islanders of the Regional Seas Claim Area and the State of Queensland and others*, Federal Court of Australia November 2001.

Scott, C. and M. Mulrennan 1999, 'Land and sea tenure at Erub', *Oceania* 70: 146–176.

Shnukal, A. 1988, 'Broken, an introduction to the creole language of Torres Strait', *Pacific Linguistics Series* C(107).

Sutton, P. 2002, 'On the translatability of placenames in the Wik Region, Cape York Peninsula', in *The Land is a Map: Placenames of Indigenous Origin in Australia*, L. Hercus, F. Hodges and J. Simpson (eds), Pandanus Books in association with Pacific Linguistics, Canberra: 75–86.

Thornton, T. 1977, 'Anthropological studies of Native American place naming', *American Indian Quarterly* 21(2): 209–228.

Wailu, A. 'Witness Statement', in *Leo Akiba and George Mye on behalf of the Torres Strait Islanders of the Regional Seas Claim Area and the State of Queensland and others*, Federal Court of Australia November 2001.

10. Pinning down Kaurna names: Linguistic issues arising in the development of the Kaurna Placenames Database

Rob Amery
University of Adelaide

Vincent (Jack) Kanya Buckskin
Kaurna Warra Pintyanthi
University of Adelaide

Kaurna people are in the process of reclaiming their identity and their language, a language that was considered to be 'extinct' by many or 'sleeping' by the people themselves (see Amery 2000a). Kaurna people have expressed the view at Kaurna Warra Pintyanthi (KWP) meetings that they wish to see Kaurna words spelt and pronounced correctly and are keen to see that Aboriginal placenames in use on the Adelaide Plains conform to the sound patterns of the language. Names that appear to be of Indigenous origin are being sifted through. Those that can be verified as Kaurna names are retained, others are discarded and some are translated into Kaurna or adapted into the Kaurna sound and spelling systems.

We are attempting to also pin down the meanings of Kaurna placenames. It can be shown (see Amery 2002) that some etymologies that have been put forward are fanciful and verifiably false. Others are highly questionable. In many cases we simply do not know. There are also difficulties in determining what a particular name relates to, or whether variants are simply spelling variations for the same word, or were in fact attempts to spell different though somewhat similar names. So pinning down the form depends on pinning down the meaning and vice-versa.

A set of principles for dealing with such uncertainty has been developed by KWP. We will give many examples where these principles can be applied and other examples where we are still at a loss as to how we should deal with the names in question.

Kaurna people are also reinstating some of the original names through Dual-Naming legislation with the help of the South Australian state government

Geographical Names Unit. Other features, notably parks and wetlands, are being named with Kaurna names that relate in some way to the geographical features, local vegetation or indeed to commemorate Kaurna ancestors (see Amery and Williams 2002; Amery and Rigney 2006). In addition, since 1980 many organisations, programs, buildings, rooms and events etc are being given Kaurna names. This naming activity began slowly, but has increased exponentially over the last few decades.

The Kaurna community has been at the forefront of efforts by Aboriginal peoples in urban areas to reinstate and strengthen an identity, a people, a culture and a language. Similar efforts are also being made in Sydney (see Troy and Walsh, 2009), Melbourne, Perth, Canberra and other centres, sometimes drawing on the Kaurna experience for inspiration and support. When the naming of Adelaide city parks was first invoked there was some concern regarding the length of some Kaurna names and perceived pronunciation difficulties (see 'Unsayable Adelaide' letter to the editor, *The Advertiser*, Monday 10 February 1997), but also a very positive and encouraging letter in response ('All South Australians can feel proud', *The Advertiser*, Saturday 15 February 1997: 24). Reportage has been factual and neutral to positive. Since then there has been no further response. Adelaideans fully accept the Kaurna names.

1. Introduction

Kaurna is the language of the Adelaide Plains, a small tract of land in South Australia extending west of the Mount Lofty Ranges from Crystal Brook and Clare in the north to Cape Jervis south of Adelaide. Various wordlists were compiled by a range of observers. A number of these wordlists include placenames, notably Teichelmann and Schürmann (1840), Williams (1840), Piesse (1840) and Wyatt (1879). Others also recorded placenames. Snippets of information from various sources were collected by Norman B. Tindale who compiled a series of placenames card files, including one of Kaurna placenames (Tindale n.d.). Compilers of books on South Australian placenames, notably Cockburn (1990), Manning (1990) and Praite and Tolley (1970) also include odd pieces of information and it is often difficult or impossible to track down the source of specific snippets of information in these publications. Chester Schultz has been engaged over the past five years in the laborious task of sifting through archives and old records in an attempt to do just this – find wherever possible the earliest records in that small window when colonists heard the Kaurna names directly from the mouths of native speakers of Kaurna. See Schultz (2011, 2012) and earlier work (Schultz 1999).

10. Pinning down Kaurna names

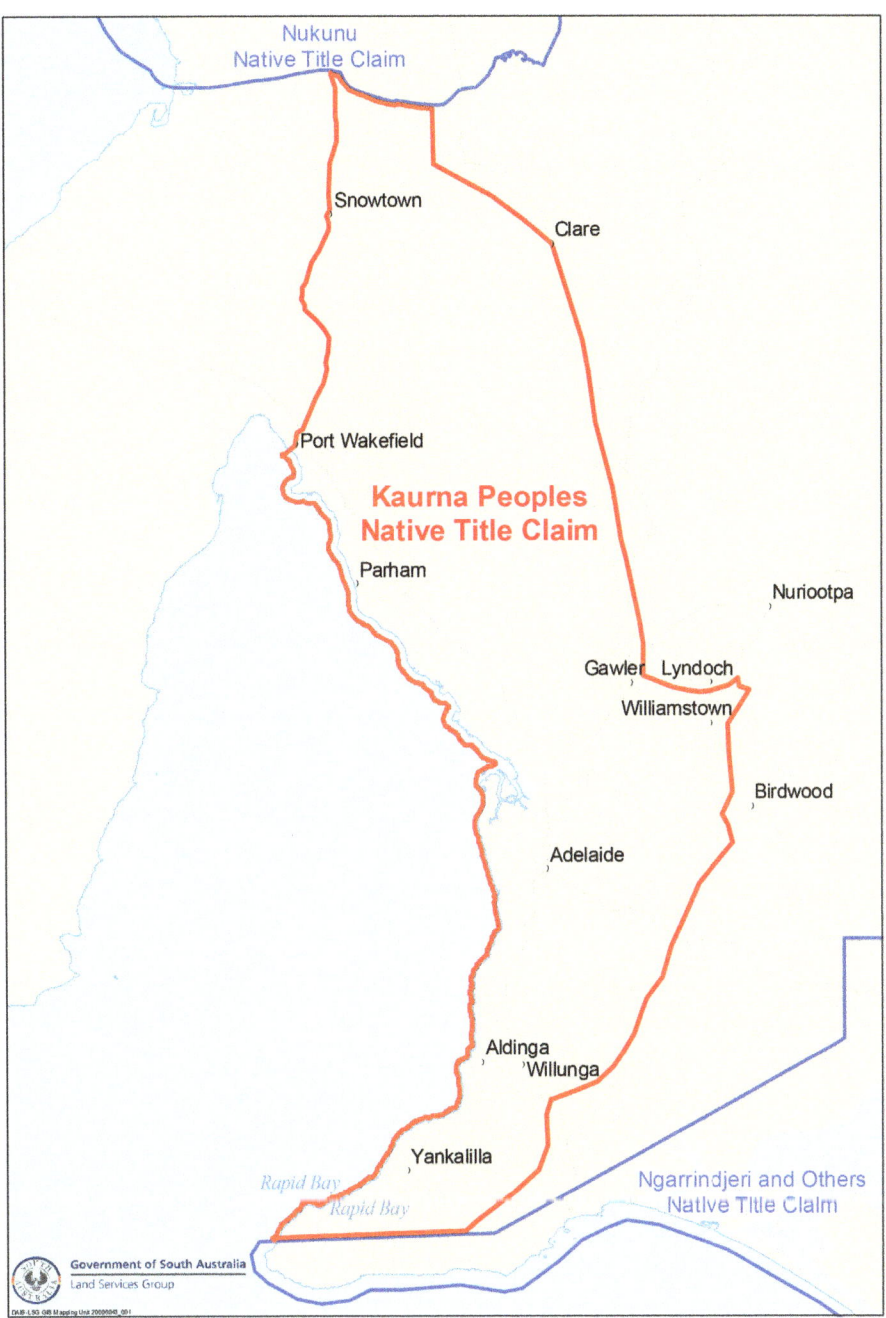

Map 1: Kaurna Native Title Claim map.

Source: Government of South Australia, Land Services Group.

Kaurna is a language that is undergoing a renaissance. It was probably last spoken on a daily basis no later than the 1860s. Many, including Teichelmann (1857), who knew the Kaurna people well, have described it as 'dead' or 'extinct' (see Amery 2000a: 49 for further details), though Kaurna people themselves would prefer to think of it as a 'sleeping' language which is being 'woken up'. The Kaurna language is being re-learnt and re-introduced on the basis of the aforementioned written records.

Placenames are of increasing interest to members of the public. Accordingly, in 2006 the City of Onkaparinga initiated a project to display Kaurna names on Google Earth maps on the internet. This project is a collaborative work between the Geographical Names Unit (GNU) of South Australia, Kaurna Warra Pintyanthi (KWP) based at the University of Adelaide (see www.adelaide.edu.au/kwp), the Tappa Iri business centre and the four southern councils (City of Onkaparinga, City of Marion, City of Holdfast Bay and Yankalilla). The GNU provides geographic information system (GIS) information, assists in locating the names and makes its archives accessible. KWP makes judgements about the form (that is, morphology, spelling and pronunciation) and the meaning of the names. The City of Onkaparinga provided overall coordination and management of the project and a reference committee was established that drew all partners together. Beanstalk, a website developer, was contracted to build the webpages and facilitate importation of data from the database, whilst the database itself was developed by the GNU and KWP. Some information is displayed publicly, whilst other more technical, controversial or sensitive material is password-protected (for the use of Kaurna people, project partners and legitimate researchers). The webpages may be viewed at http://www.kaurnaplacenames.com.

Some of Schultz's research, which is included in Schultz (1999, 2011, 2012), and write-ups of additional names is posted on the KWP webpages. Much more will be posted in due course with links from the Kaurna Placenames website.

2. Research questions

Toponymy research concerns a number of different but inter-related parameters. These inter-relationships are heightened where researchers are trying to make sense of patchy historical documentation in the absence of native speakers, as Schultz (2011) discusses in some detail. This paper investigates placenames in terms of:

i) Form

    a. What is the underlying phonemic representation?

b. How should the name be represented in public?

ii) Morphology

a. Is the name composed of several morphemes (meaningful parts)? It may consist of one or more roots plus one or more suffixes.

iii) Meaning

a. Does the name have a meaning at all? It may not.

b. What are the different documented meanings?

c. What is the evidence/counter-evidence supporting or detracting from each of these meanings?

iv) Etymology

a. What is the language(s) of origin of the name?

b. How did the name come to be applied to the particular feature or location?

v) Referent or Location

a. What geographical or physical feature does the name apply to?

b. What is the extent of the reference? Is it a specific feature able to be identified with a pin on a map, is it a bounded area, is it a diffuse, unbounded feature, or does the name operate at several levels simultaneously?

c. What is the relationship between the original name and the current entity to which the name applies?

Because of imprecise early spelling, to identify the form we need to know the meaning. To identify the meaning we need precision in the recording of the form. To judge the plausibility of a given meaning we need to understand the limits of the recording of the form and the various possibilities for its underlying phonemic representation. To know which meaning is possible or plausible, we need to know about the location. Any information about the etymology or history of the name helps to complete the picture. Morphology assists greatly in identifying the source language(s) and in turn the form, meaning and etymology.

Whilst much of the research carried out at the direction of KWP concerns placenames that have been in use for time immemorial and/or have been documented in the historical literature, research is not limited to these. Placenaming is ongoing, and with successes in the revival of the Kaurna language, new Kaurna placenaming activity is taking place. This recent activity will be discussed in section 7 towards the end of the paper, including some uncertainties that have arisen in the process.

3. The form of Kaurna placenames and their representation

3.1. Underlying phonemic representation and pronunciation

Pronunciation is being reconstructed through comparison of variant spellings employed by the same observer, different spellings of the same word employed by different observers and through comparison with related forms in neighbouring languages. We can be 100 per cent confident about the pronunciation of some words, but there is an element of guesswork with others. At times there is an exceedingly large dose of guesswork involved. For instance, there were most likely three contrasting r-sounds in Kaurna. Not surprisingly, most who recorded Kaurna placenames made no effort to distinguish between them. Even Teichelmann and Schürmann (1840), henceforth T&S, who were far better at recording Kaurna words than most, did not adequately distinguish between them. They recorded the name for the River Torrens as Karrauwirraparri (RS Karrawirra Pari)[1] with three lots of double rr's. We know from comparison with other languages that the first two sets are rolled or trilled rr's whilst the rr in T&S *parri* is a glide as in Australian English. T&S spelling is of little help in deciding the pronunciation of the r's or the t, l and n sounds, which may be interdental (tongue between the teeth), alveolar (as in English) or retroflex (tongue tip turned back).

3.2. Orthography issues

3.2.1. T&S spellings

The German missionaries compiled by far the most comprehensive records of the language and their spellings, despite some shortcomings, are reasonably consistent and systematic. For the first 20 years of Kaurna language revival efforts since the early 1990s, we employed T&S spellings and when words from other sources were co-opted they were re-spelt to fit in with T&S conventions (see Amery 2003). Most importantly T&S spellings afforded the revived language an authenticity as the words used could be more readily traced back to the original source material.

---

1 Throughout this paper, by necessity, a mixture of different spelling conventions are employed. Placenames generally appear in regular font as they appear on the map or in published sources. At times these names also appear as they would be spelt in the Revised Spelling system adopted in 2010 in which case they are preceded by the letters RS. Placenames on the Kaurna Placenames website also appear in a form adapted to T&S spelling conventions which were sanctioned by the Kaurna language revival movement prior to 2010, though these will soon appear in Revised Spelling. Regular Kaurna words and phrases appear in italics in Revised Spelling.

3.2.2. Revised Kaurna spellings (2010)

In 2010 at the urging of Buckskin, who was by that time the main teacher of the Kaurna language across multiple programs, the Kaurna language movement adopted a phonemically inspired orthography which more closely represented the distinctive sounds of Kaurna. The uncertainties in knowing how to pronounce many Kaurna words was confusing and disconcerting for students, and rather than having to frequently check with Amery, Buckskin wanted to pin down the pronunciations once and for all. This could be done once firm decisions were made about the underlying phonemic representation of each and every word based on extensive language-internal and comparative research. Orthography issues were discussed at a number of KWP meetings and several versions of the new spelling system were trialled within a PowerPoint presentation that had been prepared for the Kaurna Learner's Guide (Amery and Simpson 2013). In this way KWP members and teachers and community members at Kaurna Plains School could see what the new spelling conventions would look like. Where there is absolutely no evidence to indicate vowel length, short vowels are employed, unless there are other considerations such as to avoid a linguistic taboo. For example, Buckskin argued for the spelling of T&S *nepo* 'neighbour; friend' as *niipu*, though there is no evidence to suggest a long vowel, in order to avoid association with English 'nipple'. Likewise, if there is no evidence to suggest an interdental or retroflex consonant, then usually alveolars (t, n and l as in English) are employed, unless there is a particular need to differentiate between two similar words. The glide r as in Australian English is usually the default r-sound, unless there is evidence to the contrary.

Buckskin immediately began to use the revised Kaurna spellings in 2010 in his evening Kaurna language classes with adult students and in his day classes with adolescent students at Salisbury High School. He saw how easily students learnt the new spelling system which gave certainty and precision as to how Kaurna words should be written and pronounced. At the same time, Amery began to use revised spelling in the script of radio shows in preparation in 2010, and saw how easily participants were able to adapt to the new system, despite their previous considerable familiarity with T&S spellings. The revised spelling system was explained in depth and taught throughout 2012 and early 2013 within the TAFE Certificate III course 'Learning an Endangered Aboriginal Language (Kaurna)' where all students responded very positively. All who have actually used the revised spelling system have found it easy to understand and apply.

3.2.3. Spelling of Kaurna placenames

The spelling of many Kaurna placenames in common use that appear in the street directory or on road maps bears little relationship to the original word. Examples such as Aldinga (probably /ngaltingka/), Onkaparinga (/ngangkiparingka/), Myponga (/maitpangka/ or /matypangka/) and Patawolonga (probably /pathawilyangka/) demonstrate this.

T&S spellings were promoted up-front on the Google Earth maps on the placenames website. That was the spelling system in use by the Kaurna language movement at the time of establishment of the placenames project. In the database underpinning the website, all known spellings of the names and their sources are recorded and an attempt is being made to reconstruct the original forms. This is done using the analytic spelling system adopted by Simpson and Hercus (2004: 180) which uses lowercase letters when we are certain of the underlying phoneme and uppercase letters when we cannot tell its value with any degree of confidence. So for example in /ngALTingka/ Aldinga, there are three sources of uncertainty. The first vowel A could be a long aa [a] as in 'Bart' or a short a [ʌ] as in 'b*u*t'. The L and T could be either interdental /lhth/ with the tongue between the teeth, alveolar /lt/ as in English 'be*lt*', or retroflex /rlrt/ with the tongue tip curled back. In both the T&S spellings used up until 2010 and the revised spelling system, Aldinga will be rendered Ngaltingga.

The Kaurna name for McLaren Vale, spelt variously as Doringo, Taringa, Tarranga, Tu-run-ga, Dooronga, Doo-ronga, Daringa, Taranga, Tarangk, is even worse.[2] We can represent it as /thVRVngka/ where there are three sources of uncertainty. We know that a t-sound at the beginning of a word is always interdental, so we can confidently write /th/. However, we are not sure whether the vowel in the first syllable is /a/ or /u/ or whether it is short or long. The r-sound could be either a rolled /rr/ = [r], tapped /rd/ = [ɾ] or glided /r/ = [ɹ]. There is so much discrepancy between the sources that we are not certain what kind of vowel is in the second syllable. It is unclear whether it is [ɪ] as in 'b*i*t', [ʌ] as in 'b*u*t' or [ʊ] as in 'p*u*t'. Given so much uncertainty, we simply indicate that there is some kind of vowel present. This spelling is ideal for analytical purposes because it signals immediately the areas of certainty and uncertainty, but it is obviously less than ideal for use with the public. But any version of this particular name for public display is something of a blind guess.

Knowledge of Kaurna phonotactics helps reduce some of the uncertainty. Only certain sounds (p, th, k, m, nh, ng, w, y) are allowable at the beginning of words and every word must end with a vowel. Because Kaurna words never commence with alveolar or retroflex consonants, we decided to write the initial interdental /th/ and /nh/ sounds as t and n respectively, though they should actually be

---

2   The wide range of variant spellings raise the possibility that there may even have been two similar names for two different localities in close proximity within the McLaren Vale area.

pronounced with the tongue between the teeth. Long vowels are only permitted in the first syllable. Initial consonant clusters, with the possible exception of thR, are not permitted. Syllables in Kaurna are either CV, CVC or rarely CVCC.

3.2.4. Revised Kaurna spelling and placenames

Placenames are undoubtedly the most difficult area of the language in which to implement spelling reforms and especially so in the case of Kaurna. This is because so many Kaurna placenames have no known meaning and many were recorded by unknown individuals or as one-off instances. So there is no way of checking author spelling preferences. It is really only in the case of the four wordlists mentioned earlier, that is Teichelmann and Schürmann (1840), Williams (1840), Piesse (1840) and Wyatt (1879), that any determination can be made as to the kinds of conventions adhered to by the recorder. With questionable spellings and in the absence of a trusted meaning there are few cues by which we can relate many placenames to other recorded words. Kaurna placenames researchers, Schultz and Amery, look for plausible endings or suffixes and plausible meanings (see below), but many attempts to arrive at phonemic spellings for Kaurna placenames are really clutching at straws or making stabs in the dark and it is important that this is recognised.

Many Kaurna placenames of course are in use in the public domain on maps, in street directories and in other publications. They also appear on signage. Kaurna placenames are the most visible aspect of the living Kaurna culture in the landscape on the Adelaide Plains. The Kaurna language has no visibility in the commercial world, such as on billboards or in advertisements etc. To date there is no strong movement for the replacement of existing names or signage as with, for instance, the replacement of Peking with Beijing or Bombay with Mumbai. Adelaide City Council has recently been made aware of the revised spellings for Kaurna names for the parks and squares. In the event that signage is replaced, revised spellings may then be adopted. Indeed, new requests for names of parks, streets, trails, bridges or other named places which are put to KWP since 2011 are being spelt with revised Kaurna spellings. This results in a number of different spelling conventions being used concurrently, which is far from ideal.

In due course, the public will be made aware of the revised spellings alongside of spellings in current use. As at the time of writing the Kaurna Placenames website displays the T&S spelling alongside the heading "Kaurna Name", whereas the name in public usage appears alongside "Common Name". For example:

Kaurna Name: Wommamukurta

Common Name: Mount Barker

Additional Notes: Also recorded as Womma Mukarta, Yaktanga.

Spelling issues for the Kaurna Placenames website were discussed at the KWP meeting on 15 November 2012. The meeting resolved to create an additional field "Old Spelling" and to migrate the content of the current "Kaurna Name" category to "Old Spelling" whilst the Revised Spelling form will be inserted in the Kaurna Name field. Thus, the entry above will appear as:

Kaurna Name: Wamamukurta

Common Name: Mount Barker

Old Spelling: Wommamukurta

Additional Notes: Also recorded as Womma Mukarta, Yaktanga.

The Common Name may in fact be a Kaurna name and in the case of names presently approved by KWP it will be exactly the same as the Kaurna name as in the case of the Defence SA 23 hectare reserve named Kardi Yarta 'emu ground' (KWP Minutes, 26 October 2011). Even for some long-standing names such as Yultiwirra, the Old Spelling may be identical to the Revised Spelling, so that it is possible that all three fields may be identical.

3.3. The shape (morphology) of Kaurna words and placenames

Morphology is the intersection between form and meaning. Morphology analyses words into their smallest meaningful parts (morphemes) and is sometimes an essential step in determining possible meanings of placenames.

Most Kaurna words consist of a single two syllable morpheme. Quite a few consist of a three-syllable morpheme. Less commonly they might be a single syllable with a long vowel. Like other Australian languages, Kaurna uses case suffixes instead of prepositions and for a number of other functions, so Kaurna nouns may take quite a range of endings which sometimes occur in documented placenames.

Many Kaurna placenames appear with a location suffix *-ngga* (/-ngka/) on two-syllable roots (e.g. Nurlungga, Waitpingga, Maitpangga and Wilangga) or *-illa* (/-ila/) on three-syllable roots (e.g. Kawantilla, Yarnkalyilla and Kangkarrilla). A special concession was adopted within the revised spelling system introduced in late 2010 in relation to this locative suffix on placenames. The T&S spellings, -ngga and -illa, are retained on placenames (spelt with initial capitalisation), whilst -ngka and -ila are employed on common nouns.

As a result of this spelling convention, *nurlungka* (/nhurlungka/) means 'at the corner' but Nurlungga with exactly the same pronunciation but slightly different spelling means 'at Nurlu' (or 'at Nurlo' in its original form). The name

Nurlu 'corner; curvature' refers to 'the Horseshoe' (the bend on the Onkaparinga River at Old Noarlunga). We could use other case suffixes in other contexts such as *nurlunangku* 'from the corner' vs Nurlunangku 'from Nurlu (Old Noarlunga)', *nurlulityangka* 'in the vicinity of the corner' vs Nurlulityangga 'in the vicinity of Nurlu (Old Noarlunga)', *nurlu-ana* 'to the corner' vs Nurlu-ana 'to Nurlu', *nurlu-arra* 'alongside Nurlu' vs Nurlu-arra 'via Nurlu'.

Often placenames have been recorded both with and without the location suffix as in Tarndanya vs Tarndanyangga;[3] Warriparri vs Warriparringga and Pattawilya vs Pattawilyangga. How should the name appear on the map? Should these pairs of names be regarded as one or two names? The foregoing pairs have been listed as separate names because they now refer to distinct locations or entities. Tarndanya refers to the city of Adelaide south of the Torrens as specified in T&S (1840: 75) whilst Tarndanyangga has been used in dual-naming Victoria Square in the heart of the city. Warriparri refers to the Sturt River, whilst Warriparringga refers to the specific Warriparinga site formerly known as Laffers Triangle where the Living Kaurna Cultural Centre is located. Pattawilya refers to Glenelg, whilst Pattawilyangga refers to the Patawalonga waterway. However, in their original form and reference, these names referred to one and the same place, the place itself vs being at that place.

Kaurna also has a dual suffix *-rla* or *-dla* which contrasts with the plural suffix *-rna*. The dual suffix appears in Yuridla 'ear-two' and Pikudla 'eyebrow-two'. In the neighbouring Nukunu language, the dual suffix is *-pila*. Thus Yurrebilla is probably just another form of the name Yuridla meaning 'two ears' referring to the two peaks Mt Lofty and Mt Bonython. It is known that at the time of first contact there were several dialects of Kaurna. The fact that the neighbouring closely-related language to the north (Nukunu) uses *-pila* leads us to speculate that it could also be the form of the dual suffix in one of the more northerly Kaurna dialects. Assuming Yuridla equals Yurrebilla, how should we treat them today? Yuridla these days refers to the nearby town of Uraidla, whilst Yurrebilla refers to a walking trail at Mt Lofty. It is probably best to simply note that they most likely mean the same thing.

Often placenames consist of compounds of two, and sometimes three Kaurna words, perhaps with suffixes added as in Yultiwirra (*yulti* 'stringybark' + *wirra* 'forest'), Ngangkiparringga (*ngangki* 'woman' + *pari* 'river' + *-ngga* 'LOC') and Karrauwirraparri (*karra* 'redgum' + *wirra* 'forest' + *pari* 'river'). Name elements like *pari* 'creek; river', *wirra* 'forest', *yarta* 'soil; ground; land', *wama* 'plain'

---

3 Tarntanyangga looks like it breaks the two-syllable rule governing the *-ngga* suffix. However, Tarntanya is a reduced compound, derived from *tarnta* 'male red kangaroo' and *kanya* 'rock' as evidenced by versions of the name, Dundagunya and Dharnda anya recorded from Ivaritji by *The Advertiser* and Daisy Bates respectively. See Gara (1990: 90, 93) and Amery (2002: 177).

and *wardli* 'house; home' often appear as the second root in these compounds. *Kanya* 'rock', *mukurta* 'hill', *wilya* 'foliage', *karla* 'firewood', *yarlu* 'sea', *warti* 'tail', *warta* 'behind' are also known to occur in this slot.

Compounding is also seen in the property name Yankaponga, clearly a combination of Yankalilla and Myponga. Yankaponga is not a traditional Kaurna name but has been formed by the owners by combining two neighbouring traditional Kaurna names in the vicinity.

4. Pinning down the meanings

The meaning of some Kaurna placenames, such as Yultiwirra 'stringybark forest' or Karrawirrapari 'redgum forest river', is readily apparent, whilst for some names no meaning is given at all, nor is one readily apparent. Documented 'meanings' are found for many placenames, however, more often than not, the meaning is a source of much conjecture.

4.1. Falsifiable or questionable meanings

Whilst a wide range of meanings can be assembled for many placenames from published and archival sources, some of these are clearly falsifiable and others are highly questionable (see Amery 2002). An example will serve to illustrate the problem:

4.1.1. Maitpangga – Myponga

T&S list this name Maitpa – ngga 'Matpunga Plain', but do not list *maitpa* in their vocabulary. Wyatt (1879: 23) spells it Maippunga again without definition. According to the State Gazetteer Myponga is an Aboriginal name meaning vegetable food place. Manning (1990: 218) says "according to H.C. Talbot it is derived from *miappunga* – 'divorced wife'" and "in a poem entitled 'Aboriginal Nomenclature – By a Native' which appeared in the *Register* on 11 October 1893, says it means 'high cliffs by the sea'". Cockburn (1990: 155) says "Myponga is corrupted from *maipunga*, meaning 'locality of high cliffs'. Another assertion that it is an Aboriginal term for 'divorced wife' may be discarded." Tindale in his Kaurna Placenames card file says:

> Maitpangga = [mai] + [pa] + [-ngga]. Pa is apparently a contraction of paru, namely animal food. Probably name applies to much of the length of the creek from Section 735 to beyond 740. Several versions of the name exist, the earliest being Teichlemann & Schurmann as Maitpa and

Maitpangga. Best interpretation of the name is probably vegetable food place from [mai] and [pangkara] a term applied to swamps & lagoons. Other versions and spellings exist (Tindale n.d.)

Now *pangkarra* means 'territory' whilst *pangka* means 'lake', so for starters Tindale has confused these two words. The ending *-ngga* is simply the locative suffix seen in numerous other Kaurna placenames. Tindale's assertion that Maitpangga is derived from *mai* 'vegetable food' + *pangkara* [or *pangka*] 'swamps and lagoons' or *paru* 'meat' are clearly fanciful. None of these account for the t. Our guess is that *maitpa* had no known meaning in the 1840s. It was simply a name. Otherwise T&S and Wyatt would have most likely recorded it. We observed previously that most Kaurna words were bisyllabic. *Maitpa* is a single morpheme. It simply cannot be divided into *mai* + *-tpa*. It would be like trying to split English 'under' into the prefix un- + der. Of course der has no meaning. Neither has *tpa* in Kaurna. The *tp* cluster occurs frequently in Kaurna and is a distinctive marker of the Miru subgroup of languages to which Kaurna belongs.

4.2. Ascribing meaning to placenames

What about cases where no meaning is given in the source material? Two examples are given below to illustrate the problem.

4.2.1. Callawonga

No meaning was ever given to Callawonga as far as I know, yet Callawonga looks like it could be *karla* 'fire' + *wanga* 'grave' or *wangka* 'west' or *wangka* 'speak'. These names are plausible, especially when we take into consideration the Kaurna cultural practice of lighting a fire on the grave (Adams 1902: 9 quoted in Amery and A. Rigney 2006: 38). And if the wind can speak, for *warri wanggandi* (RS warri wangkanthi) 'the wind blows' was recorded (T&S 1840: 54) it is likely that *garla wanggandi* (RS karla wangkanthi) 'the fire speaks/crackles' is also acceptable. There are at least three plausible alternatives here and they could *all* be wrong.

4.2.2. Kanyanyapilla

Similarly for Kanyanyapilla. Is this word formed from *kanya* + REDUP + *-pila* 'DUAL' meaning something like 'two lots of rocks'? It also looks like *kanya* 'rock' + REDUP + *yapa* 'hole' + *-illa* (T&S *kanyappa* 'earth oven'). However, the addition of *-illa* in this situation would disobey the phonotactic rule of applying *-illa* to a three-syllable root. *Kanyanya* itself was recorded as 'crowd, multitude, heap' and *pilla* 'eagle'. So Kanyanyapilla looks like it might mean 'a multitude of eagles' or is it *kanyanya* 'multitude' + *-pila* 'DUAL' (ie 'two heaps')? Again there seem to be a multitude of ways of breaking this word up to make some sort of sense, but what basis do we have for doing so?

These examples were discussed in the KWP in April 2007. The meeting resolved that it is not wise to speculate wildly in cases like these. We do not want to fall into the same trap that Tindale appears to have done. Where we do not know what the meaning is, we say we do not know.

5. Etymology

Etymology concerns the origins and development of words and their meanings. In most instances, there is no documented etymology of historical Kaurna names, though we are making efforts to clearly document the etymology of current Kaurna naming activity, discussed later in section 7. Even in the absence of a documented etymology, at times the origins of a name are quite clear. At other times, they are the subject of conjecture as some of the following examples illustrate.

5.1. Combinations of Kaurna and English

In the same way that Yankaponga has combined two Kaurna placenames (discussed in section 3.3), nearby Ourponga, a property on Sampson Rd Myponga Beach, has combined English 'our' with the Kaurna element *-ponga*, and is obviously a play on words in response to the re-analysis of the Kaurna name Myponga (= my + ponga) in English with 'my' from English.[4] Of course in Kaurna Myponga is analysed as *maitpa* + *-ngga* and the morpheme *maitpa* (meaning unknown) cannot be broken down further.

Similarly, a number of better established names on the map also combine Kaurna and English elements. Such names include Warradale, Glenunga, Parafield and Tappa Pass in the Barossa (which was formerly known as German Pass but was changed to Tappa Pass during World War I and has remained so ever since).

In developing the Kaurna placenames database KWP decided to translate these names fully into Kaurna. So Warradale became Warriwaltu (RS Warriwarltu) in the knowledge that the Warra- relates to Warriparri (RS Warripari) 'Sturt River' derived from *warri* 'wind' + *pari* 'river'. Dale is the term used in northern England for 'valley', thus translated into Kaurna as *warltu* 'valley'. Similarly

---

4 Similar play on words is seen in Nash's (2011: 120–129) study of roof names on Norfolk Island, sometimes combining Norf'k and English elements.

glen is a Scottish term also meaning 'valley'. Thus Glenunga is rendered Waltungga (RS Warltungga). Para was an early corruption of *pari* 'river'. So Parafield became Parriyerta 'river-ground' (RS Pariyarta).

5.2. Names recorded by Tindale and the Berndts from non-Kaurna sources

Norman Tindale and Ronald and Catherine Berndt worked with a number of Aboriginal people from the lower Fleurieu and lower Murray regions who had some knowledge of the Adelaide Plains and associated Dreaming narratives, notably the Tjilbruke story. Some of these names are obviously Kaurna in appearance, whilst others break all the rules. Ruwarung, for instance, begins with an r and ends with a consonant. No Kaurna words recorded by Teichelmann and Schürmann (1840), Wyatt (1879), Williams (1840), Piesse (1840), Robinson (ca 1837), Gaimard (1833), Koeler (1842)[5] etc. commence with r or l. Many names that Tindale and the Berndts recorded in this area, such as Patawiljaŋk, Witawataŋk, Tulukudaŋk etc., end with the Ngarrindjeri location ending -*ngk* (or -ŋk). This suffix is equivalent to Kaurna -*ngga* /-ngka/ (often written in historical documents and appears on maps as -*nga* as in Willunga, Aldinga, Waitpinga, Onkaparinga etc.).

Some of these Ngarrindjeri-looking names are clearly originally Kaurna names but have been assimilated into Ngarrindjeri. This is not surprising, as they were recorded from Ngarrindjeri speakers. Patawiljaŋk (Glenelg) as recorded by Tindale or Patawilyandjalang as recorded by Berndt and Berndt (1993) is a clear example of this. This same name was recorded as Pattawilya by T&S (1840) and appears on the map as Patawalonga (with the -*ngga* location ending). This name is analysable in Kaurna as *patha* 'a species of gum tree' (possibly swamp gum) + *wilya* 'foliage'.

If this happens with a well-known, high-profile Kaurna name, then it is likely also that some of the other Ngarrindjeri-looking names not recorded in other Kaurna sources are also originally Kaurna names that were assimilated into Ngarrindjeri by Milerum and Karlowan (who were informants for Tindale and the Berndts).

A set of options for dealing with Ngarrindjeri-looking names were put to the KWP meeting in April 2007. These were:

1. Ignore. For example, Ngutarangk (Rapid Bay) was recorded by Meyer (1843) as the name for Rapid Bay. Meyer was documenting Ramindjeri. Others

---

5 Koeler does include *lubera* 'woman' in his word list, but this is known to be a word in common use in South Australian Pidgin English at the time. It originates from Tasmanian languages.

recorded Yattagolunga/Yatagolanga (RS Yartakurlangga) as the Kaurna name for Rapid Bay. Thus it is best to ignore Ngutarangk.

2. Translate into Kaurna. For example, Paldarinawar = *paldari* 'salt' + *-na* ?? + *-war* 'LOC' in Ngarrindjeri. This might be translated into Kaurna as *kityangga* 'salt place' or *kityakauwingga* 'salty water place'.

3. Assimilate into Kaurna phonotactics. Accordingly Tulukudangk has been rendered Tulukudangga, Ka'raildung as Karildilla and Ruwarung as Wirruwarrungga[6] (see Amery 2000b: 38).

4. Keep as it is even though it disobeys Kaurna phonotactic rules. Dulil was proposed as a possible example of this.

5. Accept some intermediate form. For example Rekarnung might be re-written as Rikarnungga with a transparently Kaurna suffix, even though it commences with r.

The Minutes record that:

> The meeting resolved to accept the first three options only (ie 1. Ignore, 2. Translate into Kaurna, 3. Assimilate into Kaurna phonotactics). The meeting totally rejected the option of accepting a name of Ngarrindjeri appearance as a Kaurna name. An intermediate form (such as Tjilbruke) might be accepted occasionally with reluctance if there were compelling reasons. (KWP Minutes, April 2007).

5.3. Placename or descriptive?

There are a number of instances where the recorded 'name' may not be a true toponym, but rather a descriptive that was misunderstood as a placename. Yatala (RS Yartala), now referring to the prison but earlier in 1846 to the Hundred of Yatala and Section 422 in the Hundred of Yatala subdivided by Osmond Gilles circa 1848 (Manning 1990: 351) and a host of other names is another particularly good case in point. T&S list *yertalla* 'water running by the side of a river; inundation; cascade'.

'Yatala' was thought at first to be the name of the Torrens River (Stephens 1839: 105). Later a variant 'Yerta-illa' was remembered by settlers as being a name for 'land on the north bank of the Torrens'; and also 'Yatala' as the name for a tract of land 'extending from Port Adelaide to Teatree Gully'. The latter was no doubt the reason for the name given to the Hundred of Yatala in 1846, and the

---

[6] The Kaurna referred to Encounter Bay as Wirramu or Wirramula, though it was known to the Ramindjeri as Ramu or Ramong. As Kaurna words do not commence with r it appears that an extra syllable has been added to the front of the Ramindjeri word and the Kaurna location suffix added to the resultant three syllable word. By analogy, Wirruwarrungga was formed from Ruwarung.

old suburb of Yatala near today's Rosewater. All of these areas were subject to inundation from either creek flooding or tides. According to Manning (1990: 351) the Dry Creek area became flooded when water flowed from the hills. The weight of evidence suggests that originally Yartala was simply a descriptive which was co-opted by the colonists in their endeavours to name things including a government schooner and subsequently Yatala Shoal and Yatala Reef as well as a suburb Yatala Vale (gazetted in 1978).

Hercus (2002: 67–68) discusses examples from Victoria such as *yaluk* meaning 'creek' in some western Victorian languages which is recorded as the name of watercourses at quite different locations. This suggests that a descriptive was probably misunderstood to be a name, as has also probably occurred in the case of Yartala in Adelaide.

Parnka is listed by T&S as Lake Alexandrina in their "Names of Places and Rivers" section (T&S 1840: 75). Is Parnka really the toponym 'Lake Alexandrina' or is it simply the word for 'lake'? Certainly Schürmann and Teichelmann believed that it was both placename and descriptive as they list *pangka* in the vocabulary section (T&S 1840: 36) as 'lake; lagoon; n.pr. Lake Alexandrina'. Hercus (2002) discusses a number of cases like these. In Paakantyi, the Darling River is known simply as Paaka '(The) River' whilst the Diamantina/Warburton is known as Karla '(The) Creek' in Wangkanguru, being the only significant rivers and creeks in their respective areas.

5.4. Relative location or placename?

Hercus and Simpson (2002: 17–18) discuss the names Cowandilla, now an inner suburb of Adelaide and Patpangga. But *kawantila* means 'in the north' and *patpangka* 'in the south'. Were these originally true placenames or descriptors of relative location from the speaker at the time of inquiry or a descriptor of relative location from some unspecified feature? Schultz (2011: 26–27) does not regard *patpangka* to be a placename but rather an area descriptor of the country from Cape Jervis north to at least Carrickalinga and perhaps Myponga Beach or up to Sellick's Hill.[7] However, Wyatt (1879) recorded Patpungga (= Patpangga) for Rapid Bay though he probably never actually visited the place himself, and as we saw earlier, Rapid Bay has its own Kaurna name, Yartakurlangga.

---

7 Protector Matthew Moorhouse recorded "Patpunga, or those inhabiting the southern coast from Mt Terrible to Rapid Bay" in his Second Quarterly Report, 14 January 1840.

6. Pinning down locations

No Kaurna placename in use today refers to precisely the same entity that it once referred to when the language was still strong and vibrant. Piltawodli (RS Pirltawardli) in the late 1830s and 1840s was a 14-acre selection of land on the north bank of the River Torrens adjacent to the present day Torrens Weir which served as the 'Native Location'. Its boundary is known with reasonable accuracy. However, it is unknown as to what Piltawodli referred to in the minds of Kaurna people before it became the 'Native Location'. Was it a specific site? Or was it even a post-contact name referring to the huts constructed there? Today it refers to a much larger expanse of parkland known otherwise as Park 01. Even the names of rivers probably only applied to certain tracts of those watercourses. For instance, Ngangkiparri 'women's river' probably applied to a tract of the Onkaparinga in the Old Noarlunga area. It is known that women would seek refuge in the ravines to the immediate east of South Rd and the area was apparently a women's sacred place. It is most unlikely that the name Ngangkiparri would have been applied to the Onkaparinga near Hahndorf in the Adelaide Hills, though we do not know the Indigenous names for upper reaches of this river.

The original location of some names, such as Yurridla (RS Yuridla), is known with some certainty because they applied to particular known features. One early source (Piesse 1840) is particularly useful in determining the precise location of a handful of names because, being a surveyor, he supplied section and district numbers for these names in the Willunga-McLaren Vale area. Unfortunately, most sources are vague as to the whereabouts of the placenames provided. Teichelmann (1857) includes a Kaurna placename Nortumbo, in an example sentence:

> *wanti-dlo na nurntidlo padni? nguntarluntya Nortumbotarra*
>
> where.to-up 2PL away-up went there-up-ALL Nortumbo-PERL
>
> 'whither are you gone away? thither in the direction of Nortumbo' (TMs *nguntarlo*)

Teichelmann fails to locate the name, and as this name was not recorded by any other observer, it could be anywhere on Kaurna country or even beyond. Tindale, in working with historical sources, is known to have mis-located at least some names.

Chester Schultz has undertaken intensive excursions throughout the region armed with descriptions from the range of historical sources available. We need to attempt to imagine the country as it was prior to changes arising from clearing the land and the impact of agriculture, roads and urbanisation. Recorded names most likely refer to springs, water sources and campsites, some of which have been identified.

7. Current naming activity

Largely as a result of the linguistic and cultural renaissance in Adelaide since 1989 (see Amery 2000a), there has been renewed interest in Indigenous names and various initiatives have been implemented to reinstate, recognise and introduce Kaurna names. Dual naming provides a means whereby original Kaurna names might be recognised for features known by other names, but there are also opportunities to apply new names to previously un-named features.

Since its establishment in 2002, Kaurna Warra Pintyanthi (KWP) has served as a forum to discuss hundreds of requests for Kaurna names and translations at its regular monthly meetings. The Geographical Names Unit and a range of local government entities regularly consult KWP in addition to other bodies.

At first thought one may think that current naming activity should be straightforward in terms of knowing what the form, meaning, etymology and location are for any given new name. As it turns out, many of the issues raised within this paper come into play in several recent new names that have been recognised or proposed in the last few years within the area of study. Several case studies will serve to illustrate.

7.1. Re-instating original Kaurna names

Warriparinga is probably the first original Kaurna name to be re-instated. Its use in recent times dates back to 1992. See Amery and Williams (2002: 259–262) for a detailed discussion of Warriparinga. Several original Kaurna names, Piltawodli (RS Pirltawardli), Tambawodli (RS Tampawardli), Kainka Wirra, have been re-instated through the Adelaide City Council Kaurna placenaming initiative. These and other initiatives are discussed in Amery and Williams (2002).

7.2. Dual-naming

Dual naming enables the original name of a geographical feature to be recognised alongside of another existing name. Hodges (2007: 393–395) provides a comprehensive overview of dual naming within Australia. Ayers Rock/Uluru (now Uluru/Ayers Rock) and Mount Olga/Kata Tjuta was the first instance of official dual naming within Australia in 1993. In 1993 the South Australian parliament accepted a set of guidelines allowing for the recognition of

Aboriginal names. In 1999 dual naming was formalised in an amendment to the *Geographical Names Act 1991*. Karrawirra Parri (Torrens River) (RS Karrawirra Pari) was the first such Kaurna name to be officially recognised as a dual name in November 2001.

Dual naming only applies to natural features thus its scope of application is restricted. For instance, Kaurna names are known for several entities, including Adelaide = Tandanya (RS Tarntanya) and Port Adelaide = Yertabulti (RS Yartapuulti). But these Kaurna names cannot be recognised as dual names. Any entity that has a postcode lies outside the scope of the dual naming legislation. The official recognition of the Kaurna names for these entities would require a name change.

7.2.1. Creek names

Dual naming only applies to original names. In 2008 The City of Campbelltown and City of Norwood, Payneham and St Peters approached KWP about the naming of 1st to 5th creeks. A series of Kaurna names, Palti Parri 'ceremony creek', Wirrabulto Parri 'remnants of a forest creek', Narni Parri 'goatsucker (nocturnal bird) creek' Morialta Parri 'eastern cascade creek' and Ngaltaitya Parri 'yabby creek' respectively were proposed based on resident fauna and flora and historical information (KWP Minutes, August 2008). It turned out that the creeks already had gazetted European names, Greenhill Rivulet = First Creek, Hallett Rivulet = Second Creek, Todd Rivulet = Third Creek, Anstey Rivulet = Fourth Creek, Ormsby Rivulet = Fifth Creek, having been named by Colonel Light in the early days of the colony, though these names are not actually in use. Only Morialta Parri = 4th Creek was accepted for recognition under dual naming legislation as the other names were newly applied names with no historical precedence. The remainder would have to be put forward as name changes if Campbelltown, Norwood, Paynhem and St Peters Councils wished to proceed with recognising the other Kaurna names.

7.2.2. Brian Nadilo – Ngutinilla Reserve[8]

A name was sought by the City of Holdfast Bay for the new reserve established following the demolition of Magic Mountain at Glenelg. KWP suggested Ngutinilla 'Ngutinai's place' in recognition of Ngutinai (spelt Ootinai in the original sources), a Kaurna man who was invited aboard ship (possibly the *Buffalo*) during the first weeks of the colony. Through the use of this name, some of the early shared history can be recognised. The dual-naming proposal was discussed by Holdfast Bay Council where it was decided by a vote of 7 to 5 to place the name of the former Mayor Brian Nadilo before the Kaurna name.

---

8   See http://www.tourism.holdfast.sa.gov.au/site/page.cfm?u=589&c=2794.

However, because many were ignoring the Kaurna name, it was later decided that the reserve should be referred to as Ngutinilla only when the name needs to be shortened (*Messenger*, 13 June 2007).

7.3. New names for previously un-named features

Other previously un-named features are sometimes being given Kaurna names. In 1996 a previously un-named creek was named Kuranye (rainbow) Creek in reference to the multi-coloured sands nearby (see Amery 1998 Vol. 2: 277). In 2007 an un-named watercourse was named Turraparri (see below). Many local government authorities are turning to the Kaurna language as a source of names for parks, reserves and wetlands. The naming proposal that was developed for the Adelaide City Council in 1996 (see Amery and Williams 2002 for details) included 22 parks then known only by numbers. All of those names have since been adopted.

7.3.1. Taikurrendi (identifying the correct form)

On 11 February 2005, a new park was opened in front of the Christies Beach Surf Lifesaving Club (see http://www.onkaparingacity.com/web/binaries?img =4838&stypen=html). A Kaurna translation was sought for the introduction section to the Draft Tappa Iri agreement document. One paragraph read:

> The Kaurna Tappa Iri Reconciliation Agreement is an outcome of working together for many years on individual projects such as the Living Kaurna Cultural Centre at Warriparinga, foreshore redevelopments at Christies Beach (Tarkarendi), Pt Willunga (Ruwaraung) and Holdfast Bay, management of the Tjilbruke Track and Red Ochre Point (Portartang) and discussion in the Tjilbruke Dreaming Forum. (Kaurna Tappa Iri Reconciliation Agreement 2005–2008, p. 3)

Here we see the use of names of Ngarrindjeri appearance (Ruwaraung and Portartang)[9] alongside Kaurna Taikurrendi (meaning 'to be mixed; together') misspelt as Tarkarendi (which means 'to name; sing') in this document. This misrepresentation in the Draft Tappa Iri agreement has caused a great deal of confusion and errors within the Kaurna translation which was done in collaboration with Kaurna people (Leonie Brodie and Buster Turner from Tappa Iri and Dennis O'Brien from KWP). I (Amery) was not aware that the park had been named Taikurrendi at that time. Because the erroneous spelling was, in fact, a legitimate Kaurna word, and it was cited in the context of a name without definition, the error could not be identified. This example shows how easily errors might arise when people are not very familiar with the language.

---

9   These two names are usually spelt Ruwarung or Ru:warung and Potartang or Potarta:ng by Tindale.

7.3.2. Turraparri – Baxendale Creek

In 2005, the Geographical Names Unit (GNU) received a request from Wirra Wirra Winery to name the creek flowing through the property into Daringa Swamp on the outskirts of McLaren Vale. A proposal had been put up to name it Baxendale Creek after one of the early settlers. The GNU consulted the Kaurna Heritage Board, and in June 2007 its Chair, Lynette Crocker advised that the creek should be named Mullawirra Para, no doubt in recognition of the Kaurna ancestor Mullawirraburka. Lynette was probably relying on Tindale who places Mullawirra erroneously near Blewitt Springs, which as Schultz (1999: 99) points out, cannot be right. The GNU then sought advice from KWP. The matter was duly considered at the KWP meeting on 18 July 2007.

The true location of Mullawirra is certainly a long way south of Willunga and McLaren Vale in the foothills near Mount Terrible (see Schultz 1999: 37–39, 99–105). If the intention is to reinforce the roots that these names have in the country (see Williams in Amery and Williams, 2002: 267) then it is probably not a good idea to apply this name as proposed.

Para is certainly an early corruption of *pari* 'river' and survives in a number of well-known placenames such as the Para River, Little Para River, Munno Para, Parafield, Parafield Gardens and Paralowie. There seems little point in reinforcing an early corruption in a new Kaurna name.

The alternative is to propose a name based on the names within the McLaren Vale area. When the location issue was pointed out, Lynette was quite happy for a local name to be used.

We immediately faced the dilemma of having to pin down the form of the name. The name for McLaren Vale was not recorded by T&S, the most reliable early Kaurna source. We saw previously that the underlying representation is /thV$_1$RV$_2$/ where V$_1$ could be /a/, /aa/, /u/ or /uu/, R could be /r/, /r/ or /rr/ whilst V$_2$ could be /a/, /u/ or /i/. That is, there are no less than 36 possible forms/pronunciations of this name. After looking at the variants and who recorded them and when, we decided that a back vowel /u/ or /uu/ was most likely in the first syllable and that /a/ was reasonably likely in the second syllable. The word *turra* 'shade; shadow; likeness' is listed in the T&S (1840) vocabulary and we know from comparison with Nukunu that its phonemic representation is /thura/. Discussion followed about the locality of the creek and the environment through which it flowed. The consensus was that this was a fitting meaning and a suitable name for the creek. Thus the KWP meeting of 18 July 2007 resolved to name the creek Turraparri (RS Turapari) 'shade river' which was accepted by the GNU and now appears on RAA maps (see https://www.raa.com.au/download.aspx?secid=294&file=documents\townmap_87.pdf).

8. Conclusion

Attempts to make sense of erroneous, conflicting, vague and ambiguous source materials present many challenges. Nonetheless, it is seen as a worthwhile pursuit to reinstate the best possible guess at the original form, pronunciation, meaning, cultural context and location of placenames in southern metropolitan Adelaide and the Fleurieu Peninsula and to ensure that these are legitimate Kaurna forms. The results of this analysis are being posted on Google Earth maps allowing the public ready access to the most accurate and reliable information we are able to assemble.

In future, the Kaurna Placenames website, along with the Kaurna Learner's Guide (Amery and Simpson 2013) and the Kaurna Dictionary (Amery and Morley forthcoming) will be the main vehicles through which the revised Kaurna spellings will be introduced to the general public.

We see this as a work in-progress where we are receptive to new evidence and open to revision. We appeal to the public for additional information about names already posted and extra names which are not yet included in the database.

Acknowledgements

We acknowledge the work of the South Australian state government Geographical Names Unit, the four southern councils (City of Onkaparinga, City of Marion, City of Holdfast Bay and Yankalilla Council) and Beanstalk Creative and Production, without whose effort and support the Kaurna Placenames website would not have been possible. We also acknowledge the untiring work of Chester Schultz who has taken on detailed and exhaustive research of Kaurna placenames since 2007 under the guidance and direction of Kaurna Warra Pintyanthi whose members volunteer their time to discuss this and other Kaurna language projects. Thanks to Chester Schultz, Gerhard Rüdiger and two anonymous reviewers for detailed comments on a draft of this paper.

References

Amery, Rob 1998, 'Warrabarna Kaurna! Reclaiming Aboriginal Languages from Written Historical Sources: Kaurna Case Study', (2 volumes), PhD thesis, University of Adelaide.

—— 2000a, *Warrabarna Kaurna: Reclaiming an Australian Language,* Swets & Zeitlinger, Lisse, The Netherlands.

— 2000b, 'Reclaiming the Kaurna language', in *Footprints in the Sand: Kaurna Life in the Holdfast Bay Area to 1850*, Y. Allen (compiler), Holdfast Bay Reconciliation Group, Glenelg: 30–40.

— 2002, 'Weeding out spurious etymologies: Toponyms on the Adelaide Plains', in *The Land is a Map: Placenames of Indigenous Origin in Australia*, L. Hercus, F. Hodges and J. Simpson (eds), Pandanus Books in association with Pacific Linguistics, Canberra: 165–180.

— 2003, *Warra Kaurna: A Resource for Kaurna Language Programs.* Kaurna Warra Pintyandi, Adelaide.

Amery, R. and J. Morley, forthcoming, *Kaurna Dictionary*, Kaurna Warra Pintyanthi, Adelaide.

Amery, R. and A. W. Rigney, with Nelson Varcoe, Chester Schultz and Kaurna Warra Pintyandi 2006, *Kaurna Palti Wonga. Kaurna Funeral Protocols.* Kaurna Warra Pintyandi, Adelaide.

Amery, R. and L. I. Rigney 2006, 'Recognition of Kaurna cultural heritage in the Adelaide Parklands: A linguist's and Kaurna academic's perspective', in *Proceedings of The Adelaide Parklands Symposium: A Balancing Act: Past – Present – Future*, University of South Australia, Adelaide, 10 November 2006.

Amery, R. and J. Simpson, for Kaurna Warra Pintyanthi 2013, *Kulurdu Marni Ngathaitya! Sounds Good to Me: Kaurna Learner's Guide*, Wakefield Press, Kent Town.

Amery, R. and G. Y. Williams 2002, 'Reclaiming through renaming: The reinstatement of Kaurna toponyms in Adelaide and the Adelaide Plains', in *The Land is a Map: Placenames of Indigenous Origin in Australia*, eds. L. Hercus, F. Hodges and J. Simpson, Pandanus Books in association with Pacific Linguistics, Canberra: 255–276.

Berndt, R. and C. Berndt, with J. Stanton 1993, *A World That Was: The Yaraldi of the Murray River and the Lakes, South Australia,* Melbourne University Press at the Miegunyah Press, Carlton, Vic.

Cockburn, R. 1990, *South Australia. What's in a name?* (Rev. ed.), Axiom, Adelaide. Original work published 1908.

Gara, T. 1990, 'The life of Ivaritji ('Princess Amelia') of the Adelaide Tribe', in *Aboriginal Adelaide,* Special Issue of the *Journal of the Anthropological Society of South Australia* 28(1): 64–104.

Gaimard, M. 1833, 'Vocabulaire de la langue des habitans du Golfe Saint-Vincent', in *Voyage de découvertes de L'Astrolabe 1826–1827–1828–1829: Philologie*, M.J. Dumont D'Urville, Ministère de la Marine, Paris.

Hercus, L. 2002, 'Is it really a placename?', in *The Land is a Map: Placenames of Indigenous Origin in Australia*, L. Hercus, L.F. Hodges and J. Simpson (eds), Pandanus Books in association with Pacific Linguistics, Canberra, 63–72.

Hercus, L. and J. Simpson 2002, 'Indigenous placenames: an introduction', in *The Land is a Map: Placenames of Indigenous Origin in Australia*, L. Hercus, L.F. Hodges and J. Simpson (eds), Pandanus Books in association with Pacific Linguistics, Canberra, 1–23.

Hodges, F. 2007, 'Language planning and placenaming in Australia', *Current Issues in Language Planning* 8(3): 383–403.

Kaurna Placenames website www.kaurnaplacenames.com a collaboration between City of Onkaparinga, City of Marion, City of Holdfast Bay, District Council of Yankalilla with the Kaurna Heritage Board through the Kaurna Tappa Iri Regional Agreement; Kaurna Warra Pintyandi; Land services Group, SA Department for Transport, Energy and Infrastructure; Linguistics Discipline, University of Adelaide; the Australian Government Department of the Environment and Water Resources; and Beanstalk Creative & Production. Launched in July 2006.

Koeler, Dr H. 1842, 'Einige Notizen über die Eingebornen an der Ostküste des St Vincent-Golfs in Süd-Australien 1837 und 1838', in *Monatsberichte über die Verhandlungen der Gesellschaft für Erdkunde*, Berlin.

Manning, G.H. 1990, *Manning's Place Names of South Australia*, The Author, Adelaide.

Meyer, H.A.E. 1843, *Vocabulary of the language spoken by the Aborigines of the southern and eastern portions of the settled districts of South Australia*, James Allen, Adelaide.

Nash, J. 2011, 'Insular Toponymies: Pristine place-naming on Norfolk Island, South Pacific and Dudley Peninsula, Kangaroo Island, South Australia', PhD thesis, University of Adelaide.

Piesse, L. 1840, 'Letter to the Editor' of the *Adelaide Guardian* dated 18 October 1839, *The South Australian Colonist* 1(19): 296.

Praite, R. and J.C. Tolley 1970, *Place Names of South Australia*, Rigby, Adelaide.

Robinson, G.A. n.d., Papers held in Mitchell Library, Sydney, A7085(6).

Schultz, C. 1999, 'Kaurna historical and musical notes', in *Kaurna Paltinna*, Chester Schultz, Nelson Varcoe and Rob Amery, Kaurna Plains School, Elizabeth: 79–121.

— 2011, 'Ask the right question, then look everywhere: Finding and interpreting the old Aboriginal place-names around Adelaide and Fleurieu Peninsula', Paper presented at the Australian National Placenames Survey Conference, SA Dept of Transport, Energy and Infrastructure, Adelaide, 2 September 2011.

— 2012, 'Feet on the Fleurieu, language on the land: Kangaroo Islanders, their Aboriginal women and local Aborigines 1831–7: the story of the guides and interpreters in the first explorations of Fleurieu Peninsula', Unpublished manuscript.

Schultz, C., N. Varcoe and R. Amery 1999, *Kaurna Paltinna: A Kaurna Songbook*, Kaurna Plains School, Elizabeth.

Simpson, J. and L. Hercus 2004, 'Thura-Yura as a Subgroup', in *Australian Languages: Classification and the Comparative Method*, Claire Bowern and Harold Koch (eds), John Benjamins Publishing Company, Philadelphia: 179–206.

Stephens, J. 1839, *The Land of Promise,* Smith, Elder & Co., London.

Teichelmann, C.G. 1857, Dictionary of the Adelaide dialect, MS 4vo. pp. 99 (with double columns). No. 59, Bleek's Catalogue of Sir George Grey's Library dealing with Australian languages, South African Public Library.

Teichelmann, C.G. and C.W. Schürmann 1840, *Outlines of a Grammar, Vocabulary, and Phraseology, of the Aboriginal Language of South Australia, Spoken by the Natives in and for some Distance Around Adelaide*, Published by the authors at the native location, Adelaide.

Tindale, N.B. n.d., Kaurna place names card file, Tindale Collection, South Australian Museum, Adelaide.

Troy, J. and M. Walsh 2009, 'Reinstating Aboriginal placenames around Port Jackson and Botany Bay', in *Aboriginal Placenames: Naming and Re-Naming the Australian Landscape,* Harold Koch and Luise Hercus (eds), Aboriginal History Monograph 19, ANU E Press and Aboriginal History Inc., Canberra.

Williams, W. 1840, 'The language of the natives of South Australia', *South Australian Colonist* 1(19): 295–296.

Wyatt, W. 1879, 'Some account of the manners and superstitions of the Adelaide and Encounter Bay tribes', in *The Native Tribes of South Australia,* J.D. Woods (ed.), ES Wigg, Adelaide: 157–181. Original MS with corrections in Barr Smith Library Special Collections, University of Adelaide.

11. One name for one Place – but it is not always so

Luise Hercus
The Australian National University

1. Introduction

Aboriginal placenames represent a very ancient layer of the vocabulary, just as placenames do in European traditions: extensive work has been done on European river names which are said according to some scholars, to form the most ancient layer of the vocabulary, preceding the arrival of the Indo-Europeans (Vennemann 1994). For a traditional Aboriginal person, as for older Europeans the world map was territorially very much smaller than it is for people now in the days of the 'global village'. It was, however, infinitely more detailed and meaningful. We will look at several aspects of Aboriginal placenames in the light of this:

(i) Placenames may be old, but there is not an eternal one-to-one relationship between a place and its name: there are cases of duplicates in name, on the one hand, and dual naming on the other;

(ii) Placenames may be old, but they are not immutable, and there are cases where one can see new placenames evolve; and

(iii) Aboriginal Placenames have special significance in the chronology of the creation of the landscape.

2. More than one place with the same name

The fact that there is not a one-to-one relationship between a place and its name is clear from the many instances where there are two or more places with the same name.

For the eastern Lake Eyre Basin we have the remarkable list compiled by J.H. Reuther of over 3000 placenames with their explanations, and the associated map by Hillier (1904). This list, which comprises volume 7 of the Reuther MS (translated in *The Diari*, 1981), contains a surprising number of 'duplicates': two or sometimes even three places can share the same name. The explanations and the comparison with the Hillier map make it clear that these duplicates refer to separate and different locations, often in different people's country. There is enough similarity between the languages involved to make this quite feasible, but sometimes there are reasons for doubt in the identifications. For instance there are three places in this list called by the name 'Daku-ngarra-ngarra',[1] which was said to refer to a heart-shaped sandhill. One of these is attributed by Reuther to a Wangkangurru Ancestor and is assigned to Wangkangurru country, but the word 'daku' sandhill is not known in Wangkangurru, where the word for 'sandhill' is *mudlu*. Even if in isolated instances the multiple locations with one name are doubtful, there is still plenty of evidence of this practice, and the same situation can be seen in those placenames that have survived into modern times. We will look at the reasons behind these duplications. The data on which this study is based are language recordings and fieldtrips undertaken since 1965 in the Lake Eyre Basin.

2.1. Copying a name

The use in Australia of European names like 'Newcastle' is usually due to nostalgia: a desire to name a township after an English township. This kind of translocation of a placename is extremely rare in Aboriginal topography, but it does occur. One striking example is the translocation of the Arrernte name *Antherrtye*. It is originally a common noun, defined as follows:

> a large rocky hill or mountain, mountain range or chain of large hills (Henderson and Dobson 1994).

People further south, in the Lake Eyre Basin, both Arabana and Diyari, interpreted this as a specific name for the Macdonnell Ranges, which to them were a mysterious, distant and very high mountain range, the home of several important Ancestors, including the Native Cat *Malpunga,* the hero of the Urumbula song cycle. Siebert in his correspondence with A.W. Howitt, compares the range spelt variously as 'Antiritcha', and 'Antirtja' to Mt Olympus, the Greek 'Mountain of the Gods'. He writes about one of the Two Men of mythology being sent

> nach dem Götterberg Antirtja, dem Australischen Olymp.

> 'to the mountain of the Gods, Antirtja, the Australian Mt Olympus'.

> (document 347, a letter sent from Bethesda-Killalpaninna, 28 August 1899, p. 2).

---

1   We follow the convention of writing Aboriginal words from early documents within quotation marks, and words that are taken from modern transcriptions in italics.

In document 334 of the same collection Siebert calls 'Antirtja' 'the holy mountain', cf. also Howitt 1904: 785. The Macdonnell Ranges rise to over 1500 metres with Mt Zeil. Arabana people borrowed this name for a low but rocky range on the west side of Lake Eyre, under 200 metres high, admittedly rising from close to sea level. This range includes Mt Perrypollkot[2] (*Pirri-palkanha* 'Splitting their claws' from the Emu History), Mt Robinson (*Yaltya-Wati* 'Frog-Path', because the Ancestral Frogs clambered right up to the top in pursuit of their enemies), and Mt Toodlery (*Thurliri* 'Rocky Tableland'). As is evident from the names, a number of important myths traverse this range and so Arabana people had their own *Anthritya*, sometimes pronounced *Nganthritya*, though not of Olympic proportions.

2.2. Names from common features

A name may be descriptive and refer to some obvious and commonplace attribute: this is one of the main reasons why two or more places can end up having the same name.

2.2.1. Bird names

This attribute may be the presence of particular creatures.

Finches love to congregate around water, and so it is not surprising to find sources of water called after them. On the western side of Lake Eyre in Arabana country there are two places simply called *Yatyapara-nha* 'Finch' (the final *-nha* is just an optional proper noun marker). One *Yatyapara-nha* is the Tarlton[3] spring near the headwaters of Hope Creek, in the Mt Margaret Range, the other is Paisley Pond[4] in the Paisley Creek, hence the name served also for the Paisley Creek (see Hercus and Potezny 1999: 165). These places once named *Yatyaparanha* are only some 50 km apart, but in a world where each place was so much more significant and transport was not mechanised this did not seem to lead to any confusion. Unfortunately in neither case has the name survived on modern maps.

Other birds too figure in more than one placename: there are for instance several *Paku-Paku* 'Bellbird' creeks, *Kukunka* 'Brown Hawk' creeks and places called 'Eaglehawk's nest'. There are also duplicate placenames involving other creatures, such as 'Ant-water' and 'Mosquito creek', but as the names of these creatures vary a lot between languages, multiple identical forms are not so common.

---

2 All the locations given here are in decimal degrees using the Geocentric Datum of Australia (GDA) 1994. Mt Perrypollkot is -27.7468 Latitude, 136.2160 Longitude.
3 -28.5384 Lat., 136.1154 Long.
4 -29.2928 Lat., 136.6928 Long.

Indigenous and Minority Placenames

2.2.2. Plant-names

Dikirri is the term for 'swamp cane-grass' in Yaluyandi (once spoken on the Diamantina near Goyder Lagoon) and neighbouring languages. This plant is particularly common in wet areas, and so it is not surprising to find a number of swampy waterholes called by that name: there are four in the Birdsville-Bedourie area. Three of these appear on modern maps: the vagaries of English spelling however are such that these duplicated placenames always seem to turn out to be written in different ways:

1. Dickeree[5] waterhole on the Diamantina just south of Birdsville;
2. Dickerrie[6] waterhole below Old Annandale on Eyre Creek;
3. Dickery[7] waterhole near the Kalidawarry ruins, not far from the junction of the Mulligan with Eyre Creek;
4. *Dikirri* is also the original name of the waterhole where Old Alton Downs[8] homestead was built in South Australia on an Eyre Creek channel near the Northern Territory border. This name does not appear on modern maps.

Kurla is a widespread name for 'sandhill cane-crass'. The name *Kurlanha,* with the optional proper noun suffix *–nha,* is used for two separate locations. English spelling has made them look very different from one another:

1. Goolong Springs,[9] near Marree;
2. Coolina[10] waterhole, at the Macumba Bend.

The latter site has a mythological background as well as the simple descriptive one. It is on the track of the Ancestor *Intara* from Mt Arthur[11] to the Ilkildana waterhole[12] on the Alkaowra Channels. In one of the verses of this cycle, *Intara* travels at night to get home quickly with the precious pounding stone that he has taken. He gets disoriented, and so he collects some sandhill cane-grass from a dune near a waterhole to light a bright fire so that he can see. He sees his own track and sings 'This is the way I have come just now!' This waterhole, Coolina, was therefore named after the cane-grass.

Karingala is the name for a scented kind of water-mint in Arabana-Wangkangurru and Kuyani. There are several places named after it, one is a small watercourse,

---

5   -26.0350 Lat., 139.1945 Long.
6   -25.2800 Lat., 138.4100 Long.
7   -24.4454 Lat., 138.8888 Long.
8   -26.1219 Lat., 138.9412 Long.
9   -29.6563 Lat., 138.1479 Long.
10 -27.2807 Lat., 136.5279 Long.
11 -27.4928 Lat., 135.9742 Long.
12 -27.1946 Lat., 136.6125 Long.

location uncertain, near Nilpinna Spring[13] in Arabana country. Another *Karingala* is a long way to the south on Finniss Springs Station. It is by the Screechowl Creek and is now called 'Woolshed Springs'. Yet another *Karingala* is the original name of Duck Waterhole[14] not far from Duck Bore near the Woodmurra Creek, and it is shown on T.G.H. Strehlow's map (Strehlow 1971). A fourth and fifth are still found on modern maps: Curranullina[15] Spring, now a bore, on Peake Creek and Karingallanna[16] waterhole in Wangkangurru country on the lower Warburton.

Similarly there are at least two sites named after the 'Ruby Saltbush' *Kudnampira*, and several others saying 'full of Eremophila bushes' *Yarda-purrunha*, e.g. Yardaparinna Creek and Waterhole[17] close to the Macumba homestead. It seems that duplicates of this kind are accidental and there is no other connection between the sites of identical name.

2.2.3. Names from the actions of Ancestors

In the stories of the Ancestors events are often repeated. The Two Men of Initiation introduce the use of knives in initiation: they arrive just in time and save youths from initiation by fire. This happens at Finniss Swamp[18] near Lake Eyre South, and so this place was called *Wibma-Malkara* 'History-time Initiation'. There was another History-time Initiation at North Hawker Springs[19] near Mt Margaret, so this place was also called *Wibma-Malkara*.

In the myth of the creation of Lake Eyre, the Ancestor *Wilkuta* tries to find a place to spread out the huge kangaroo skin, which ultimately forms the lake. He tries to spread it in a number of places and each time a tiny wren *yurilya* calls out shrilly telling him 'don't put it here, I need room for all my little children'. In memory of these events there are a number of sites called *Yurilya(nha):*

1. Eurelyana Hill,[20] and the nearby Eurelyana Creek, which is a tributary to the Peake Creek.

2. Eurilyna Spring,[21] south of Lake Cadibarrawirracanna.

---

13 -28.2097 Lat., 135.6901 Long.
14 -27.6398 Lat., 136.0735 Long.
15 -28.0857 Lat., 135.5509 Long.
16 -27.7609 Lat., 137.6383 Long.
17 -27.2090 Lat., 135.6986 Long.
18 -29.5921 Lat., 137.4111 Long.
19 -28.4192 Lat., 136.1930 Long. The Arabana name for this site, Wibma-Malkara, is noted in the current Gazetteer.
20 -28.3455 Lat., 135.2553 Long.
21 -28.9333 Lat., 135.4437 Long

Indigenous and Minority Placenames

3. *Yurilya* was also the name of the Margaret Spring,[22] just south of Francis Swamp, where the little wren again stopped the Lake from being spread out.

The journey of *Wurru,* the name of the ancestral White-face Heron is reflected in the placename *Wurrunha*, which is an alternative name for Brinkley Springs[23] (see section 3.2) to the east of Mt Margaret, and also in the Woorana[24] waterhole. These names are obviously connected as they follow the myth over the landscape.

Names from the deeds of Ancestors however need not be connected: some may originate from separate minor stories, which may have been forgotten; one such is the name *Katilkanha,* which means 'jaw' in Arabana-Wangkangurru and neighbouring languages. This still survives in the name of a waterhole and the ruins of a station, 'Cadelga',[25] adjacent to a waterhole of the same name, in the far north-east of South Australia, near Haddon's Corner. It was also the name of a waterhole in the location where Big Blyth Bore[26] is now near Mt Denison on Anna Creek. There is no obvious connection between the two.

Wabma-karda(ya)pu 'Snake-head' in Arabana features in several unconnected stories and there are sites with that name. It was the traditional name of Hamilton Hill,[27] near Coward Springs. This hill is now part of a reserve, which is called 'Wabma Kadarbu Mound Springs Conservation Park'. There is another *Wabma-karda(ya)pu*, belonging to a different story on the lower Neales, close to Lake Eyre and that is written as 'Warmakidyapoo Waterhole'[28] on modern maps, adjacent to a 'Warmakidyapoo Hill'. Similarly there are several 'Snake-skin' waterholes. There are several 'Fingernail' and 'Toe-nail' places too, as well as 'White smoke' and 'White ground'. These similarly named sites have no apparent connections with one another.

A particular site is usually seen as part of the landscape and part of stories, not as an isolated feature, and there is therefore much less chance of confusion than there would be if one viewed things from a European perspective. This duplication of names never seems to lead to confusion, somehow the names always occur amid sufficient background to be correctly identified. They are part of a web of stories.

A glance at modern maps makes it clear that the Aboriginal names are more varied than the European ones, this is to some extent because the European names are practically all in one language, English, but the Aboriginal names are in many different languages. The main feature however is that Aboriginal

---

22   -29.2175 Lat., 136.3418 Long. The Arabana name for this site, *Yurilya*, is noted in the current Gazetteer.
23   -28.5040 Lat., 136.3079 Long.
24   -27.6493 Lat., 136.6849 Long.
25   -26.0855 Lat., 140.4091 Long.
26   -28.0723 Lat., 136.0554 Long.
27   -29.4576 Lat., 136.8543 Long.
28   -28.1430 Lat., 136.7731 Long.

placenames are 'lively' through their connection with stories. They make the introduced names seem endlessly dull and repetitive: one need only think of the seemingly infinite number of names like Salt Creek and Welcome Springs and Creeks, and places called Dinnertime and Breakfast Time, Five Mile and any other number of miles. Yet these European names originally were meaningful in the context of life on particular stations. Just like the Aboriginal duplicate placenames they did not lead to confusion when used within their context: however, when stations were split up or boundaries changed or homesteads moved they lost their original significance, whereas the Aboriginal names were permanently relevant to the Aboriginal view of the landscape.

The Aboriginal placenames reflect Aboriginal views on life and are an integral part of storytelling. Telling stories in the traditional environment must have been somehow an 'insider' affair: the audience already knew something about it all. The storyteller might mention the main protagonists by name once or twice near the beginning, but normally did not bother with names later on – except for some asides to the audience like 'cunning old fellow that Crane'. It is not the same with placenames – a recital can almost be a series of placenames – but there is still scope for that familiarity, and so instead of naming a creek the speaker might say 'you know that box-creek coming down' or instead of naming a swamp 'you know that cane-grass swamp behind there'. This is probably why we have so many places called *Dikirri* and *Karingala*. With station life this practice continued into English, usually with loss of the original name: hence the numerous places called Box Creek, Wattle Creek, Gum Creek and Canegrass Swamp. There are 10 Canegrass Swamps in the South Australian Gazetteer alone, but that number is easily surpassed by the 25 Gum Creeks.

3. Dual naming

3.1. Naming in adjacent languages

Dual naming is much less common than the duplication of names. There are just a few places that have dual naming because they are at the boundary between two groups speaking different languages.

Sometimes the name from one language simply gets adapted to the sound-system of the second language: there is a difference of pronunciation, not a difference of name. This has happened with the Lower Southern Arrernte name *Utyerre* 'Springs', the traditional name for 'Dalhousie Springs', with the accent on the second syllable. The Arabana-Wangkangurru pronunciation is *Wityira*, with the stress accent on the first syllable, and this is the pronunciation that is reflected in the name Witcherrie Mound[29] which survives on modern maps, and it has been re-established with the naming of the Witjira National Park. It was one name that had split in two according to the two different sound systems of two different languages. A parallel situation is found when an Arabana-Wangkangurru word is pronounced by Arrernte speakers. *Aruwolka* is a waterhole, not named on maps, but located by the Wangkangurru elder, Mick McLean in the vicinity of Coolina waterhole (see section 2.2.2) on the same northern outlier channel of the Macumba, in an area which was said to be shared by Arabana, Wangkangurru and Arrernte. He was telling an Arrernte story, and he consistently pronounced the name as *Arrwewelkente*, in the manner of an Arrernte speaker, not as *warru-(w)alkanta* 'appearing white-coloured' as he would have done had he been speaking Wangkangurru. This name is formed from Wangkangurru *warru* 'white', *-w-* is a glide consonant, *alka* means 'colour' and *-nta* is the present tense reflexive marker (Hercus and McCaul 2002: 44).

Nganta-ngantanha 'Stopping' was the name of the Gregory Creek, near Lake Eyre South. This is where the Willie Wagtail was stopped when he was trying to fly away stealing the fire, in the form of a fire-stick. The Kuyani name *Thinta-thinta* 'willie wagtail' for the nearby Tinta-dintana[30] Creek belongs to this story. Arabana people use their pronunciation of this name *Tyinti-tyintinha*.

Dual naming can involve actual translation. The best-known example is the name of the Macumba. During the west-east part of its course, below the present day Macumba Station, this river formed the boundary between Southern Arrernte to the north and Arabana to the south. The floodplain is a vast expanse of dark red gibber. In the 'History Time' *Maka-thakapa* 'the Fire-striker', who was nearly bald and had just one little strand of hair, was teased by some boys 'you've got lice in that little strand of hair, ha ha!'. He lit a fire which raged along the river burning them and everybody who lived there as far as the *Maka-thadninha* 'Fire-stopping' Swamp, not marked on maps, just above Woorana[31] waterhole.

The name Macumba belongs to this story and is derived from Arabana *Maka-wimpa* 'fire track'. The Arrernte version of this name is *Uringka* 'fire-track' and the two terms were used by senior Arabana and Arrernte speakers respectively. Only the Arabana name has survived on modern maps.

3.2. Alternative names

Places may have two names, one being an alternative name, a kind of nickname. These nicknames tend to be ephemeral, and there are very few such alternative

---

29   -26.4382 Lat., 135.5268 Long.
30   -27.6493 Lat., 136.6849 Long.
31   -29.5071 Lat., 137.2709 Long.

names recorded. *Parra-parranha* 'The very Long One' is an example of a site that has an alternative name. It is a well in the Central Simpson Desert. *Parra-parranha* was so called because people had to dig a very long tunnel to get down to the water. The explorer Lindsay in his report wrote this name as 'Burraburrina'. In the 'History Time' the Two Boys, followed by their mother travelled through there on their way to the east, bringing with them the use of feathers in ceremonies. They camped and were cooking two emus. The older boy went down the well to fill up his waterbag. The younger boy brought the emus back to life and they ran off making their loud grunting sound. Hearing this the boy down in the well got such a shock that the bag slipped from his hands. This is why the place also got the alternative name *Yunga-kurdalayangu* 'his waterbag slipped down (out of his hands)'.

Another place with two Aboriginal names is Brinkley Spring (see section 2.3). It was called *Thurru-thurrunha,* 'The Hard One'. It also came to be known as *Wurrunha* 'Crane', because the one box-tree standing there represented the Old Man Crane of mythology.

4. New placenames

Placenames are an old layer of the vocabulary, but as with any living system, a new name could be created, when for any reason a site came to be recognised as a distinct site. The way this could happen gives us some insight into the traditional formation of placenames.

4.1. *Ngunarndula*, 'Lilies' a descriptive name in the making

Thanks to the way in which Wangkangurru people cherished their traditions it is possible to see how the kind of descriptive naming seen in section 2.2.2 could have come about. In the early years of the 20th century a Wangkangurru man who had gone to the Killalpaninna Mission dreamt that a spirit showed him the landscape around Lake Eyre and gave him the songs which he called collectively the *Kudnarri* 'floodplain' songs, as some verses related to the floodplain of the Cooper. He taught the songs to younger people. The Wangkangurru and Diyari speaker Leslie Russell, *Wanga-pulanha* 'Two Mornings', and his cousin Jimmy *Wanga-mirri* 'Many Mornings' who worked with both L. Hercus and P. Austin learnt these songs from the old man and Leslie added to them. He 'found' a verse about a particularly large patch of beautiful Crinum lilies, *ngunarndula* growing on the eastern side of the Kopperamanna[32] crossing. It is a distinctive site, easily

---

32 -28.6019 Lat., 138.7116 Long.

accessible: a track goes through there on the way to a bore, which is adjacent to the Swan Rocks *Kandri-mukunha* (Horne and Aiston 1924: 141), important in mythology. Some of these verses have been analysed by P. Austin (1978: 530). Because of that special verse this particular place in the floodplain came to be associated with Crinum lilies. People would speak about the site as if they were giving a placename: 'I'll show you *Ngunarndula*'. It had become recognised as 'The Lily Place'. Aboriginal people gradually all moved away from that area, and the name is sinking into oblivion, as is its association with the song, now, when the people who could sing it have died.

4.2. *Yuru-pula pantirda* 'Two Old Men had a fight', an action name in the making

In the 1860s or '70s a duel to the death took place between two Kuyani men. There had been a long-standing feud between the Kuyani people from around Mirrabuckinna, north of Lake Torrens, and those from the Gregory. The two protagonists belonged to the opposing factions and also had a grudge against each other. The event was so horrendous that it became legendary, and a Kuyani song was made about it. In the 1960s a few people still knew this song and everybody in the Lake Eyre South area seemed to know about the fight and commented on the futility of it all. The two men killed each other with boomerangs on the southern edge of the *Wimparanha* Whimberina Waterhole[33] south-west of Finniss Springs, and so this spot was known to the Arabana people who had come to live in the area by the Arabana name *Yuru-pula pantirda* 'Two Old Men had a fight'. There were said to be many broken boomerangs lying about – but we did not see any. This name was regarded as a placename, but as few Aboriginal people now live in the area on a permanent basis, memory of the name and its origin is fading.

5. Many associations, but one name

The network of myths that connects together the Lake Eyre Basin is so complex that naturally the paths of Ancestors cross one another. One place may have been visited by several Ancestors. This is all viewed chronologically: the comments made by traditional people about placenames imply that the Dreamtime or 'History Time', as it is often called in the Lake Eyre Basin, was not altogether timeless, but had its own inner sequence. It is viewed normally that an Ancestor created or found a place and at the same time named it. It was somehow a system of first-come, first-served: whoever came first to a place, found it as it was or

---

33 -29.8812 Lat., 137.3880 Long.

created it, was the one to name it. Thus it is usually taken for granted that the Two Old Man Snakes created many springs on their journey down the western side of Lake Eyre. They were, however, not the only ones on the scene at that time: they coincided with the HFire Striker, who brought about the formation of the Macumba, the Fire-track (see section 3.1). They got burnt by the Fire and only just managed to escape, and that is how they came to name the Melon Spring,[34] *Palku-wakanha* 'Body-black', because they had been blackened by the Fire. They still saw that Fire when they have reached much further to the South:

> They saw the fire which was burning (far way on the Macumba) as related in the Fire History), the smoke kept on billowing up, they both watched it, and they climbed up on the hill, the Yarrapolina Hill, to have a look at the country to the north. (And they said one to the other, speaking in Arabana): 'It's (still) burning over there, old man my friend!' They watched it in the distance. (L.A. Hercus, MS, p. 7).

There are many other examples of contemporaneity in the 'History Time'. Ancestors are apt to make rude observations about others they encounter, and this can be reflected in placenames: the name may reflect the activities of two or more Ancestors. The Emus camp on a high sandhill near Duff Creek.[35] They see the Ancestor *Thudnungkurla* 'The Erotic Old Man', the main character of another long History. He is camped by a claypan below. He bends down to pick up his bag, and they make an obscene anatomical observation about him. That is why that claypan has the absurd name *Manha-warirndanha,* which of course always had everybody laughing when they heard it, and people do not forget that claypan.

One of the most crowded places in the 'History Time' was Primrose Springs[36] called *Papu Ngalyuru* 'Green Egg'. The Emus, the Kangaroo whose skin forms Lake Eyre, and the Fish and Crane all travelled through there, visiting this high mound-spring. As its name implies, the Wangkangurru elder Mick McLean said, 'the Emus must have been there first, *ularaka* (Histories) could travel same place different times'. Although there may be different stories for a place, there is only one which first explains the name.

In the traditional culture of the Lake Eyre region placenames were much more significant, evocative and meaningful than what they are in modern times. They represented an ancient layer of the vocabulary, mostly reflecting the activities of Ancestors of the 'History Time'. The system was nevertheless flexible, as is shown by the duplication of placenames and double naming, and the way in which new placenames could be created.

---

34   -28.2647 Lat., 136.0778 Long.
35   -28.5347 Lat., 135.8333 Long.
36   -28.1464 Lat., 136.3824 Long. The Arabana name is noted in the Gazetteer.

References

Austin, P. 1978, 'A grammar of the Diyari language of north-east South Australia', unpublished PhD thesis, The Australian National University.

— 1981, *A Grammar of Diyari, South Australia*, Cambridge University Press, Cambridge.

Henderson, J. and V. Dobson 1994, *Eastern and Central Arrernte to English Dictionary*, IAD Press, Alice Springs.

Hercus, L.A. MS, Yurkunangku and Kurkari, (deposited at AIATSIS, Canberra).

Hercus, L.A. and V. Potezny 1999, '"Finch" versus "Finchwater": a study of Aboriginal Place-Names in South Australia', *Records of the S.A. Museum* 31(2): 165–180.

Hercus, L. and K. McCaul 2004, 'Otto Siebert: the missionary ethnographer', in *The Struggle for Souls and Science, Constructing the fifth Continent: German Missionaries and Scientists in Australia*, Walter Veit (ed.), Occasional Papers 3, Strehlow Research Centre, Alice Springs: 36–50.

Hillier, H.J. 1904, 'Map of Reuther's Gazetteer of 2468 placenames in north-eastern South Australia', Unpublished map, South Australian Museum, Adelaide.

Horne, G.A. and G. Aiston 1924, *Savage Life in Central Australia*, Macmillan, London.

Howitt, A.W. 1904, *The Native Tribes of South-east Australia*, McMillan, London.

Lindsay, D.M.S, Report on a Journey from Dalhousie to the Queensland Border (January 1885), South Australian Museum, Adelaide.

Reuther, J.G. 1981, *The Diari. Translated into English by P.A. Scherer*, AIAS microfiche no. 2, Australian Institute of Aboriginal Studies, Canberra.

Siebert, O., Letters to A.W. Howitt. Howitt Collection, Melbourne Museum Archive.

Strehlow, T. G. H. 1971, *Songs of Central Australia*, Angus and Robertson, Sydney.

Vennemann, T. 1994, 'Linguistic reconstructions in the context of European prehistory', *Transactions of the Philological Society* 92, Blackwell Publishing, Oxford: 215–284.

12. Why did squatters in colonial Victoria use Indigenous placenames for their sheep stations?

Fred (David) Cahir

Federation University Australia

The archival records of many squatters in 19th century Victoria (formerly known as the Port Phillip District) often contain brief references to the processes involved in and decisions that led to the naming of their pastoral leases. This documentation is hardly surprising given that a squatter wishing to obtain a pastoral license would have to register a legal document with the colonial government, stating among other things the name of the run. What is perplexing is why a large number of pastoralists chose an Indigenous name – given that squatters were not under any instructions to bestow 'native names' whenever possible – unlike the surveyors who came after them.

Most etymological discussions, in Australia at least, have largely centred on the placenames of towns, cities and geographical features such as rivers, mountains and lakes. This paper aims to explore whether the reasons offered by contemporary writers and toponymists such as Cole (1991), Carter (1995), Randall (2001) and Furphy (2002) about why Indigenous placenames were adopted by the colonial usurpers for towns, cities and geographical features also mirror the stated reasons and symbolic intent of 19th century Victorian pastoralists who chose to use Indigenous placenames when naming their pastoral leases or private places.

Names are words, they are special words – that we use to identify a person, a thing or a place. Names are *aide de memoirs* that are capable of evoking powerful emotions. By way of personal example my eldest brother's name is Patrick. He was named after Patrick Edwards, the pilot of my father's bomber aircraft, who during the Second World War sacrificed his life so that his crew, including my father, could live. The name 'Patrick' then, in my family's household, symbolises a love and friendship pregnant with sacrifice, yet in many other households it is 'just' a name.

Conversely, placenames sometimes act to facilitate cultural inclusivity or exclusivity.

Discussion about Indigenous vocabulary in Australia being used by non-Indigenous people for naming natural and built features in the landscape are commonly placed into two appropriation categories, namely: imperialist and pragmatic.

The appropriation of Indigenous names whether it is for houses, suburbs, streets or geographical features has long been argued by historians and geographers to be a vehicle for cultural subordination. By way of example Hartley (1988) contended that 'As much as guns and warships, maps have been the weapons of imperialism.' Writing specifically of the colonisation process in Australia, Rosaldo (cited in Birch 2003: 154) coined the phrase 'imperialist nostalgia' to describe how the dominant culture in Australian society, the colonisers, having altered or destroyed the culture of the 'other', then appropriate it for their own gain, whilst at the same time denying their own complicity in the often aggressive devastation of the culture they have displaced. This argument is persuasive and Birch (2003) considers it is substantiated by an analysis of Sir Thomas Mitchell's journals which clearly demonstrate that as a representative of British colonial power he attached names to landscapes which were designed to legitimise the legal ownership of the culturally dominant group. This was the case whether the name was a non-Indigenous or an Indigenous one; exemplified by the fact that Mitchell (cited in Birch 2003: 155) noted 'I have always gladly adopted Aboriginal names'. Birch (2003: 155) contends that 'Mitchell was a surveyor, taking control of the land by charting it on a map. By naming features, he placed a symbolic British flag on each of them. The land was charted, ordered and labelled, becoming a colonial possession'. Mitchell is also an exemplar of colonial appropriation of Aboriginal language for the purpose of place naming for pragmatic reasons. Two pragmatic reasons for place naming are postulated by Kostanski (2003: 18–19) which Kostanski has termed: 'Colonial historical identification' and 'Anglo-Indigenous historical identification'. Kostanski notes for instance that Mitchell sought to appropriate territory for the British Crown and also had as his objective in bestowing Anglo placenames a desire to achieve recognition and fame for his surveying work and 'believed that this could be obtained through naming places of the Australian landscape'. In addition, Kostanski also draws directly upon Mitchell's journals of 1836 which reveal that 'The great convenience of using native names is obvious ... so long as any of the Aborigines can be found in the neighbourhood ... future travellers may verify my map. Whereas new names are of no use in this respect' (Mitchell 1838: 174).

But what of the 19th century pastoralists who occupied Aboriginal lands in what is now known as Victoria? Were they too willingly practising a colonialist practice of cultural theft when they appropriated Indigenous placenames for their sheep stations? It is necessary to first establish their pedigree before answering this question. It is not often articulated but the first wave of pastoralists who sought to occupy the Port Phillip District of New South Wales, as it was known until 1850, were considered illegal trespassers by the Colonial and British authorities and the newspapers of the period, hence the term 'squatter'. The squatters themselves were acutely aware of their precarious legal position and were very keen to shore up all possible credibility as legal landholders they possibly could. In a series of letters (Mercer 1838) between two squatters at Port Phillip – John Wedge and George Mercer, it is possible to discern a palpable concern with their tenure on the lands they had claimed and the importance they placed on keeping in with Government sanction by enacting a treaty and being on the best possible terms with the Aboriginal people of Port Phillip.

> The arrangements made by Sir Richard Bourke [Governor of New South Wales] to relieve us from the engagements with the Natives, by the Government taking upon itself the fulfillment of the terms agreed upon, is also prejudicial to our interests; for the Natives still expect to receive from our hands [manuscript underlined] the fulfillment of the Treaty – Nor can they be made to understand the true bearing of Sir Richard Bourke's arrangement, – and in fact, it is incumbent on those of the Association who have formed establishments still to contribute very largely to the Natives on their periodical visits; – and thus the onus of keeping up the friendly intercourse that was established by the [Batman's] treaty of 1835, devolves upon us; and be it remembered that it is the only instance of an intercourse being established with the Natives of new Holland, if with any others without bloodshed. – This ought in fairness to be taken into consideration by the Government, and to weigh in our favour (Mercer 1838, n.p.)

In this context we can see that, unlike Mitchell who possessed the imprimatur (and responsibilities) of imperial power to name and claim for the Crown, the squatters were undertaking a risky land grab for purely pecuniary purposes.

Having come across the Bass Strait with their thousands of sheep the predominately Scottish squatters immediately commenced to name the surroundings they had come to occupy as their own. Of course the landscape was not devoid of placenames as prior to permanent colonisation sealers, whalers, runaway convicts, exploration parties and two failed convict settlements had mapped and recorded many Indigenous names which are still with us today, including: Geelong, Werribee, Corio and Anakie. These early non-Indigenous sojourners had also bestowed many non-Indigenous names upon the Port Phillip District in the decades before, including: Convincing Ground, Western Port, Portland and Sealer's Cove.

The Western colonisers had a long tradition themselves of place naming according to criteria such as geography. This is evidenced by one of the instructions given to Robert Hoddle, the Government Surveyor at Port Phillip, upon commencement of his surveying work in July 1837 which was to: 'assign to each Parish a name founded on the native appellations of any hill or place therein'. Two years later in 1839 Hoddle (Clark 1998: 28) gave some indication of the difficulty and lack of relish he found in following this instruction, stating to G.A. Robinson (Chief Protector of Aborigines in Port Phillip, 1838–1850) that he (Hoddle): 'pieces the Aboriginal names of localities – it was ordered by the government'. The squatters it should be remembered had no such imperative from any governmental authority about how to name their pastoral leases. The only placenames etiquette they observed was their own. Sadly, we have few surviving records of squatters committing to paper the reasons why they chose one name over another for their pastoral leases. By conferring with Billis and Kenyon's (1932) list of pastoral licencees of the Port Phillip District we do know that of the hundreds of squatting runs which quickly developed into what is now Victoria that the majority maintained 'existing Aboriginal designations' (Wallace 2005: 156). This is perplexing given Cole's (1991: 138) study of Victorian placenames which found that 'Western peoples tend to use possessive, commemorative and commendatory names far more frequently than descriptive names'.

Why did such a large percentage of squatters choose to use Indigenous names for the lands they were usurping from the Indigenous custodians? Some of the reasons for their naming practices are arguably straightforward. For example there is some evidence to suggest (Matthews 1974) that a small number of squatters merely followed their age-old tradition of bestowing placenames after individuals, as Anglo-Saxons have a long tradition of doing so. A number of placenames for towns and districts in England are thought to originate from the celebration of prominent individuals such as Gig of Ipswich, Glot of Glossop and Dudda of Dudley. Aboriginal name lists from 19th century non-Indigenous records provide us with some evidence that the process of naming one's station after an Aboriginal person almost certainly did occur. By way of example Morangourke Station may refer to Murrangurrk, Moorabbin Station to Murrobin, Truganina Station to Truganinni, Bungall Station to Bungil Jem, and Tarra Creek Station to Charlie Tarra. Another likely reason for squatters to use Aboriginal language in the naming of their pastoral runs in the 19th century was the continuation of the British convention of naming of places after a prominent geographical feature. By way of example, Wormbete, a sheep station in south-west Victoria named by Henry Hopkins (Koenig 1935: 89) in 1837, reputedly was conferred this name as 'the word Wormbete meant lake with a blackfellow's mound'. Similarly, another squatter in the western district named his station Yan Yan Gurt, which was supposed in non-Indigenous squatter memories to mean in the local Wathawurrung language 'ever flowing streams', presumably indicating the presence of permanent water. Other geographical placenames of Aboriginal significance were also handed down (Koenig 1935: 89) by non-Indigenous squatters which clearly memorialised Aboriginal occupation and evidence of permanent settlement such as 'Carrung-e Murnong [near the township of Birregurra] a native name meaning house of yams. The yam grew well in this parish and consequently yam refuse was plentiful in the ashes and ovens around which the natives built their camps.'

Toponymists (see Redmonds 2004; Reilly 2003; Kostanski 2009) are acutely aware that a placename is not a random thing. The motivational psychology for the naming of a place depends on a range of factors and must take into account innumerable causes including historical setting, stage of cultural development of the name conferrer and their social, political, religious or patriotic background. Was the naming process a desire to commemorate Indigenous individuals and thereby to record their attachment and even loyalty to those Aboriginal individuals?

Before we answer that question it is interesting to note that there are a significant number of sheep stations which appear to have been named after the resident clan names (see Clark 2005a). If we take the Ballarat region as a representative example there are at least four sheep stations that bear the resident clan name, namely Carngham Station, Caranballac Station, Kuruck-Kuruck Station and Wardy Yalloak Station. In recent times historians (Cahir 2001; Clark 2003; Broome 2005) have increasingly come to the conclusion that an appreciable number of squatters when initially taking up their runs in Port Phillip (Victoria) often conferred with and had very amicable relationships with clan heads who offered some degree of 'education' to the squatters in the way of bush lore. Often this tutelage was in the form of hunting, finding water and gaining a modicum of understanding about Aboriginal customary laws, and possibly these squatters bestowed the clan name to their stations as a type of pacifying gift or even as a symbol of colonial reciprocity – it is difficult to know. Some semblance of the degree to which Aboriginal tutelage about Aboriginal placenames was respected by colonists, though still couched in paternalistic tones, can be gleaned from Governor La Trobe's (2006) journal (3 October 1842) which describes his arduous travels through the Port Phillip District accompanied by the Native Police and also notes an occasion where he is instructed about Aboriginal placenames:

> Alone through the ranges leaving Waraneep [Warenheip] some miles to the right, the Cornish and Taylor's hut, 20 m. [miles], then 11 m. to Thomas', afterwards Beveridges. Struggle in the forest above; meet George Airey, on to Stieglitz 4 m. & 12 to Moore and Griffiths. It was at Mollison's on the morning of the 2nd that my black trooper "Dr Bailey", gave me a lesson about native names. "Mittern" -, "-Minutedon, -Momiteden, - Momitaten, -Momateden, - Momatzeden-, Monmacedon!" (La Trobe 2006: 3 October 1842)

It is possible of course that the squatters who named their sheep stations did so purely because they felt the Indigenous names 'sounded good'. Many colonists expressed their admiration of the Aboriginal names on the basis of their 'euphonious qualities'.

Squatters in the early period of colonialism such as the Kirklands who took land west of Ballarat at Trawalla (a Wathawurrung name believed to mean 'much rain') considered that the Indigenous names were preferable to English ones. Katherine Kirkland (1845: 27) wrote: 'Boning Yong is a native name and means big mountain. I like the native names very much: I think it a great pity to change them for English ones as it is often done'. Kirkland's sentiment about a preference for the Aboriginal names over English ones in Australia was not isolated. A decade later Samuel Mossman (1853), an adventurer on the Victorian goldfields mirrored Kirkland's approbation of native names:

> Not that we condemn the application of her Majesty's name to this beautiful province but when scarcely a town, river or hill is found without some official's name, from the Premier down to the lowest clerk in the office, names that seldom possess euphony – the system is fulsome. The native appellations are far more characteristic and pleasing to the ear.' (Mossman 1853: 75)

Another proponent of local names William Westgarth (cited in Ross 1911: 63) exclaimed 'One is apt to wonder how that picturesque and beautiful river came to be called the Hopkins' and then Westgarth queried why give such starched, hard names, when there are Eumeralla, Wannon, Doutagalla, Modewarre, Yarra Yarra, and countless other such natural and genial modulations to be had for the asking?'. More credence is given to the euphonious sound of Aboriginal names argument by Mundy (1852: 191) who weighed into the debate claiming emphatically that: 'Some of the native names of places are grandly sonorous and polysyllabic; it is well when they are retained by the English possessors of the lands instead of substituting vulgar and unmeaning European titles'. Three decades later the discussion about the merits of native names in Victoria was still burning brightly, the focus now squarely it would seem on the musical sounding attributes of Aboriginal placenames and some little deference to Aboriginal people. It is also observable that there is a call to an emerging nationalism and doubly to acknowledge the beauty of the savage Australian bush:

> Oh, spare the native names! 'Twere hard indeed
>
> Were "Tinpot Gully" handed down to fame
>
> As record of an old Australian name.
>
> Does "Murderers Flat" imagination feed

With aught of noble? Nay, we rather love

Words that possess the murmur musical

Of distant streams that through the forest fall,

Or sound of branches rustling high above:

Best Langi-Ghiran for the Eagle's Land,

Marida-Yallock for the Pleasant brook,

Corio, Yarra, sounds that well express,

In the strange language of a dusky band

Who caught their lesson from fair Nature's book,

The barbaric beauty of the wilderness. (Cuthbertson 1880 cited in Cooper and Brown 1987: 43)

Other squatters merely revealed that they had adopted Indigenous names for their runs without providing any explicit reasons for doing so. Robert von Stieglitz's (1878, n.p.) squatting run was named 'Ballanee' and he refers in his journal to two neighbours who bestowed Wathawurrung names to their sheep stations: 'Cowie and Steed gave their new run the native name of Bunjeeltap ... my neighbour called his station "Ballynue", the native name.' Alexander Thompson (Croll and Wettenhall 1937: 29), squatting also on Wathawurrung land in the Geelong district recorded that his station 'Kardinia, is the aboriginal word for sunrise'. There is some evidence that the prolific naming of stations with local Indigenous names is not simply a superficial fondness of the rhythmic sounding native names. More complex interfaces are arguably at play which have only recently been considered by Australian historians including the argument that some settlers possibly adopted local names that sounded similar to names from back home – such as Ballan and Buchan.

The extent to which Aboriginal culture and heritage has been employed to confer Australian national identity has become a contentious issue in Australian historiography. Furphy (2002) for instance is adamant that 'the use of Aboriginal place names in Australia is not an example of sensitive cultural interplay' whilst Griffiths (1996: 5) argues that: 'Throughout their history making, Europeans sought to take hold of the land emotionally and spiritually, and they could not help but deny, displace and sometimes accommodate Aboriginal perceptions of place. They were feeling their way towards the realisation that becoming Australian would, in some senses, mean becoming "Aboriginal"'. The records left by squatters in the early period of colonisation in Victoria certainly support this supposition. Cahir (2001) has presented as evidence of transmogrification the archival records of significant numbers of pastoralists and their workers who stated explicitly and implicitly that they had acquired a workable knowledge of the Indigenous languages where they had taken up a sheep station. It is worthwhile briefly exploring what the extrinsic and intrinsic motivations behind the invaders learning an Indigenous language were as this will allow us some insight into their place naming rationale.

Indigenous language acquisition on the colonial frontier, Cahir (2001) argues, was predominantly tied up with conferring with clan heads. Squatters often recorded, as noted previously, how they actively employed or enlisted the assistance of clan heads on their sheep stations and gathered an abundance of vital socio-economic intelligence from them. William J.T. 'Big' Clarke (1980), a squatter in the Ballarat region (at one time considered the wealthiest man in Australia) was like many other squatters in revealing that a friendly clan head had shown him his new country, guided him to local waterholes and boasted in later years of his knowledge of their language. Many squatters acknowledged that they enjoyed or endured mutually binding relationships with Indigenous people through language and assigned relationships. This was often evinced by name swapping, conferring of names and assigning of familial relationships. Clark and Cahir (2011) for example have considered the prevalence of Europeans who were recognised as deceased clan members who had returned to life and Cahir (2001) has identified the recording by squatters in colonial Victoria of the exchange of names. John Fawkner, considered one of the colonial founders of Melbourne wrote in his journal (15 December 1835 cited in Billot 1982: 21) of his discovery that Derrimut, a Boonwurrung man, had 'changed names with me this day'. In a similar vein Georgina McCrae (23 June 1843 cited in Niall 1994: 192), a pastoralist also on Boonwurrung country, wrote of the Boonwurrung's desire to 'exchange names with her children'. McCrae considered it a 'compliment to be received with good grace'. Some squatters listed the great benefits to be gained from appropriating elements of Indigenous language and culture (both material and intellectual). It seems clear that the benefits were predominately wrapped up in economic pragmatism such as the protection of their stock or securing a reliable labour force, a fact evinced by Foster Fyans (1842, n.p.), first Police Magistrate in the Port Phillip District who noted 'on my arrival here in 1837 I found scarcely an establishment in this neighbourhood without natives being employed thereon; many of them doing extremely well.'

There were also very significant degrees of indigenisation occurring on the early colonial frontier which was arguably about connecting with the land. Squatters, it has been suggested (Furphy 2002), were casting around for a new identity and certain elements of Aboriginal culture such as placenames were admissible. The evidence for this supposition is, by its very nature, as difficult to prove as it is to disprove and there are many critics. Birch (cited in Furphy 2002: 60) is sceptical about the notion of adopted native placenames and argues it 'does not represent or recognize an Indigenous history' whilst Rackham (cited in Redmond 2004: xi) is particularly cautious in this regard and has accused toponymists of 'clutching at straws and reading into place names more than they can say' and there is some validity in this concern. Dissenting voices such as Curthoys (cited in Furphy 2002: 60) argue there is adequate evidence to contend that 'white Australians have been involved in a mythological quest to forge relationships with the landscape through literature and legend'. Cahir (2001) goes further and has argued there are sufficient accounts in the early records which clearly demonstrate that elements of Aboriginality were powerfully attractive and highly sought after by some squatters. Some squatters who had significant inter-cultural relationships with Aboriginal people on their sheep runs displayed their affinities via a number of out-workings. Samuel Winter Cooke (cited in Forth 1980: 3), a squatter in the south-west district of Victoria whose diaries contain many references to a living together/living apart relationship with the local clans chose the name Lake Condah for his station house as he believed (incorrectly) that the name meant Black Swan in the native language. Moreover, he instructed his brother upon his death to: 'on no account bury me in any cemetery, and if my body is taken to Murndal [the sheep station's name was a Marr word for thunder] I would like to be buried in the stones where the blacks are buried.' Some squatters penned poetry using Indigenous language, others noted minor usage of Indigenous language interspersed with English such as 'borack' for No, 'mia mia' for hut/shelter and the use of the call 'Coo-ee'. Some evidence of this non-Indigenous longing to belong can be gleaned from the golden anniversary reminiscences of Western district (Victoria) squatter, J.L. Currie in 1894 (*Camperdown Chronicle*, n.p.) who reflected upon the naming of several sheep stations he had 'entered into possession of' in 1844. Currie noted that the naming process involving Aboriginal names was not done immediately upon usurping Aboriginal land, which arguably indicates a degree of feeling for the local language is observable. Whilst it is a long theoretical bow to draw, perhaps the Australian land which Carter (1995: 403) contends was 'unknowable' for the colonists, was after some time of association with the rhythms of Aboriginal seasons and eco-cultural occurrences with place – knowable: in some small degree attainable through associative knowledge and personal relationships with the previous 'occupiers'.

> The native name of the head of the spring is Anakie-boonnook. There was a strong tribe of natives, with some very fine men amongst them, owing I have no doubt to the abundance of food. In the swan egg season great numbers collected – the Elephant Marsh, Laggoon, Bailles Lake, Murnong Kiln Swamp, and c., were all favourite and extensive breeding places for waterfowl. The run was not named for some time after occupation by us. When this became necessary, and by official request,

it was named Gelengla. This I believe, was the aboriginal name for the spring at the head of Gelengla creek now Ti-Tree. The name Larra was the native name for the locality of a spring in the horse paddock ... It was pronounced by some Lawur, Larr-ach, and Larra. The last was adopted as being the best of the three, but after the name had been too well fixed to be altered, another pronounced it Lawarra, a much finer name than either. (*Camperdown Chronicle*, 28 April 1894, n.p. cited in Currie n.d, n.p.).

Even in more recent times, Wendy Lowenstein (1972: 4), a 20th century oral historian noted that in remote parts of Australia 'the old timers have a distinctive way of pronouncing local place names, and that all over Australia where men had lived and worked with Aboriginals they themselves used pidgin English as part of their everyday speech, so that they spoke of being "proper cold" or "proper hungry"'.

From a purely survivalist point of view there were some sound reasons for the squatters to name their pastoral station or 'runs' a local Indigenous name.

The bush was an inhospitable place even for experienced squatters. J. Kerr (1872) duly noted 'To be lost in the bush in Australia is indeed a most forlorn and bewildering position', a fact not lost on Robert von Stieglitz (1878, n.p.), a pastoralist in the Ballarat region who described how he became totally disoriented on his new station and was rescued from perishing in the bush by Murrydeneek, a Wathawurrung clan head. Von Stieglitz, who as previously mentioned bestowed on his station an Aboriginal name and had been saved by a local clan head whom he befriended, is an exemplar of the station placename origins conundrum: for Stieglitz (1878) also openly avowed his fear of Aboriginal people, noting that on account of the local clan being 'very dangerous' he had cooperated with a neighbour to make 'blue pills' (a euphemism for strychnine) to use on the local clans. This dualism in behaviour – the befriending of clan heads, conferring of Aboriginal names for their sheep runs and deep seated murderous stance – was not an anomaly on the colonial frontier. However, many other squatters expressed their admiration for the assistance and tutelage they received from their Aboriginal mentors. George McCrae (1911: 25), a squatter at Port Phillip gave tribute by noting: 'They not only guided us accurately, but taught us many lessons in bushcraft, and in the mode of approaching game, which perhaps we should never have picked up otherwise.' Sometimes the lessons for the white squatters, or chastisement in this instance, were about naming places. Clark (2005b: 172) noted how G.A. Robinson recorded the views of his Aboriginal companions on the suitability of the name 'Monkeys Gully' in Gippsland: 'Natives joked said what for call it Monkey Creek no monkeys only opossum, said white fellow plenty stupid call it what for no give it another name.' It is certainly feasible that squatters named their stations after Aboriginal placenames for the purely pragmatic reason that in the case of becoming lost they would be able to ask directions from an Aboriginal person and receive very clear directions to their sheep run. Thorpe (1935: 1) draws our attention to a critical aspect of place naming for Aboriginal people which also may have played a role in non-Indigenous squatters also adopting Aboriginal names for localities around their pastoral leases: food and water. Thorpe notes simply that 'while many of the meanings may appear frivolous, yet one cannot but notice that the factor of food and water enters largely into Aboriginal nomenclature.'

Conclusion

Historians have long paraphrased the strong disparagement exhibited towards Australia's Indigenous people but surprisingly have overlooked the degree of cultural accommodation that also took place at both a conscious and subconscious level. Many authors and historians discussing the appropriation of Indigenous placenames have failed to seriously consider the duality of expressions with which the squatters considered the Indigenous people. There is a considerable body of evidence to contend that a significant degree of unconscious transmogrification occurred amongst the squatters, the early usurpers of Aboriginal land in Victoria that invoked the linking of Aboriginal placenames to land and a sense of belonging. The reasons by squatters in colonial Victoria for the widespread use of Aboriginal placenames for their sheep stations is multifarious and importantly includes a growing sense of longing to belong.

References

Billis, R.V. and A.S. Kenyon 1932, *Pastoral Pioneers of Port Phillip*, Macmillan, Melbourne.

Billot, C.P. (ed.) Melbourne's Missing Chronicle being the Journal of Preparations for Departure to and Proceedings at Port Phillip by John Pascoe Fawkner, Quartet Books, Melbourne.

Birch, T. 2003, '"Nothing has changed": the making and unmaking of Koori culture', in *Blacklines: Contemporary Critical Writing by Indigenous Australians*, M Grossman (ed.), Melbourne University Press, Carlton, Vic.: 145–159.

Broome, R. 2005, *Aboriginal Victorians: a History since 1800*, Allen & Unwin, Crows Nest, NSW.

Cahir, F. 2001, 'The Wathawurrung people's encounters with outside forces 1797–1849: a history of conciliation and conflict', unpublished MA thesis, University of Ballarat.

Camperdown Chronicle, 28 April 1894, [cited in Currie, L. c.1890s, Scrapbook, State Library of Victoria (SLV), MS 8243].

Carter, P. 1995, 'Naming place', in *The post-colonial Studies Reader*, H. Tiffin, G. Griffiths and B. Ashcroft (eds), Routledge, London: 395–410.

Clark, I. 1998, *The Journals of George Augustus Robinson, Chief Protector, Port Phillip Protectorate, volume 2: 1 October 1840– 31 August 1841*, Heritage Matters, Melbourne.

— 2005a, 'Value of Victorian Aboriginal clan names for toponymic research', *Globe*, no. 57: 13–16.

— 2005b, 'George Augustus Robinson: his value as a resource for place names research', Victorian Historical Journal 76(2): 165–179.

Clark, I.D. and F. Cahir 2011, 'Understanding *Ngamadjidj*; Aboriginal perceptions of Europeans in nineteenth century western Victoria', *Journal of Australian Colonial History* 13: 105–125.

Clarke, M. 1980, *Big Clarke*, Queensberry Hill Press, Carlton, Vic.

Cole, L. 1991, 'Changing town names in Victoria', *Victorian Historical Journal* 62(3–4): 137–142.

Cooper, D. and P.L. Brown 1987, *The Challicum Sketch Book, 1842–53*, National Library of Australia, Canberra.

Critchett, J. 1992, *A Distant Field of Murder: Western District Frontiers, 1834–1848*, Melbourne University Press, Carlton, Vic.

Croll, R.H. and R. Wettenhall 1937, *Dr. Alexander Thomson: a Pioneer of Melbourne and Founder of Geelong*, Robertson & Mullens, Melbourne [Vic.].

Forth, G. 1980, 'The Winter Cooke Papers', *La Trobe Journal* 25: 1–8.

Furphy, S. 2002, 'Aboriginal house names and settler Australian identity', *Journal of Australian Studies* 26(72): 59–68.

Fyans, F. 1842, Letter from Foster Fyans to Governor LaTrobe, CSIL Add88F, Mitchell Library, NSW.

Griffiths, T. 1996, *Hunters and Collectors: the Antiquarian Imagination in Australia*, Cambridge University Press, Cambridge, Melbourne.

Hartley, J.B. 1988, 'Maps, knowledge, and power', in *The Iconography of Landscape: Essays on the Symbolic Representation, Design, and Use of Past Environments*, D. Cosgrove and S. Daniels (eds), Cambridge University Press, Cambridge [England], New York: 82–102.

Kerr, J.H. 1872, *Glimpses of life in Victoria by a Resident*, Edmonston & Douglas, Edinburgh.

Kirkland, K. 1845, *Life in the Bush by a Lady*, William and Robert Chambers, Edinburgh.

Koenig, W.L. 1935, *The History of the Winchelsea Shire*, Winchelsea Shire Council, Winchelsea, Vic.

Kostanski, L. 2003, 'Toponymic dispossession and spurious etymologies: Town names of the Murray River', unpublished Hons Thesis, Monash University.

— 2009, 'What's in a name?: Place and toponymic attachment, identity and dependence', unpublished PhD thesis, University of Ballarat.

La Trobe, C.J. 2006, *Charles Joseph La Trobe: Australian Notes 1839–1854*, Tarcoola Press, Yarra Glen, Vic.

Lowenstein, W. 1972, 'A collection of oral history, traditions and folk lore in the La Trobe Library', *La Trobe Journal* 9: 3–15.

McCrae, G. 1911, 'The early settlement of the eastern shores of Port Phillip bay with a note on the Aborigines of the coast', *Victorian Historical Magazine* 1(1): 1–24.

Matthews, C.M. 1974, *How Place Names Began, and how they Develop*, Lutterworth Press, Guildford.

Mercer, G. 1838, Letter from John Wedge to George Mercer, 2 July 1838, SLV, MS 8340, BOX 975/3(e).

Mitchell, T. 1838, *Three Expeditions into the Interior of Eastern Australia, with descriptions of the recently explored region of Australia Felix, and the present colony of New South Wales, Volumes 1&2*, T&W Boone, London.

Mossman, S. and T. Banister 1853, *Australia Visited and Revisited: A narrative of recent travels and old experiences in Victoria and New South Wales*, Addey and Co., London.

Mundy, G.C. 1854, *Our Antipodes, or, Residence and Rambles in the Australasian Colonies: with a glimpse of the gold fields*, Richard Bentley, London.

Niall, B. 1994, *Georgiana: A Biography of Georgiana McCrae, Painter, Diarist, Pioneer*, Melbourne University Press, Carlton South, Vic.

Randall, R. 2001, *Place Names: How they Define the World and More*, Scarecrow press, London.

Redmond, G. 2004, *Names and History*, Hambledon and London, London.

Reilly, Alexander 2003; 'Cartography and Native Title', *Journal of Australian Studies* 79: 3–14.

Ross, S. 1911, 'The history of settlement in the Western District of Victoria', *Victorian Historical Magazine* 1(2): 51–72.

Thorpe, W. 1935, *List of New South Wales Aboriginal Place Names and their Meanings*, Australian Museum, Sydney.

Von Stieglitz, R. 1878, *Reminiscences of R.W Von Stieglitz*, SLV, MS BOX 391/4.

Wallace, Bernard 2005, 'Naming Victoria's south west', *Victorian Historical Journal* 76(2): 147–164.

13. Multiple Aboriginal placenames in western and central Victoria

Ian D. Clark

Federation University Australia

In a recent paper on transparency versus opacity in Australian Aboriginal placenames, Michael Walsh (2002: 47) noted that in 'Aboriginal Australia it is relatively common for a given place to have multiple names'. In providing an overview of multiple naming practices Walsh (2002: 47) stated the 'simplest case is one place having two names. Such doublets can be intralectal or crosslectal. For intralectal doublets where there are two names for the one place in the same lect, both placenames may be opaque, both transparent, or one opaque and one transparent. … The same applies to crosslectal doublets where two names for the one place come from different lects'. Walsh (2002) observed that he was unclear on how multiple naming works and what its function is. Other than some case studies (Schebeck 2002 re Flinders Ranges, Sutton 2002 re the Wik region, Cape York, and Tamisari 2002) we are yet to gain a comprehensive picture for Aboriginal Australia. This paper adds to this discussion through a consideration of multiple naming in western and central Victoria using the results of research conducted by Clark and Heydon (2002) into Victorian Aboriginal placenames. The paper refers to examples from three languages in central and western Victoria Kulin, Wathawurrung, and Maar.

1. Intralectal doublets

In the study area, it has been possible to identify 20 intralectal and 12 crosslectal doublets.

Lake Buloke: *Banyenong* – Banye is said to mean 'burning of roots and stumps' and 'nong' 'the past' (Chauncy in Smyth 1878 Vol. 2: 205); *Buluk* is the descriptive Kulin word meaning swamp/lake, which suggests this may not be a placename (Hartmann in Smyth 1878 Vol. 2: 176; Blake et al. 1998: 118). Buluk is found elsewhere in Lake Buluk (Lake Bolac) and Bulukbuluk (the name of a swampy area near Mt Macedon (see Clark and Heydon 2002).

Lake Coorong: *Gurrong* is a common Eastern Kulin word for 'canoe' (Blake 1991: 112); the meaning of *Yarrak* is unknown, although it is found in the name of the local clan Yarrakaluk meaning Yarrak people (Hartmann in Smyth 1878 Vol.

2: 176) which may favour the primacy of Yarrak. Gurrong is found elsewhere in Coorong Swamp near Rupanyup; Mount Gorong in the Moorabool Shire; and Mount Korong near Wedderburn (see Clark and Heydon 2002).

McKenzie Falls: *Migunang wirab* – a Jardwadjali placename meaning 'the blackfish cannot get any higher up' (Thornly in Smyth 1878 Vol. 2: 63); and *Kurnung* which means 'a hill or impediment of any kind' as well as river (Surveyor General in Smyth 1878 Vol. 2: 201; Blake 1991: 112). Wirap (blackfish) is also found in Kuwirap (Kooweerup) and Djeriwirap (Clunie) (see Clark and Heydon 2002). Kurnung is found elsewhere in Kurnung (Badger Creek) and Kurnung-kurnung (Koonung Koonung Creek) (see Clark and Heydon 2002).

Mt Arapiles: *Djurid* – the meaning of which is unknown, however it is found in the name of the local clan – Djurid baluk (Robinson Jnl 4/4/1845); *Kawa* is a Kulin word meaning 'mountain, large mountain' (Hercus 1992: 23), and may not be a placename, but a descriptive word (Thornly in Smyth 1878 Vol. 2: 60; Surveyor General in Smyth 1878 Vol. 2: 199; Blake et al. 1998: 123). Kawa is seen in Mount Gowar near St Arnaud and in Kawa-panyul the name for a hill near Moonambel (see Clark and Heydon 2002).

Mt Elephant: *Djerrinallum* is a Wathawurrung placename meaning 'nest of sea swallows, terns' (Dawson 1881) [according to Porteous in Smyth 1878 Vol. 2: 214 this name means 'A hill of fire'], and is also the name of a local clan Djerrinallum gundidj.[1] Willam/yellam is the Woiwurrung, Boonwurrung, Daungwurrung word for camp/nest (see Blake 1991); *Larra* is the Wathawurrung word for 'stony' (Porteous in Smyth 1878 Vol. 2: 179; Blake et al. 1998: 141), however one source identifies Larra as the name of a spring at a homestead near Mt Elephant (Surveyor General in Smyth 1878 Vol. 2: 193).[2] Larra is also the name for a small township (Lara) near Geelong. It is possible then, that Larra is descriptive, or a microtoponym – referring to a nearby spring.

Mt Erip: *Yirrip* is the Kulin word for ironbark tree (Blake 1991: 121); the meaning of *Nollo* is unknown (Porteous in Smyth 1878 Vol. 2: 179). Robinson noted that this hill was 'celebrated among the natives for supplying the choice wood for their spears' (Clark 2000b: 158). Yirrip is also the name of a farming district (Yeerip) near Lake Mokoan; Yerrip Hill on Jacksons Creek in Sunbury; and an Aboriginal name for Pleasant Creek – Stawell (see Clark and Heydon 2002).

Mt Korong: *Korong,* Gurrong the Eastern Kulin word for 'canoe' (cf. Lake Coorong above) (Robinson Jnl 13/4/1847; Blake 1991: 112) and *Burrabungale* containing banyul/banhul a Kulin word meaning 'mountain' (Mitchell Jnl 5/7/1836; Blake

---

1 Clans are likely to be named after the locations.
2 There are two separate nouns in some Kulin languages – lar (with a dot under the r) 'camp, nest, home' and lar 'stone'.

1991: 106). Banyul is found elsewhere in Banyule Flats Reserve in Heidelberg; Lianganuk banhul (Mount Alexander); Bergerer panhul (an unidentified hill near Mitchellstown); Kawa-panyul (see above discussion for Mt Arapiles); and Pillawin-panyul (The Pyrenees) (see Clark and Heydon 2002).

Mt Macedon: *Geboor* (Mitchell Jnl 30/9/1836, confirmed by Robinson in Clark 2000b: 219) and *Tarehewait* (Robinson Jnl 21/1/1840).

Mt Napier: *Murroa* (first recorded by Mitchell Jnl 10/9/1836 and later confirmed by Robinson 1841) and *Taapuuk*, meaning unknown, however, the local clan was named Taapuuk gundidj (Robinson Jnl 5/5/1841) which would seem to give primacy to the latter name.

Mt Poolongoork: *Bula(ng)goork* meaning 'the two women' and *Mecornam*, meaning unknown (Porteous in Smyth 1878 Vol. 2: 179).

Murchison: *Boolumbel,* meaning unknown (Horsburgh 1850 in Clark 1999: 58) and *Mungallook*, yaluk = 'river, creek' (Robinson Jnl 6/11/1843; Blake 1991: 121).

Stockyard Hill: *Bapel* meaning 'fat' (Porteous in Smyth 1878 Vol. 2: 179), similar to bepul identified by Hercus (1986: 199) as the Djadjala (dialect of Wergaia) word for fat, also kidney-fat; and Powerwil, presumably a reference to *Barwal*, the Kulin word for 'island' (Robinson in Clark 2000b: 152; Blake 1991: 107). Barwal is seen elsewhere in reference to French Island and Swan Island (see Clark and Heydon 2002). A swamp at Tyntynder near Swan Hill is also known as Bapel (see Clark and Heydon 2002).

Swan Hill: *Barbariook* meaning unknown (Massola 1968: 46) and *Merterrukpert*, 'platypus' (Gummow in Smyth 1878 Vol. 2: 176). There is also a crosslectal *Wanilu* which is what people said in more recent days (Hercus, pers. comm. 25 June 2013).

Swan Island: *Barwal* (Morgan 1967: 7), the generic Kulin word for 'island' (Blake 1991: 107) (see discussion for Stockyard Hill); and *Woorang-a'look* which 'describes the rushing sounds of the surf through the narrow opening between the island and the mainland' (Lang 1865 in Smyth 1878 Vol. 2: 217). Blake and others (1998: 134) confirm that warri is the Wathawurrung word for sea, and warriyn is the adjoining Woiwurrung word.

Condah Swamp: *Konda* is the Dhauwurdwurrung word for 'water' (Dawson 1881; Mathew Papers 1907; Krishna-Pillay 1996: 214); *Tyarrk* refers to the common reed *Phragmites australis* (Dawson 1881; Krishna-Pillay 1996: 196; Blake 2003: 139). Krishna-Pillay considers 'quondum' is equivalent to 'parreeyt' meaning 'water'. There are many instances of Tyarrk elsewhere in Victoria, including

Langanong-djark the endonym for Ashens (Wilson in Smyth 1878 Vol. 2: 177);[3] Tjarrk the endonyms for Framlingham (Lane in Smyth 1878 Vol. 2: 187); Kelly Swamp (Robinson in Clark 2000b: 100); a swamp on Koort Koort Nong pastoral run (Scott in Smyth 1878 Vol. 2: 185); a swamp near Larra homestead (Dawson 1881: lxxxii); Olinda Creek (Robinson Jnl 30/8/1840); a creek near Mt Campbell (Robinson Jnl 27/5/1840); and finally the Melbourne suburb of Toorak.

Griffiths Island: *Mallin* (Robinson Jnl 28/4/1841) meaning 'island' and confirmed in the name of the local group Mallingundidj (Blake 2003: 109); and *Meerring* (Robinson Jnl 27/8/1841) meaning 'eye, hole in the ground' (Krishna-Pillay 1996). Mallin is found elsewhere in Kurnnamaleen, 'little islands' on the west side of Lady Bay near the mouth of the Merri River (see Dawson 1881: lxxx), and Kurtbaulen 'islands of stone', a descriptive name for the Stony Rises (see Scott in Smyth 1878 Vol. 2: 182). Meerring is seen elsewhere in Martung-mirring 'big eye', the name of a marsh in the vicinity of Lake Purrumbete (Scott in Smyth 1878 Vol. 2: 182); and Yatt mirng 'white eye', the name for a sink hole at Mount Rouse (Dawson 1881: lxxxiv) and a crater in Tower Hill Island (Dawson 1881: lxxxiv).

Lake Gnotuk: *Ngutuk-killingk* the Marr word 'my/your lake' (Lane in Smyth 1878 Vol. 2: 187; Krishna-Pillay 1996: 179) and *Yammercurrermudjoke*, of unknown meaning (Robinson in Clark 2000b: 88). Killingk is found in at least another 12 placenames including Korangamitj killingk; Kunawarr killingk; Yelingamadj killingk; Kilambidj killingk; Pertobe killingk; and Yambuk killingk.

Lady Julia Percy Island: *Din mar* 'this blackfellow here' (Dawson 1881: lxxix; Krishna-Pillay 1996: 193) and *Tirngoona* 'where the sun go away longa night' (*Port Fairy Gazette*, 26 August 1902; Krishna-Pillay 1996: 207).

Mt Eckersley: *Kang-beem-beem* meaning 'hill/mountain-head' (Robinson Jnl 27/5/1841; Krishna Pillay 1996: 174, 175, 186; Blake 2003: 104, 106) and *Yiyar*, also found in the local clan named Yiyar gundidj (Robinson Jnl 25/6/1841). Beem is found elsewhere in Butj-peem (Mt Eccles) (Lane in Smyth 1878 Vol. 2: 187); and Kartbimyoke 'large head' the name of an unidentified hill near Heywood (Robinson Jnl 28/5/1841). Kang is seen in Pinnambul kang (Mt Clay) (Robinson Jnl 18/5/1841); Wukrnnumbol caark (Mt Garvoc) (Lane in Smyth 1878 Vol. 2: 187); Karngeeyang (Keayang Home Station south of Terang) (Lane in Smyth 1878 Vol. 2: 187); and Lehurra kang (Mt Leura) (Lane in Smyth 1878 Vol. 2: 187).

---

3 Endogenous names are those given by an ethnic group to features in their own language area; exogenous names are those given to these features by external ethnic groups.

2. Crosslectal doublets

In the case of these crosslectal doublets seven are mountains, two are lakes, one is a promontory, and two are localities. In the case of the mountains and the promontory these features are clearly observable from the vantage point of the adjoining lect. The locality Hexham and the two lakes are on the margins of the lects concerned.

Franklinford: this placename falls within the Djadjawurrung dialect area. *Larng-i-barriamul* and *Willam-i-barriamul* both mean nest/camp/home (lar(ng)/willam) of the emu (barriamul) (Robinson Jnl 19/11/1841, Surveyor General in Smyth 1878 Vol. 2: 195, Blake 1991: 106; Hercus 1986: 207; 1999), however Larng-i-barriamul is endogenous and Willam-i-barriamul is exogenous. Willam is the Woiwurrung, Boonwurrung, and Daungwurrung word for camp/nest (see Blake 1991) and is found elsewhere in Willam-i-murring 'tomahawk-house' (Mount William Quarry near Lancefield) and Willam-wyn (camp/hut fire) (Pentland Hills) (see Clark and Heydon 2002). Lar is the Djadjawurrung, Djabwurrung, Wembawemaba, Djadjala, and Wathawurrung equivalent (see Hercus 1986) (q.v. discussion regarding Mt Elephant, above) and there are many examples of its usage including Larngikurrurk 'home of the magpie' (Cardinal Hill); Larngidorn 'nest of the bell-bird' (Doctors Creek); Larngiguragurg 'home of female kangaroos' (Mount Hollowback); Larngigure 'home of kangaroo' (Laanecoorie Reservoir); Larngikalkal 'dogs camp' and/or 'resting place of cicada'; Larngiyin 'camp of the moon' (Mount Misery); and Larnuk containing the possessive marker -uk 'his/her/its camp' (Mount Widderin Cave) (see Clark and Heydon 2002).

Hexham: *Bulla-bulla*, the Djabwurrung word meaning 'good' (Lane in Smyth 1878 Vol. 2: 187), and *Petereet*, the Dhauwurdwurrung name for the masked lapwing (formerly called spurwinged plover) (Goodall in Smyth 1878 Vol. 2: 187; Dawson 1881; Krishna-Pillay 1996: 179; Blake 2003: 135).

Mt Emu: known to local Wathawurrung people as *Tarecurrumbeet* (Robinson Jnl 5/8/1841), and to the Marr people as *Narrowhane* (Goodall in Smyth 1878 Vol. 2: 187).

Mt Langi Ghiran: *Larngidjerin* 'home of the black cockatoo' (Robinson Jnl 10/7/1841), the local Djabwurrung name; but neighbouring Wathawurrung named the feature *Corrong-ah-jeering* 'house/camp of cockatoo' (Tyers 1840 in Smyth 1878 Vol. 2: 216; Blake 1991: 112; Blake et al. 1998). Charles Tyers recorded the Wathawurrung name as referring to Mt Cole, which adjoins Mt Langi Ghiran, however its similarity with Langi Ghiran suggests he has misunderstood his source. According to Dawson (1881) the local Djabwurrung word for black cockatoo was 'wiran', a reference to the Banksian cockatoo (or red tailed black cockatoo; *Calyptorhynchus magnificus*). Chauncy (1862–66 in Smyth 1878), notes that 'gherin' is a reference to the yellow-tailed black cockatoo (funereal cockatoo; *Calyptorhyncus funereus*); however in support of Dawson, Blake and others 1998: 101 note that *djerrin* is 'black cockatoo with red'.

Mt Sturgeon: *Wurgarri* meaning 'black' is the local Djabwurrung name for this feature (Robinson Jnl 26/6/1841; Hercus 1986: 254), the local clan was named Wurgarri gundidj; the Giraiwurrung knew the feature as *Tolelokewearr* (Robinson Jnl 5/5/1841). *Malubgar* is a second Djabwurrung name recorded in the literature, meaning 'that mountain there' and is probably not a placename (Robinson Papers in Clark 2000b: 135).

Mt William: *Duwul* the local Djabwurrung language name meaning 'The Mountain' (Robinson Jnl 3/8/1841) – the local clan was known as Duwul baluk; *Worranneyan*, is recorded as the Giraiwurrung name for this mountain (Robinson Jnl 13/7/1841).

The Pyrenees: known by the local Djadjawurrung as *Pilliwin-panyul*, containing 'bili' 'stomach', panyul = hill (Robinson Jnl 27/2/1840; Blake 1991: 106), and seen in the local group name 'Pilliwin baluk' and to the adjoining Wathawurrung as *Peerick* (Tyers 1840 in Smyth 1878 Vol. 2: 216), possibly a reference to beerik, native cat (Surveyor General in Smyth 1878 Vol. 2: 199).

Wilsons Promontory: known to the eastern Kulin as *Wammun* (Robinson Jnl 27/4/1844) and western Ganai as *Yiruk* (Massola 1968: 53).

Lake Colac: *Kulak*, the Gulidjan word for 'sand' (Dawson 1881: lxxx; Krishna-Pillay 1996: 198); the Wathawurrung knew the lake as *Koram* (Porteous in Smyth 1878 Vol. 2: 179; Surveyor General in Smyth 1878 Vol. 2: 193).

Lake Gnarpurt: *Ngarpurt* a Marr placename of unknown meaning (Porteous in Smyth 1878 Vol. 2: 179) and *Kongiadigallock*, an exogenous Wathawurrung placename possibly containing yaluk the Kulin word for 'creek/river' (Morgan 1967: 36; Blake et al. 1998: 133).

Mt Kerangemoorah: known to the local Gulidjan as *Korrangermurrer* (Robinson Journal 27/3/1841) and as *Worayan* to their Wathawurrung neighbours (Porteous in Smyth 1878 Vol. 2: 179).

Mt Shadwell: *Boorook* or *Boorook kang*, a Giraiwurrung toponym meaning 'head mountain' (Robinson Jnl 4/4/1841; Scott in Smyth 1878 Vol. 2: 181; Goodall in Smyth 1878 Vol. 2: 187) [translated as 'a cold in the head' (Porteous in Smyth 1878 Vol. 2: 214)], and the local clan was named Boorook gundidj; and *Dooroobdoorabal* was the Wathawurrung name for this feature (Tyers 1840 in Smyth 1878 Vol. 2: 216).

3. Intralectal triplets

Michael Walsh (2002: 48) noted that some places have more than two names. In the study area it has been possible to identify nine toponymic triplets – six intralectal and three crosslectal.

Arthurs Seat: three Boonwurrung (Kulin) names have been recorded for this feature: *Momo*, *Tubberrubberbil* (Robinson Jnl 28/7/1840) and *Wonga*. Tubberrubberbil is possibly confused with Tubba Rubba Creek. Thomas (in Smyth 1878 Vol. 1: 55) noted that Wonga, a Woiwurrung clan head 'was born at Wonga (Arthur's Seat) and thus has the name'. Blake (1991: 96) noted that the adjective 'some' was 'wonga' in eastern Kulin.

French Island: *Bellarmarin* (Thomas 1840 map), *Bawal* (Haydon in Gooch 2006: 20; Blake 1991: 92), the descriptive Kulin word for 'island', *Woone* (Smyth field book in Gooch 2006: 272) and *Jouap* (Thomas 1841 map) (but Haydon gives the name of a lagoon on the island as Tooaiup (Gooch 2006: 272). O'Callaghan (1918: 92) has suggested that 'Tyaba' means 'worm'.[4] Jouap survives today as Tyabb, a township on Western Port Bay, not too distant from French Island.

Victoria Range: three names have been recorded for the Victoria Range: *Billiwin*, containing 'bili' 'stomach' (Surveyor General in Smyth 1878 Vol. 2: 202), after which the local clan Billiwin balug was named (Clark and Harradine 1990: 51), *Bareng* meaning 'river' (Surveyor's Returns, 1869–70; Surveyor General in Smyth 1878 Vol. 2: 199), and *Larneyannun*, containing 'lar(ng)i' 'the nest/camp of ...' (Robinson in Clark 2000b: 150)

Lake Condah: there are three names in the primary sources for this lake – all within the Marr language – *Koondoom* meaning 'water' (Mathew Papers 1907; Krishna-Pillay 1996: 214; Blake 2003: 169); *Karrap* meaning 'lake' (Lane in Smyth 1878 Vol. 2: 187); and *Tyarrk*, a reference to the common reed *Phragmites australis* (Dawson 1881: lxxxxii; Krishna-Pillay 1996: 196) (q.v. discussion regarding Condah Swamp, above). *Gundidj* meaning 'belonging to' (Stahle 1880 in Howitt Papers) is a fourth name recorded for this topographical feature however this is unlikely to be a placename and Clark (1990) has argued that Stahle has misunderstood his Aboriginal sources.

Mt Pierrepoint: *Allowween* (Robinson Jnl 1/7/1841), *Culmurri* (Robinson in Clark 2000b: 129), and *Parreeyt*, a Marr word meaning 'water' (Robinson Jnl 13/11/1843; Dawson 1881; Krishna-Pillay 1996: 214; Blake 2003: 169). Parreeyt

---

4 Hercus (pers. comm. 13 June 2013) has suggested that it is possible that O'Callaghan may have been thinking of the Arrernte tyape 'grub'.

is seen elsewhere, for example, 'Mumpareeyt' 'bottom of the water' (Spring Creek, near Mt Rouse); and 'Lapeeyt parreeyt' 'salt water' (a locality on the Hopkins River) (see Clark and Heydon 2002).

Port Fairy: *Puyupkil*, a reference to *Mesembryanthemum* or pig face, and the name of the local clan Puyupkil gundidj (Robinson in Clark 2001b: 18; Krishna-Pillay 1996: 193), *Tarngunnet* (Robinson in Clark 2000b) a placename similar to that recorded for Lady Julia Percy Island (Tirngoona, see above) which was translated as 'where the sun go away longa night'; and *Nyamat* meaning 'sea, ocean, sea water, wave' (Robinson Jnl 28/4/1841; Lane in Smyth 1878 Vol. 2: 187; Krishna-Pillay 1996: 198; Blake 2003: 198).

4. Crosslectal triplets

Mt Ida: *Borebine* [Daungwurrung] (Robinson Jnl 27/5/1840); *Dayderric* [Daungwurrung] (Robinson Jnl 27/5/1840); *Dyerndemal* [Djadjawurrung] (Robinson Jnl 29/11/1842).

The Grampians: *Gariwerd*, the Jardwadjali/Djabwurrung name for the mountain range meaning 'The Mountain Range' (Robinson Jnl 11/6/1841; Clark and Harradine 1990: 44); *Murraibuggum*, containing marree meaning 'stone', the Dhauwurdwurrung name (Tyers 1842 in Smyth 1878 Vol. 2: 66; Krishna-Pillay 1996: 206; Blake 2003: 192); and *Tolotmutgo*, the Wathawurrung name for these mountains (Tyers diary 26/2/1840). In addition to these three names, there are two other attributions found in the literature: *Duwul*, a Kulin word meaning mountain, that also refers specifically to Mt William (Dawson 1881: lxxxii); and *Kawa*, a Kulin generic word meaning 'abrupt mountains' and probably a descriptive word and not a placename (Wilson in Smyth 1878 Vol. 2: 178; Blake et al. 1998: 123).

Mt Gellibrand: *Worcanweluc*, the local Gulidjan name (Robinson Jnl 25/3/1841); and *Loo-larrung-oo-lak*, its Wathawurrung name, recorded by Tyers (Jnl 19/10/1839; also see Tyers 1840 in Smyth 1878 Vol. 2: 216). Robinson (Jnl 13/11/1843) recorded a third name for Mt Gellibrand, *Nolarric*, however, its language of origin is unknown.

5. Conclusion

This study has found 19 possible intralectal doublets in the study area. Of these, perhaps nine may be based on errors in that descriptive words have been mistaken as placenames, for example, buluk the generic Kulin word for lake, kawa the generic Kulin word for mountain/large mountain, barwal the Kulin word for island and mallin, the Marr equivalent. Others may be examples of confusion between names of the primary feature, such as a mountain, and a microtoponym of a feature near the mountain, such as a spring – this was the case at Djerrinallum. Other examples suggest a misunderstanding between the Aboriginal source and the recorder – such as Ngutuk-killingk which means 'my/your lake'. The situation regarding intralectal doublets was similar with intralectal triplets – it was difficult to find examples where all three names had integrity – many were confusions between generic words for features such as islands, rivers, water, lake, and sea. In the case of cross-lectal placenames, the situation has greater clarity and all 12 examples studied here are considered to have integrity. In two cases both crosslectal names have the same meaning – Larng-i-barriamul and Willam-i-barriamul both mean 'nest/camp/home of the emu' and Larng-i-djerin and Corrong-ah-jeering both mean 'nest/camp/home of red tailed black cockatoo'. Similarly with crosslectal triplets all three examples were considered to have integrity. This study has not been able to show how multiple naming worked, nor its function, but it nevertheless has added to the ongoing discussion by providing some understanding of the situation in western Victoria.

References

Blake, B.J. 1991, 'Woiwurrung, the Melbourne Language', in *The Handbook of Australian Languages*, Vol. 4 The Aboriginal Language of Melbourne and other Grammatical Sketches, R.M.W. Dixon and B.J. Blake (eds), Oxford University Press, South Melbourne: 31–124.

— 2003, *The Warrnambool Language – A Consolidated Account of the Aboriginal Language of the Warrnambool Area of the Western District of Victoria based on nineteenth-century sources*, Pacific Linguistics, Research School of Pacific and Asian Studies, The Australian National University, Canberra.

Blake, B.J., I.D. Clark and S.H. Krishna-Pillay 1998, 'Wathawurrung: the language of the Geelong-Ballarat area', in *Wathawurrung and the Colac Language of Southern Victoria*, B.J. Blake (ed), Pacific Linguistics, Series C, Vol. 147, Research School of Pacific and Asian Studies, The Australian National University, Canberra: 59–154.

Clark, I.D. 1990, *Aboriginal Languages and Clans, an Historical Atlas of Western and Central Victoria, 1800–1900*, Monash Publications in Geography, No. 34, Department of Geography, Monash University, Clayton.

— 1999, *A History of the Goulburn River Protectorate Station at Murchison, 1840–1853*, A Report to the Heritage Services Branch, Aboriginal Affairs, July.

Clark, I.D. (ed.) 2000a, *The Journals of George Augustus Robinson, Chief Protector, Port Phillip Aboriginal Protectorate*, Volumes 1–6, Heritage Matters, Clarendon [Cited as Robinson Jnl].

— 2000b, *The Papers of George Augustus Robinson, Chief Protector, Port Phillip Aboriginal Protectorate*, Volume 2, Heritage Matters, Clarendon.

Clark, I.D. and L.L. Harradine 1990, *The Restoration of Jardwadjali and Djabwurrung Names for Rock Art Sites and Landscape Features in and around the Grampians National Park*, A submission to the Place Names Committee on behalf of Brambuk Inc. and the Koorie Tourism Unit, Victorian Tourism Commission, Melbourne.

Clark, I.D. and T.G. Heydon 2002, *Dictionary of Aboriginal Placenames of Victoria*, Victorian Aboriginal Corporation for Languages, Melbourne.

Dawson, J. 1881, *Australian Aborigines; the languages and customs of several tribes of Aborigines in the Western District of Victoria*, Robertson, Melbourne.

Gooch, R. 2006, *Frontier French Island*, Prahran Mechanics Institute Press, Prahran.

Hercus, L.A. 1986, *Victorian Languages: A Late Survey*, Pacific Linguistics Series B-No. 77, Department of Linguistics, Research School of Pacific Studies, The Australian National University, Canberra.

— 1992, *Wembawemba Dictionary*, The Author, Canberra.

Howitt, A.W. Papers, State Library of Victoria, Ms. 9356.

Krishna-Pillay, S.H. (ed.) 1996, *A Dictionary of Keerraywoorroong and Related Dialect*, Gundidjmara Aboriginal Cooperative, Warrnambool.

Massola, A.S. 1968, *Aboriginal Placenames of South-east Australia and their Meanings*, Lansdowne Press, Melbourne.

Mathew, J. Papers, Australian Institute of Aboriginal and Torres Strait Islander Studies, Canberra, Ms. 950.

Mitchell, T.L. 1996, *Three Expeditions into the interior of Eastern Australia with the Descriptions of the Recently Explored Region of Australia Felix, and of the Present Colony of New South Wales*, 2 Vols, Brian A. Kelly, Maryborough [first published 1839] [cited as Mitchell jnl].

Morgan, J. 1967, *The Life and Adventures of William Buckley Thirty-two years a wanderer amongst the Aborigines of the then unexplored country around Port Phillip, now the province of Victoria*, Heinemann, London [First published 1857].

O'Callaghan, T. 1918, *Names of Victorian Railway Stations with their origins and meanings, together with similar information relative to the Capital Cities of Adelaide, Sydney, Brisbane and a few of the Border Stations of New South Wales and South Australia*, HJ Green, Acting Government Printer, Melbourne.

Schebeck, B. 2002, 'Some remarks on placenames in the Flinders', in *The Land is a Map: Placenames of Indigenous Origin in Australia*, L. Hercus, F. Hodges, and J. Simpson (eds), Pandanus Books in association with Pacific Linguistics, Canberra: 140–156.

Smyth, R.B. 1878, *The Aborigines of Victoria: with notes relating to the habits of the natives of other parts of Australia and Tasmania*, 2 Volumes, Victorian Government Printer, Melbourne.

Surveyor's Returns 1869–70, Surveyor General Inward Correspondence, Miscellaneous Surveyors' Returns 1869–70, Department of Natural Resources and Environment, Melbourne, 1 folder [Copy is held by the Victorian Aboriginal Corporation for Languages, Melbourne].

Sutton, P. 2002, 'On the translatability of placenames in the Wik region, Cape York Peninsula', in *The Land is a Map: Placenames of Indigenous Origin in Australia*, L. Hercus, F. Hodges, and J. Simpson (eds), Pandanus Books in association with Pacific Linguistics, Canberra: 75–86.

Tamisari, F. 2002, 'Names and Naming – speaking forms into place', in *The Land is a Map: Placenames of Indigenous Origin in Australia*, L. Hercus, F. Hodges, and J. Simpson (eds), Pandanus Books in association with Pacific Linguistics, Canberra: 87–102.

Thomas, W. 1840 map of Western Port [reproduced in Moorhead, L.M. 1971, Mornington in the wake of Flinders, Shire of Mornington, Mornington].

Thomas 1841 map in Thomas, W Papers, Sixteen volumes and eight boxes of papers, journals, letterbooks, reports, correspondence, etc, Mitchell Library, Sydney, uncatalogued Mss, Set 214, Items 1–24.

Tyers, C.J. Diaries and Letterbooks, La Trobe Library, Melbourne, Ms. 8151.

Walsh, M. 2002, 'Transparency versus opacity in Aboriginal placenames', in *The Land is a Map: Placenames of Indigenous Origin in Australia*, L. Hercus, F. Hodges, and J. Simpson (eds), Pandanus Books in association with Pacific Linguistics, Canberra: 43–49.

14. Dissonance surrounding the Aboriginal origin of a selection of placenames in Victoria, Australia: Lessons in lexical ambiguity

Ian D. Clark
Federation University Australia

When studying the history of some 3,400 Aboriginal toponyms in Victoria, Australia, the majority of placenames were found to have no equivocalness or ambiguity about them (Clark and Heydon 2002). Although it was not possible to find meanings for every one of these Aboriginal placenames, in terms of historical accounts and folk etymology there was no ambiguity – the vast majority of the placenames are accepted in the source material as being of Aboriginal origin. This paper concerns some 26 placenames for which there is dissonance or a lack of agreement about whether or not they are Aboriginal in origin. These names are considered in some detail in an effort to resolve their lexical ambiguity and an attempt is made to explain the reasons for the ambiguity and to find any patterns and causal factors. The merits of the claims and counter claims in each case will be examined and an attempt made to categorise the assertion of Aboriginal etymology as either grounded in the historical evidence, or likely to be explained by folk etymology – that is, a false meaning based on its structure or sound that may lack historical basis but has been accepted through common practice, or explained as a false etymology that neither accords with historical evidence nor equates with folk etymologies.

A critical issue when considering toponymic etymology is the fragility of toponymic knowledge and the concomitant difficulty of learning about the origins of placenames. Who is the custodian of toponymic histories and who keeps alive the history and memory of placename making at the local level? Is this history a thing of fragments recorded in local histories, or preserved in oral and family histories, or part of a database or register kept by local museums and historical societies and local government? In many cases we no longer know the circumstances by which places were given names, and even less are we able to reconstruct the toponymic history of most places, that include details of who gave the places names, and the reasons behind their adoption. Furthermore, toponymic attachment is not a monolithic phenomenon; we should expect heterogeneous etymologies where there exist divergent associations with their own vernacular *raison d'etre*. Thus in many cases, polysemy is likely to be normative and monosemic etymology the exception. Another real possibility is that most placenames are likely to be onomastic palimpsests, in that they represent accumulated iterations, glosses, or etymologies laid one over the other. Thus divergent etymologies need not require validation, but rather recognition that interpreting a placename is a dynamic process in which the etymology of a given placename may change over time and change for different iterations.

In some cases it may not be possible to resolve the lexical ambiguity and the equivocalness must therefore remain. Furthermore, in the context of colonial placename making, it has to be acknowledged that there may be numerous instances of Aboriginal placenames in their Anglicised form having the appearance of being non-Aboriginal in their origin (such as 'Cherrypool', an Anglicisation of Djarabul, see Clark and Heydon 2002: 58). Likewise there may be several names that owe their origin to exogenous names that appear to be similar to local Aboriginal words and the similarity is purely co-incidental but one that fails to withstand critical scrutiny (for example, Dimboola and Baddaginnie). In other cases the ambiguity may be deliberate. For example, Buchan in eastern Victoria (which is discussed in more detail below) is a contested toponym, with some sources attributing it as a Scotch name, whereas others suggest it is a contraction of Bukkan-munjie, a local Aboriginal name meaning 'place of the bag'. However, without hard evidence to the contrary the similarity between Buchan and Bukkan-munjie may be accidental; then again, the Scottish Buchan may have been conferred because of its similarity to the local Indigenous toponym, so the polysemy is deliberate and not accidental.

The methodology that will be followed will be to examine the entries of the various reference books for Victorian placenames, such as Saxton (1907), O'Callaghan (1918), Martin (1944), Massola (1968), Blake (1977), and Clark and Heydon (2002), and when relevant consider local histories and regional placenames studies such as Gardner (1991, 1992, 1996), Tully (1997) and Sinnott (2003). Kostanski (2009: 184) has discussed the methodological difficulties and limitations of toponymic books such as those of Massola (1968) and Blake (1977) that may in part explain the lack of rigour in their research.

1. Acheron

Acheron is the name of a river, a settlement, an Aboriginal station, gold diggings at Swamp Creek, a gap in the Great Dividing Range, a pastoral run, a ridge in the Black Range State Forest, and a scenic road called the Acheron Way (Sinnot 2003). Saxton (1907: 5) considered it was a 'Classical name'. According to Martin (1944: 5) Acheron Way 'was the name of a river in Epirus (north-west ancient Greece), regarded in awe as connected with the underworld'. Blake

(1977: 22) commented 'in 1839 Fletcher and Coburn took up their stn [station] between Acheron and Rubicon rivers, naming it after ancient Greek river which reputedly flowed to underworld'. Massola (1968) does not assert that Acheron is an Aboriginal placename. Barry Blake (2001 in Clark and Heydon 2002) considers it is a distortion of the Aboriginal name 'Ngaragon'. Sinnott has argued that Les Blake (1977) was

> unaware of the Aboriginal (Taungurong) name for the river: Agaroon (Neumayer) or Nyaggeron. Barry Blake has suggested that the original Taungurong word was Ngaragon. However, Cockburn and Fletcher would have been well placed to modify the Taungurong name or names to Niagaroon and Acheron, as the two men were the first licensees (1839) of both pastoral runs. (Also, Europeans often failed to hear or record the initial ng- in Aboriginal words). Acheron is the Latin spelling of Greek Ackheron (Αχέρων) "River of Woe", from akhos (αχος), distress. The Acheron was one of the rivers of the Underworld or kingdom of Hades, and also the name of a river in Epirus, Greece. (Sinnott 2003: 11)

This placename may be an example of polysemy, in that the first European settlers heard Ngaragon and used 'Acheron' in its place, or then again its similarity may be purely coincidental.

2. Avoca River

The town of Avoca takes its name from Avoca River. According to Saxton (1907: 7) and O'Callaghan (1918: 24), the river was named by Major Mitchell in 1836. 'Sutherland vol. 1, p. 87, says that Mitchell gave the name 'moved, doubtless, by the "clearest of crystal and brightest of green" which Tom Moore has so sweetly celebrated in the Irish Valley'. Martin (1944: 8) clarifies that this is named after the Irish river identified with the 'sweet vale' of the poet, Moore. Blake (1977: 27) noted that the Vale of Avoca is in County Wicklow, Ireland. Wajnryb (2006: 10) also considers the name is a literary name after Thomas Moore's poem 'Sweet Vale of Avoca'. Mitchell (1839 Vol. 2: 169) named the river on 10 July 1836, his entry is fact of matter and gives no reason: 'At three miles beyond the pass, we crossed a deep creek running westward, which I named the Avoca, and we encamped on an excellent piece of land beyond it'. Massola (1968) does not assert that Avoca is an Aboriginal placename.

In the Brock family papers, in a list of Aboriginal placenames 'Boca' is given as the Aboriginal name for the river. Alexander Brock squatted at Coonooer station, on the Avoca River, north of St Arnaud, and his diary spans from 1846–1852. Tully (1997: 84) considers Boca is a Djadjawurrung word for 'dog', however this is not supported by primary Djadjawurrung sources such as J. Parker (in

Smyth 1878 Vol. 2: 159), which show that Djadjawurrung, consistent with other western Kulin dialects, called a tame dog 'kal' and the wild dog or dingo 'wilker'. A Djadjawurrung clan was known as the Galgal baluk (that is 'dog people'; see Clark 1990: 158). Djadjawurrung names for segments of the Avoca River include:

- 'Bangyeno banip' waterholes in the river south of Avoca with associations with the mythical bunyip;
- 'Djub-djub-galg' a camping place on the river where djub (melaleuca) was abundant;
- 'Natte yaluk' yaluk = river/creek, near Natte Yallock township;
- 'Witji bar' witji = basket grass, bar = river, referring to the river south of Charlton; and,
- 'Yangeba' yang = to sit (i.e. camping place), bar = river, the lower reaches near Lake Bael Bael.

In the Yorta Yorta language, which is a non-Kulin language, baka is their word for tame dog (Hercus 1986: 260) so it possible that Boca is a poor hearing of the Yorta Yorta baka, but this language area is quite a distance away from the Avoca River, so this is unlikely. It is more likely that Boca is Djadjawurrung pidgin for Avoca.

3. Ballan

In terms of dictionaries of Victorian placenames, there is a consensus that Ballan is a toponym transplanted from north Ireland. For example, according to Saxton (1907: 8), Ballan was named by 'Mr. Robt. Von Steiglitz [sic] after a property in the north of Ireland, where he was born'. The *Ballan Times* accepted Saxton's interpretation (*Ballan Times*, 21 November 1912 in Ballan Shire Historical Society 1989: 4). Thomas O'Callaghan (1918: 25) was more expansive 'The village of Ballan was surveyed in 1850 by Assistant Surveyor Malcolm. Mr. Hoddle, in forwarding the plan, wrote that His Honour the Superintendent had named the village "Ballan". That was the name of a pastoral station close to the village, and then owned by Robert von Stieglitz. He had named it after an estate in Ireland'. O'Callaghan identified his information sources as W. Thorn, Chief Draughtsman, Lands Department, and J.G. Saxton's (1907) publication. Later dictionaries, such as A.E. Martin (1944: 8) and L.B.J. Blake (1977: 30) are derived from Saxton and O'Callaghan and do not add any further information. Massola (1968) does not assert that Ballan is an Aboriginal placename. The possibility that Ballan may have an Aboriginal origin was first raised in Clark and Haydon (2002: 21), and revolves around Ballan being a contraction of Ballindyapp. Robert William von Stieglitz occupied a run he named 'Ballan' (Ballen), 4,836 acres on the right bank of the Werribee River at Ballan in April 1838, and his brother, John Lewis von Stieglitz occupied an adjoining run named 'Ballanee', 16,000 acres north of

Ballan in 1838 (Billis and Kenyon 1974: 170). Emma von Stieglitz (nee Cowie), wife of John, has provided us with a pictorial record of early Ballan, and one water colour sketch is entitled 'First settlement at Balindyeapp, Ballan, 1839. Victoria'. A second sketch is entitled 'Balindyeapp, Port Phillip, Septr. 1839'. In an edited publication of Emma von Stieglitz's sketchbook, the editor K.R. von Stieglitz has noted that 'Robert von Stieglitz's original quarters on the Balindyeapp, Ballindyapp, or Ballan station (there were numerous spellings) stood on the crest of slope immediately west of the Werribee' (von Stieglitz 1964: Figure 1, n.p.).

Thus it is argued here that Ballan, which is a likely contraction of Balindyeapp, was favoured by von Stieglitz because of its similarity with his birthplace in Ireland. This may be an example of what Kostanski (2009: 177) has understood as 'Anglo-Indigenous placename production, wherein the primary aim of adopting an Indigenous name for colonial landscape identification reflected an imperialist vision, overlooking or little concerned with the true meaning of significance of the names', in this case, Balindyeapp. Thus Ballan may be another example of polysemy, or then again its similarity may be purely coincidental.

4. Balnarring

Balnarring is a beach resort south of Bittern on the western shore of Western Port Bay. It is most probably a corruption of the name of the early pastoral run taken up by the Meyrick brothers (Alfred, Maurice) and their cousin Henry in 1840 called 'Ballanrong' (Billis and Kenyon 1974: 114). Variant spellings of the station name include 'Ballyrungen' (Meyrick 1939: 135); Ballanarong; Ballanrong; Ballarong; Ballyrangue; Ballerangan (Meyrick 1939: 171). Meyrick (1939: 171) is clearly of the view that it is an Aboriginal placename as he notes that 'Ball or Balla meaning a camp is very common' and cites his source as A.S. Kenyon. According to Massola (1968: 8), Balnarring is from Balbalnarring, bal = camp, narring = hair, beard. Blake (1977: 32) posits that it is 'possibly fr. Abor. bael, gumtree, and "narang", little, or fr. Ballymering, Irish bally for "land belonging to"'. Gardner (1996: 27) has translated the name as 'hair camp'. Barry Blake (1991: 82) notes that the east Kulin word for 'beard' is 'ngarrin'; 'hair' is 'yarra', 'camp' is 'yilam' or 'wilam' which also mean 'bark'; 'red gum' is 'bial', and 'little' is 'waigurrk' or 'wayibu'. The Aboriginal origin of the placename Balnarring is contested only by Les Blake, and given the weight of the evidence supporting an Aboriginal origin, Blake's Irish etymology may be regarded as spurious.

5. Barham River

This refers to the Barham River, in south-west Victoria, near Apollo Bay. According to Massola (1968: 9), the name is a contraction of Burrum Burrum, meaning large, big. Blake (1977: 33) considers the name 'derives from Kent, England; however Barham may represent anglicising of Abor. n. for stream, burrum burrum, which possibly refers to big stones in river bed'. Pascoe (in Clark and Heydon 2002) suggests the name means muddy, presumably a corruption of 'burrum', seen elsewhere in western Victorian placenames such as Burrumbeep, Burrumbeet, and Burrumbite.

6. Beulah

Beulah is a small town in the southern Mallee region of Victoria, some 395 km north-west of Melbourne. According to O'Callaghan (1918: 29), the placename is derived from the Biblical Beulah from Isaiah 62, 4. 'Thou shalt no more be termed Forsaken, neither shall thy land any more be termed Desolate, but thou shall be called Hephzi-bah and thy land Beulah, for the Lord delighteth in thee, and thy land shall be married' (Martin 1944: 14). Massola (1968) does not assert that Beulah is an Aboriginal placename. According to L. Blake (1977: 39f), 'various meanings such as Abor. Belar, red ochre; Biblical, fruitful land; and Eng. Names, e.g. B. Spa in Norwood, have been given but first selector Alex McKenzie from Beauly, Scot'. Les Blake is the only source for the dissonant etymology, and it may be disregarded as mere speculation on his part.

7. Bonn

According to Massola (1968: 11), the name means 'ashes'. This translation was first published by District Surveyor Philip Chauncy (in Smyth 1878 Vol. 2: 204) from information he obtained in 1862–66, from Aboriginal people at Swanwater near St Arnaud. This translation is confirmed by Barry Blake (in Clark and Heydon 2002). However, according to Les Blake (1977: 44), it derives from the German city Bonn on the Rhine River in what is now the state of North Rhine-Westphalia. Les Blake is the only source for the dissonant etymology, and the problems with his interpretations have already been discussed.

8. Buchan

Buchan is the name of a village, river and tourist cave in Gippsland. Howitt (1904: 80) observed that Bukkan-munji is 'now written Buchan, and is supposed to be a Scotch name given by some early settler from North Britain. It should properly be spelled as I have written it, being the native name for the bag in which the Kurnai carries various articles. Bukkan-munji means "bag there" or "the place of the bag"'. George Augustus Robinson (Jnl 22/6/1844 in Clark 2000a) has suggested another etymology *a propos* another placename similar to Bukkan-munji: 'Fish are called munje, hence the compound Munberlemunje and so on'. William Thomas (in Pepper and De Araugo 1985: 120) considered it derived from Buccan 'stack of rocks with a hole in it'. This rendition is supported by Roberts (1977: 14) who locates Bukkan munji at the Buchan River and Tarra Creek junction where the rock folds. Saxton (1907: 13) in one entry asserts it has its origin in Scotland, however in 'Additions and Corrections' he notes 'Native name for the bag in which the Kurnai carries various articles. Buk Kan Mungi means "bag there" or the place of the bag. The Native Tribes of S.E. Australia, A.W. Howitt, 1904. Instead of Scotland' (Saxton 1907: 3). Martin (1944: 18) has recorded that 'Buk kan, natives' word for a bag they carried. Buk Kan Mungi was said to mean 'place of the bag'. According to Massola (1968: 14), Buchan is derived from 'Bukkan-munji, bag there, the place of the bag'. Blake (1977: 49) notes that in 1839 it was the name of Bayliss' station derived from buchan buchan, smoke-signal expert, or bukkan munjie, place of grass bag. Seddon (1994: 62) accords the meaning 'women's article'. The Buchan Sesquicentenary Committee (1989) translates mungie as water. Clark (1999) notes that bukin; bugin in Wiradjuri also refers to a medicine man of supernatural ability. Gardner (1992: 17) translates Bukkanmungie as 'place of the woman's bag'. This placename may be an example of polysemy, a toponym with multiple etymologies that was deliberately selected because of its polysemy.

9. Mount Buller

According to Saxton (1907: 13) named 'After Charles Buller of the Colonial Office'. According to Martin (1944: 18), 'christened by Mitchell, 1835, after an official in the Colonial Office. Natives knew it as Marrang'. Smyth (1878 Vol. 2: 196) lists Marrang as the Aboriginal name for Mount Buller. Massola (1968: 14) confirmed that Marrang meant 'the hand', or 'an edible root'. Presumably he is referring to the eastern Kulin marnang or marnong = hand (Blake 1991: 8), and murnong the eastern Kulin word for the daisy yam *Microseris lanceolata* (Gott and Conran 1991: 6). Blake (1977: 182) posits the Aboriginal name is 'Bulla Bulla, i.e. two'. However, Blake (1991: 96) has given bulabil or bindjirri as the eastern Kulin word for two. Robinson (Jnl 11/5/1840 in Clark 2000a) provides the name Marinebut (sometimes transcribed as Warinbut), as the Daungwurrung name for Mount Buller, although Smyth (1878 Vol. 2: 196) lists Warrambat as the Aboriginal names for Mount Timbertop and Mount Terrible. Presumably Marine and Marrang are cognate. Robinson (1844 in Clark 2000b: 201), notes that buller is the Dhudhuroa word for mountain; however Clark and Heydon (2002) acknowledge that the similarity with Mount Buller may be purely coincidental. Sinnott has the following entry:

> Named by Sir Thomas Mitchell in 1835 after Charles Buller, a friend in the Colonial Office. Claims that it was named by Baron Ferdinand von Mueller in 1853 (first European to climb it) are unfounded as Mount Buller appears on Thomas Ham's Map of Australia Felix (1847) and is listed by Wells in 1848. Aboriginal (Taungurong) names: Marrang (Smyth, 1878), Warrinbut (Clark & Heydon). Les Blake mentions another Aboriginal name, Bulla Bulla, meaning two: this is dubious). Clark & Heydon point out that buller is also a Dhudhuroa word for mountain. (Sinnott 2003: 103)

The non-Indigenous origin of the placename Mt Buller is well attested, and its similarity with an exogenous Aboriginal word for mountain is probably coincidental.

10. Callawadda

Callawadda is the name of a pastoral district 29 km north of Stawell in the southern Wimmera region of Victoria. The locality formed part of John Robertson's 'Robertson's Station', some 22,400 acres on the Richardson River, north of Navarre; first taken up in February 1845 (Billis and Kenyon 1974: 272). Massola (1968) does not assert that Callawadda is an Aboriginal placename, however Blake (1977: 58), suggests the name is a corruption of an Aboriginal word for 'tall timber and plain', but fails to indicate his source. He posits that it 'may also be mis-spelling of Cadwallada which derives fr. Cadwaladr. Grandson in the fifth century of Cadwallan, ruler of North Wales'. Cadwalader or Cadwallader, which mean 'Battle Arranger' or 'Great General', are common names in Wales. Callawadda may be a transposition of Cadwallader, however until further research is undertaken, the etymology of Callawadda must remain unclear.

11. Caper Kelly

According to the Surveyors' returns 1869–70 and Surveyor General (Smyth 1878 Vol. 2: 200), Caper Kelly is the native name of a large salt lake in far western

Victoria. It has not been possible to locate this lake. This name is very similar to capercaillie or capercailzie (literally 'horse of the woods'), *Tetrao urogallus*, the name of a large European woodland grouse in Scotland, and caper-kelly is one form of pronunciation. The similarity between this apparent Indigenous placename and the common name of a European grouse may be coincidental.

12. Darnum

Darnum is the name of a small town south-east of Warragul in the Shire of Baw Baw. According to Saxton (1907: 21) it is a native name meaning 'parrot'. O'Callaghan (1918: 40), repeats Saxton's gloss and sources it from Bunce (1856: 33) and Smyth (1878 Vol. 2: 191); however I have not been able to substantiate the Smyth reference. There is a reproduction of Bunce's list in Smyth (1878 Vol. 2: 138). This definition is accepted by Massola (1968: 19) and Barry Blake (1991: 87). Copeland, in a local history of the Warragul Shire, noted the following:

> "Darnum" is supposed to have acquired its name when the various small townships along the railway-line were taxing the ingenuity of official minds to christen and tabulate with appropriate names. This particular locality emerged from the unknown and un-named, it is said, from an exclamation of the late Sir Thomas Bent. This irascible old politician was annoyed with the suggestions made by different ones, when he expressed a desire to have the place called something it would be known by, and it was not clear whether he said "Darn 'em" or "D___' em", but the milder expression appears to have been chosen, with a slight alteration and arrangement in spelling, to denote the little railway township. However, Darnum it has remained ever since. (Copeland 1934: 485)

Martin (1944: 29), asserts that 'it is generally believed that it was derived from an exclamation frequently used by Thomas Bent, Victoria's rugged premier' in 1904. Blake (1977: 79), believes the placename is the 'ancient n. for Doncaster, Eng., but is also Abor. word for parrot'. Gardner (1992: 12) suggests it almost certainly refers to the crimson rosella *Platycercus elegans* or the eastern rosella *Platycercus exemius*. This is an example where folk etymology has generated a popular explanation that is not grounded in the historical literature.

13. Lake Drung Drung

Drung Drung is the name of one of three lakes some 16 km south-east of Horsham. Samuel Wilson (in Smyth 1878 Vol. 2: 178) confirms that Drung Drung is a native name, but he does not provide a meaning. Saxton (1907: 22) considers it a native name meaning 'spoiling'. According to Martin (1944: 32) it is an Aboriginal name meaning 'much spoiled'. Massola (1968: 20) extends the meaning to 'spoiling, spoiled, ruined'. Blake (1977: 85) also notes that Drung is the name of an Irish village in County Donegal. Les Blake is the only source for the dissonant etymology, and it may be disregarded as speculation on his part.

14. Ecklin

Ecklin is the name of a swamp and a rural locality south of Terang, in western Victoria. Massola (1968: 21) noted that the Aboriginal name for Ecklin Swamp was Ecklin yalloack. This name was sourced from Lane in Smyth (1878 Vol. 2: 187), and contains yaluk the widespread Kulin word for creek. Blake (1977: 90) has raised the possibility that Ecklin is 'from Scot. L. Eck (*linn*, pool)'. Again Les Blake is the only source for the dissonant etymology, and may be disregarded as speculation.

15. Half-way Inn, Glenorchy

According to Wilson (in Smyth 1878 Vol. 2: 178), the local Aboriginal name for this locality was 'Greech', meaning 'fat'. Wilson noted that Aboriginal people 'assure me it is the native name, although the meaning suggests an English origin'. There is some similarity with the neighbouring Wembawemba word for 'fat' 'guradj' (Hercus 1986: 185); however, Barry Blake (in Clark and Heydon 2002) is convinced that 'greech' represents the English word 'grease', thus it is another example of misunderstood Aboriginal pidgin.

16. Jim Crow Hill

This was an early name for Mt Franklin, and was the name of a creek, range, and goldfield north of Daylesford. 'Mt Franklin' named after Sir John Franklin's visit to the Loddon Protectorate station in 1843 displaced 'Jim Crow Hill'. According to Saxton (1907: 36) Jim Crow Hill was 'Named by Capt John Hepburn. Capt. Bacchus, who accompanied him, asked what name should the ranges have, and Hepburn replied: Jim Crow, after a popular song'. Morrison (1967: 41) explains that the origin of the name 'Jim Crow' has intrigued many for a long time.

> Some believe it is the name of a former 'king' of the local Loddon tribe of Aborigines. Etymologically, the term "jim crow" was used for various implements, as for example, a "jemmy", which is a miniature form of a

bent crow (bar) and, somehow, the idea of bending or twisting seems to be implicit in its derivation. A device for bending iron bars was one time termed a "jim crow". About 1835, an American negro, James Rice who was a rather popular "song and dance" comedian wrote and popularised a song, the chorus of which was: "Wheel about and turn about and do just so, Turn about and wheel about and jump Jim Crow". Set to a catchy tune it swept the world, as similar songs do today. ... There seems to be no reason, to doubt the accuracy of the story that the application of the term "Jim Crow" to this region, stems from a trivial incident wherein Capt. Bacchus, riding on horseback between "Lalgambook" and Koorocheang with Capt. Hepburn, called to his companion, "What do you think we should call these ranges?" Hepburn (perhaps with the maddening refrain churning in his mind) replied: "Call them Jim Crow!" (Morrison 1967: 41)

Quinlan has noted that Mount Franklin

> which the early squatters called Jim Crow and the natives knew by the name of Lalgambook. John Hepburn used the name Jim Crow to refer not only to the mount itself but to the creek below it and to the district. Edgar Morrison who, in 1965, published the memoirs of Edward Stone Parker under the title *Early Days in the Loddon Valley*, believes that Jim Crow derives from the chorus of an American minstrel song, popular at the time of the first overlanders. It seems quite feasible, as he suggests, that the behaviour of this winding creek recalled to someone like the Mollison brothers the popular jingle, 'Hop a little, stop a little, jump Jim Crow'. Later, when the aboriginal station was established there, many took it for granted that the word referred to the natives. (Quinlan 1993: 99)

According to Blake (1977: 133), overlander Alexander Mollison's records list the district as 'Jumcra', 'Aboriginal name for which meaning not traced; "Jim Crow" was minstrel song from U.S.A. 1835'. Randell (1979: 222) in a history of the Coliban district explained that Mollison took up two stations in the vacant land immediately west of his Coliban station in early May 1840, naming the Loddon run 'Jumcra, probably an aboriginal name. The second run was called Boughyards. The men soon corrupted the first name into Jim Crow'. Tully (1997: 87) supports the view that Jumcra was corrupted to Jim Crow.

17. Kaneira

This is the name of a railway station and township on the Bendigo to Nandaly line in north-west Victoria. According to Saxton (1907: 38) and O'Callaghan (1918: 56), the station was named by 'Mr. Breen, the surveyor, after a man named

Kiniry'. Martin (1944: 47) notes 'Was originally Kiniry, or something similar, the name of an early settler'. According to Blake (1977: 138), 'word either Abor. for place where snake was seen, or corrupt version of n. of settler, Kiniry'. This is another example of a placename whose etymology has been interpreted by Les Blake without independent verification and is therefore Blake's interpretation and is likely to be spurious.

18. Kaniva

Kaniva is a town in the west Wimmera region. According to O'Callaghan (1918: 56), probably 'a corruption of "Kanizba", the name of a town in Hungary. A large number of Germans and Austro-Hungarians were amongst the earliest land selectors in that locality'. Presumably O'Callaghan is referring to Nagy-Kanisva, a town in the county of Szala, in southwest Hungary. 'The aboriginal name for the place was "Budjick" meaning "tomahawk"'. O'Callaghan cites St Eloy D'Alton 'Notes on the early settlement of the Wimmera' as his source. D'Alton was an Engineer in the Dimboola Shire in the early 1890s and the first Dimboola Shire Secretary. Massola (1968: 27) confirms that Budjick means 'stone axe'. Blake (1976: 59) in a history of Nhill and west Wimmera, notes that the name Kaniva was conferred to the locality in 1881 by the Post Master General, after the name of a shepherd's hut on the old station which recalled Kinnivie, near Durham, England. Blake (1977: 139) states that station plans show Kinivae as 'n. of shepherd's hut on pre-emptive right; Kinnivie is locality SW of Durham, England'. Landt (1961: 14), in a local history of Kaniva, notes that '"Kinivae" was six miles north-west of Kaniva's present site shown on early maps and was the name given to the Overseer's Hut on Tatiara, Woolshed Hill. Kaniva itself was originally called "Budjik Hill". Professor Browne suggests that the hut took its name from Kanziba [sic] in Hungary, suggesting that perhaps a Hungarian shepherd may have named the hut'. The identity of Professor Browne is not known. Wesson (2001: 72) is the only source that suggests Kaniva is an Aboriginal word, meaning 'snake asleep'. I suspect Wesson has considered Kaniva to be a variant of Kaneira (see above). Although the non-Indigenous origin of this placename is contested, there is very little support for it having an Aboriginal origin.

19. Kenmare

Kenmare is a farming district near Lake Hindmarsh. Massola (1968: 28) asserts Kenmare is an Aboriginal word meaning 'kangaroo'. This seems unlikely as the local word for grey kangaroo was 'gure', red kangaroo 'bara', and black-faced mallee kangaroo 'gudji' (Hercus 1986: 269). Blake (1977: 140) argues that it is 'named after Eire estate near Lake Killarney, owned by Lord Kenmare in nineteenth century'. The etymology of Kenmare is unclear; however, Massola's interpretation is not supported by linguistic analyses.

20. Langi Willi

This is the name of a pastoral station near Skipton. Massola (1968: 30) considers that this name means 'the home of Willie (the home of William Mitchell, a pioneer at Skipton)'. Blake (1977: 155) concurs with Massola adding that Mitchell held the station from 1852–59. Claud Notman (1939: 18), in a history of Skipton, noted that the run's name was originally Bamgamie until it was purchased in 1852 by William Mitchell who changed its name to 'Langi Willi'. Robert Scott (in Smyth 1878 Vol. 2: 182) includes Langi Willi in a list of native names and gives its meaning as 'W. Mitchell's homestead'. If this is correct then Langi Willi is a fabrication comprising one Aboriginal word and one English word, and is comparable to another nearby station name 'Langi Logan' (the home of Logan). Langi, or more correctly larng-i-, is a widespread Kulin word that means 'the home of', and is seen elsewhere in placenames such as Langi Ghiran, Langi Kal Kal, Larnebarramul, and Larngibunja. Wile (pronounced willie) is the widespread Kulin word for 'possum' (Hercus 1986: 276), thus Langi Willi may mean 'home of possums' (Clark and Heydon 2002), however it seems more likely that Langi Willi is an Aboriginal – English composite. This is consistent with Kenyon's (1968: 3) promotion of the use of Lar to compose a house name using a mixture of Aboriginal and English words: 'Words may be made up. For instance, all words for ground or earth also indicate camp. Thus Lar, Larne, Laane, Langi all mean ground, camp or home, and may also be used as a prefix similarly to that fine name Langilogan, or Mr. Logan's homestead'. Another example of a composition using the prefix Langi, is Langi Morgala, the name for the Ararat Museum, roughly meaning 'home of yesterday' (see Kenyon 1968: 13).

21. Morwell

This is the name of a river and township in the La Trobe Valley in Gippsland. Legg (1992: 28) has documented that the first variant 'Morewell' dates from 1844. Massola (1968: 36) claims that it is derived from 'More willie', meaning 'woolly possum'. Blake (1977: 180) accepts Massola's position. Gardner (1992: 16) considers it is a Gunnai word that means 'inhabitants of the swamp' and he believes it is unlikely that the name is derived from one of a number of places in England on the Tamar River near Plymouth including Morwell Rocks and

Morwell Abbey. Stephen Legg (1992: 28–29, 32) in a history of Morwell Shire has undertaken a detailed analysis of the name and documents five interpretations – that it is derived from the name of a nearby hotel; that it is a corruption of Maryville; that it is named after the town of Morwell on the Morwell River in Cornwall; that it has an Aboriginal origin; and finally, that it gets its name from Morwell Street in London. Legg concludes that the Aboriginal explanation has the most integrity and is the only one that can 'survive critical examination'. He concludes that it is derived from 'morewill' meaning 'woolly possum' and he considers this 'a fitting tribute to the Ganai who pioneered the land' (Legg 1992: 34). The only difficulty with this *bon mot* is that the Ganai word for possum is 'wadthan' (see Smyth 1878 Vol. 2: 96) and not 'wile' or 'wollert' which are Kulin words, a situation that Legg (1992: 32) was cognisant of.

22. Narbethong

Narbethong is the name of a township some 87 km north-east of Melbourne. Saxton (1907: 49) notes that it is a native name, meaning 'cheerful, lively, humorous'. According to Martin (1944: 63), it is an Aboriginal word meaning 'cheery'. Massola (1968: 38) agrees with Martin, adding the gloss 'lively'. Blake (1977: 198) notes that it was named 'by surveyor John Wrigglesworth in 1865 as Nar Be Thong; Abor. word for cheerful or a cheerful place'. Bunce (1856: 8, 27) records Narbethong as meaning cheerful and lively. Bunce (in Smyth 1878 Vol. 2: 144) in a list of east Kulin vocabulary, includes 'Narbeethong – Lively; Narbethong – Cheerful, fun, levity; Karbeethong – Mirth' (Bunce in Smyth 1878 Vol. 2: 140), and Carbeenthon or carbethon – Gay, cheerful, hilarity, humorous, play, to sport, to chuckle, to laugh, glad, gleeful, merry (Bunce in Smyth 1878 Vol. 2: 137). Blake (1991: 98) lists 'narbethong' as the east Kulin word for 'lively'. Sinnott (2003) accepts that Narbethong is an Aboriginal word. John Green, the superintendant of the Coranderrk Aboriginal station at Healesville informed John Mathew (Papers) that it is 'not a local Aboriginal word' but it is difficult to know what Green means by this comment as Bunce's vocabulary covers east Kulin which includes the Narbethong district. Green may be suggesting that it is not a placename. Symonds (1982: 54), in a history of Healesville acknowledges that the name is said to have come from the Aboriginal word for 'A cheerful place' but a local claims that the name derives from Narbeth, Wales, from where the Fisher family originated from. Sinnott (2003: 114) dismisses this claim.

23. Porepunkah

According to O'Callaghan (1918: 78) 'there are two accounts given as to the origin or derivation of this name. First:-An Indian officer who was with a party of "diggers", called the place Porepunkah – "pore" and "punkah" being two Hindoo words signifying respectively, "wind" and "blower". The name was given during a storm. Second:-Derived from a native name of somewhat similar pronunciation, signifying, "meeting of the waters", and having reference to the junction of the Buckland and the Ovens rivers'. O'Callaghan's source was Edward John Delany, Secretary of the Shire of Bright. Martin (1944), Blake (1977), and Gardner (1991) have accepted the Hindu explanation and Massola (1968) the Aboriginal explanation. The goldfield origin explanation may be suspect as the station name 'Portpunka' or 'Port Punka' (Billis and Kenyon 1974) or 'Point Punkah' (Lloyd and Nunn 1987: 7) was used from 1846, at least five years before gold digging commenced. Gardner notes that the run

> was taken up by William Walker and Co. in 1846; Walker was a banker and trader who spent much of his life in Calcutta. Indian coolies were imported in 1846 by Captain Robert Towns to work on Walker's stations and almost certainly worked here. The name is derived from the Hindi words for wind and blower, literally the name of a primitive cooling fan and almost certainly referred to the cold wind off the mountains. Also called Port Punkah and Point Punkah. Massola incorrectly has this as being of Aboriginal origins. (Gardner 1991: 17f)

Carol Sonogan (2011) suggests that Port Punkah may be derived from the Hindi term 'punka walla' which referred to a slave boy fanning a large rug to create a small breeze, or punka'. She postulates that given that the Port Punkah freehold provided the river-crossing place for a number of adjacent runs, the name may reflect its water association as well as the Indian connection. However, she believes it is more likely an 'attempt to assign personal meaning to the foreign sounds of an already-existing Indigenous name'. Sonogan (2011: 3) suggests a possible literal translation of Porepunkah is puwa pungga, head+stone, with an underlying meaning of 'man's head'.

24. Timor

Timor is the name of a creek and a farming district north-west of Maryborough. Flett (1975: 83) notes that the town of Coxtown on the Bet Bet Creek was surveyed in 1856 by Hugh Fraser and named 'Timor' 'although the new name went unknown for a long time'. Blake (1977: 257) fails to add to Flett's information. P.C. Crespigny (in Smyth 1878 Vol. 2: 180) lists Timor as a native name of 'unknown meaning' of a 'creek running through Adelaide Lead into the Bet Bet Creek'. At first glance it is tempting to draw parallels with the Island of Timor and the Timor Sea, north-west of Australia, which is a variant of the Malay word 'timur' meaning 'east'.

25. Underbool

Underbool is the name of a railway station on the Ouyen to Pinnaroo line in the Mallee region of north-west Victoria. According to O'Callaghan (1918: 92), from information he obtained from A.S. Kenyon, it is a native name, 'probably from 'wimbool', the ear, 'bool' means 'water', native name of waterholes'. Martin (1944) accepts O'Callaghan's interpretation. Massola (1968: 50) renders the name 'Undera-bool' meaning 'abundance'. Hercus (1986: 261, 290) confirms that the local word for 'ear' was 'wirimbul', and 'water' was 'gadjin'. Blake (1977: 264) suggests that on '30 October 1861 surveyor Dr Neumayer camped there and district received German n. Underbolt'.

26. Warracknabeal

This is the name of a town in the Wimmera region of Victoria that takes its name from a local pastoral station. District surveyor, Philip Chauncy (in Smyth 1878 Vol. 2: 208), recorded the original native word as Wurranjibeel', referring to Warracknabeal station on Yarriambiack Creek, and gives it the following signification: 'Wurra, lip; ngi, its; beal, flooded gum tree – ie., lip of a flooded gum tree'. He noted that he obtained this information from native speakers at the Wimmera. Howitt (1904: 54) interpreted it as 'plain of red gum tree'. Saxton (1907: 66) notes that it is a native name meaning 'large gum trees'. O'Callaghan (1918: 94) reproduces Chauncy's information. Martin (1944: 85) translates the name as 'large gums'. Massola (1968: 51) renders the name '*warrak*, plain, *na*, of, *beal*, red gum tree (*Eucalyptus rostrata*)'. Priestley (1967: 3) in a history of Warracknabeal translated it as 'redgum trees shading the creek'. Linguist Luise Hercus (1986: 214; Clark and Heydon 2002) analysed the name as Wurungi-bial 'mouth of creek with red gum trees'. Blake (1977: 273) notes that 'although in 1932 Mrs G.H. Warrack of Edinburgh claimed n. came fr. her family and *nabeal* (Gaelic), of the ravine, the Abor. origin is usually accepted: fr. word for fringe of gum trees about hollow, or flooded red gum trees; in 1878 spelt Werracknebeal'. The Warrack family claim seems to be spurious. The pastoral run was named 'Werracknabeal' by Andrew Scott in 1845 with his sons Robert and Andrew (Billis and Kenyon 1974: 137).

27. Conclusion

This paper has considered 26 Victorian placenames that are the subject of etymological dissonance. It has been argued that two of them (Boca [Avoca] and Greech [Grease, Halfway Inn, Glenorchy]) are best explained as instances of misunderstood Aboriginal pidgin. In nine cases the origin of the placenames is well-attested, and the similarity with non-Aboriginal or Aboriginal placenames may have been instrumental in their adoption or perhaps the similarity is purely coincidental: Acheron; Ballan; Barham; Buchan; Mount Buller; Caper Kelly; Morewell; Porepunkah; and Timor. One case, Langi Willi, is best explained as an Aboriginal-English composite. Jim Crow Hill is an example of an Anglicisation of an Aboriginal placename, Jumcra, which has misled subsequent researchers who were unaware of the preceding Aboriginal name. Of the remaining 13 cases, they may all be explained as examples where despite the earliest evidence attesting to an Aboriginal or non-Aboriginal origin they have been subject to speculative or spurious etymology – for example, Blake (1977) is the source of eight instances: Balnarring; Beulah; Bonn; Callawadda; Lake Drung Drung; Ecklin; Kaneira; and Underbool; Massola (1968) one instance – Kenmare; Wesson (2001) one instance – Kaniva; and local historians and genealogists a further three – Darnum, an example of erroneous folk etymology (Copeland 1934); Narbethong (a spurious claim based on a genealogical connection with Narbeth, Wales, in Symonds 1982); and Warracknabeal (a spurious claim from the Warrack family of Edinburgh reproduced in Blake 1977).

Other possible conclusions to be drawn are that some of these toponyms may be examples of polysemy; that is that they are toponyms with multiple meanings, and ones that may have been selected deliberately because of this polysemy (for example, Acheron, Ballan, Beulah, and Buchan are prime examples); and secondly, that they may be onomastic palimpsests, representing accumulated iterations, glosses, or etymologies laid one over the other, literally the accumulation and reinforcement of toponymic ideas over time (examples of this include Jim Crow Hill, and Morwell). It is common to find placenames with contested histories – a careful reading of any placename dictionary will reveal many examples. Thus for some of the examples considered in this study, it is possible that of the various explanations that exist some or all may have integrity.

References

Ballan Shire Historical Society 1989, *A Pictorial History of the Shire of Ballan*, Ballan Shire Historical Society, Ballan.

Billis, R.V. and A.S. Kenyon 1974, *Pastoral Pioneers of Port Phillip*, Stockland Press, North Melbourne.

Blake, B.J. 1991, 'Woiwurrung, the Melbourne Language', in *The Handbook of Australian Languages* Vol. 4 The Aboriginal Language of Melbourne and other Grammatical Sketches, R.M.W. Dixon and B.J. Blake (eds), Oxford University Press, South Melbourne: 31–124.

Blake, L.J.B. 1976, *The Land of the Lowan: 100 Years in Nhill & West Wimmera*, Nhill & District Historical Society, Nhill.

— 1977, *Placenames of Victoria*, Rigby Ltd, Adelaide.

Brock family papers, La Trobe Library, State Library of Victoria, Melbourne, Ms. 10554.

Buchan Sesquicentenary Committee 1989, *Bukan-Mungie 150 years settlement in the Buchan District 1839–1989*, Buchan Sesquicentenary Committee, Buchan.

Bunce, D. 1856, *Language of the Aborigines of the Colony of Victoria and Other Australian Districts*, Thomas Brown, Geelong.

Clark, I.D. 1990, *Aboriginal Languages and Clans, an historical atlas of western and central Victoria, 1800–1900*, Monash Publications in Geography, No. 34, Department of Geography, Monash University, Clayton.

— 1999, 'In quest of Nargun and Nyols: an ethnohistory of the Buchan Caves Reserve and the Cape Conran Coastal Park', Unpublished report to Andrew Long and Associates for Parks Victoria, Heritage Matters Ltd, Melbourne.

Clark, I.D (ed.) 2000a, *The Journals of George Augustus Robinson, Chief Protector, Port Phillip Aboriginal Protectorate*, Vol. 1: 1 January 1839 – 30 September 1840, Heritage Matters, Clarendon.

— 2000b, *The Papers of George Augustus Robinson, Chief Protector, Port Phillip Aboriginal Protectorate*, Vol. 2 Aboriginal Vocabularies: South East Australia, 1839–1852, Heritage Matters, Clarendon.

Clark, I.D. and T.G. Heydon 2002, *Dictionary of Aboriginal Placenames of Victoria*, Victorian Aboriginal Corporation for Languages, Melbourne.

Copeland, H. 1934, *The Path of Progress From the Forests of Yesterday to the Homes of To-Day*, Shire of Warragul, Australia.

Flett, J. 1975, *Maryborough Victoria Goldfields History*, The Poppet Head Press, Glen Waverley.

Gardner, P.D. 1991, *Names of the Victorian Alps*, Ngarak Press, Ensay.

— 1992, *Names of East Gippsland*, Ngarak Press, Ensay.

— 1996, *Names of the Latrobe Valley and West Gippsland*, Ngarak Press, Ensay.

Gott, B. and J. Conran 1991, *Victorian Koorie Plants: some plants used by Victorian Koories for food, fibre, medicines and implements*, Yangennanock Women's Group, Hamilton.

Hercus, L.A. 1986, *Victorian Languages: A Late Survey*, Pacific Linguistics Series B-No. 77, Department of Linguistics, Research School of Pacific Studies, The Australian National University, Canberra.

Howitt, A.W. 1904, *Native Tribes of South-East Australia*, Macmillan & Company, Limited, London.

Kenyon, J. 1968, *The Aboriginal Word Book*, Lothian Publishing, Melbourne [First printed 1930].

Kostanski, L. 2009, 'Toponymic books and the representation of Indigenous identities', in *Aboriginal Placenames: Naming and Renaming the Australian Landscape*, H. Koch and L. Hercus (eds), The Australian National University E Press and Aboriginal History Incorporated, Canberra: 175–188.

Landt, T.M. 1961, *The Story of the Kaniva District 1845–1961*, Brown, Prior, Anderson, Melbourne.

Legg, S.M. 1992, *Heart of the Valley: A History of the Morwell Municipality*, City of Morwell, Morwell.

Lloyd, B. and K. Nunn 1987, *Bright Gold: The Story of the People and the Gold of Bright and Wandiligong*, Histec Publications, Brighton East, Melbourne.

Martin, A.E. 1944, *Placenames in Victoria and Tasmania*, NSW Bookstall Co, Sydney.

Massola, A. 1968, *Aboriginal Placenames of South-east Australia and their meanings*, Lansdowne Press, Melbourne.

Mathew, J. Papers, Australian Institute of Aboriginal and Torres Strait Islander Studies, Canberra, Ms. 950.

Meyrick, F.J. 1939, *Life in the Bush 1840–1847: A Memoir of Henry Howard Meyrick*, Thomas Nelson And Sons Ltd, London.

Mitchell, T.L. 1839, *Three Expeditions into the Interior of Eastern Australia with the Descriptions of the Recently Explored Region of Australia Felix, and of the Present Colony of New South Wales*, 2 Vols, 2nd edition, Boone, London.

Morrison, E. 1965, *Early Days in the Loddon Valley*, The Author, Yandoit.

— 1967, *Frontier Life in the Loddon Protectorate: Episodes from Early Days, 1837–1842*, The Author, Yandoit.

Notman, G.C. 1939, *Out of the Past: The Story of Skipton 1839–1939*, Skipton Centenary Committee, Skipton.

O'Callaghan, T. 1918, *Names of Victorian Railway Stations with their origins and meanings, together with similar information relative to the Capital Cities of Adelaide, Sydney, Brisbane and a few of the Border Stations of New South Wales and South Australia*, HJ Green, Acting Government Printer, Melbourne.

Pepper, P. and T. De Araugo 1985, *What did happen to the Aborigines of Victoria Vol. 1 The Kurnai of Gippsland*, Hyland House, Melbourne.

Priestley, S. 1967, *Warracknabeal: a Wimmera Centenary*, Jacaranda Press, Melbourne.

Quinlan, L.M. 1993, *Here My Home The Life and Times of Captain John Stuart Hepburn 1803–1860 Master Mariner, Overlander and Founder of Smeaton Hill*, Victoria, Oxford University Press, Melbourne.

Randell, J.O. 1979, *Pastoral Settlement in Northern Victoria*, Vol. 1 The Coliban District, Queensberry Hill Press, Melbourne.

Roberts, L. 1977, *A Brief History of the Buchan District and Schools prepared for the Buchan School Centenary*, Buchan School Committee, Buchan.

Saxton, J.G. 1907, *Victoria Place-Names and Their Origins*, Saxton and Buckle, Clifton Hill.

Seddon, G. 1994, *Searching for the Snowy, an Environmental History*, Allen & Unwin, St Leonards.

Sinnott, N. 2003, *Place-Names of the Alexandra, Lake Eildon and Big River Area of Victoria*, Friends of the Alexandra Library, Alexandra.

Smyth, R.B. 1878, *The Aborigines of Victoria: with notes relating to the habits of the natives of other parts of Australia and Tasmania*, 2 vols, Victorian Government Printer, Melbourne.

Sonogan, C. 2011, 'Porepunkah – Of Rocks and Men', Placenames Australia Letter of the Australian National Placenames Survey, March: 1, 3–4.

Sutherland, A. 1888, *Victoria and its metropolis past and present*, 2 vols, McCarron, Bird & Co, Melbourne.

Symonds, S. 1982, *Healesville History in the Hills*, Pioneer Design Studio, Lilydale.

Tully, J.D. 1997, *Djadja Wurrung Language of Central Victoria including Placenames*, The Author, Dunolly.

Von Stieglitz, K.R. (ed.) 1964, *Emma Von Stieglitz Her Port Phillip and Victorian Album*, Fullers Bookshop, Hobart.

Wajnryb, R. 2006, *Australian Placename Stories*, Lothian Books, South Melbourne.

Wesson, S. 2001, *Aboriginal Flora and Fauna Names of Victoria: as extracted from early surveyors' reports*, Victorian Aboriginal Corporation for Languages, Melbourne.

15. Duel-Names: How toponyms (placenames) can represent hegemonic histories and alternative narratives[1]

Laura Kostanski
Federation University Australia

1. Introduction

Of central import to this study is the rarely cited notion that 'it is not spaces which ground identifications, but places. How then does space become place? By being named' (Carter, Donald and Squires 1993: xii). Carter and others are among the few who have overtly linked the process of naming to the creation of places from space and their theoretical cohort include Claude Levi-Strauss (1962) who noted that place is named space, and Tim Cresswell (2004: 10) who asserted that 'when humans invest meaning in a portion of space and then become attached to it in some way (naming is one such way) it becomes place'. This concept of place positioning human landscape interactions is of integral importance to this research in that it is thought to be toponyms which symbolise this interaction and identification. This paper contributes to the developing field of cultural toponymy by examining whether the social and cultural role of toponyms can be partly defined through a theory on toponymic identity. Essentially, this paper asks 'can toponyms contribute to social, cultural and historical identity formation or recognition in similar, yet distinguishable, ways to places?'.

The impetus for this research came about as a result of the Victorian State Government's proposal in 1989 to remove colonially-allocated toponyms for features in the Grampians National Park (as it was then officially recorded in the Victorian State Register of Place Names) and restore Indigenous names. Within geographical literature it is asserted that recognition of Indigenous and non-Indigenous places gives inhabitants a stronger sense of identity (Taylor

---

[1] The title of the paper was inspired by the happenstance occurrence of a transcriber returning some of the interview manuscripts with the phrase 'duel-name' utilised instead of the correct 'dual-name' where the participants or researcher were discussing the official recognition of two names for one place. It was evident that the transcribers were translating what they heard into the written word, and not being familiar with the concept of dual-naming, and hearing the tones of the interview discussions, must have assumed that duel-naming referred to a process of contesting a name for a place.

1992; Wong 2002). Indeed, one of the general arguments used by government agencies (including the United Nations Group of Experts on Geographical Names) for following the process of reinstating Indigenous toponyms in the landscape is that the names will help reassert Indigenous identity and aid in recognising the Indigenous connections to the landscape (UNGEGN Working Group on the Promotion of Indigenous and Minority Group Place Names 2007). Yet there is currently not enough research nor theories published on the determinants of toponymic identity to support these arguments. The purpose of this paper is therefore to fill this gap in knowledge regarding toponymic identity.

If governments are to talk of reinstating Indigenous toponyms as a nexus from which to provide more tenable identification with the landscape for both Indigenous and non-Indigenous people, then this paper aims to explore and build a strong theoretical framework upon which to base these assertions. This paper will firstly summarise details regarding the case study, data collection and participant identification methods before providing an outline of the theoretical background underpinning the research. The discussion will then move into an analysis of the key themes of the case study data in relation to the existing literature on place identity, before finally offering a summary of the results and explanation of the proposed theory of toponymic identity.

2. Case study

2.1. Background to case study and methods

The Grampians (Gariwerd) National Park covers 170,000 hectares containing ancient mountains, rocky escarpments and Indigenous rock art. The area is popular with tourists for mountain walking, rock climbing and learning about Indigenous art and cultural heritage, whilst the area around the park is populated by farming and tourism-based communities.

The traditional custodians of this landscape are the Jardwadjali and Djabwurrung peoples, whose traditional boundaries dissect the area. The Djabwurrung and Jardwadjali peoples have names for sites and areas within the contemporary National Park area, with one of the mountain ranges known as *Gariwerd*.

In 1836 Thomas Mitchell, then Surveyor Mitchell named the area after a place in his home country of Scotland, where the name Grampians is used to refer to a range of mountains. The mountains were originally referred to as *Mons Graupius*, the meaning of which is unknown, except for the fact that 'mons' refers to 'mountain' (Fraser 2005: 66).

As the landscape is a mental construct, Richard Baker (1999: 33) argues that we must see it as a cultural construct, and should thus observe it as the physical form of social and political ideologies. Mitchell's seemingly simple act of place-naming at once transferred the legal and cultural identity of the landscape from Indigenous possession and understanding to colonial possession and control. From 1836 onwards the European names defined by Mitchell and the colonists who followed him, became the official government records of the landscape. Maps, addresses, electorates and government zones all came to identify with the area as *Grampians* in essence. The Jardwadjali and Djabwurrung were dispossessed from official records by an act of toponymy. In the Grampians (Gariwerd) area, this lessening of status began in 1836 and predominated until 1989, when the Victorian Government announced its intention to restore the Indigenous names within the National Park.

2.2. The 1989–1990 name restoration debate

In March 1989 the Hon. Steve Crabb, Minister for Tourism with the Victorian Labor Government, introduced the process of Indigenous toponym restoration in the National Park. Steve Crabb agreed to be interviewed for this research and when asked why he had started this process, he stated that there were two reasons. The first, which is relevant to the focus of this paper, pertained to the idea that

> one of my experiences of having sort of tramped around the Grampians was that one of the most fascinating things about it was the Aboriginal heritage that was there ... there was a whole lot of quite mystical stuff there that wasn't there, it wasn't very well interpreted and a lot of the time there were wire cages around it or it was hidden because they didn't want people to know it was there and none of the rest of the Grampians reflected it so there was ... stuff with silly names ... like "Elephant's Hide"... (Crabb, Steve, interview 2006)

In essence, Steve Crabb's proposal to restore the Indigenous names came from his desire to 'correct' what he perceived to be the historical 'wrongs' of removing Indigenous toponyms from the landscape. [His second reason – a desire to promote tourism – is discussed in (Kostanski 2009).]

At the time of Steve Crabb's proposal to investigate the traditional Indigenous names for the National Park area, the government regulations which guided naming practices in the State of Victoria, stipulated that there was only the possibility of having 'one place and one name'. The implications of this regulation meant that for the Indigenous toponyms to be restored, the colonial toponyms would have to be removed, and therein the problem and the fuel for public reaction lay. This regulation and its implicit notion that the restoration of Indigenous toponyms could only be enacted with the removal of existing, predominantly Anglo-Celtic, toponyms was the catalyst for overwhelming political and community reaction to the proposals.

The 12 months following the original proposal saw continued public and political debate, mostly negative in substance. The most informative of the reactions to the changes were those from individual members of the community. These responses were recorded as letters to the editors of rural and metropolitan newspapers, and as signatures on petitions during the debate. The letters were both supportive and negative, and their contents highlighted the key concerns the community had about the research and the proposal to restore Indigenous toponyms.

2.3. Methods and participants

In total 141 letters and 94 newspaper reports or editorials were collated for the purposes of this research. In addition, 114 participants in the original debate were sent questionnaires, of which 48 were returned. Further to this, 45 people were interviewed for this research program between October and November 2006. The interviews involved asking the participants open-ended questions, which related to their sense of place and toponym.

In this paper where a name appears by itself, such as 'Doug' or 'Anita' this is a pseudonym used to identify oral-history and/or interview participants. Where a name appears with a surname, and is not followed by a reference indicating that it is a quote taken from a media source, this is the real name of an oral-history and/or interview participant who explicitly gave permission for their real name to be used because of their political or key stakeholder role in the initial name restoration program.

3. Theoretical background

Toponyms are, by their very description, names for places. As such, this paper explores human interactions with places and their names through theories related to place and place attachment, as will now be discussed. The focus here is on place itself, as the research of this paper centres on *place* names.

3.1. Sense of place and place attachment

Many geographical and psychological researchers have developed their own *sense of place* theories over the past 40 years, and often there is criticism within the literature (Patterson and Williams 2005; Pretty, Chipuer and Bramston 2003: 274) of the lack of a distinct theory being a hindrance to the progression of the study. Nonetheless, to create a structured basis for this research the study of 'sense of place' has been designated as the overarching study of 'place attachment' and 'place interference', with place attachment consisting of 'place identity' and 'place dependence'. This grouping has been determined based on recent research by various geographers (Hidalgo and Hernandez 2001; Jorgensen and Stedman 2006; Williams and Vaske 2003; Shamai 1991).

Shamai (1991: 347) asserts that sense of place is an umbrella concept that includes other concepts such as place attachment, national identity and regional awareness. Hidalgo and Hernandez (2001: 274) assert that a general description of place attachment defines it as 'an affective bond or link between people and specific places'. They posit that place attachment takes two forms: emotional and physical (Hidalgo and Hernandez 2001: 279). Jorgensen and Stedman (2006: 316) note that place attachment is a concept that can be included under the term 'sense of place', along with the constructs of place identity and place dependence. These two terms identity and dependence are similar to Hidalgo and Hernandez' social and physical, and considering recent literature by Williams and Vaske (2003) and since then others (Sharpe and Ewert 2000; White, Virden and van Riper 2008) this paper will defer to the terms *identity* and *dependence*. Williams and Vaske (2003) also classify place attachment under the term 'sense of place', but go further than Jorgensen and Stedman and state that identity and dependence are correlated concepts which are sub-constructs of place attachment.

Some theorists note that place attachment, identity and dependence (along with sense of community) are separate but related concepts (Pretty et al. 2003) whilst others state that place dependence and identity are models of person-place relationships (Shumaker and Taylor 1983). During the research phase of this program the most convincing theoretical assertion was promoted by Williams and Vaske (2003) who stated that place identity and dependence were constructs of place attachment. Williams and Vaske (2004: 5) assert that there are two different forms of attachment to place. The first they label 'place dependence' and describe it as a *functional* attachment to place which 'reflects the importance of a place in providing features and conditions that support specific goals or desired activities' and also 'suggests an ongoing relationship with a particular setting'. The second form of attachment to place Williams and Vaske label 'place identity', which they assert is an *emotional* attachment to place. Further, they posit that place identity 'generally involves a psychological investment with the place that tends to develop over time'. In addition to this is the theory that place identity does not have to result from particular experiences with the place, yet place identity 'enhances self-esteem … increases feelings of belonging to one's community … and is an important component of communications about environmental values and policies'. Thus, Williams and Vaske defined place attachment as occurring in two distinguishable forms, that of the emotional and that of the functional. [The focus for this paper is the emotional attachment, discussion of the functional attachment can be found in (Kostanski 2009).]

3.2. Place identity

For Sharpe and Ewert (2000: 218) the term place identity is a second component of place attachment, which is linked to 'the emotional and symbolic nature of person-place relationships'. This theme of the emotional nature of person-place interactions is explored by Proshansky (1978) who determined that place identity is a subconcept of self-identity. Hernandez and others (2007: 311) concur with this notion of place identity being a component of personal identity and Twigger-Ross and Uzzel (1996: 210) expanded upon Proshansky's notion of place identity to claim that it is 'not a separate part of identity concerned with place, but that all aspects of identity have place-related implications to a greater or lesser extent'. Thus, the literature allows that personal identity is intrinsically linked to place identity, as part of a larger emotional or cognitive experience of sense of place.

As place identity is intrinsically linked to personal identity, many theorists note that official and local recognition of personal and collective forms of identity and attachment is extremely important. Taylor (1992: 32) asserted that 'recognition by others of the person one is, is central to having a meaningful life'. It can be argued that in instances such as the study area, where the government proposed to remove non-Indigenous names, the negative sentiment from some sectors of the community was borne out through anxiety of their identity being ignored and a perception that their identity was unimportant. Whether the theories of place identity can be extrapolated to explain people's emotional links to toponyms will now be explored.

4. Components of place and toponymic identity

From the literature review, and initial analysis of the data, it can be said that the construct of place identity is composed of four key elements: *history/memory*, *community*, *emotions* and *actions/events*. Thus, this section of the paper will explore these four key components individually, giving consideration to the discussion of place identity, and questioning in each instance whether similar identification with toponyms can be found in the research data.

4.1. History and memory

First, we should explore why history and memory are considered to be components of place identity, and by extension toponymic identity. Lowenthal states that 'remembering the past is crucial for our sense of identity ... to know what we are confirms that we are' (1997: 197). Further, Hoelscher and Alderman (2004: 347) have theorised that 'together, memory and place conjoin to produce much of the context for modern identities'. Abrahamson notes that communities occupy their own geographical areas with which they become intimately associated. He argues that through this process of identification 'areas acquire symbolic qualities that include their place names and social histories' (Abrahamson 1996 cited in Ramsay 2003). As the literature asserts that place identity is partly formed through history and memory, it needs to be ascertained whether toponymic identity can also be formed through history and memory. An analysis of the research data in regards to participants' linking of history and memory to the toponyms can shed light on whether this phenomenon exists.

Furniss (2001: 284) has noted that with colonial histories, such as that promoted until the late twentieth century in Australia, an 'imagined linearity' of themes is deployed by the constant referral to 'discovery', to 'firsts' and to 'pioneers'. This referral to discovery and pioneers was notable in the research data, especially from those who opposed the renaming proposal. For example, Digby Crozier (1989), former member of parliament for the Liberal Party (in opposition at the time), asserted in his letter to the editor that the naming proposal was an 'assault on our history and the enduring links with the countries of origin of our pioneering forebears ... these names evoke an undoubted affinity'. He explicitly linked the use of non-Indigenous names with the history of the places as he knew and understood them. For Crozier, identity is linked to the toponym which represents and connects him to the history he knows of the case study area.

There were many others like Crozier who asserted similar sentiments. For instance, Vivian Day (1990: 2) wrote 'I think this is a cause worth fighting for, to uphold the respect of the pioneers and the likes of Major Mitchell and his party, who risked their lives to explore and name such a beautiful spot in which to live'. Further to this were the words of J. Atchison, a representative of the Australian Council of Scottish Clans, which intimated that the 'section of the community which descended from the Scottish pioneers and settlers ... [were] concerned to see their history and heritage under threat' (Editor 1989). The inference by Day and Atchison is that by removing the non-Indigenous names the links to colonial history would be lost and would be a sign of disrespect for their toponymic identity which hinged on notions of colonial exploration and settlement in the case study area.

Tuan (1991: 688) has noted that 'normally only a socio-political revolution would bring about a change of name ... the new name itself has the power to wipe out the past and call forth the new'. In addition to the sentiments of Day and Atchison were arguments that removing the non-Indigenous names would be akin to removing colonial history from the landscape, map and community. These remarks can be contextualised in regards to the theory of Crane (1997: 1372) who posits 'that the future might mourn is the projection of nostalgia; it is also the supposition of historical thinking, which charges itself with the preservation of what would be lost both mentally and materially'. For most it is important to pass down historical meaning through the names for places with which they identify. In this manner, where previously it has been argued that it is place identity which helps to connect a population with their history, it can be seen that it is toponymic identity which also connects a population with their history.

It is argued by Furniss (2001: 285) that the imagined linearity of colonial history erases 'any prior Indigenous history, suggesting instead that the land and its inhabitants somehow did not exist, or their existence was unimportant, until they were "found" and incorporated into Western systems of knowledge'. Similarly, Lewicka (2008: 213) notes that 'events that happened before the group settled down in a place are assigned less significance and are less frequently recalled than events that are a part of the group past'. Sentiments of the non-existence of Indigenous history, or unimportance of Indigenous history, to the case study area were often borne out in the letters. For example, Anne Pietsch (1990a: 12) asserted that 'Aboriginals never lived in the Grampians. They only visited and hunted there as they preferred the open spaces'. Further to this, Eric Beale wrote that

> what is important is that the mountains were named in 1836 as the Grampians and that is what they have been known as here and all over the world for the last 150 years. As for Crabb's crazy statement that "the white man wiped out thousands of years of civilisation" I simply ask what civilisation? Does anybody know what he is talking about? Does he know himself? (Beale 1989)

The promotion of colonial history is necessarily one which is biased in favour of the mainstream society at the time. Thus, it can be asserted that Beale, and others of a similar sentiment, formed a toponymic identity similar to place identity, through the linking of history to the toponym.

Withers (2000: 534) has noted that with the creation and perpetuation of colonial history and the inevitable production of colonial maps as a technique with which to acquire and possess the landscape, 'natives were either "mapped out" of their own spaces or falsely "mapped in". In those terms, matters of authority ... become questions of authenticity: who, if not "the native voice", can give definitive orthographies and meanings to names?'. The question of authenticity for the Indigenous names was a common theme in the research data. J. Fitzsimmons (1989: 12) asserted in one letter that 'there is some question as to the validity of any Aboriginal place name recommendations ... this is based on the claim there are no true descendents of the Grampians' original inhabitants left'. For Fitzsimmons, being connected to a name meant that the descendents who gave the name had to still be in constant connection with the landscape. Further to this was the statement by F.R. Churton (1990: 59) that 'Aboriginals had no alphabet nor written records. How then can anyone give a correct name and spelling of so-called Aboriginal place names?' It was common in the data for participants to question the validity of the names, and this was summed up eloquently by Ern Golding (1990) in his letter, where he stated that 'Old "Mulga" would have been the only person with an understanding of the names, true meanings, if there are any ... he stated he was "the last full blooded aborigine in Victoria"'. For Churton and Golding an ignorance of colonial translation and transcription processes whereby colonists recorded Indigenous words in official records and other now-historical manuscripts, meant a questioning of the veracity of the proposed names. It can be contended for this colonially biased perception of landscape connection, not to mention the ignorance of the existence of an ongoing Indigenous presence in the area, that Fitzsimmons', Churton's and Golding's toponymic identity related strongly to a colonially-verifiable historical connection.

Cr Robert LoRicco (1989b) of the Shire of Stawell, noted that the reinstatement of Indigenous names would recognise the Indigenous history and rights to land recognition. Indeed, LoRicco was insistent that the reinstatement of the Indigenous names would reassert Indigenous identity in the study area:

> European settlement has lasted only some 200 years but there has been an Aboriginal presence of some 17 to 20,000 years. The Aboriginal people now have the opportunity to re-establish and re-assert their cultural heritage and we should assist this process. ('Grampians name change debate', *The Colac Herald*, 2 June 1989: 7)

The councillor is discussing the notion that the reinstatement of the names is linked to respecting land tenure and Indigenous identity. Thus, for this councillor the notion of place and name are inextricably linked, the toponym is a symbol of the history of a place and current attempts should be made to help change this situation.

The perceived need to identify with colonial history and names, or to assert the suitability of Indigenous names, saw the narratives associated with identity diverge according to the memories that people associated with the names. The proposition is clear here that a toponym can be a symbol of multiple identities, and the use of two toponyms for one place can be a strong reminder of the multiple place histories and cultural identities which exist for a locale. At this point in the discussion attention needs to be given to notions of how collective or community cultures influence the creation and interpretation of place, and perhaps toponymic, identity.

4.2. Community

The presence or non-existence of Indigenous people in Australia and the region was a consistent 'fact' mentioned many times by various research participants. The minority status of Indigenous Australians was often used as support for the arguments of why colonial history and community connectedness was more important than Indigenous history. Clive Johnson (1990: 17) in his letter was able to recognise that Indigenous histories exist, but he was not willing to acknowledge them further than they had been already. He asserted that 'I don't for one minute deny Aborigines their place in history, but there is already an abundance of Aboriginal place names across Australia, far in excess of their percentage of the population'. Importantly, R. Pietsch (1990b: 10) questioned whether the community, as she perceived it, was going to 'have to become a radical minority group to be heard?'.

George Seddon (1997: 15) theorised that the words of the landscape carry 'cultural baggage' that may 'imply values and endorse power relations'. For Johnson and Pietsch the values of their community, as they understood them, had colonial interpretations as mainstream accepted notions of identity. Jackson (1989: 151) asserts that 'racism in Britain and similar societies is a dominant ideology ... racism refers to a set of ideas and beliefs that have the weight of authority behind them; they are enshrined in statutes and institutionalised in policy and practice'. The fact that predominantly non-Indigenous names were present in the landscape served to reinforce these notions of local, and by extension national, identity being that created by colonists and perpetuated by their descendants. This community identity was therefore bound to, and represented by, the toponyms. Penrose and Jackson (1994: 206) assert that 'Aboriginal land claims challenge the apparent "neutrality" of the hegemonic culture' and it could be extended here to assert that the proposal to reinstate Indigenous names was a challenge to the mainstream, colonially-defined local and national culture. As stated by Graham in an oral history interview, 'we really thought it was a whole lot of hogwash because to us there were the Grampians, had always been the Grampians and everybody that we, you know, talked to or associate with referred to them as the Grampians'. Graham's community was those whose identity was formed with the name Grampians, and he was asserting therefore that it was in the interest of community that the name Grampians be retained.

For those who supported the renaming proposals they reported that recognising the Indigenous names for the places would lead to the conferral of a greater sense of Indigenous identity. For instance, Bruce Henry (1990: 10) noted that 'the real opposition to the proposed name changes comes from white Australia's ongoing refusal to recognise Aboriginal prior ownership ... the renaming of the Grampians ... serves to recognise this ownership'. Similarly, Louise in her interview asserted that while she didn't personally think the reinstatement of Indigenous names was important, 'I imagine the Indigenous people ... feel having their original names back would make them belong to the country more again'.

For those opposed to the proposal, many acknowledged an ignorance or non-acceptance that Indigenous people are part of the community. For example, C. and D. Hey (1990: 37) wrote in a letter that 'we were raised in the Grampians area and did not see any Aboriginals in the district until recently ... where are these people from?'. K.W. Dadswell (1989) asserted that 'the people of the area will ALWAYS cherish and call the range "the Grampians"'. Similarly, M. Albrecht (1990: 18) argued that 'it is our heritage and not his [Steve Crabb's] to toy around with. The Grampians forever!'.

Pretty and others assert that 'discursive evidence that a place has become integrated into one's self-identity is re-enacted in "I" and "me" statements regarding the place'. Likewise, it can be argued that for statements such as those from the Heys and Albrecht, that the use of 'we' and 'our' denote an affinity they feel with the community around themselves. This community of 'our' and 'we' is that which rejects the renaming proposals and identifies with a colonial heritage. In this sense, it can be seen that toponymic identity does exist, and is reinforced by connection to community. Indeed, Wong (2002: 454) posits that 'a key source of [identity] beliefs is the culture(s) or community(ies) in which a person is located', and similarly it can be contended that a source of identity are the toponyms recognised by the community.

The notions of inclusion and exclusion, or insiders and outsiders, are fundamental to an understanding of community and national identity. Don Johns asserted in his interview that 'since then [1836], everyone has known it as the Grampians, worldwide. Now, why change the name? I mean, its rubbish in my opinion. ... I'm not a racist but I think what we're doing sometimes is like kow-towing to them and so forth, we're dividing'. Johns notes here that by 'everyone' knowing the area as the Grampians, the normal attitude is to accept that the community identity is that which is represented by the colonial names. As discussed by Salecl (1993: 102) 'national identification with "our kind" is based on the fantasy of an enemy, an alien who ... threatens us with habits, discourse and rituals which are not "our kind"'. This was exposed in the interview with Doug who asserted that they [the government] should have kept Grampians and underneath if they wanted in brackets put Gariwerd because it's the Caucasian people's taxes that are paying for the running and the maintaining and keeping the Grampians afore and they are the most populated, the majority of the population. It's not that we have a thing set against that but to completely take history and completely change it to something that no-one refers to, or relates to, or understands… (Doug, interview, 2006)

It can be seen in Doug's narrative that he perceives the non-Indigenous population to have credentials for deciding which names will be used in the landscape. Interestingly, Salecl (1993: 106) asserts that in the process of othering 'the fantasy of how the other lives on our account is lazy, exploits us etc is repeatedly recreated in accordance with our desire'. Doug's assertion that it is Caucasian people who pay taxes, leads to the obvious conclusion that he believes the community to comprise of non-Indigenous tax-payers who have a right to make decisions on cultural heritage and inclusion, and Indigenous non-tax-payers who 'live off the system'. For Doug, the non-Indigenous names are a part of his identity, and the connection has been made to this identity through his understandings of the community around him.

As has been seen from the discussion of communities, there are groups in society which determine who is included as 'normal' and who is perceived as an 'outsider'. In this way place identity is partly formed by community definitions of inclusion and exclusion. Similarly, it can be seen that toponymic identity is partly formed through personal and community identification with particular community understandings of what is condoned as 'normal' and what is condoned as being from 'outside'. People are more likely to form an identity with toponyms which are perceived by them to be 'normal' than those which are considered 'foreign'.

4.3. Emotions

The previous discussion, in this paper, of inclusion and exclusion in relation to place identity leads into an exploration of what is defined as appropriate and not appropriate behaviour in a place. As posited by Manzo (2005: 83) 'the dynamics of exclusion and creating spaces of belonging have a powerful effect on people's emotional relationship to places'. Thus, within the cultural roles defined by community, the emotional effects of feeling included and excluded can play a major role in the formation of identity. Emotions, as a component of identity, assist in determining what is construed as acceptable behaviour in a place.

For Tim, an Indigenous representative who currently works in Halls Gap, the time of the proposed renaming was extremely emotional. He stated in an oral history interview that 'at the time we felt there's recognition of true ownership of Aboriginal people but also our identity, who we are as a people'. James, another Indigenous man who has cultural connections to the case study area, noted that he knew 'the Aboriginal community were very happy about it, about the idea. And it just gives us a bit more recognition that we're not ... a dead culture'. For Tim and James, the proposed renaming was an emotional time acknowledged by both of them, and others, to be an important step towards the wider community acknowledging and accepting Indigenous heritage in the case study area.

On the opposing side of the debate, Stawell Shire Council wrote to the Victorian Government and asserted that the proposed renaming posed 'an emotional threat to the history and heritage of descendants of original pioneers' (Lo Ricco 1989a: 36). Writers such as Florence Schulz (1990: 18) opined that 'As a child I could see the Grampians range from our kitchen window, ... and later had the misfortune to lose my mother as a result of an accident in the Grampians. I could not and will not ever accept any other names for the beauty spots there'. For Schulz the name 'Grampians' emotionally connected her to the memories she held with the area. The possibility of using other names to identify the places in the case study area was impossible because for her the proposed Indigenous names would not hold those same emotional connections.

Fred Redeker (1989) posited in a letter that it was not appropriate behaviour for the Victorian Government to propose the renaming, as it would go against mainstream values. He asserted that 'giving the land or the rights back to Aborigines and suggesting to rename places to pacify some of the stirrers ... and suggesting it is for the good and rights of the poor, exploited or displaced existing tribes ... I say baloney'. In a similar vain an anonymous writer to the *Hamilton Spectator* (Anon. 1989: 8) asserted that 'to force that name onto the English speaking people ... would not work... The ownership of a piece of land, or indeed the whole world, does not lie within a tribe or race that used to live there, but with the people that live there now'. For Redeker and the anonymous writer the notion of the name change occurring due to external forces outside of their community, such as the Government or Indigenous people, was anathema to their emotional understandings of what was acceptable behaviour in the case study area.

Barry noted that the decisions of what was perceived as acceptable and not acceptable in the mainstream community could be likened to the emotional reaction people feel when they have 'built a house and ... developed your garden ... you get really attached to the way it is and you don't really want to see that change. When you sell it and you move away suddenly the garden is ripped out and people completely change it and you feel really hostile against that lot'. He went on to assert that 'people don't like things not staying the way they are if they are comfortable with it'. Graham in his interview also noted that 'people don't like change really. Well, they can accept change in small degrees but not across the board I think, it sort of throws people right out of whack and that is when the sparks flow'.

Essentially, Barry and Graham indicated that the emotional reactions the mainstream community, those in power, felt to changes was one of hostility when what they perceived to be unacceptable behaviour was occurring in their community. Their sense of ownership was visibly under threat, and the emotional reaction occurred as a voicing of perceived power being illegitimated by an action which was deemed to be out of place in the community. For a proposed name change to have this effect on a community and its inhabitants points to the notion of emotions being a component of toponymic identity.

Tuan (1991: 685) notes that 'individual words ... impart emotion and personality, and hence high visibility, to objects and places'. Similarly too, the proposal to restore Indigenous names in the case study area brought high-visibility to Indigenous heritage and according to Tuan's reasoning, the proposal brought emotional reactions. A strongly negative emotional reaction to the raising of visibility to Indigenous heritage was enunciated by Anthony Toben in a letter to the editor where he stated that

> All nations have shameful skeletons tucked away in their cupboards, many of them speaking about unspeakable crimes committed against someone else. But surely ... there is nothing to be gained from digging up the smut of the past ... I would question those people's motives who continuously wish us to feel guilty about past events ... the guilt industry has us emotionally mulling in our own moral disgust ... this moral egoism, this "me and my feelings" attitude fails to offer us worthy explanations of past events. (Toben 1990: 10)

Community forces of power and control affect people's emotional reactions to change where it is perceived to be against the favour of those in power. For those who are in power, the emotional reaction is negative and can be linked to feelings of the actions being invalid and against the notions of community identity. For those who are out of power, the emotional reaction is positive and can be linked to feelings of resistance and contentment that the formerly neglected identity is being recognised.

4.4. Events/actions

Jedrej and Nuttal (1996: 123) assert that 'the landscape is a living landscape and place names are mnemonic devices that trigger recollection of particular activities'. Zerubavel (2003: 42) noted that places 'play a major role in identity rhetoric' and he proposed that events such as the hajj to Mecca, or romantic couples visiting the site of their first date are examples of pilgrimage which bring 'mnemonic communities into closer "contact" with their collective past'. Indeed, the contention of Zerubavel's argument is that memories of place imbue a present-day identity on the users or inhabitants of the place. This place identity is almost the glue which holds community groups together through a shared understanding of their collective past.

Chow and Healey (2008: 371) assert that 'place meaning is in part created and confirmed through in-place-experiences' and as such it could be argued following the previous analysis in this paper that the experiences which create place also create names. Thus, experiences which brought about the original and then subsequent renaming of places in the case study area could be said to have brought meaning and therefore identity to the people who associate with the area. The ongoing maintenance of the names from 1836 until 1989–1990 led to the confirmation of perceptions of community power, inclusion and exclusion.

The experiences which are deemed to be important by a community are memorialised in various ways. Similarly to the arguments posited by Zerubavel, Lewicka (2008: 214) posits that 'places remember and they do it though their monuments, architectural style of their buildings, inscriptions on walls etc. For people who reside there, the traces play the function of "urban reminders", the "mnemonic aids" to collective memory'. The decision on which monuments are erected and which events are memorialised is a constant battle between those included in the community and those excluded from it. I would argue that based on the research data analysed so far in this paper, that in a way similar to buildings and inscriptions on walls, events and actions are remembered by placenames. In this way, in their memorialisation of actions and events, communities utilise toponyms as mnemonic devices for their collective identity.

5. Conclusion

As stated in the introduction to this paper, the intention was to create a theory (or theories) of the constitution of toponymic identity. Place identity is an emotional function of place attachment (Sharpe and Ewert 2000) and is linked to the symbolic nature of place relationships (Williams and Vaske 2003). In addition, the formation of place identity can dictate within a community what actions should occur in a place and how people should behave within a particular setting (Proshansky, Fabian and Kaminoff 1983).

It was seen that personal and community identity can be tied to a toponym(s) in a similar way to which it can be linked to places. The discussion in part focused on the power dynamics of place inclusion and exclusion exhibited by communities. It was argued that the existence of non-Indigenous names in the landscape served as constant reminders of colonial history and 'ownership' of the landscape. It was this colonial history that many opponents of the name change supported, as they argued that removal of non-Indigenous names would remove their emotional connections to colonial history and sense of community. Concomitantly, those in the community who identified with the Indigenous names were jubilant at the proposal because they believed it to be an acceptance of Indigenous identity in the case study area, and they connected with the Indigenous names. Thus, it was argued that toponymic identity can exist in a similar way to place identity, with a distinction being made because the connections to history and community by the participants was linked strongly to the names rather than the places themselves. Obviously, the constructs of place and toponymic identity are strongly correlated, as places would not exist without names, and names would have no purpose without places.

References

Albrecht, M 1990, 'Grampians', *The Wimmera Mail-Times*, 8 August 1990: 18.

Anon. 1989, 'Not a racist', *Hamilton Spectator*, 24 June 1989: 8.

Baker, R. 1999, 'Land is life: a cultural geography of australian contact history', in *Australian Cultural Geographies*, Elaine Stratford (ed.), Oxford University Press, South Melbourne: 25–47.

Beale, E. 1989, 'Name change "clap trap"', *Hamilton Spectator*, 1 April 1989.

Carter, E., J. Donald and J. Squires (eds) 1993, *Space and Place: Theories of Identity and Location*, Lawrence & Wishart, London.

Chow, K. and M. Healey 2008, 'Place attachment and place identity: first-year university undergraduates making the transition from home to university', *Journal of Environmental Psychology* 28: 362–372.

Churton, F.R. 1990, 'Risky business, native names', *The Sun*, 7 June 1990: 59.

Crane, S. 1997, 'Writing the individual back into collective memory', *The American Historical Review* 102(5): 1372–1385.

Cresswell, T. 2004, *Place: A Short Introduction*, Blackwell Publishing, Melbourne.

Crozier, D. 1989, 'Bugara Off, Mr Crabb!', *Hamilton Spectator*, 1 April 1989.

Dadswell, K.W. 1989, 'Stand on Grampians name "arrogance"', *Stawell Times-News*, 14 April 1989.

Day, V. 1990, 'Appalled at name change proposal', *Stawell Times-News*, 17 July 1990: 2.

Editor 1989, 'Council of Clans and an elderly woman object to name change', *The Age*, 12 May 1989.

Fitzsimmons, J. 1989, 'Crabb's audacity in renaming mountains must be opposed', *The Age*, 30 March 1989: 12.

Fraser, J. 2005, *The Roman Conquest of Scotland: The Battle of Mons Graupius AD84*, Tempus, Gloucestershire.

Furniss, E. 2001, 'Timeline history and the Anzac myth: settler narratives of local history in a North Australian town', *Oceania* 71(4): 279–298.

Golding, E. 1990, 'Mulga not tinkit fit', *Warracknabeal Herald*, 10 July 1990: 8.

Henry, B. 1990, 'Name changes show justice to Aborigines', *The Age*, 18 August 1990: 10.

Hernandez, B., C. Hidalgo, M. E. Salazar-Laplace and S. Hess 2007, 'Place attachment and identity in natives and non-natives', *Journal of Environmental Psychology* 27: 310–319.

Hey, C. and D. 1990, 'Grampians and "local" blacks', *The Sun*, 22 June 1990: 37.

Hidalgo, C. and B. Hernandez 2001, 'Place attachment: conceptual and empirical questions', *Journal of Environmental Psychology* 21: 273–281.

Hoelscher, S. and D. Alderman 2004, 'Memory and place: geographies of a critical relationship', *Social and Cultural Geography* 5(3): 347–355.

Jackson, P. 1989, *Maps of Meaning: An Introduction to Cultural Geography*, Unwin Hyman, London.

Jedrej, C. and M. Nuttall 1996, *White Settlers: The Impact of Rural Repopulation in Scotland*, Penguin Press, Luxembourg.

Johnson, C. 1990, 'Crabb must go', *The Wimmera Mail-Times*, 8 June 1990: 17.

Jorgensen, B. and R. Stedman 2006, 'A comparative analysis of predictors of sense of place dimensions: attachment to, dependence on, and identification with lakeshore properties', *Journal of Environmental Management* 79: 316–327.

Kostanski, L. 2009, '"What's in a Name?": Place and Toponymic Attachment, Identity and Dependence. A case study of the Grampians (Gariwerd) National Park name restoration process', PhD Thesis, School of Business, University of Ballarat, Ballarat (Australia).

Levi-Strauss, C. 1962, *The Savage Mind*, University of Chicago Press, Chicago.

Lewicka, M. 2008, 'Place attachment, place identity and place memory: restoring the forgotten city past', *Journal of Environmental Psychology* 28: 209–231.

Lo Ricco, R. 1989a, 'Grampians name change', *The South Gippsland Sentinel-Times*, 14 June 1989: 36.

Lo Ricco, R. 1989b, 'Grampians name change debate', *The Colac Herald*, 2 June 1989: 7.

Lowenthal, D. 1997, *The Past is a Foreign Country*, Cambridge University Press, Cambridge.

Manzo, L. 2005, 'For better or worse: exploring multiple dimensions of place meaning', *Journal of Environmental Psychology* 25: 67–86.

Patterson, M. and D. Williams 2005, 'Maintaining research traditions on place: diversity of thought and scientific progress', *Journal of Environmental Psychology* 25: 361–80.

Penrose, J. and P. Jackson (eds) 1994, *Constructions of Race, Place and Nation*, University of Minnesota Press, Minnesota.

Pietsch, A. 1990a, 'What's in a name?', *The Weekly Times*, 8 August 1990: 12.

Pietsch, R. 1990b, 'Letter from Names Committee', *Ararat Advertiser*, 25 August 1990: 10.

Pretty, G., H. Chipuer and P. Bramston 2003, 'Sense of place amongst adolescents and adults in two rural Australian towns: The discriminating features of place attachment, sense of community and place dependence in relation to place identity', *Journal of Environmental Psychology* 23(3): 273–287.

Proshansky, H. 1978, 'The city and self-identity', *Environment and Behaviour* 10: 147–169.

Proshansky, H., A. Fabian and R. Kaminoff 1983, 'Place identity: physical world socialisation of the self', *Journal of Environmental Psychology* 3: 57–83.

Ramsay, G. 2003, 'Cherbourg's Chinatown: creating an identity of place on an Australian Aboriginal settlement', *Journal of Historical Geography* 29(1): 109–122.

Redeker, M. F. 1989, 'Stirrers', *Wimmera Mail-Times*, 5 April 1989.

Salecl, R. 1993, 'National identity and socialist moral majority', in *Space & Place: Theories of identity and location*, Erica Carter, James Donald and Judith Squires (eds), Lawrence & Wishart, London: 101–111.

Schulz, F. 1990, 'Renaming horrifies', *The Wimmera Mail-Times*, 8 June 1990: 18.

Seddon, G. 1997, 'Words and weeds: some notes on language and landscape', in *Landprints: Reflections on Place and Landscape*, George Seddon (ed.), Cambridge University Press, Cambridge: 15–27.

Shamai, S. 1991, 'Sense of place: an empirical measurement', *Geoforum* 22(3): 347–358.

Sharpe, E. and A. Ewert 2000, *Interferences in Place Attachment: Implications for Wilderness*, www.wilderness.net/library/documents/Sharpe_3-29.pdf.

Shumaker, S. and R. Taylor 1983, 'Toward a clarification of people-place relationships: a model of attachment to place', in *Environmental psychology: Directions and Perspectives*, N. Feimer and E. Gell (eds), University Press, New York: 219–251.

Taylor, C. 1992, 'The politics of recognition', in *Multiculturalisam*, ed. Amy Gutman (ed.), Princeton University Press, Princeton: 25–73.

Toben, Dr A. 1990, 'Guilt industry', *The Wimmera Mail-Times*, 13 July 1990: 10.

Tuan, Y.-F. 1991, ',Language and the making of place: a narrative-descriptive approach', *Annals of the Association of American Geographers* 81(4): 684–696.

Twigger-Ross, C. and D. Uzzell 1996, 'Place and identity processes', *Journal of Environmental Psychology* 16(3): 205–220.

UNGEGN 2007, *Report of the UNGEGN Working Group on the Promotion of Indigenous and Minority Group Place Names*, United Nations, New York.

White, D., R. Virden and C. van Riper 2008, 'Effects of place identity, place dependence, and experience-use history on perceptions of recreation impacts in a natural setting', *Environmental Management* 42: 647–657.

Williams, D. and J. Vaske 2003, 'The measurement of place attachment: validity and generalizability of a psychometric approach', *Forest Science* 49(6): 830–840.

— 2004, *The Measurement of Place attachment: Validity and Generalizability of a psychometric approach*, 2002 [cited March 2004]. Available from www.fs.fed.us/rm/value/docs/psychometric_place_attachment_measurement.pdf.

Withers, C. 2000, 'Authorizing landscape: "authority", naming and the Ordnance Survey's mapping of the Scottish Highlands in the nineteenth century', *Journal of Historical Geography* 26(4): 532–554.

Wong, J. 2002, 'What's in a name? An examination of social identities', *Journal for the Theory of Social Behaviour* 32(4): 451–463.

Zerubavel, E. 2003, *Time Maps: Collective Memory and the Social Shape of the Past*, University of Chicago Press, Chicago.

16. Water for country, words for water: Indigenous placenames of north-west Victoria and south-west New South Wales

Edward Ryan

La Trobe University

In dry land people search for water, in any land people search for meaning in landscapes. This paper continues previous explorations of placenames of Indigenous origin of north-west Victoria and south-west New South Wales begun in 'Blown to Witewitekalk' (Ryan 2002) approaching that region as a geographical, cultural and linguistic entity in order to draw out such meanings. Names for country can be as localised or region wide as the creation figures that placed them on the land and so the question of the existence of placenames for areas of country rather than just specific localities will be considered. Both those 'regional' names and more specific placenames will be examined in the light of their origin as variously; sites of significance in creation stories, reflections of natural features or local flora, and additional types of placename origin. All examples will be considered in the light of the Aboriginal sources where identifiable and the relationships those specific informants had to particular places across the region.

The cultural landscape from which the placenames explored in this paper derive relate to the physical landscape of north-west Victoria and south-west New South Wales. The region in question stretches from the Grampians in the south on northwards past the Murray River to beyond Balranald, and from west of the South Australian border to the central Victorian hills and the Campaspe River. These limits, given the imperfect nature of our knowledge and the ongoing tensions of colonialism, are inevitably both arbitrary and contentious but are based effectively on the extent of the 'limits of affinity' of the Wergaia – the traditional people of my home area. The Wergaia language is a north-western 'western Kulin' language, so named after the common word for man, others of which are Yardwadjali to the south and Wemba Wemba and Perapa Perapa to the north-east and Nari Nari away to the north around Hay. A number of other languages distinct from Kulin such as Yari Yari, Yitha Yitha and Dadi Dadi were also traditionally spoken in the region from around Mildura upriver past Robinvale. The speakers of these languages associated socially and culturally with their neighbours including speakers of a sub-group of north-west Kulin languages which display influence from these non-Kulinic tongues. This sub-group included Ladji Ladji, Mathi Mathi, Wathi Wathi, Weki Weki and Boraipur, the language of the Ngarkat away to the west. These particular languages differed from other nearby Kulin languages most obviously in terms of placenames in having the particle 'i' added to nominative forms familiar from other western Kulin tongues. Hence *galk* – tree/bone in north-west 'standard' Kulin becomes *galki* in this group which is described comprehensively in *The Mathi Group of Languages* (Blake et al. 2011). Similarity of language was not the sole marker of social alliance as can be seen from this mixed picture. In terms of how 'limits of affinity' might be defined the testimony of Captain Harrison who was probably a 'doctor' or 'cleverman' with family links to Morton Plains, Carr's Plains and Swanwater in the southern Mallee and east Wimmera, to the ethnographer A.W. Howitt is of prime importance (Howitt, n.d. – a).

Captain Harrison told Howitt that the Gamutch (Black Cockatoo) and Krokitch (White Cockatoo) moiety divisions extended west a long way towards Wellington and down beyond Mt Gambier where 'another language came in & people would kill him if he went among them'. He also knew the tribes on the Murray Dadi Dadi, Mathi-Mathi, Wati-Wati up to where about Hay another 'language' came in where the Wiradjuri were. Included within the bounds of the area to the west, Captain mentions, is country of the Buandik people who spoke a non-Kulin language. Beyond them though, 'down beyond Mt. Gambier', lay country where a different moiety system pertained. But amongst the people of the Murray, Captain mentions that another moiety system also prevailed as those people were divided between Kilpara and Mukwara – Crow and Eaglehawk. Again there is a mix of language families in this area to the north though he mentions only the area beyond Hay where the Wiradjuri were as where a new 'language' began. The peoples he lists, however, even those to the immediate south of the Wiradjuri, did not intermarry with them and limited their overall contacts with them in order to avoid conflict. The bounds of Wergaia social relations were thus shaped by both affinity of language and social order, as well as their limits.

While the situation in which placenames developed was clearly complex, the question arises of where scholars find them in a part of Australia in which the traditional languages have not been spoken for many years. Sources are varied and include the written accounts of explorers and pastoralists, missionaries, ethnographers and surveyors. The great bulk of placenames examined in this study stem from the maps those surveyors created, a source which provides important spatial as well as linguistic information.[1] The greatest level of cultural context and detail comes, as might be expected, from the random accounts

---

1 The majority of cartographic material consulted is found in the Victorian Public Record Series (VPRS) 15899 or VPRS 5920.

taken from Aboriginal people themselves and recorded by the small group of Europeans interested enough to do so, such as R.H. Mathews and A.W. Howitt in the late 19th and early 20th centuries and Luise Hercus in the 1960s. The region has a dryland ecology, as does much of Australia away from the coastal fringe, and a common concern of both Aboriginal and European people is and has been, access to water. Accordingly this survey begins by looking at placenames referring to water.

Dialectal variants on a common word for water occur in many of the languages of the region – *gadjin/gaden/gadini/gayini* – and as will be seen it does feature in placenames. Catiabrim (water + spring) is located at Mt Elgin in the northern Wimmera, Moochargatchin (to pick up + water) to the east on the Yarriambiack Creek, Wa-wa-catchi (to follow + water) further east again while Porp-a-gatyein (head + water), Becatyin (mud + water) and Tulgamuruy catyin ('water of the visitors') are found in the southern Wimmera. The nominal forms appear to be straightforward in derivation and certainly the descriptive notation 'chalky or lime water' next to Becatyin on the source map does neatly accord with the literal meaning of muddy water. These nominal forms could however also stem from the travels across the land of creation figures and the verbally based forms listed here certainly would. Tulgamuruy Catyin is found in Smyth (1878 Vol. 2: 178) where it is accompanied by a gloss which illustrates both the benefit and the difficulty of working with such sources; benefit in that *gadjin* the relevant word for water is featured but difficulty remains in the absence of a reference to visitors. The initial part of the placename however is clearly based on *telgug* the word for good and certainly in the context of the gloss good water would be sought for visitors, though again the visitors in question would be creation figures. What we might call 'good water' placenames are also found in the form of Towalky alias Tualka Creek in Weki Weki country near Boundary Bend on the Murray and Curndualk again on the Murray upstream from Swan Hill.

A further number of water related placenames is found across the region featuring *brim*, the word for spring. Brim is found at two locations in the Wimmera and Brimin at two in the Mallee. More complex forms are found such as Bim Bim a Nouchie (springs + mythological figure) at Lake Tyrell and Coonubrin (excrement + spring) at Lake Timboram to its east. The water at Coonubrin was salty which may indicate the name was descriptive of spoilt water. Similarly Gretchie Brem in the northern Mallee was glossed as bitter or salty spring in a list of words taken from Sam Kinnear at the site of the old Ebenezer Mission in the 1930s (Massola n.d.). Sam was born at the mission while his father came from Lalbert and his mother was a Wemba Wemba woman from Long Lake and his use of an initial consonant cluster when writing this placename confirms his family's linguistic origins in the eastern part of Wergaia country. The Gretchie Brem spring features as a camp in a narrative featuring the Bram Brothers, the main creation figures for the region, where the brothers battled *Djine-djinedj* the tawny frogmouth, which reinforces the different levels of association and meaning embodied in placenames (Mathews n.d.).

There are many other water sources that are descriptive in a different sense, utilising shape or size as a basis for a placename. Included in this group we find the word *bili* for belly, as in the following instances: Muckbilly (alongside + belly) known from two locations on the Wimmera River and Yarriambiack Creek and the remarkable Billyjumbuck (belly + sheep) featuring the pidgin word for sheep. This may indicate the development of a very new yet traditional placename or perhaps that the word which became attached to sheep had other associations previously. There is another word often found as a placename element associated with water; spelt variously Jackel or Jackle. It is found in the name of an early pastoral run, Jackel ba Jackel, along the outlet creek to the north of Lake Albacutya. It is also found as the original name for Lake Lonsdale in the southern Wimmera and referring to a swamp on the Mt Elgin run in the form Torongyjackle where the first part of the name can be read as *tjurung* = long (Smyth 1878 Vol. 2: 206). Given the spatial context of these placenames it could be assumed that Jackel was a nominal form similar to *bili* (belly) relating to an enclosed area of water or an alternative nominal form based on the word *dja* (ground). When we return to the Bram Brothers narratives though we find that Kangaroo formed the Wimmera River, including the outlet channel from Lake Albacutya, and *grazed* (my emphasis) about Lake Albacutya. It can then be seen that the verb *djaga* = to eat forms the base of all three placenames with Jackel ba Jackel being read as *djagila djagila* – 'to go on eating greedily' and Torongyjackle meaning a long area of grazing at that location. In traditional times all these waterways and the edges of lakes and swamps would have been regularly burnt to form new grass and attract kangaroos and other herbivores and so placenames can illustrate the links between cultural and environmental cycles. This is further emphasised by the sourcing of much Bram Brothers narrative from Henry and Teddy Fenton of the Dyakkal Balluk division of the Wergaia, based at Lake Albacutya (Mathews n.d.).

Difficulties of interpretation also present themselves when we look at the placenames Chuangpille from Wonwondah Station in the southern Wimmera and Churingabull well to the northward on Morton Plains, as they could be read as *tjuwerung* + *bili* (long + belly) or *tjuwerung* + *pil* (long + 'having'). The second form where *-pil* is a variant of the more common grammatical morpheme *-wil* for 'having' thus reads as 'the long one' – a nickname for the emu used by Wemba Wemba speakers. It is difficult to judge which is the correct etymology here as while we do not have tokens of Yardwadjali and Wergaia speakers using anything other than the standard form *gauir* for emu, that does not mean the alternate form was not employed. Certainly emus feature elsewhere in the region in placenames through their formal name as discussed below. Stepping away from water sources we have a clear instance of the belly word in the placename for the Victoria Ranges section of the Grampians where the traditional name is Billyweane (belly + fire). This may originate from a story connected with the creation of the range through volcanic activity as there are similar stories connected with the volcanic plains of south-west Victoria as well as an account from Mt Talbot to the west of the Grampians of conflict between Eagle and Cockatoo who alone held fire, where cockatoo was struck on the head letting out fire which 'raged across the land' (Officer, C. n.d.).

An entry from Sam Kinnear's wordlist further illustrates the complexity of naming practices, as bechurnnma winyap is glossed as mountain duck fire. Certainly *bidjengal* and *wanjab* are the local words respectively for mountain duck and fire but without a detailed contextual narrative it is impossible to conceive what a mountain duck fire might represent. Other fire-centred placenames are at least partly readable with the Kinnear wordlist and Luise Hercus' (1986: 212) informants providing *walbana ngadje* – 'they are burning the little fellow', with the little fellow being a widely found mythological figure. That placename refers to a location on the Wimmera River as does Walpana Muya from cartographical sources where the first part of the name again clearly represents 'they are burning' whilst the second could be *manja* which translates as 'hand' or *munja* which translates as 'yam'. A yam being burnt might well be a more everyday occurrence but a burnt hand might more readily fit a relevant creation narrative – without which we can draw no further conclusion. It is unclear if 'the Walpa country' to the north of Murrayville held that name before a parish of that name was formed in the early 20th century but it would at least be an apt placename for much of the year. Another form based on *walpa* in Walpeup certainly existed as a placename attached to a plain prior to the creation of parishes, though at a slightly different location to the current town between Murrayville and Ouyen.

Ngadje, the 'little fellow' who was burnt on the Wimmera River, was as noted a widely cited form of mythological creature who attacked people at night. This creature appears in many placenames beyond the burning place on the Wimmera and his springs at Lake Tyrell such as Dowar Natchic in the Wimmera where he is clearly struck (from *dauwa* – 'to strike'), Natimuk (ngadje + alongside), and the opaque forms Naghywerrie, Grambonatchie and Nutte Carenn from across the region. He also features in the stand-alone placename of Natya near Tooleybuc and was said in the colonial period to inhabit particular waterholes. Other figures with such associations include Witjewitj who was linked with a well in the desert between the well-known Devon Downs rock shelter and Loxton in the South Australian riverland. Robert Tarby Mason recorded for Norman Tindale how Witjewitj was greatly feared for killing people and Mason's people would never linger at the well because of it (Tindale n.d.). Devon Downs itself was named traditionally Naud Naud after another figure well known across the Mallee and Wimmera. The presence in the landscape of these figures or 'powered men' as Tarby Mason called them confirms the cultural and linguistic continuity between that country of the Ngarkat and adjacent Kulin speaking areas of Victoria and New South Wales. It can also be seen how the association of feared figures with these dryland water sources would preserve them from over exploitation and limit the potential for inter-tribal contact and conflict as 'outside' travellers did not pause for long at them on their journeys. While the well known 'bunyip' (*banib*) was linked with particular waterholes across the region in a cautionary fashion, other such associations showed the limits of affinity mentioned above: as Captain Harrison's countryman Morton Plains Bobby when quizzed by A.W. Howitt dismissed the Wiradjuri creation figure Biami as a dweller in a waterhole on the Wimmera River (Howitt, n.d. – b).

Anything connected with these 'powered men' left an imprint on the landscape that is readable through placenames. Across the region there are axes, clubs and bags, both water and carry bags, left embedded in place. And there are placenames composed of isolated verbal forms that make no sense whatever on their own – but form part of larger narratives when read in conjunction with other names across country. Near the Wimmera River in the placenames Jolem and Jollymuck (waterbag + alongside) – we find waterbags (*djul*) much where they might expect to be found. Mulkra (*malgar*) a waddy shield is found on the Murray River in the Riverine language area though the name is widespread to the south and Batchicar (*badjiga*) an axe found on the Yarriambiack Creek. More intriguingly in the early 1860s the pastoralist Suetonius Officer recorded in his diary how he rode across the plains from his head station at Murray Downs on the Murray River near Swan Hill to 'Tumble Down Waddy' – a name which appears to be English rather than a bowdlerised Aboriginal Word (Officer, S. n.d.). Given that in the colonial period someone who was said by Aboriginal people to have 'tumbled down' had died or indeed been killed, this may represent an event beyond a waddy falling. While it is not possible to determine the precise location of Tumble Down Waddy it was in the same general area as Cunnienyook Station. This placename is clearly based on the word *gani* for waddy and can clearly be read as *gani-nyuk* – 'his waddy' and so through examining placenames in two languages it can be established that some form of violent event occurred in the area in the ancestral time.

Similar events are inscribed on the landscape elsewhere. Towan lies to the south of the Murray between Swan Hill and Lake Tyrell, surviving as a locality name and it is also the original name of Long Lake, the home place of Sam Kinnear's mother Sarah Smith, near Lake Boga. It presents an unusual difficulty in that there are two equally valid readings as Towan could stem from *duwang* (pigmy possum) or alternatively *dauwan* ('they strike'). In a placename list from Swan Hill in Brough Smyth though we find 'Towan' glossed as 'being speared' and *dauwa* has a more particular meaning of being struck with a weapon or wounded. It is thus much more likely that Towan represents 'they spear', particularly given that there is a placename a little to the south in Towaninny, which translates as 'they strike the neck', as well as the example from the Sam Kinnear list mentioned above of Dowar Natchie which is glossed as 'chop 'is neck', with 'him' being the mythological figure *ngadye* recorded in other placenames as discussed above. Importantly the narrative of the Bram Brothers conflict with *Djire-djiredj* the Willie Wagtail links the Brothers with their cousin the turtle and Lake Lalbert, which was originally set in a great plain on which Towaninny was located. Spears were not used in that struggle but the narrative links to the area show it to have been an area where ancestral beings were joined in combat.

Beyond the known 'powered men' and their actions and belongings reviewed above a range of everyday creatures feature in the placenames of the region, in particular birds. This is unsurprising as birds take a central position in the moiety systems and narrative traditions of the region to such an extent that while traditionally Aboriginal people greeted strangers with *njanja yauir* (what meat) in order to establish how to relate to each other, in later times in English they would discuss what 'their birds' were – even though the system encompassed more than just bird figures. Jenep (*djinab*) the Sulphur Crested Cockatoo exists as a placename near the Yarriambiack Creek and 'larnee jinnep' – his landing place or more literally his camp lies further west. There is also Perrit Perrit (*beredj beredj*) in the west Wimmera and a number of instances of Coonawar (*gunuwar*) the swan across the region. Wahpool Ngurrum Tyrill just to the east of Lake Tyrell probably reflects star lore as such material from that area refers to a male and female crow and the first part of the name Wahpool (*wabul*) refers to two crows while Tyrill (*direl*) means sky. Frustratingly the middle word is untranslatable but this may be rectified when Aboriginal astronomy of the region is considered in an informed and rigorous manner. We also find the white cockatoo or corella at Kathica (*gadjegar*) on the Richardson River near Donald and his foot far to the west at Mt Elgin in the form Tenunggatiga (*djine + gadjegar*). While these may have been the locations of increase sites they would all have formed part of broader ancestral narratives which are now lost.

Fortunately some lore does survive in regard to the emu (*gauir*). While Wemba Wemba people favoured a nickname for the emu there is at least one instance of the proper name from their country in the early pastoral station name Giaour, located to the north of the Murray. There are also two extant pastoral maps from widely spaced parts of the region which record in English 'kangaroo and emu plains' and while no explanation of what that might mean is given, it is clearly a carryover from the Aboriginal cultural landscape. The main surviving narrative we have featuring emus relates again to the Bram Brothers with the most detailed version taken down by R.H. Mathews from residents of Ebenezer Mission north of Dimboola in the 1890s with the relevant section beginning in the northern Mallee at Wombegrak or Cow Plains Station – now the village of Cowangie (Mathews n.d.). Crow was chased from there by a fearsome giant emu whose name was rendered as Ngindyal by R.H. Mathews and Tchingal by A.W. Howitt. Crow was pursued south to the Grampians where he went through a tunnel and the giant emu in pursuit split the mountain, forming Rose's Gap or Barregowa (path + emu), the path of the emu which was named from the event.

Between these two locations, part of the Ebenezer Mission Station was formed from Bonegar Station which could possibly be read as dust of the emu. When petitioning the government for more land for the Mission in the 1860s and 1870s the residents led by Philip Pepper and Jackson Stewart mentioned Bonegar as a place where they and their ancestors 'always liked to go', so it was certainly a place of importance to them (VPRS 44). Lake Hindmarsh was also of importance to them and there we find that Rocky Point was originally known as Garndagauer (Smyth 1878 Vol. 2: 176) which could possibly read as 'nose of the emu'.

While these places fall within the range of the giant emu's tracks their meaning is not readily verifiable as they are not mentioned in the narrative remnants which survive and they exist in only one or two examples. Nevertheless discussion of their meaning is rendered possible when a cultural context exists for the placenames themselves, a context which illustrates that while these animals may take everyday form, they are as likely to be 'powered' as are the other figures.

There is another range of placenames in those that do not feature animals in any form but are based on plants. These names are often relatively simple and direct in form and in addition to further cultural information can provide an insight into the historical ecology of this much changed region. Widji, the word for basket grass occurs widely as in Witchice in the Wimmera, Wichi-pel (basket grass + 'having') at Antwerp on the lower Wimmera River, Witchi at Polkemmet Station in the southern Wimmera and the well-known Wycheproof (basket grass + head) referring to a basket grass hill. Other general references to forms of grasses and groundcovers are also widespread. Jarrok (reeds) appears as a placename on the Lalbert Creek and lower Avoca River in the southern Mallee as well as near Mt Talbot in the southern Wimmera. There are also compound forms featuring reeds such as Tallijark (tongue + reeds) on the Murray and Buckanyany-jowk for Duck Lake in the Wimmera – glossed as 'reedy neck – descriptive of the shape of this lake' in Smyth (1878 Vol. 2: 178). Certainly the second morpheme refers to the neck and the final one to reeds so even without the meaning of the first morpheme it appears this placename gloss has some validity.

On the Murray we find Booyup (pigface), in the sand-hill country of the western Mallee is Patchywallock (grass + porcupine grass) and Karrun (lignum) in the east Wimmera. Moving to bushes we find Jope (*djub*) in the south-west Wimmera as well as the important camping spot of Djub Djub Galk near Charlton, and Cutya (bitter quandong) on the outfall of the Yarriambiack Creek. Banksia occurs in placenames in the south and east Wimmera at Warrock Plains, Woorack, and Wurruck Wurruck. Golden wattle occurs at a number of locations across the region, reflecting its physical spread. *Galk* the generic name for tree also features in a range of locations such as Witchagulk (little + tree) on Morton Plains, Bairbargulk and Gartanagalk in the Wimmera though both of these are only partly readable. *Galk* also features in Calcalcebeal (tree + tree + redgum) which related to a redgum forest near Mt Talbot. The Redgum occurs in many placenames such as Bael on Morton Plains, Nurrabial down in the Wimmera, and Goorucbeale (sand + redgum). Lake Bael-Bael refers to numbers of trees while Baelapungit (redgum + wire rush) also gives a detailed description of a place on the Murray.

Finally there is a reference to the yellow gum in Papp Plains in the east Wimmera and Bapcha (yellow gum + ground) at two locations elsewhere in the Wimmera, as well as Gourteebap glossed as 'clump of white or yellow gums' in Sam Kinnear's wordlist. The morpheme *gurt* occurs in many other placenames across the region but lacks contextual material to clarify its meaning, although the final morpheme in Gourteebap is clearly *bep* (yellow gum). Most of these plant related names take a simple form and could be read as simply descriptive of the region's ecology. Others such as Witchagulk (small + tree) on Morton Plains feature in Bram Brothers narratives and as lore from Mt Talbot states that 'trees formerly had the power of locomotion', plants are as likely as animals to be 'powered' in cultural landscapes and the placenames that illustrate them (Officer, C. n.d.).

It is unsurprising that placenames featuring plants appear at a range of locations across a region regardless of background narratives given the comparable physical spread of the plants. Placenames themselves can recur at widely spaced intervals across a region and illustrate a range of factors impacting on language spread. Witchagulk on Morton Plains is replicated as Witewitekalk further west which reflects the localisation of regional creation narratives. Boomboon in the Yardwadjali area of the Wimmera and Poonboon north of Swan Hill in Wadi Wadi country illustrate the amount of commonality amongst Kulin type languages as well as a linguistic puzzle as the northern example of this probable nominal form does not feature the '-i' ending expected in the Mathi sub-group. Instances of Mournpul at the lakes in Ladji Ladji country and in the country between the Richardson River and Yarriambiack Creek in Wergaia country follow this pattern. Instances occur where the Mathi sub-group '-i' ending does appear though and clarifies language boundaries. Waitchie (golden wattle) west of Swan Hill as distinct from Wergaia *wadj* shows the reach of Wati Wati, as Lepi (manna) to the west of Piangil as opposed to Wergaia *lerəb* shows the extent of Wati Wati or Weki Weki. Further pairs are found with Wennca located near Pine Plains in Wergaia country and Wennga further north in Yu Yu territory, which as a Riverine language is linguistically distinct. In this case as there is not a great overall distance between the locations concerned the adjacent but unrelated languages may have influenced each other. Derrick also occurs in Yu Yu country and is apparently matched by Terrick Terrick in Barapa Barapa country hundreds of miles away to the east. It is possible that *djarug* (yam) is intended here given that it was a staple traditional food commonly found on the Terrick Plains but analysis is greatly restricted by the limited extent of Yu Yu vocabulary surviving. The country of Riverine languages can be identified in part by the presence of monosyllable placenames such as Pom on the Murray as they do not appear in Kulinic languages. At the other extreme we have instances of placenames comprised of phrases such as Mebimdonudgawanginaroong and Murmenon Yannane Merong from near Lake Tyrell, the latter of which probably features the verb 'to walk', *yanga*. A number of other phrase or sentence length placenames survive from the lower Murrumbidgee River though equally as opaque as these examples. Placenames thus provide clues into questions of historical linguistics as well as historical ecology but most of which must remain unanswered due to paucity of material.

The range of types of placenames explored above demonstrate how the land is culturally encoded in a variety of ways. Names for place as a concept in itself and for terms encompassing discrete areas such as clan or language areas remain to be explored. 'Country' is generally glossed in wordlists from across the region as *dja,* as are 'ground' and 'earth'. There are no tokens of *dja* extant though as a placename in its own right in the way for instance that *bial* and *buyub* exist as stand-alone names that may refer to single examples of a redgum tree or pigface. *Dja* is found however as a morpheme in more complex placenames such as Tiega in the central Mallee which could mean 'hopping mouse ground' and Panitya near Murrayville and Tya-moonya near Lake Albacutya which clearly mean 'small ground' and 'yam ground' respectively. Sam Kinnear's aunt Mrs Esther McGuinness contributed 'jabomungul' as a word for 'country' to a vocabulary (Mathew n.d.) and while it is not fully readable it is likely to describe the quality of a particular place as does Tiega, Panitya and Tya-moonya, rather than representing a broader area or 'country' in a general sense.

There are two remaining placenames that do refer to identifiable larger areas of country: Wityelibar glossed in Smyth as 'Avon River and country' and Wandyin Marungu glossed in the same source as 'Morton Plains country' (Smyth 1878 Vol. 2: 176). 'Avon River and country' certainly defines a specific area and could reflect the clan estate of a number of clan groups or the geographical location of the river and surrounds. Whilst the name itself is difficult to read there is a Wemba Wemba form for creek *withe birr* (small + creek/pathway) which may be relevant given the Wergaia/Yardwajali cognate of *withe* could readily be written as Witye. As this is only a partial translation and there is little in the way of cultural records from the area it is not possible to analyse this placename further. Wandyin Marungu on the other hand presents greater opportunity. While the first word is unreadable the second is clearly *marung* for Murray Pine and early maps of the area showed pines were plentiful. An animate or 'powered' view of the landscape also features pines as a giant pine tree grew in ancestral times on the shore of Lake Buloke at the south of 'Morton Plains country' which the ancestors of the local people used to climb to the sky-land to hunt there. One day when the people had poor hunting they ate one of dogs of the creation figure *Djiwan*[2] (the grey shrike-thrush) who in retaliation placed live coals at the root of the tree which caused it to fall (Howitt n.d. – a). When it fell, members of the local group were left behind in the sky and the pine kernels formed 'a paved road' across Morton Plains to Lake Tyrell, an area that matches the eastern Wudjabalug dialect of Wergaia. Part way across the plain to the north from Lake Buloke lies Tchumm Lake, referred to in pastoral papers from 1850 as 'Chian waterhole'. Clearly this is a rendering of and reference to *Djiwan*. From that smaller lake, Tatchera Creek takes water in flood years northward again to where it joins up with the Tyrell Creek and eventually reaches Lake Tyrell. Tatchera is derived from *djədjera* from 'fork of a tree' and so that watercourse may represent a branch of the pine tree as it fell. Certainly the narrative runs across the land in the same way that this and other water courses do with those 'words for water' and other animate landscape features shaped and named by 'powered' men and women still existing as placenames today to those who wish to read the land. The Tatchera Creek lies a short distance to the west of my home-place and *Djiwan* in physical manifestation often hops a short way ahead of me as I move across the land. With such persistence and the use of a combination of cultural, historical and environmental sources and forms of knowledge it is clearly possible to take the placenames left to us and again illuminate the land.

References

Blake, B.J., L.A. Hercus, S. Morey, and E. Ryan 2011, *The Mathi Group of Languages*, Pacific Linguistics, Canberra.

Hercus, L.A. 1986, *Victorian Languages: A Late Survey*, Pacific Linguistics, Canberra.

---

2 This figure is written in A.W. Howitt's manuscripts 'Xurn' and was erroneously written as 'Kurn' in Ryan (2002).

Howitt, A.W. n.d.(a), MS 1053, State Library of Victoria, Melbourne

— n.d.(b), MS 759, Museum Victoria, Melbourne.

Massola, A. n.d., The Aldo Massola Collection: historical photographs principally from Victoria, A1 BW, Australian Institute of Aboriginal and Torres Strait Islander Studies, Canberra.

Mathew, J. n.d., MS 950, Australian Institute of Aboriginal and Torres Strait Islander Studies, Canberra.

Mathews, R.H. n.d., MS 8006, National Library of Australia, Canberra.

Officer, C. n.d., MS XM 1514, Museum Victoria, Melbourne.

Officer, S. n.d., MS 9891, State Library of Victoria, Melbourne.

Pastoral Run Plans n.d., VPRS15899, VPRS 5920, VPRS 44, Public Record Office of Victoria, Melbourne.

Ryan, E. 2002, 'Blown to Witewitekalk', in *The Land is a Map: Placenames of Indigenous Origin in Australia*, L. Hercus, F. Hodges and J. Simpson (eds), Pandanus Books in association with Pacific Linguistics, Canberra: 157-164.

Smyth, R.B. 1878, *The Aborigines of Victoria: with notes relating to the habits of the natives of other parts of Australia and Tasmania*, 2 Volumes, Victorian Government Printer, Melbourne.

Tindale, N., n.d. MS AA338 131/2, South Australian Museum, Adelaide.

17. Obtuse anglers: The linguistics and ethnography of fishing ground names on Norfolk Island

Joshua Nash
University of Adelaide

When I first lived in Arviat [Canada], the sea was a blank space to me. I did not know the names of the headlands, the reefs, the islands, or the other places along the coastline. I did not know the stories associated with the sea, and I had no personal experiences on the sea. In the beginning I was utterly confused. My journeys on the open water or sea ice were disorienting. I did not know where I was or where I was going, and I relied completely on the hunters with whom I travelled. However, as time moved on, I began to develop an understanding of the sea. I became familiar with the places along the coastline, and I began to hear the stories that were situated in specific places. I began to make connections between these places, and I began to have memorable experiences of my own in specific places at sea. (Tyrell 2006: 228)

1. At sea

The toponymic processes involved in the naming of fishing grounds represent significant examples of place-creation. They are brought into existence by the human need to name and remember locations at sea. These utilitarian placenames are rarely mapped; they are easily forgotten and are some of the most ephemeral aspects of a people's toponymic inventory:

> It is not much use taking bearings if they are not accurately recorded for future reference. The human memory for such details is fickle and the eye is easily deceived. ... It is asking a lot to try to carry details of 4 points in the mind for each fishing point that may be worked. It is imperative that they be recorded, and it is a good idea to mark them on an Admiralty chart in similar manner [sic] to that used in our sketch. (Hardy 1974: 227)

Fishing ground names are a subcategory of hydronyms, names for water features. They are transient cultural capital; the offshore location of these *no places* which become *place(s)* through naming can be lost when terrestrial markers, such as trees and houses, are altered or removed. As I will demonstrate, there is a large amount of grammatical variation in the linguistic form and cultural status of fishing ground names. Despite a large amount of interest in the anthropology of fishing (Acheson 1981) and specifically the anthropology of fishing in Oceania (Johannes 1981), there has been little interest in the relationship between the naming of fishing grounds and the relevance of these names to formal linguistic and ethnographic analysis.

This paper is divided up as follows: the historical and theoretical background into the role of fishing ground names in toponymy is given; the relevance of fishing ground names to Norfolk toponymy and Norf'k, the Norfolk Island language, is outlined; a tagmemic analysis of Norf'k fishing ground forms is presented to account for the formal structure of these names; an analysis of a single fishing ground name is used to explore the role Norf'k fishing ground names hold in Norfolk toponymy as a whole and how fishing ground names can contribute to the writing of Norfolk's toponymic ethnography. To the best of my knowledge, a similar analysis has never been attempted in Australia or elsewhere. The closest study is given in Blair (2006).[1]

2. Collecting *no-names*

To collect fishing ground names I dealt with older members of the Norfolk population. I utilised maps when interviewing knowledgeable people and asked whether they remembered places, who lived there, who named the places, and what activities were carried out in these places. Many remember the names of places and their locations but in many cases they did not know who named them, and why they were named such. I would often probe in order to understand how people came to acquire esoteric knowledge such as fishing ground locations. Informants told me they would simply go out fishing with the old fishermen when they were around ten years old and the old fisherman told the younger men where the old places were. The men knew who *Johnnies* and *Frankies* were named after; they worked with them, had a beer with them after work, and their children played together. Because of the insular nature of Norfolk as a closed, island society, an *insular toponymy* developed. This insular toponymy served not only a linguistic and practical social function involving communication – they became vital economic tools and provided a means of adapting ecologically to a place. Fieldwork in these places is a reliable method to access this insider knowledge and these insular toponymies.

---

1   My analysis draws heavily on Nash (2011: 136–145). Fishing ground data is given in an appendix to this document which can be found at http://digital.library.adelaide.edu.au/dspace/handle/2440/71015.

Nine fishermen (only males) were interviewed over 15 interviews to compile a corpus of fishing ground names and historical information. In order to carry out this process I liaised with and interviewed five Norfolk fishermen over three field trips in 2008 and 2009. These interviews involved creating an offshore map of Norfolk which incorporated both the plotting of locations to names and documenting the history of these names. Seventy-three fishing ground names were elicited during this time. Obtaining fishing ground name data was initially a sensitive issue. This was because the location of these names had traditionally been almost sacred insider knowledge that would not normally be shared with the community. These fishermen are *obtuse anglers*. Their knowledge is obtuse, the angles used to line up fishing grounds are astute. After I had established rapport with the group of fishermen with whom I worked intently, both onshore and offshore, I could freely ask questions about their fishing grounds. Common questions I posed to the fishermen were: what is the name of the fishing ground?, who named it and when was it named?, where is it and how do you locate it?, and what kinds of fish would you catch there?

My field research on Norfolk Island with fishermen who still remember and use these fishing marks and the visual triangulation system has shown that knowledge of these fishing marks is exclusively the realm of the older predominantly male members of this community. This knowledge is not gender specific per se. But because few women fish on Norfolk Island, women have less access to fishing ground knowledge. Any such knowledge, if known to women at all, typically consists of a few common names that are overheard when spoken by male relatives or associates. While the map presented in map 4 depicts fishing ground locations as accurately as possible, it is the cultural and ecological links to language and place that are integral to this paper rather than exact locations.

3. Norf'k introduced

Norf'k stems from the language which emerged on Pitcairn Island from 1790 in a small community comprised of Tahitian and English speakers. All the Pitcairn Islanders were moved to Norfolk Island in 1856. This marks the beginning of Norf'k as a form of the language of Pitcairn which has undergone changes due to its transplantation to a new environment.

Norf'k is spoken by around 300 people on Norfolk Island. As an endangered language recognised by the United Nations Educational, Scientific and Cultural Organization (UNESCO 2007), and the only other language within Australia and its territories co-official with English with the passing of the *Norfolk Island Language (Norf'k) Act* (2004) (Administration of Norfolk Island 2004),

Norf'k is a key element of Australia's linguistic and cultural heritage. Various social and political stigmas associated with the language during the last 100 years, especially in the education system (Mühlhäusler 2007), have meant the language has suffered severely. Documenting Norf'k fishing ground names is not only important for documenting an important element of the lexicon of an endangered language, but also in putting forward fishing ground names as a key aspect of a language's placename lexicon which deserves theoretical consideration. Norf'k fishing ground name data are extremely valuable to the Norfolk Island community.

4. Fishing ground name analysis

A quote from Forman contextualises the status of fishing ground names:

> The fishermen of the Coqueiral [Brazil] share a generalized knowledge of the area of the sea and the aspect of the land which comprise their fishing universe. The possibility of maximizing individual production rests on their ability to locate particular species of fish according to market values in different seasons. Towards this end they have elaborated a complex system of named fishing grounds and landmarks. The location of the fishing grounds by visual triangulation and the knowledge of the distribution of fish within them in given seasons are transmitted over generations. (Forman 1967: 417)

Apart from Capel's (1977) description of colloquial names for fishing grounds in coastal South Australia, the most comprehensive descriptions of fishing ground names are Hovda (1961) for the western coast of Norway and Forman (1967) for mangrove-based fishing in areas of coastal Brazil. Blair's (2006) account of the neighbourhood-based narrative of fishing shots in the Gippsland Lakes in Victoria and Gaffin's (1996) analysis of fishing grounds in the Faeroe Islands as part of his ethnography represent the key significance of fishing ground names as a part of oral culture and memory rarely documented by ethnographers. Blair lists fishing shot names like 'Gilly's Snag', 'Silver Shot Slunk' and 'Coaler's Rack'; Gaffin gives Faeroe Islands names like 'Shag Bank' and 'Aksal's Spot'.

Norfolk fishing ground names have arisen in relation to particular elements of Norfolk's topography and represent an intimate relationship between language, landscape, and culture where toponymy is viewed as a useful access point. It is worth remembering Mühlhäusler's statement:

> Memories are not factual records of events but socially negotiated. Etymologising for any language is a mixture of factual information and socially acceptable accounts. (Mühlhäusler 2006: 110)

Fishing is an important livelihood and defining cultural activity on Norfolk. However, modern GPS technology and a decreased need to depend on fishing for sustenance mean many of these names are just a memory, which is quickly fading. Two quotes from Kurlansky's (1999) depiction of pioneering fishermen in North America in his book *Cod: A Biography of the Fish that Changed the World* illustrate the need to document the cultural significance of fishing ground names against the inevitability of loss over time:

> These are the fishermen who stand sentry over the cod stocks off the headlands of North America, the fishermen who went to sea but forgot their pencil. (Kurlansky 1999: 1)

> Only today, having forgot a pencil, they head over to the other boat where the three-man crew is already hauling cod with handlines. After a few jokes about the size of this sorry young catch, someone tosses over a pencil. They are ready to fish. (Kurlansky 1999: 3)

Norfolk fishing ground names are culturally elaborate and significant. Many of these are shallow reefs and crevices and have been found through experimentation and trial and error over time. It becomes clear when interviewing older people on Norfolk Island that people know fishing ground names exist and were and are still used. Most people, however, do not know the names, the history of the names, e.g. who named them first and who continues to use them, why some names were named in the way they were, and where fishing grounds are located. This could be due to several reasons, the most obvious being lack of usage, loss of memory, and secrecy:

> A fisherman rarely teaches the art of lining up a specific fishing spot, and a boy's apprenticeship consists largely of curiosity and persistence. While a fisherman is always delighted to have a young apprentice help to augment his catch, he avoids taking him to a preferred spot. (Forman 1967: 422)

Shallow Water came into being through trial and error from fishing experience and was passed down through generations. It exists as a non-exact even transient offshore location created through intimate knowledge of the sea and its location in terms of the terrestrial topography:

> Just at the start of *No Trouble* you find *Shallow Water*. When you line the *Alligators Eye* with *Mount Pitt* and follow that line out until you get a little narrow gap in the pine trees at Byron Burrell's place at *Duncombe Bay* near the *Captain Cook Memorial*. The reef is very shallow and comes up to about 35 metres depth. *Shallow Water* is the general name of a fishing area which covers about a mile square. (Bev McCoy, Norfolk Island, 2009)

Indigenous and Minority Placenames

Capel's (1997: 5) description of 'Fred's Ground', named after the shark which was once seen in the area offshore from Adelaide (Map 1), and Hovda's (1961: 257) description of the fishing ground 'Seta' off the shores of Karmøya near Stavanger on the west coast of Norway (Map 2) depict how names of fishing grounds prior to GPS were located, recorded, and remembered.

Fishing off the coast of Norfolk Island has taken place for more than a century. There is no extant fishing ground knowledge used before 1856. While there were possibly fishing grounds located and used prior to 1856, my informants were not aware of any of these names or locations. However, it is likely any offshore fishing would have used similar grounds and similar triangulation techniques to those used by the Pitcairners after they arrived on Norfolk. Göthesson (2000) lists several Pitcairn fishing grounds, e.g. 'Side for Parkin's', 'Pulawana Bank', and communication with Pitcairn Islanders indicates there is a similar system of triangulation on Pitcairn:

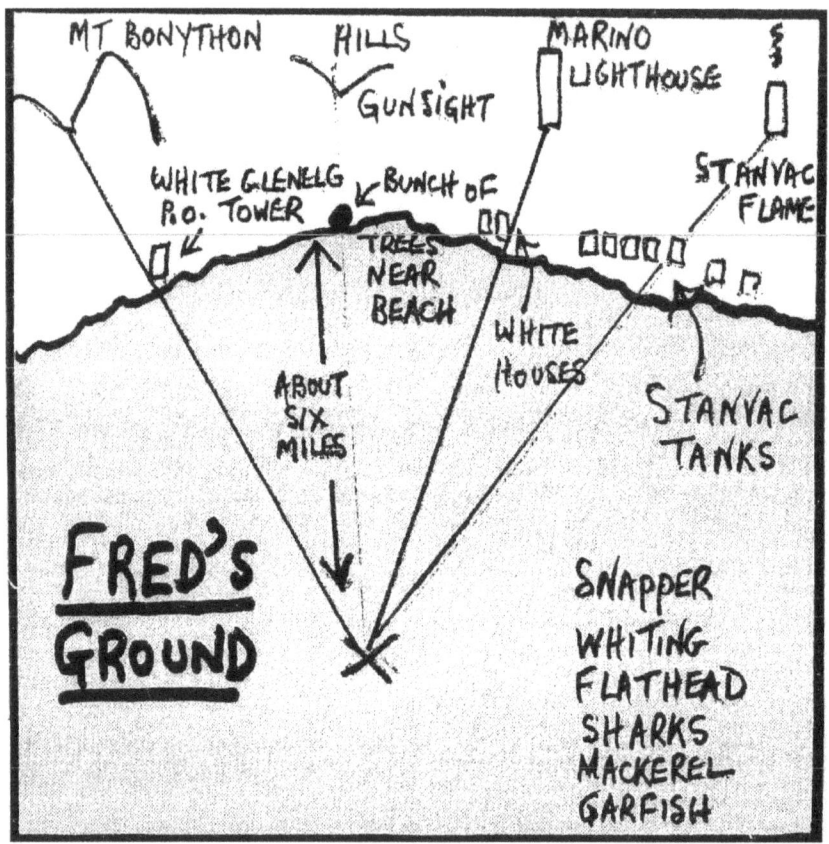

Map 1: Map of 'Fred's Ground' off the coast of Adelaide.

Source: Capel (1997: 5).

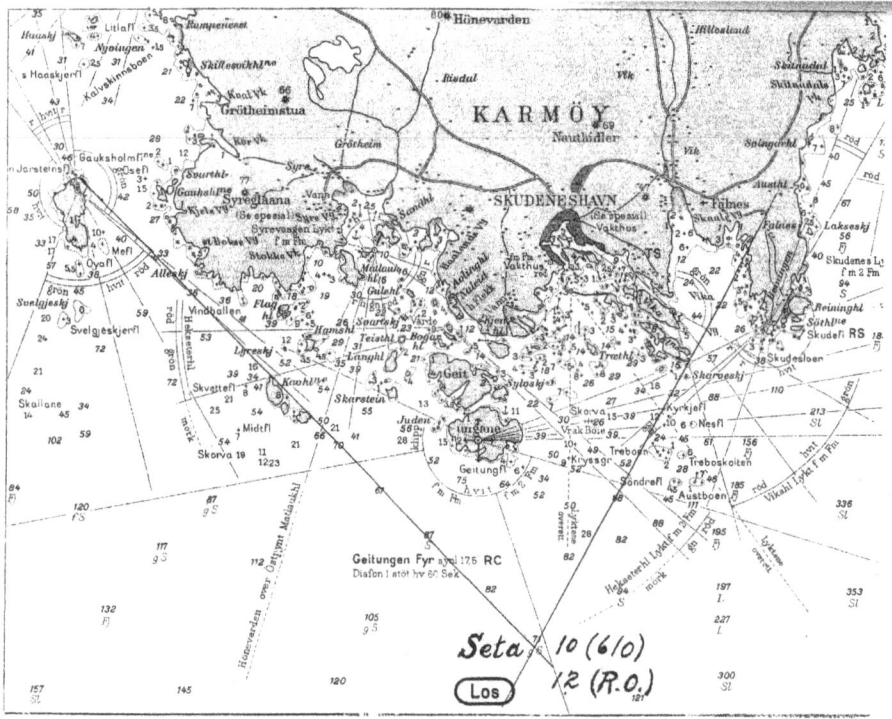

Map 2: Map of location of the fishing ground 'Seta' off Karmøya, Norway.

Source: Hovda (1961: 257).

> We have many names offshore, e.g. 'Har road fer Cookies', 'Har Rooster', 'Out har Bear', 'Har Speckle Side', 'Headache', 'Matt en Dowley'. The marks are taken from ridges or trees lined up with the coastline or Island. These have been passed down through the generations. (Meralda Warren, email, 24 March 2008)

Starting with oared boats, then single piston motors that enabled fishermen to travel further away from the island, and eventually boats that could travel up to 30 kilometres away from Norfolk for commercial fishing, fishermen still rely on distinct landmarks on Norfolk to gain offshore bearings. When trees are chopped down and other landmarks such as houses and electricity poles are removed, marks are lost. Image 1 shows how Norfolk's coastline appears from the sea and some of the terrestrial features fishermen use when lining up fishing grounds:

Image 1: Offshore view looking west to Norfolk Island's north coast.

Source: The author, 2009.

A map documenting Norfolk fishing ground names is given in Map 3.

Map 3: Norfolk Island fishing ground names map.

Source: The author, 2011.

While Map 3 presents fishing grounds as fixed locations, their positions are variable and commonly cover large tracts of open ocean. The geographical patterns in this map are:

1. Most of fishing grounds are located close to the two major launching piers on Norfolk Island, *Kingston* (south) and *Cascade* (north).

2. Getting to the majority of grounds does not require much travel. As a result, the grounds closer in to shore are older and grounds further from *Cascade* or *Kingston* are newer. This is because there was a need to search out newer grounds after older grounds were gradually fished out.

3. There are many fishing grounds in *The Passage*. Due to the volcanic nature of the Norfolk Ridge (Green 1973), there are many reefs located just beneath the surface of the ocean, especially near Nepean Island and Phillip Island.

There are a number of linguistic patterns in the fishing ground data:

1. Fishing ground names can be named after people and usually take the form of a proper noun + possessive, e.g. *Powders, Tilleys, Frankies*. Other syntactic variants occur in connection to the obligatory semantic component, e.g. *Powders* can occur as *Dar Side fer Powders* or *Dar fer Powders* (see section 5 tagmemic analysis).

2. Uninflected proper nouns can be fishing grounds, e.g. *Acme* (a boat used for fishing), *Arcadia* (named after the passenger ship *Arcadia*, which passed by when this ground was named).

3. ((English/Norf'k) definite article) + noun (+ noun) is productive, e.g. *The Crack, The Gardens, The Thumb, Ar Saddle, Dar Milky* Tree, *Dar Fig Valley, Dar Boomerang, Convict Store, Offie Bank* ('offie' is the Norf'k name for the fish, trevally). These are all descriptive names which describe either the water surrounding the ground, e.g. *The Gardens*, or terrestrial features used in lining up marks, e.g. *Dar Horg*. (Looking back to Norfolk on this mark, there is a topographical feature in the cliff which looks like a big black hog lying down.) *Ar* and *dar* are in free variation in all these forms. Choice is determined by certain pragmatic constraints, i.e. when Norf'k is spoken, Norf'k articles are used.

4. Animal and plant names can be metaphorically applied to fishing grounds, e.g. *Whales Hump* (named such because it uses the topographical feature of the same name in its marks), *The Gardens* (named after the seaweed found in the area).

5. Fishing grounds can take spatial prepositions, e.g. *Up the Norwest, Out orn ar Milky Tree, Down to the East, Down ar Graveyard*.

6. There are fishing grounds that have arisen through humour, e.g. *Oodles* (where you catch oodles of fish), *No Trouble Reef* (there are lots of fish in this area so you have no trouble catching fish here), and *Horse and Cart*. There is confusion as to the history of *Ar Yes! / Ikes*; either it was named because when the fish start biting, someone once exclaimed 'Ar yes! They're down there', or because it was named after Ike Christian. *10 O'Clock Bank* has a similar story – this is the time fish in this area are caught.

Many fishing grounds have multiple names. For example, *Eddys*, named after Eddy Yeaman, is also known as *Dar (Side) fer Yeamans*. Other examples of fishing ground name variants are:

1. *Alfreds /Dar Side fer Alfreds / Dar fer Alfreds*
2. *Ma Nobbys / Dar House fer Ma Nobbys / Dar fer Ma Nobbys / Dar fer Nobbys*
3. *Graveyard/ Dar Graveyard/Down ar Graveyard*
4. *Milky Tree / Out orn ar Milky Tree*
5. *Whales Hump / Dar Whales Hump*
6. *Up the Norwest / Out the Norwest / Up ar Norwest / Out ar Norwest*
7. *Ar Yes! / Iyes / Ikes / Ikeys / Side fer Iyes*
8. *Dodos / Ar Side fer Dodos*
9. *Gun Pit / Ar Gun Pit / Out ar Gun Pit*
10. *Ar Saddle / Out ar Saddle*

Making a distinction between the linguistic status of fishing grounds is not clear. Because these names have developed over time and have developed unofficially, they illustrate a high level of grammatical variability and embedded cultural understanding. Anthroponymous fishing grounds, e.g. *Gootys*, *Alfreds*, were named by Norfolk Islanders after Norfolk Islanders. While their formal structure is similar to English forms, the semantic component of names such as *Gootys* has an insider cultural meme linked to fishing places and the people who fished there. It could be claimed because Gooty was a Norfolk Islander who spoke Norf'k, this name *is* a Norf'k name. In a similar fashion, the English topographical name *Gun Pit* can be prefixed with the Norf'k article *ar* to form the fishing ground name *Ar Gun Pit*. This would most likely occur when Norfolk Islander fishermen speak Norf'k.

5. Tagmemic analysis of Norf'k toponyms

Norf'k toponyms are often obtuse and idiosyncratic; many bear little resemblance to English toponyms, e.g. *Johnny Nigger Bun Et* (Johnny Nigger Burnt It), *Down Side Monty Drown* (literally, 'down place Monty drown'), *Dar House fer Ma Nobbys* (Ma Nobby's House), *Out ar Station* (Out at the Melanesian Mission Station), *Side ar Whale Es* (literally 'place the whale is') and *Dar Coop* (The (Chicken) Coop). Because of the building block or slot-like nature of many Norfolk toponyms, a tagmemic analysis is appropriate. I use tagmemics and a description of slots to indicate whether tagmemes are obligatory or optional.

In order to test the acceptability of variations in the common Norf'k toponym form, i.e. *Dar ... fer ...-s*, Norf'k speakers were queried about the acceptability of the six forms. The degree of approval from most favourable to least favourable form was conducted with ten informants. I use the fishing ground name *Dar House fer Ma Nobbys* (Ma Nobbys House) because it is a typical and prevalent Norf'k toponym form.[2] There are at most five tagmemes in this form. However, the patterns can be applied to any other Norf'k toponym, comprising the form *Dar... fer ...-s*. Of the six forms presented below, only the first three were acceptable to my informants, for all toponyms:

1. *Dar House fer Ma Nobbys*
2. *Ar House fer Ma Nobbys*
3. *House fer Ma Nobbys*
4. **Ma Nobbys House*
5. **Ar/Dar House fer Ma Nobby*
6. **Ma Nobby House*

Dar House fer Ma Nobbys differs significantly from the suggestion of the English 'Ma Nobbys House'. Although an equivalent English translation of the Norf'k name rather than the literal 'The House of Ma Nobbys', it was not considered an acceptable Norf'k form because it did not conform to the common pattern. This name is not used by Norf'k speakers; using the English would not only seem to appear as not conforming to the system, but comprises a variant of the name which would not be considered Norf'k.

The use of *ar* or *dar* has no structural, functional or semantic significance apart from possible pragmatic marking of specificity by the use of *dar*, e.g. 'which house? *Dar* House fer Ma Nobbys'. The form of §3 indicates that *ar* and *dar* are optional. 'Ma Nobbys House' is considered English by Norf'k speakers and §4 and §5 are not considered possible Norf'k names. The nucleus of the standard Norf'k toponym form consists of five tagmemes with a specific function for each:

Formula:	Article	+ Generic Noun	+ Preposition	+ Proper Noun	+ Possessive
TAGMEME	1	2	3	4	5
	(a) *Dar* (b) *Ar*	House	fer	Nobby	-s
	The	House	of	Ma Nobbys	POSS

---

2 I analyse 'Ma Nobbys', with optional 'Ma', as a single lexical unit. 'Ma Nobby' and 'Nobby' are synonymous.

1. (a) *Dar* (b) *Ar*: Form is optional. There are two phonological variants but the forms in free variation are subject to the pragmatic constraint marking specificity. Inclusion is optional except when the conditions in §2 occur.

2. *House*: Inclusion is optional based on a key cultural understanding that the place being referred to is known. If excluded, tagmeme 1a is obligatory.

3. *Fer*: It is obligatory in all cases except when only tagmeme four and five are present. Realisation does not change form.

4. *Ma Nobby*: Inclusion is obligatory. This tagmeme is always a male or female proper noun, the combination of a name status term like *Ma* or *Pa* and a proper noun or nickname.

5. *–s*: Inclusion is obligatory. Realisation does not change form.

Possible syntactic variations are:

1.	Dar	House	fer	Ma Nobbys
2.	Ar	House	fer	Ma Nobbys
3.	-	House	fer	Ma Nobbys
4.	Dar	-	fer	Ma Nobbys
5.	-	-	-	Ma Nobbys

Forms which are not possible are:

1.	* Ar	-	fer	Ma Nobbys
2.	* Dar	House	fer	Ma Nobbys
3.	* Dar	-	fer	Ma Nobbys
4.	* Ar	-	fer	Ma Nobbys

The tagmemic analysis accounts for all toponyms adhering to the five-tagmeme forms. This system can be applied to generics such as 'side' (place), e.g. *Dar Side fer Honeys*, pine, e.g. *Dar Pine fer Robinsons*, and pool, e.g. *Dar Pool fer Helens*. The analysis shows that tagmemes §1a/b, §2 and §3 comprise the core syntactic element of this toponym form. The combination of tagmemes §4 and §5 constitutes the semantic or cultural element of these toponyms. When the generic element represented by the tagmemes §1a or §1b, §2 and §3 or §1a and §3 are present, the core semantic element appears sequentially second. This has implications for understanding the relationship between Norf'k syntax, semantics and social dynamics on Norfolk Island, i.e. what is semantically central does not necessarily appear sequentially first.

Patterns from the tagmemic analysis pose the semantic element (§4 and §5 combined) as central to the social and historical meaning of a toponym. Names such as (*Dar Side fer*) *Martys*, (*Dar fer*) *Johnnies* and (*Dar Pool fer*) *Helens* emphasise the personal (semantic) element of toponyms, and the part they play

Indigenous and Minority Placenames

in understanding toponym location, spatial description and history within the social ecology of Norfolk. The analysis reveals that a core syntactic element is related to a core semantic element. It emphasises the difference between the interrelatedness of obligatory and culturally central aspects and optional aspects that are culturally peripheral.

6. *Ar Yes!* / *Ikes*

Borrowing from Heidegger, Ingold's (2000: 172–188) 'dwelling perspective' emphasises the need to evaluate toponyms in terms of how people construct notions of self, personhood and identity. I use the fishing ground name doublet *Ar Yes!* / *Ikes* to illustrate how social worlds and 'neighbourhood' – i.e. situated communities – are created through place-knowledge and how the intricacies of these names are partial descriptions of the toponymic ethnography of the Norfolk Islanders. *Ar Yes!* / *Ikes* explicates how such names and linguistic ephemera become embedded in landscape through the localisation of intricate cultural knowledge.

Ar Yes! / *Ikes*, north-west of Phillip Island in *The Passage*, has two possible histories. A Norfolk Island informant explained:

> The reason this ground is called *Ar Yes!* is because when your line hits the bottom and the fish start biting, you say 'Ar yes! They're down there!' There are two marks. The first lines up the pine trees on *Collins Head* across *High Point* on Nepean, and the second one involves travel west until a little rock on Phillip Island comes out in the cliff like a head. It's about three or four miles from *10 O'Clock Bank*. You mainly catch trumpeter, sweet lip (red emperor), and red snapper there. *Ikes*, another name for the same ground, refers to Isaac 'Ike' Christian. *Iyes* is another name for the same place. (Bev McCoy, Norfolk Island, February 2008)

Side fer Ikes/Iyes was also elicited according to patterns presented in the tagmemic analysis.

Ar Yes! / *Ikes* is still known to many Norfolk Island fishermen. No informants knew who had originally named this place. It can be assumed, however, that it was one of the most frequented fishing grounds, as several informants knew of it. The name and the place are connected to a much larger cultural and toponymic network. The fact that it is unknown outside of fishing history and fishing name usage on Norfolk Island means this name 'belongs' to a particular network of people, names, and relationships. A past exists in this name, linked to a particular event (ar yes!) and person (Ike), and these activities and remembrances occur within or with reference to this specific place and name. The name *Ar Yes!* /

Ikes animates the event and person Ike as an actor, something or somebody represented and recalled in and through landscape. Ultimately, the doublet is a cultural description of place – it also poses a name as a lineage of knowledge and information that is used pragmatically during daily fishing life and livelihood.

Basso's (1996) place theory presents names as living things within Apache metalinguistics. Living names then can be considered 'healthy' and 'vital' linguistic, social and cultural property. *Ar Yes! / Ikes* lives in a similar way because the name remains a positive cultural and linguistic artefact for the memory of the event of catching fish and Ike in the minds of Norfolk fishermen. It is known through the activity of fishing and interacting with other fishermen. There appear to be no specific social prohibitions to passing knowledge of this place to others, but Norfolk fishermen are often reluctant to disclose such information to the uninformed or those who do not have any need to know this history – that is, they wonder why non-fishers and people who do not use these areas would be interested in knowing this name. Names and locations of fishing grounds are particularly guarded as such names articulate closely with the political economy of subsistence and small-scale commercial fishing on Norfolk. Those with knowledge of such places, in particular their locations, are then viably able to access the resources therein. There are certain people who are long term residents of Norfolk Island, generally mainlanders, who fish regularly and yet are generally not told about such locations.

Myers' (1986) perspective on language, self, and the solidification of identity in and on landscape can be applied to this fishing ground. It is assumed Ike himself did not name *Ar Yes! / Ikes* but rather others endowed the place with his name. They have linked and materialised – that is, made durable through mnemonic practices – Ike's self and identity to this place through naming. Linking through naming renders this fishing ground into the historical and linguistic landscape of Norfolk. Ike, the person, is made real through linguistic means – the name *Ar Yes! / Ikes* – and through embodied practices of using, inhabiting, and moving through place – the name is remembered and the place personalised, localised, and created.

From Ingold's (2000) 'dwelling perspective', *Ar Yes! / Ikes* as a place and a person comes into being as an agent in a particularised social and ecological setting. Ingold is careful to distance his 'dwelling perspective' from what he calls a 'building perspective'. This building perspective rests on an assumption that human meaning is separated from substance; that is, meaning is inscribed on the natural (real) environment from a separate (virtual) plane of mental representation (2000: 178). From this perspective, as Ingold states, "worlds are made before they are lived in … acts of dwelling are preceded by acts of worldmaking" (2000: 179). The building perspective therefore presents a pre-existent natural world overlayed by a tapestry of human meaning that precedes interaction with the environment. Meaning in this perspective must be created in consciousness and affixed to the environment prior to any human engagement with it (2000: 177, 191). Ingold posits we may better understand the relationship between human beings and their environments – and the forms they build in their imaginations or in the physical world – by beginning with the context of their practical relationship and involvement in their surroundings (2000: 5, 177).

Linguistic worlds are created and affixed to objects in the environment before the users of a language interact with it. Language, in this sense, exists in a mental space separate to the environment. This division appears all the more stark when considering the settlement of the Pitcairn Islanders from a building perspective; the Pitcairners brought Pitkern to a new environment (Norfolk Island) and affixed meaning to it on the basis of existing cultural schemas. An ecolinguistic perspective, on the other hand, does allow these processes of affixing to be seen as preceding or fully separable from experiences of living and dwelling in this environment. Following Ingold's parallel argument about home construction (2000: 186), I assert while humans have the capacity to envision and consider linguistic forms "in advance of their implementation", they can not merely import these forms into the world from a mental location completely detached from it, their thoughts are inseparable from their unavoidable inhabitation of that same world.

While place-naming could be conceived of in a Saussurean sense as the act of attaching of pre-envisioned linguistic forms to undifferentiated space, acts of naming similarly cannot be detached from human activity and their engagements with their environments. The name *Ar Yes! / Ikes* has become embedded and immersed in a living lifeworld and is signified by the fact that it exists and is used. People privy to this name can locate, interact with and move through these worlds created by and within the world created by *Ar Yes! / Ikes*. This perspective sees toponyms, and here *Ar Yes! / Ikes*, metaphorically as names and processes existing within the world (in a place) – in the minds of a select group (language and thought) and in an actual place, although this place, or acculturated space, cannot be set apart or seen aside from the people who interact with it. The name, the memory, the person, the place, and the location of the place and the fishing activities associated with the place 'dwells' and lives in the minds and actions of the people who use the name. The linguistic manifestation of *Ar Yes! / Ikes* – the formal structure and semantics – is only one element in understanding and realising the importance of the pragmatic usage of the name, what the name represents and the realisation of where the name exists and 'dwells'. The placename itself must be located within the series of contemporary and historical social relationships and activities that enliven it as a place.

Carter (1988) offers a historical cartographic perspective that can be employed to understand the placement of *Ar Yes! / Ikes* within the historical creation of

Norfolk toponymic history. The creation and use of the name *Ar Yes!* / *Ikes* is a method to claim toponymic space (Crocombe 1991). It is also a method of culturally loaded and embedded linguistic colonisation. It is through knowledge of names via the conduit of language that place-knowledge involves and implies a greater access to and increased 'right' to use the place. Place-knowledge and language use is articulated through and connected with the political and social economy of placenames – the stakes related to knowing and 'unknowing' names also involve access to the location of the fishing ground and the use of the fishing ground. Carter (1988) argues colonising occurs through mapping and creating places from spaces. This process is made clear by and through naming – the personification of names and the processes of naming are methods of 'micro-colonisation' that have become remembered. Those who remember the name re-enact the colonisation of the name and the place-space the name represents. There is a degree of ownership associated with the knowing of names, their location in time–space and the mental and physical maps of these places that come to be used.

7. Coming back to shore

The esoteric nature of fishing ground names on Norfolk Island represents the role toponyms play in establishing ecological links to place and people through language. Many fishing ground names are semantically transparent and are readily remembered by informants. However, if the history of a name is forgotten, it can still be affixed to the offshore landscape.

The process of acquiring fishing ground names on Norfolk Island took a significant amount of time. This reflects the degree of apprehension about giving insider information to outsiders. Norfolk Island toponymy is *insular* and inaccessible to outsiders, its anglers obtuse. This could be due to Norfolk's remoteness, its much more marked ethnic and cultural boundaries, and the result of English and Norf'k toponyms creating a complex linguistic ecology.

Norfolk Island fishing ground names are indeed a part of an *insular toponymy*: they are an extremely guarded element of Norfolk's linguistic and social past. Large amounts of this history have been lost because such knowledge was never documented. It is likely that taking large amounts of toponymic knowledge to the grave, in the past and possibly still in the present, is in accordance with well-established cultural memes which solidify stark insider-outsider dichotomies of Norfolk's insider society. Moreover, such dichotomies emphasise the strong societal allegiances on Norfolk through restricting access to the transmission of toponymic knowledge to outsiders, whether they are from outside Norfolk or outside the respective circle which is granted access to this knowledge. It is possible Norfolk's acceptance of its stronger historical and cultural ties to Britain, Pitcairn Island, and Tahiti rather than to Australia and to a lesser extent New Zealand exacerbates some of the suspicion outsiders from the inner core of Norfolk society feel when attempting to access linguistic information like toponyms. A quote by Latham (2005: 41) succinctly summarises the insularity of Norfolk Island society:

> [I] did want to try and understand what made the place tick. It made me wonder if Norfolk Island really wanted to be understood. No one ever said jump in my truck or boat and I'll show you what's important to me. No one offered to show me their island, their world, the one they so desperately wanted to protect and honour. I was never invited to anything by an elected representative of an island which claims to be misunderstood, misrepresented and maligned by mainland media and politicians. I got the feeling it enjoyed its ambiguity, it helped cloud everything over. 'It takes time to understand this island,' locals kept saying, which is not surprising because so few were willing to explain it. (Latham 2005: 41)

References

Acheson, J.M. 1981, 'Anthropology of fishing', *Annual Review of Anthropology* 10: 275–316.

Administration of Norfolk Island, 2004, *Norfolk Island Language (Norf'k) Act 2004*, Administration of Norfolk Island, Norfolk Island.

Basso, K.H. 1996, *Wisdom Sits in Places: Landscape and Language among the Western Apache*, University of New Mexico Press, Albuquerque.

Blair, S.L. 2006, 'Shooting a net at "Gilly's Snag": the movement of belonging among commercial fishermen at the Gippsland Lakes', unpublished PhD thesis, University of Melbourne.

Capel, D. 1977, *Dave Capel's 50 Favourite Offshore Fishing Spots*, Advanced Marketing, Adelaide.

Carter, P. 1988, *The Road to Botany Bay: An Exploration of Landscape and History*, Faber & Faber, London.

Crocombe, R. 1991, 'Naming and claiming in the South Pacific', *Journal of the Pacific Society* 14(1): 216–234.

Forman, S. 1967, 'Cognition and the catch: The location of fishing spots in a Brazilian coastal village', *Ethnology* 66(4): 417–426.

Gaffin, D. 1996, *In Place: Spatial and Social Order in a Faeroe Islands Community*, Waveland Press, Prospect Heights.

Green, T. H. 1973, 'Petrology and Geochemistry of Basalts from Norfolk Island', *Journal of the Geological Society of Australia* 20(3): 259–272.

Hardy, W. 1974, *The Saltwater Angler,* Fifth edition, Murray, Sydney.

Hovda, P. 1961, *Norske Fiskeméd: Landsoversyn og to gamle médbøker.*: Universitetsforlaget, Oslo.

Ingold, T. 2000, *The Perception of the Environment: Essays in Livelihood, Dwelling and Skill*, Routledge, London.

Johannes, R.E. 1981, *Words of the Lagoon: Fishing and Marine Lore in the Palau District of Micronesia*, University of California Press, Berkeley.

Kurlansky, M. 1999, *Cod: A Biography of the Fish that Changed the World*, Vintage, London.

Latham, T. 2005, *Norfolk: Island of Secrets: The Mystery of Janelle Patton's Death*, Allen & Unwin, Crows Nest, NSW.

Mühlhäusler, P. 2006, 'The Norf'k language as a memory of Norfolk's cultural and natural environment', in *Referred Papers from the 2nd International Small Island Cultures Conference*, H. Johnson (ed.), Small Islands Cultures Research Initiative, Sydney: 104–111.

Mühlhäusler, P. 2007, 'The Pitkern-Norf'k language and education', *English World-wide* 28(3): 215–247.

Myers, F.R. 1986, *Pintupi Country, Pintupi Self: Sentiment, Place, and Politics among Western Desert Aborigines*, University of California Press, Berkeley.

Nash, J. 2011, 'Insular toponymies: Pristine place-naming on Norfolk Island, South Pacific and Dudley Peninsula, Kangaroo Island, South Australia', unpublished PhD thesis, University of Adelaide. http://digital.library.adelaide.edu.au/dspace/handle/2440/71015.

Tyrell, M. 2006, 'From placelessness to place: an ethnographer's experience of growing to know places at sea', *Worldviews* 10(2): 220–238.

UNESCO 2007, Degree of Endangerment of the Norf'k Language (Norfolk Island, South Pacific), document.

18. Sámi placenames, power relations and representation[1]

Kaisa Rautio Helander
Sámi allaskuvla, Sámi University College, Norway

Language plays an important role in forming the social world and it is used to construct and shape social and political reality. According to Clark and Dear (1984: 84), "language is studded with signs, icons or symbols, which may carry meanings in excess of the simple word being used". Power relations are also institutionalised in language, at the same time as it functions as a means of social contact and communication. Language has the effect of including or excluding various groups and individuals according to their perception of the linguistically created "reality" (Clark and Dear 1984: 83–88). As Taylor (1985: 258) points out, "it is language which enables us to draw boundaries, to pick some things out in contrast to others. Thus through language we formulate things, and thus come to have an articulated view of the world".

Battiste and Henderson (2000: 74) write, concerning the significance of language in the ordering of the world, that "the people who have the power to decide what a thing will be called have the power to decide reality". It is precisely because placenames are a part of language, that they contribute to forming an image of the world, and thus also placenames can be used to influence a real perception of the world. The use of placenames, particularly in official contexts, is often connected to political aims (see e.g. Helander 2009a, 2013; Carter 2011; Berg and Kearns 2009; Kearns and Berg 2002; Clark and Kostanski 2012; Wilkinson, Marika and Williams 2009; Jordan 2009).

In this article, I shall examine how placenames can be used as part of a conscious effort to form representation. I shall pay special attention to what has happened to Indigenous Sámi placenames as the powers that be have, with the help of placenames, shaped representation to suit their own political aims. At the same time, this article also provides examples of what happens to traditional Sámi placenames in oral use when subjected to a written culture that is governed according to different criteria.

The noun *Sápmi* is used as a proper name, denoting the area, while the adjective, *Sámi*, is used in a more general sense, when referring to languages and placenames, thus, *Sámi languages* and *Sámi placenames*.

---

[1] The original paper was published in North Sámi language in Sámi dieđalaš áigečála 1/2011, pp. 19–41 under the title, 'Sámi báikenamat, válddi relašuvnnat ja representašuvdna' (available from: http://site.uit.no/aigecala/sami-diedalas-aigecala-1-2011-helander/). Minor revisions have been made for the English language version.

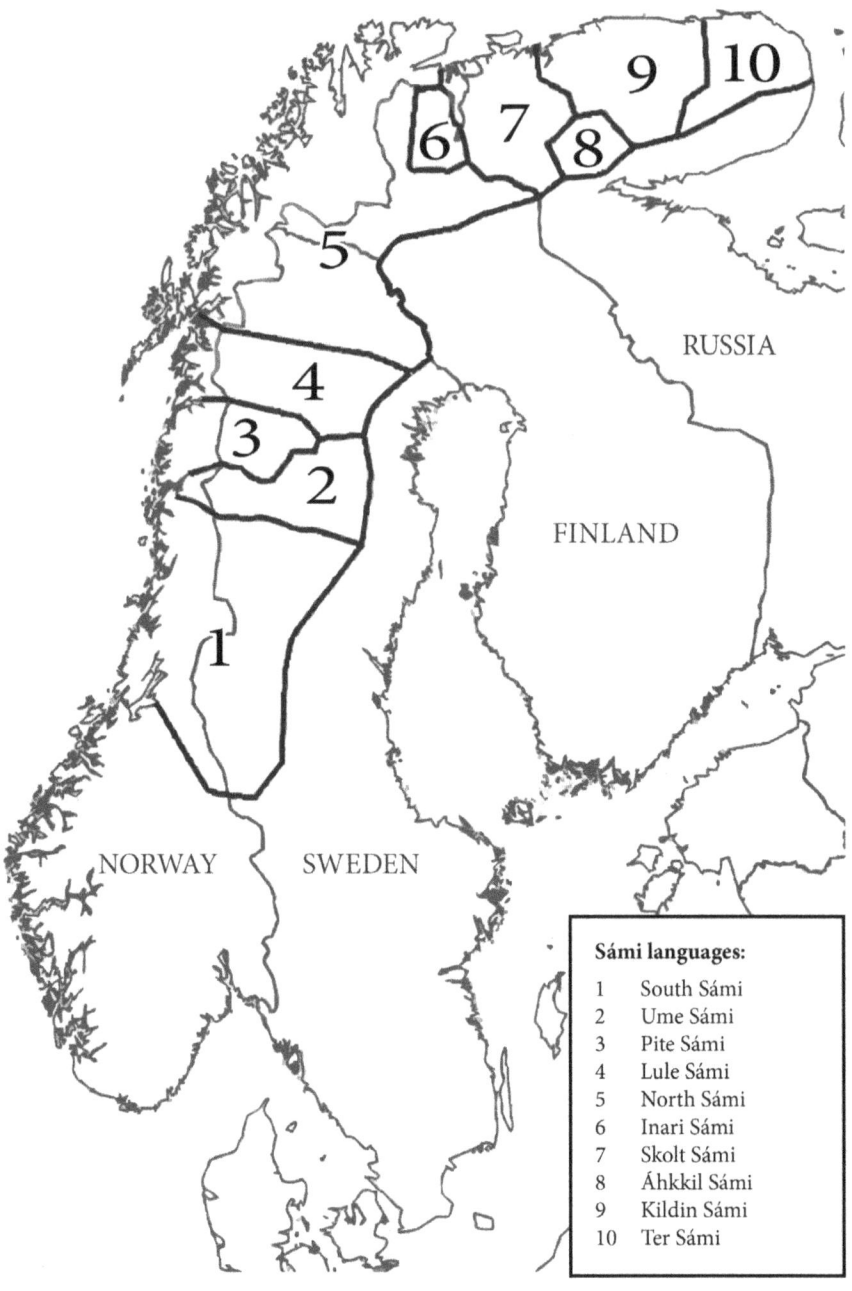

Map 1: The Sámi languages and the traditional settlement area called *Sápmi*.

Source: Map edition by Johan Isak Siri.

Sápmi is the name of the area traditionally inhabited by the Sámi people and which lies in the Artic region of four nation states, Norway, Sweden, Finland and Russia (Map 1). The borders of these nation states were first drawn through the Sámi speaking area in the middle of the 18th century (see section 3 for further details). The Sámi languages are Indigenous languages in the Nordic countries as well as in Russia's Kola Peninsula. The Sámi languages do not have official status throughout the whole of the Sámi area, and have only recently started to acquire some of the language rights that are a matter of course for the majority languages in the Nordic countries. North Sámi has the strongest legal protection of all the Sámi languages. (Helander 2006; Aikio 2002; Sammallahti 1998.) In this article, examples of Sámi placenames are primarily North Sámi language names.

1. What is representation?

Representation is defined as "the cultural practices and forms by which human societies interpret and portray the world around them and present themselves to others" (Cloke, Crang and Goodwin 2005: 12). With a set of practices meanings are constructed and communicated. Hence, representations not only reflect reality, but they help to constitute reality. If one accepts that representation is an active, constitutive practice, then it follows that knowledge cannot be neutral or innocent of power relations (Johnston et al. 2000: 703–704). Representation is a consciously constructed image, formed to suit society's social and political purposes. "Representations of landscape are culturally determined, dependent on who is doing the 'seeing'." (Smith 2003: 72; see also Agnew 1998: 11–12; Helander 2009a).

As Paasi (1996a: 20) notes, "the signs and texts, particularly maps and cartography, which have been employed to illustrate and visualize this 'geography' – the space of geopolitics – have always been social and political instruments of power in the division of space" (see also Harley 2001). Hence, geography is also drawing and visualising the abstract and invisible boundaries of power which emerge from social practices and inherent human relations (Paasi 1996a: 20).

Power constructs are often examined in historical cartography, however, it is important to bear in mind that power relations are not just restricted to historical cartography, or to cartography at all for that matter. The structures of power relations can also clearly be seen in other historical and present-day activities such as, for instance in the administration of land-ownership, on road-signs and in other official naming practices (see e.g. Helander 2008, 2013; Kostanski and Clark 2009). Production of maps, administration of land-ownership, signposting of roads and other official use of nomenclature, all support one another and can thus be used to reinforce and maintain representation.

Historically, it is mostly western, eurocentric representations that have governed and influenced the perception of the world. The question is namely, on whose terms, from whose perspective and for whose benefit representation is shaped and, furthermore, what kind of relationship is there between power structures and representations. Smith writes of the management of history, a factor that augments the power to control representation:

> History is also about power. In fact history is mostly about power. It is the story of the powerful and how they became powerful, and then how they use their power to keep them in positions in which they can continue to dominate others. (Smith 2004 [1999]: 34)

Nevertheless, as Smith (2004 [1999]: 29–30) argues, "history is important for understanding the present and reclaiming history is a critical and essential aspect of decolonization." With respect to the official use of placenames, representation and the study, from a historical perspective, of how it continues and is maintained, reveals that representation is a construct that has been built up over a long period of time. A change in representation will often provoke opposition from precisely the majority population as the current placename discussion in Norway clearly demonstrates (a more detailed account of this in section 6) (see also e.g. Puzey 2009, 2011, 2012; Carter 2011; Matthews 2011; Kostanski 2009, 2011; Amery and Williams 2002). This kind of opposition is, therefore, also clearly an example of neo-colonial power structures. Analysing representation that has been shaped by placenames, it is also possible to examine why present-day Indigenous communities so often struggle to get their placenames recognised in official use. Demands to change long held representations are, therefore, part of Indigenous peoples' self-determination and toponymic decolonisation process. Hence the principal challenge of this process is the question of how to change long standing representations.

2. The reinforcement through placenames of the European colonial representation

Examination of colonial naming-processes and their results shows how placenames have been used to emphasise certain aspects of the real world and thus influence the form of representation. Harley (2001: 181) uses the term *toponymic colonialism* when referring to the renaming processes commonly employed in Indigenous regions, whereby placenames are given to localities that already traditionally bear names in the Indigenous language. This kind of renaming is linked most definitely to representation and, more precisely, to the formation of a certain type of representation.

Toponymic colonialism is a term that also adequately describes other colonial naming practices in addition to renaming. There is also often discussion about which placenames are chosen or recognised for official use, which are silenced and which names of places are prioritised or emphasised in official use of toponyms. Another central question is who has the authority to decide which placenames are to be recognised in official use and in which language. (Cf. also Helander 2013.)

Since the end of the 15th century, European peoples have, as a result of colonialism, transferred their placename tradition to regions with Indigenous populations. It is possible to trace, since the time of Columbus, the ways in which European names have become established in colonised regions. Todorov describes the naming-methods employed by Cristóbal Colón or Christopher Columbus as follows:

> At the beginning, we observe a kind of digram: the chronological order of the baptisms corresponds to the order of importance of the objects associated with these names. These will be, successively, God, the Virgin Mary, the King of Spain, the Queen, the Royal Prince. - - Later on, having more or less used up the religious and royal hierarchies, he resorts to a more traditional motivation. - - Columbus knows perfectly well that these islands [or places] already have names - - others' words interest him very little, however, and he seeks to rename places in terms of the rank they occupy in his discovery, to give them the right names; moreover nomination is equivalent to taking possession. (Todorov 1984 [1982]: 27–28)

Many kinds of renaming strategies have been used in all colonial regions, among others commemorative names, constructed according to various different motives, such as: places named after European seafarers *Cook Island* or *Mount Cook*, after captain James Cook or *Tasmania* and *the Tasman Sea*, after the Dutchman Abel Tasman. Even the name of entire continents such as *America*, is a commemorative name, the background to which being the name of the Florentine explorer Amerigo Vespucci. (MacKinnon 2009; Hodges 2007; Schwartz 2003; Berkhofer 1978).

When adapting names from Europe to the colonies, the transferrence of names was often employed. A common variation of this method was to add for instance the adjective *new* as an attribute to pre-existing European names. Very many names were constructed according to this model, such as from English, *New England*, *New York*, *New Plymouth*, *New South Wales* and also *New Zealand*, which had originally been given the Dutch name *Nieuw Zeeland* (Latin *Nova Zeelandia*), on the basis of which the present-day English form of the name was established as New Zealand.

Through this method of naming, European naming tradition was transferred to a new context in such a way as to maintain, at one and the same time, a connection both to existing locations in the region of origin as well as to the naming models. This model supports eurocentric thinking, in which the world is divided, as a result of colonialism, into, from the European perspective, the Old World and the New World (see also Jacob 2006: 205).

This practice of naming is linked both to a nostalgia for the native land and to colonial projection. It has a function of a symmetrical axis that favours this doubling, the reflection of the Old World upon the New World. It represents a symbolic taking possession of a territory before the actual event. (Jacob 2006: 205.)

The role of colonial placenames has been to serve as a sort of linguistic stamp and symbol, something with which Europeans could mark places and regions and demonstrate ownership of the colonial regions. When, however, Indigenous peoples' placenames were silenced as a result of toponymic colonialism, it reinforced the perception of a terra nullius – as if the regions were not inhabited before the arrival of the Europeans. Thus, taking possession of these regions was legitimised through placenames (for greater detail see e.g. Miller 2008; Harley 2001; Byrnes 2001; Strack 2011; Black 1997; Blaut 1993). For this reason, placenames given by Europeans have been extremely significant as symbols, reinforcing ownership-rights to the regions of which they gradually took possession. In addition, representation is built up through the placenames, which, in turn, reinforce the colonisers' settlement history.

Characteristic of toponymic colonialism is the forming of representation, with which the perception of colonial ownership and domination is reinforced. According to Jacob (2006: 205), "the toponym is thus a signature, a claim of precedence and of symbolic ownership, analogous to the political and colonial mastery suggested by the name of the sovereign."

Naming a place anew is a widely documented act of political possession in settlement history. Equally, the taking away of a name is an act of dispossession. Silencing Indigenous toponymy "must be like being written out of history" (Harley 2001: 178–180; cf. also Ormeling 1983). Toponymic colonialism also has strong ties to the writing of history and to that representation, which is constantly being formed in the conscious writing of history. This is also referred to by the aforementioned Linda Tuhiwai Smith (2004 [1999]: 34) in her description of the management of history. The conscious writing of history, for its part, reinforces the perception of colonial peoples' ownership rights (see e.g. Miller 2008).

The history of European colonialism also demonstrates how maps have been used as a powerful means of visualisation, to establish and strengthen colonial representation (see e.g. Warhus 1997; Whitfield 1998; Edney 2009). Maps "were a medium in a wider colonial discourse for redescribing topography in the language of the dominant society" (Harley 2001: 179). "Thus maps are powerful images that helped to shape and reinforce the colonial view by authorising control and appropriating the land through its representation" (Smith 2003: 72). Through maps, and thus also through their choice of placenames, it is possible to control the world, since through these, information can be limited and shaped (cf. Turnbull 1993; Paasi 1996b; Häkli 2002).

"Although governments and those with political power had always used maps as a means of demonstrating and confirming the control they sought to exercise over space, it was not until the beginning of the nineteenth century that mapmaking became fully absorbed into the apparatus of the state." (Blacksell 2006: 31). State-sponsored topographical and toponymical surveys are key instruments for the expansion and consolidation of central government. They aid the internal colonisation of the nation-state as well as the incorporation of overseas territories. (Daniels 1998: 114; Godlewska 1995; Bassett 1994.) Thus in the 19th century, states started to control map-making in a more systematic way, in order to form maps in accordance with their own nationalistic objectives. Maps were extremely important in forming and consolidating nation-states' territorial representations. In the 19th century, maps started to become useful in the portrayal of national power, and with maps, it was easy to show, in a very tangible way, national territories. With the help of maps, an image of the nation-state was created in the mind of the people, and thus maps served the objectives of imagined communities (cf. Anderson 1991; also e.g. Kosonen 2000).

3. Representation in Sápmi – examples of the use of placenames in Norway

From here on, I shall examine the treatment of Sámi placenames, as an example of how placenames in the Nordic region have been used in shaping representation. In particular, I use the situation in Norway as an example of how, during the creation of nation-states, placenames have been a principal means of reinforcing a written narrative of national history, as well as territorial representation. Placenames on maps played an important role in visualising the nation-state's territorial image. The placenames of landed properties shaped the representation of the Norwegian people's settlement and settlement history. For this reason, during the period of nation building, the authoritites began to consciously control the use of placenames in Sámi areas (Helander 2008, 2009a).

It is, however, important to remember that the shaping of the representation of Sámi areas does not just begin during the process of nation-state building, but has a much longer history. As I have previously explained, the start of European colonialism, particularly in regions outside Europe, is reckoned from the end of the 1400s and the voyages of Columbus. The Sámi regions' contacts with the surrounding peoples go back way before the 15th century, and, as regards trading links and the taxation of Sámi in particular, have roots going back to prehistoric times. The most important literary evidence of the taxation of Sámi is the account given by Ottar to Alfred King of Wessex at the end of the 9th century (Hansen and Olsen 2004; see also Hansen 2011).

Though states' interest in Sápmi is over 1,000 years old, literary documents from the Sámi regions only exist from the end of the 16th century. Placenames are also mentioned in sources from that time, since they were used in administrative documents such as tax and court records, letters and other documents. The sources show in what ways the various different authorities, in their various different languages, have used placenames and recorded them in documents. Placenames have been documented in many languages, such as Danish, Norwegian, Swedish, Finnish and Russian, as the surrounding states had been competing for territory in the Sámi regions in the preceding centuries, before these regions were divided between the nation-states as territory, for the first time in the year 1751. Thus we can trace in Sápmi, the same competition for ownership of areas of land that we see in European colonialism. In the history of the Nordic countries, the terms *private Sámi*, *common Sámi* and *common areas* are used. These terms show how the surrounding peoples and governing states divided the Sámi regions among themselves as their own sphere of interest, and controlled Sámi ownership e.g. through taxation- and trading rights.

Placename use in Sámi regional sources does not give a true picture of Sámi name use as a part of oral traditon, since, for the most part, this is silenced in the sources. As Bergsland (1974: 1) writes, Sámi history has been written by others than the Sámi for others than the Sámi. This has also meant that Sámi placenames have been documented according to other criteria and requirements than those of the Sámi (see also Helander 2004a, 2008; Bergsland 1991; Hansen and Olsen 2004).

The fact that written sources contain few Sámi language placenames does not mean that those places have not had Sámi names. It means, rather, that the authorities managed to get by with the Scandinavian macrotoponyms of the main centres that already existed at the time. (Frette 1984: 69; Helander 2008: 65–66.)

It is significant, that placenames in historical sources were, for a long time, on the macro-level, so that the names of Sámi siidas (or tribes) and main areas and the biggest localities were mentioned. The placenames found in these written sources are macro-toponyms for those localities, to which outside society has given names on the basis of its own needs and requirements. These documents also show that other language naming in Sápmi was not always widely used at the outset of settlement history, but that it was rather used as administrative-historical documentation, which demonstrates the interests the governing states or peoples had in the Sámi regions (Helander 2008: 148). The majority language use of nomenclature in historical documents has, however, over time, built up a false impression of settlement history. In Norway in particular, Norwegian etymological name-studies have also been used in explanations of settlement history that are used in the Sámi region in interpreting the settlement history of the Norwegian people (cf. Rygh 1924 etymological explanations; Helander 2008: 86–87). It is precisely because the sources lack systematic documentation about how the Sámi themselves have used placenames, that the silencing, in turn, has reinforced the false impression that a Sámi settlement history was also in fact lacking.

However, a detailed examination of Scandiavian placenames also reveals how naming and naming practices have often had Sámi language names both as their starting-point and model. Frette (1986) has explained the *anger (-n)* 'fiord' -names on Norway's northernmost coast as being Norwegian language names constructed on the basis of Sámi placenames. The locations' original Sámi names have been adapted to the Norwegian name-system, such as in North-Troms Sám. *Gohppi* 'round bay; inlet' + Nor. *angen* > *Koppangen* and Sám. *Čoalbmi* 'sound' + Nor. *angen* > *Kjølmangen*. What we have here, are examples of the transferrence model, in which Sámi names are the basis for the construction of Norwegian names, which are then, in this particular naming practice, adapted to the Norwegian -*anger*-name model.

On the other hand, many centuries of Norwegian administrative toponym use may also have had an effect on the use of original Sámi names, as shown by the example of the Norwegian *Porsanger* and Sámi *Leavdnja*. The Sámi name, *Leavdnja* was originally used as the name for the whole region. In addition, the loan-name *Porsáŋgu* also became established, loaned from the Norwegian name, *Porsanger*. The use of this loan-name has had such an effect, that the placename *Leavdnja* has gradually aquired another use, and is therefore, in current Sámi, almost always used as the name of a town, and no longer exclusively as the name of the whole region (Helander 2008: 46–47).

In such cases where a Sámi name is recorded in historical sources, it is usually written according to other languages' antiquated orthographical principles, as shown by the name forms *Polmak* (in Sámi *Buolbmát*) and *Karasjok* (in Sámi *Kárášjohka*). Such written forms gradually became established, particularly as the names of towns or villages, more precisely in Norwegian-speaking name use.

The same type of processes have also occured with respect to other Indigenous peoples' placenames, as other language authorities have proceeded to write Indigenous names on the basis of their own languages. Gordon has written about a similar loan-process involved in the transfer of names from the oral language of the Iroquois tribe in North America to the written name-tradition of the colonial people:

> Iroquois place-names, like their language, existed primarily in oral form. Whites recorded Iroquois place-names phonetically in their own written languages. When Indian place-names were needed in white documents concerning land grants, treaties, laws and settlements, they were usually recorded by a white law clerk. This procedure introduced Iroquois place-names into official white oral and written usage, thus also establishing them in white place-name landscape. (Gordon 1984: 222)

When Iroquois names were used in the colonial peoples' documents, it meant that the names became established in the placename landscapes of the white man, as Gordon describes the process. Kostanski and Clark (2009: 189) use the term *Anglo-Indigenous* to describe the type of Australian Indigenous placename that has been transferred to an English speaking context, in connection with cartographic work. Hence, this is the same type of name-loan process as in the Sámi regions, where Sámi placenames are used in written contexts, and thus become established in Norwegian. Suitable examples of this would be, among others, the names *Alleknjarg*, *Sirma*, *Stallogargo*, *Sarves* and *Haldde*, which are old orthographic forms of Sámi placenames, but which are used in these forms, particularly in a Norwegian context (see also Helander 2009b).

4. Conscious renaming in Sámi regions intensifies in the 19th century

The structures of European colonialism were tightened at the end of the 1800s, at the same time as the process of nation-state building was started (cf. Yazzie 2000: 39). It is worth noting, therefore, that by the time of the nation-state building process, the treatment of Indigenous peoples and minorities had been linked to many centuries of colonialism. The aim of the nation-state was to build a representation of a mono-lingual, mono-cultural society. The treatment of placenames therefore, also demonstrates similar methods of toponymic colonialism to those demonstrated in the naming processes of historical colonialism. The official use of Sámi placenames in the Nordic countries was also restricted, particularly from the 1800s onwards, as part of the nation-building project. Prioritising and linguistic selection of placenames were practised as a powerful strategy, with which the nation-states could reinforce the perception of a 'We', in accordance with national ideological objectives.

In Norway, the first piece of legislation concerning the Norwegianisation of Sámi placenames was implemented in 1876, when an amendment dealing with minority names was added to the Finnmark Land Purchasing Act (which had been revised in 1863) (Helander 2004b: 109). With this legislation, the use of Sámi placenames was regulated according to the aims of Norwegianisation policy. From the 1870s on, official use of placenames in Norway was closely controlled, in accordance with more strictly defined aims. Placenames in Sámi regions had been Norwegianised well before the amendment to the Land Purchasing Act, as explained in the previous section, but the Norwegianising of names had not, until that point, been regulated in such detail or so obviously controlled by central government authorities as it came to be from the 1870s onwards (Helander 2008, 2009a).

The authorities in Norway linked the Norwegianisation of Sámi placenames to sections in the Land Purchasing Act and to recommendations for map-making. As I have explained in the previous section, there had long been Norwegian placenames in the Sámi regions at the macro-toponymic level. In Scandinavian sources that describe the Sámi regions located in present-day Norway, the Norwegian names are, to begin with, mostly in coastal areas, however, Norwegian naming has gradually expanded, from the coast to the fiords and ultimately to the interior. This naming history is, therefore, very similar to the colonial naming process of the Europeans, as described in other regions. Regions were colonised first at the coast, as Cronon (2003: 19–20) describes in the case of New England in the colonisation of America, "for many years, the only New England known to Europe was near salt water" (see also Harley 2001: 169–195; Hodges 2007: 383–384).

As, among other things, the making of topographic maps was started in Norway, and the sale of land became more strictly regulated through the Land Acts of the 19th century, the authorities also found it necessary to extend Norwegian naming to include micro-toponyms, in particular, locations of Sámi settlement. From that time, a conscious Norwegianisation of Sámi placenames was set in motion, with the clear aim of forming a suitable representation for the nation of Norway. Two toponymic strategies were employed in this process: *toponymic silence* and *toponymic subjugation* (for more detail, see Helander 2008, 2009a).

Toponymic subjugation is a consciously employed hierarchy, in which the Indigenous placename is subjugated in relation to the majority language placename. In 1876, an amendment was added to Norway's Land Purchasing Act, which stated:

> Landed property shall be given a Norwegian name, and any potential Sámi and Kvæn name shall be added in brackets. (Reg. 1876 § 3 f.)

With this provision, a clear hierarchy was created, in which Sámi settlement names were subjugated in relation to Norwegian names. Toponymic subjugation was also emphasised in cartographic recommendations from the 1880s, particularly in cases where a place did not previously have any kind of name in Norwegian. According to the recommendations, the Sámi name was to be translated into Norwegian and the translated form was then be given priority as the correct name. The Sámi name was to be put in brackets (NGO 1886; Instr. 1895: 23).

Toponymic subjugation is a strategy in which places' original Sámi names are accepted in official use. With the hierarchy, however, the impression is created that the Norwegian names are the correct and proper names and that the Sámi names are just some kind of additional name. It is worth noting, that often, only the Sámi name was in oral use, and the Norwegian name was merely a constructed name, based on political decisions, yet it was still given priority. A feature of consciously constructed Norwegian placenames is that Sámi placenames serve as the starting-point or model for them, in that they are either translated or adapted from Sámi to Norwegian. It was often even the case that the local inhabitants had to translate the names for the cartographers. (Helander 2009b.)

The construction of placenames led to many types of manufactured Norwegian names, since the translation of placenames is, methodologically speaking, a difficult and sometimes even impossible process. (Helander 2008; cf. also e.g. Short 2009.) (The linguistic loan-methods of the Norwegianisation of placenames are analysed in greater detail in Helander 2007, 2008, 2009b.)

The clear aim of toponymic subjugation was to establish Norwegian names and to eliminate Sámi names. Sámi names were, nevertheless, needed as an aid until the use of the Norwegian names became properly established. The objective of toponymic subjugation was, therefore, similar to that of the Norwegianisation of the school: in the view of the authorities, the Sámi language was only fit to serve as an aid until the time when it was rendered obsolete by Norwegian.

Another power-strategy with which the official use of Sámi placenames was to be controlled, and which has heavily influenced representation, is *toponymic silence*. According to this strategy, the Sámi placename was not officially recognised at all. Toponymic silence was used in Norway, both in selecting names for landed properties as well as in the making of topographic maps. The use of this strategy was decided in the year 1902, with a provision of the Land Purchasing Act:

> "surveyed landed property is to be given a Norwegian name" (Ot.prp. 1901).

In this way, the toponymic silencing of the Sámi names of settlements was used in conjunction with land ownership and the formation of a settlement-historical representation. This provision in the Act had a great effect, to the extent that the names of Sámi settlements have remained, almost excusively, in oral use and have not been recognised in any kind of written context such as land-registers, cadasters, maps or road-signs (see also Daniels 1998: 115).

The toponymic silencing of Sámi placenames was already a common strategy in historical sources. Thus the toponymic silence from the end of the 19th century was, by no means, a new method, but, rather, a continuation of a model that had long been employed in the Sámi regions. What is, however, worth mentioning is that in the 19th century, the conscious construction of Norwegian placenames increased significantly, including at the micro-toponymic level. With the silencing of Sámi names and the priority given to Norwegian names, the Norwegian names were established in the kind of micro-level localities that had not previously had any oral tradition at all as regards parallel Norwegian names. (Helander 2008: 148–149; cf. also Helander 2004a: 75–77.)

5. The effects on representation of toponymic subjugation and toponymic silence

The examples from Table 1 show how toponymic subjugation and toponymic silence have been used against the official use of Sámi placenames. The table contains the names of Sámi settlements from the area around Girkonjárga in Mátta-Várjjat, in the easternmost part of the county of Finnmark in northern Norway. The names have been written as they were marked on three maps from the 1800s. The examples show that, on ethnographic maps from the years 1861 and 1888, Sámi placenames are marked, for the most part, in toponymic subjugation, i.e. they are written in brackets under the Norwegian name. When the topographic map (Æ5 Neiden) was published in the year 1893, not one Sámi settlement name was recognised, and these names, in use in oral tradition, had been silenced in official use.

The examples from Table 1 show how toponymic subjugation is easily changed to toponymic silence. The examples also show that the silencing of Sámi settlement names gives the impression that, in the course of approximately 30 years, a language shift has occured, since the silencing of all the settlement names is easily interpreted as a silencing of Sámi settlement history and of the Sámi language. Hence, with the toponymic silencing of placenames, a representation is created that supports the perception of a Norwegian settlement area thus giving a false impression of both Sámi settlement history and of the state of the Sámi language.

Table 1: From the toponymic subjugation to the toponymic silencing of Sámi settlement and hamlet names in the area around Girkonjárga in Mátta-Várjjat (according to Helander 2008: 153–154).

Friis (1861-1): Ethnographic map	Friis (1888-2): Ethnographic map	Æ5 Neiden (1893): Topographic map
Dimesholm (Timberrovve)	Dimesholm Timberrovve	Dimesholmen
Braselv (Guollevæijokka)	Braselv (Guolleveijokka)	Braselven
Storbugt (Nirvagoppe)	Storbugt (Nirvagoppe)	Storbugten
Leervaagnæs (Ruovvenjarga)	Leervaagnæs (Ruovvenjargga)	Steinskjærneset
Skogerönæs (Salamgæčče)	Skogerönæs (Salamgæčče)	Skogeröneset
Höbugt (Nuovisgoppe)	Höbugt (Nuovisgoppe)	Höibugten
Junkerelv (Lonkesjokka)	Junkerelv (Lonkesjokka)	Lonkoselven
Buholm (Čaigak)	Buholm (Čaigak)	Buholmen
(Oažželuokta) Stonga	Staanga	Staanga
Piselvnes (Akkalanjarg)	Kirkenes (Akkolagnjargga)	Kirkenes
Ropelv (Jurrajokka)	Ropelv (Jurrajokka)	I Ropelven
Guocagoppe	Strømbugt Guocagoppe	Strømbugten
Sandnæs (Goadda)	Sandnæs (Goadda)	Sandnes

Source: Compiled from Friis (1861, 1888); Neiden (1893).

This representation is also reinforced by the series of books entitled Norske gaardnavne (Norwegian farm names), which contains the collected names of settlements from the end of the 19th century, arranged according to county (see e.g. Rygh 1924). In these books, the area from the counties of Trøndelag in the south to the county of Troms in the north, has no mention of Sámi settlement names, but only of official cadaster names. Thus, even this literary data maintains the toponymic silence with respect to Sámi settlement. In the series' section on Finnmark (Rygh 1924), mention is made of Sámi settlement names, but even in this section, the Norwegian names are, in most areas, indicated as the primary names and written in bolder lettering than the Sámi names. The way the book emphasises the Norwegian names while subjugating the Sámi names reinforces the representation, according to which, the Norwegian names are the correct names and the Sámi names just some sort of additional names. The lexical semantic etymology of the composite elements of the Norwegian names also supports the view that these Norwegian names were original. Such interpretations, however, do not take into consideration the loan processes that link these Norwegian names to the Sámi names in the surrounding area (Helander 2008: 90–95). This series of books still carries weight in Norwegian speaking circles and is, therefore, still reinforcing an old, established representation from the Norwegianisation period.

Both toponymic subjugation and silence are powerful strategies that have greatly influenced the way representation in Sámi areas has been shaped over time through placenames. As regards land purchasing, the Norwegianisation of Sámi settlement names was completed in the year 1902 through a provision of the Land Act, for, since that time, settlement names were to be only in Norwegian. Characteristic for the name use in maps has, to this day, been that the Sámi names of settlement areas have been silenced. Thus, in maps, a two-way division appeared, with the subjugated use of Sámi names in uninhabited areas and the exclusive use of Norwegian names in settled areas. Thus, topographic maps have also supported the representation, as if all areas of settlement were Norwegian speaking and inhabited by Norwegians, and Sámi life and culture were considered nomadism (Helander 2008; 2009a: 257–258).

The emphasis on naming in settlement areas, rather than uninhabited areas, has also been a contributory factor in building up the western world's characteristic dichotomy of civilised culture and untamed nature. Settled areas were areas of civilised culture and the priority given to Norwegian placenames in such areas supported this perception. According to the writing of history that occurred in Norway in the 19th century, fixed-dwelling, agrarian, Norwegian-speaking people were able to form history and have the right to own land. The Sámi way of life, on the other hand, was defined as nomadism, which did not qualify for the right to own land. Thus a representation formed through placenames also reflects the history of Sámi rights (Helander 2008: 84–85; cf. also Agnew 1998: 36; Blaut 1993: 25; Miller 2008: 26–29).

The recognition of Indigenous placenames in official use divides similarly into two spheres in other Indigenous areas, with on the one hand, names of natural features and on the other, names of settlements. For example, in the state of New South Wales in Australia, a name-policy has been in force since 2001 which supports the use of dual placenames. It is now possible to have both the Aboriginal and European name in parallel official use. In practical terms, this means that Indigenous names can now be added to European names already in use (Geographical Names Board of New South Wales 2010: 1). It is significant, however, that in the recommendations for this bi-lingual or dual name use, there is one principle restriction: dual names may apply in the case of natural features (such as mountains, rivers, lakes and other features of the natural environment), but the names of suburbs, towns or streets must be in one language only (Geographical Names Board of New South Wales 2010: 1). This means that only the English names of towns and cities that have been in official use until now, will continue to be the official names of those towns and cities. This restriction is also, therefore, an example of how Indigenous names are not recognised as the names of inhabited or settled areas, but only as the names of natural features. Hence, even this regulation maintains the representation, according to which, aboriginals belong in nature or natural surroundings but not in urban environments.

6. Maintenance of representation in Norwegian Sápmi and present-day linguistic landscape

As road-building in Norway gradually expanded during the 20th century, village names also started appearing on road-signs. These made use of the same Norwegian placenames that had been documented in, among other records, land registers and various types of maps, such as *Karlbotn, Nyborg, Furuflaten, Skardalen, Snubba, Kjøpsvik* and *Drag*. It is only since 1990 and the Place Name Act (Lov 1990), that it has been possible to officially recognise the Sámi names of settlements and villages on an equal standing with the Norwegian names. Official recognition of Sámi names is part of a current decolonisation process, which means changes in power-constructs and equal prestige in the use of the Sámi names from an oral tradition as in the Norwegian placenames. Since the 1990s, therefore, many Sámi village names have been proposed for official use, as parallel names to the aforementioned Norwegian village names, *Karlbotn ~ Stuorravuonna, Nyborg ~ Rovvejohka, Furuflaten ~ Vuošvággi, Skardalen ~ Skárfvággi, Snubba ~ Duorga, Kjøpsvik ~ Gásluokta* and *Drag ~ Ájluokta*. Not one of these parallel Sámi village names has yet (2013) been introduced into official use, especially on road-signs.

Road-signs are a very visible part of linguistic landscape. According to Shohamy (2006: 110), "the presence (or absence) of language displays in the public space communicates a message, intentional or not, conscious or not, that affects, manipulates or imposes de facto language policy and practice". Road-signs in Sámi regions that have names only in Norwegian are still representing the authorities' Norwegianisation policy and the views of the dominant or governing culture (cf. Ben-Rafael 2009: 49).

Road-signs are very powerful, since we see them a lot and thus their name-use has an even greater effect on people's day-to-day use of language and their perception of the real world than maps. Thus linguistic landscape formed by placenames has also supported exactly the same mono-lingual Norwegian representation that has, through a conscious naming policy, been built up in Norway throughout the whole of the 20th century. The maintenance of a representation built up over a long period of time is a central element in the strategies employed by the powers that be. According to Ben-Rafael (2009: 40), it is still common practice for the power-culture, through its hegemony, to control linguistic landscape. The nation-state is a perfect example of this, where only the national language is used as the recognised language in linguistic landscape. "The more the power-relations principle plays a role in linguistic landscape structuration, the more this aspect might be the object of confrontations, or wars of words", as Ben-Rafael (2009: 47) also calls this type of confrontation. Public space and linguistic landscape can be an arena for ideological battles (Shohamy 2006: 110–111).

In Norway, changing the silence of settlement names has proved to be a difficult process. Proposed Sámi language village names have, since the 1990s, provoked various confrontations, media-discussion and, more recently, fierce opposition to Sámi placenames on social media (e.g. Helander 2006, 2013; Oskal 2003; Johnskareng 2008; NRK 2011; cf. also Dal Negro 2009). A characteristic feature of this opposition is its capacity to influence, in particular the view of the various local authorities. What this means in practice, is that the toponymic silencing of Sámi settlement names continues and official recognition, particularly of village names, is progressing only sporadically (Helander 2013).

According to Backhaus (2007: 5), "public signs are a specific type of semiotic sign in that they too stand for something other than themselves". The addition of Sámi village names to road-signs is interpreted and perceived as a symbol of Sámi rights. Sámi village names proposed for road-signs are regarded, therefore, as the visual sign of Sámi rights. The opposition, therefore, to the official use of Sámi town and village names is not just an opposition to road-signs, but to Sámi rights in general and thus also to linguistic and settlement historical rights (Helander 2013). The opposition to public use of Sámi village names in Norway, particularly on road-signs, also shows that official use of Sámi village names is perceived as a threat, to the whole mono-lingual, mono-cultural representation of settlement areas, which was consciously built up during the 20th century.

7. Conclusion

In this article, I have discussed how the use of placenames is often linked to political aims and how placenames are used to construct a representation. More particularly, I have shown, through the analysis of the use of Sámi placenames, how both toponymic silencing and toponymic subjugation have been employed as powerful strategies that have, with the help of placenames in Sámi areas, reinforced the aforementioned erroneous representation. A deeper study of placenames also shows how a division has been created between settlement names and the names of natural features in such a way that Sámi settlement names are the most adversely affected by toponymic silencing. The methods of toponymic colonialism in Sámi areas are very similar to placename-constructed representations in other Indigenous regions, since it is especially through toponymic silencing that the official use of other Indigenous placenames is also, to a great extent, controlled and politicised.

According to Battiste (2000: xix), postcolonial societies do not exist. Rather, the colonial mentality and structures still exist in all societies and nations and the neocolonial tendencies that resist decolonisation in the contemporary world. As exemplified in this article, neocolonialism also includes *toponymic neocolonialism*, since societies retain the power-structures and methods of implementation with which the official use of Indigenous placenames is still controlled and resisted. Characteristic for toponymic neocolonialism is precisely the retention and maintenance of long-held representations. It is necessary to further research the methods and effects of toponymic colonialism and neocolonialism in order to find more robust methods to promote the process of toponymic decolonisation.

References

Agnew, J. 1998, *Geopolitics: Re-visioning World Politics*, Routledge, London – New York.

Aikio, A. 2002, 'The geographical and sociolinguistic situation', in *Siiddastallan: From Lapp Communities to Modern Sámi Life*, J. Pennanen and K. Näkkäläjärvi (eds), Publications of the Inari Sámi Museum nr 5, Siida Sámi Museum, Inari: 34–40.

Amery, R. and G. Y. Williams 2002, 'Reclaiming through renaming: the reinstatement of Kaurna toponyms in Adelaide and the Adelaide Plains', in *The Land is a Map: Placenames of Indigenous Origin in Australia*, L. Hercus, F. Hodges and J. Simpson (eds), Pandanus Books and Pacific Linguistics, Canberra: 255–276.

Anderson, B. 1991 [1983], *Imagined Communities: Reflections on the Origin and Spread of Nationalism,* Revised edition, Verso, London.

Backhaus, P. 2007, *Linguistic Landscapes: A Comparative Study of Urban Multilingualism in Tokyo,* Multilingual Matters 136, Multilingual Matters, Clevedon – Buffalo – Toronto.

Bassett, T.J. 1994, 'Cartography and empire building in nineteenth-century West Africa', *Geographical Review* 84(4): 316–335.

Battiste, M. 2000, 'Introduction: unfolding the lessons of colonization', in *Reclaiming Indigenous Voice and Vision*, M. Battiste (ed.), UBC Press, Vancouver – Toronto: xvi–xxx.

Battiste, M. and J. Y. Henderson 2000, *Protecting Indigenous Knowledge and Heritage: A Global Challenge,* Purich Publishing Ltd, Saskatoon.

Ben-Rafael, E. 2009, 'A sociological approach to the study of linguistic landscapes', in *Linguistic Landscapes: Expanding the Scenery*, E. Shohamy and D. Gorter (eds), Routledge, New York – London: 40–69.

Berg, L. D. and R. A. Kearns 2009, 'Naming as norming: "Race", gender and the identity politics of naming places in Aotearoa/New Zealand', in *Critical Toponymies: The Contested Politics of Place Naming*, L. D. Berg and J. Vuolteenaho (eds), Ashgate, Surrey – Burlington: 19–51.

Bergsland, K. 1974, 'Synsvinkler i samisk historie', *Norsk Historisk Tidsskrift* 53: 1–36.

— 1991, 'Stedsnavn som historisk kilde', in *Sámi kulturmuittut. Samiske kulturminner. Báikenammačoaggima giehtagirji,* H. R. Mathisen, Keviselie (ed.), Romsa: 61–66.

Berkhofer, R. F. Jr 1978, *The White Man's Indian: Images of the American Indian from Columbus to the Present,* Alfred A. Knopf, New York.

Black, J. 1997, *Maps and History: Constructing Images of the Past,* Yale University Press, New Haven – London.

Blacksell, M. 2006, *Political Geography. Routledge Contemporary Human Geography Series*, Routledge, London – New York.

Blaut, J.M. 1993, *The Colonizer's Model of the World: Geographical Diffusionism and Eurocentric History,* The Guilford Press, New York – London.

Byrnes, G. 2001, *Boundary Markers: Land Surveying and the Colonisation of New Zealand*, Bridget Williams Books, Wellington.

Carter, L. 2011, 'The Big "H": naming and claiming landscapes', in *Making our Place: Exploring Land-use Tensions in Aotearoa New Zealand*, J. Ruru, J. Stephenson and M. Abbott (eds), Otago University Press, Dunedin: 57–69, 220–222.

Clark, G. L. and M. Dear 1984, *State Apparatus: Structures and Language of Legitimacy*, Allen & Unwin, Boston.

Clark, I. and L. Kostanski 2012, 'Reintroducing Indigenous place names – lessons from Gariwerd, Victoria, Australia, or, How to address toponymic dispossession in ways that celebrate cultural diversity and inclusiveness', in *Proceedings of the 22nd International Congress of Onomastic Sciences, Section 5 Geographical Names*, Edizioni, Pisa: 517–532.

Cloke, P., P. Crang and M. Goodwin 2005, *Introducing Human Geographies*, Second edition, Hodder Arnold, Oxon.

Cronon, W. 2003 [1983], *Changes in the Land: Indians, Colonists, and the Ecology of New England*, Hill and Wang, New York.

Dal Negro, S. 2009, 'Local policy modeling the linguistic landscape', in *Linguistic Landscapes: Expanding the Scenery*, Elana Shohamy and Durk Gorter (eds), Routledge, New York – London: 206–218.

Daniels, S. 1998, 'Mapping national identities: the culture of cartography, with particular reference to the Ordnance Survey', in *Imagining Nations*, York Studies in Cultural History, G. Cubitt (ed.), Manchester University Press, Manchester – New York: 112–131.

Geographical Names Board of New South Wales 2010, 'Dual naming – Supporting cultural recognition', Land and Property Management Authority, Sydney. Available from: http://www.gnb.nsw.gov.au/__data/assets/pdf_file/0004/58837/P1021001_DualNaming.pdf (accessed 28 March 2011).

Edney, M. H. 2009, 'The irony of imperial mapping', in *The Imperial Map: Carthography and the Mastery of Empire*, J. R. Akerman (ed.), The University of Chicago Press, Chicago – London: 11–45.

Frette, T. 1984, 'Samiske og finske navn i eldre skriftlige kilder', in *Den 3. nasjonale konferansen i namnegransking*, B. Helleland (ed.), Universitetet i Oslo, Oslo: 69–73.

— 1986, 'Noen synspunkter på -anger (-angen)', in *Årsmelding 1985*, Institutt for namnegransking (Norsk stadnamnarkiv), Universitetet i Oslo, Oslo: 66–79.

Godlewska, A. 1995, 'Map, text and image: the mentality of enlightened conquerors: a new look at the Description de l'Egypte', *Transactions of the Institute of British Geographers*, New series, 20(1): 5–28.

Gordon, J. J. 1984, 'Onondaga Iroquois place-names: an approach to historical and contemporary Indian landscape perception', *Names* 32(3): 218–233.

Hansen, L. I. 2011, 'Norwegian, Swedish and Russian "tax lands" in the North', in *Taxes, Tributes and Tributary Lands in the Making of the Scandinavian Kingdoms in the Middle Ages,* Trondheim Studies in History, S. Imsen (ed.), Tapir Academic Press, Trondheim: 295–330.

Hansen, L. I. and B. Olsen 2004, *Samenes historie fram til 1750,* Cappelen Akademisk Forlag, Oslo.

Harley J.B. 2001, *The New Nature of Maps: Essays in the History of Cartography,* Paul Laxton (ed.), The Johns Hopkins University Press, Baltimore – London.

Helander, K. R. 2004a, 'Muhtin fuomášumit báikenamaid njálmmálaš ja čálalaš anus Norgga beale davimus Sámis', in *Samiske landskapsstudier,* L. M. Andreassen (ed.), Dieđut 5, 2004, Sámi Instituhtta, Guovdageaidnu: 72–86.

— 2004b, 'Treatment of Saami settlement names in Finnmark in official Norwegian place name policy', in *Landscape, Law and Customary Rights,* M. Jones and A. Schanche (eds), Dieđut 3, 2004 2nd ed., Sámi Instituhtta – Nordic Sámi Institute, Guovdageaidnu: 102–121.

— 2006, 'The legalization of Saami place names in Norway', in *Proceedings of the International Conference on Minority Names / Indigenous Names and Multilingual Areas,* K. Gildemacher, F. Ormeling and A. Versloot (eds), GeoNames 2005, Utrecht University, Utrecht: 52–58.

— 2007, 'Sámi báikenamaid dáruiduhttin uniovdnaáigge ja dárogiela namaid lonenvuogit', in *Sámit, sánit, sátnehámit. Riepmočála Pekka Sammallahtii miessemánu 21. beaivve 2007,* J. Ylikoski and A. Aikio (eds), Suomalais-Ugrilaisen Seuran Toimituksia 253, Suomalais-Ugrilainen Seura, Helsinki: 137–159.

— 2008, *Namat dan nammii. Sámi báikenamaid dáruiduhttin Várjjaga guovllus Norgga uniovdnaáiggi loahpas,* Dieđut 1, 2008, Sámi allaskuvla, Guovdageaidnu.

— 2009a, 'Toponymic silence and Sámi place names during the growth of the Norwegian nation state', in *Critical Toponymies: The Contested Politics of Place Naming,* L. D. Berg and J. Vuolteenaho (eds), Ashgate, Surrey – Burlington: 253–266.

— 2009b, 'Renaming Indigenous toponymy in official use in the light of contact onomastic theories', in *Proceedings of the 23nd International Congress of Onomastic Sciences,* York University, Toronto: 492–500.

— 2013, 'The power of administration in the official recognition of Indigenous place names in the Nordic countries', in *Names: People, Places, Perceptions and Power*, Multilingual Matters. Forthcoming.

Hodges, F. 2007, 'Language planning and placenaming in Australia', *Current Issues in Language Planning* 8(3): 383–403.

Häkli, J. 2002, 'Mapping the historical sense of Finland', *Fennia* 180(1–2): 75–81.

Instr. 1895, *Instruks for detaljemåling.Norges geografiske opmåling*. Kristiania, Kart-samlingen, Statens kartverk, Hønefoss.

Jacob, C. 2006, *The Sovereign Map: Theorethical Approaches in Cartography throughout History*, The University of Chicago Press, Chicago – London.

Johnskareng, Á. 2008, 'Viđat rasisttalaš reivve ožžon', *Ávvir* 1 April: 4–5.

Johnston, R.J., D. Gregory, G. Pratt and M. Watts (eds) 2000, *The Dictionary of Human Geography*, Fourth edition, Blackwell Publishing, Malden – Oxford – Victoria.

Jordan, P. 2009, 'Place names as ingredients of space-related identity', *Wiener Schriften zur Geographie und Kartographie* 18: 33–39.

Kearns, R. A. and L. D. Berg 2002, 'Proclaiming place: towards a geography of place name pronunciation', *Social & Cultural Geography* 3(3): 283–302.

Kosonen, K. 2000, *Karttaja kansakunta. Suomalainen lehdistökartografia sortovuosien protesteista Suur-Suomen kuviin 1899–1942*, Suomalaisen Kirjallisuuden Seuran Toimituksia 793, Suomalaisen Kirjallisuuden Seura, Helsinki.

Kostanski, L. 2009, 'Toponymic books and the representation of Indigenous identities', in *Aboriginal Placenames: Naming and Re-naming the Australian Landscape*, Harold Koch and Luise Hercus (eds), Aboriginal History Monograph 19, ANU E Press and Aboriginal History Incorporated, Canberra: 175–187.

Kostanski, L. 2011, 'Signs of the times: changing names and cultural values in Australia', *Onoma* 46: 251–274.

Konstanski, L. and Ian D. Clark 2009, 'Reviving old Indigenous names for new purposes', in *Aboriginal Placenames: Naming and Re-naming the Australian Landscape*, H. Koch and L. Hercus (eds), Aboriginal History Monograph 19, ANU E Press and Aboriginal History Incorporated, Canberra: 189–206.

Lov 1990, Lov 18. mai 1990 nr. 11 om stadnamn. Available from: http://www.lovdata.no/cgi-wift/wiftldles?doc=/app/gratis/www/docroot/all/nl-19900518-011.html&emne=STADNAMNLOV*&& (accessed 19 December 2012).

Matthews, P. W. 2011, 'Wanganui and Whanganui: a clash of identities', *Onoma* 46: 167–208.

McKinnon, M. 2009, *Place Names: Te Ara – the Encyclopedia of New Zealand.* Available from: http://www.TeAra.govt.nz/en/place-names (accessed 27 November 2009).

Miller, R. J. 2008, *Native America, Discovered and Conquered: Thomas Jefferson, Lewis and Clark, and Manifest Destiny,* University of Nebraska Press, Lincoln – London.

NGO 1886, *Brev fra Norges Geografiske Opmaaling 23.12.1886 til Den Kongelige Norske Regjerings Forsvarsdepartements arméafdeling,* Hovedarkivet, Statens kartverk, Hønefoss.

NRK 2011, *Samiske skilt provoserer.* Available from: http://www.nrk.no/nyheter/distrikt/nordland/1.7495194 (accessed 1 April 2011).

Ormeling, F. J. 1983, *Minority Toponyms on Maps: The Rendering of Linguistic Minority Toponyms on Topographic Maps of Western Europe,* Elinkwijk Bv, Utrecht.

Oskal, N. 2003, 'Samisk offentlighet og demokrati på norsk', in *Samer, makt og demokrati. Sametinget og den nye samiske offentligheten,* B. Bjerkli and P. Selle (eds), Gyldendal, Oslo: 318–337.

Ot.prp. 1901, Ot.prp. nr. 20 (1901-1902), *Angaaende udfærdigelse af en lov om afhændelse af statens jord og grund i Finmarkens amts landdistrikt,* Den norske regjerings underdanigste indstilling af 13de mars 1902, som ved kongelig resolution af 15de mars s. a. naadigst er bifaldt.

Paasi, A. 1996a, *Territories, Boundaries and Consciousness: The Changing Geographies of the Finninh-Russian Border,* Belhaven Studies in Political Geography, John Whiles & Sons, New York.

— 1996b, 'Inclusion, exclusion and territorial identities', *Nordisk Samhällsgeografisk Tidsskrift* 23: 3–17.

Puzey, G. 2009, 'Opportunity or threat? The role of minority toponyms in the linguistic landscape', in *Proceedings of the 23nd International Congress of Onomastic Sciences,* York University, Toronto: 821–827.

— 2011, 'New research directions in toponomastics and linguistic landscapes', *Onoma* 46: 211–226.

— 2012, 'Two-way traffic: how linguistic landscapes reflect and influence the politics of language', in *Minority Languages in the Linguistic Landscape,* D. Gorter, H. F. Marten and L. Van Mensel (eds), Palgrave Macmillan, Basingstoke: 127–147.

Regl. 1876, *Reglement angaaende Fremgangsmaaden ved Afhændelse eller Bortforpagtning af Statens Jord og andre den tilhørende Herligheder i Finmarkens Amts Landdistrikt i Henhold til Lov af 22de Juni 1863.* Givet ved Kongelig Resolution af 6te Mai 1876, Kristiania.

Rygh, O. 1924, *Norske gaardnavne. Navne paa matrikulerede jordeiendomme i Finmarkens Amt*, Udgivne med tilføiede forklaringer af J. Qvigstad og Magnus Olsen, Attende bind, W.C. Fabritius & Sønner, Kristiania.

Sammallahti, P. 1998, *The Saami Languages: An Introduction*, Davvi Girji, Kárášjohka.

Schwartz, S. I. 2003, *The Mismapping of America*, The University of Rochester Press, Rochester – Woodbridge.

Shohamy, E. 2006, *Language Policy: Hidden Agendas and New Approaches*, Routledge, London.

Short, J. R. 2009, *Cartographic Encounters: Indigenous Peoples and the Exploration of the New World*, Reaction Books, London.

Smith, A. 2003, 'Landscape representation: place and identity in nineteenth-century Ordnance Survey maps of Ireland', in *Landscape, Memory and History: Anthropological Perspectives*, P. J. Steward and A. Strathern (eds), Pluto Press, London – Sterling – Virginia: 71–88.

Smith, L. T. 2004 [1999], *Decolonizing Methodologies: Research and Indigenous Peoples*, Zed Books, London.

Strack, M. 2011, 'Bounding the land: cadastral framework on the Taieri', in *Making our Place: Exploring Land-use Tensions in Aotearoa New Zealand*, J. Ruru, J. Stephenson and M. Abbott (eds), Otago University Press, Dunedin: 101–114, 225–227.

Taylor, C. 1985, *Human Agency and Language,* Philosophical papers 1, Cambridge University Press, Cambridge.

Todorov, T. 1984 [1982], *The Conquest of America*, Harper Perennial, New York.

Turnbull, D. 1993 [1989], *Maps are Territories: Science is an Atlas,* A porfolio of exhibits, The University of Chicago Press, Victoria.

Warhus, M. 1997, *Another America: Native American Maps and the History of Our Land*, St Martin's Press, New York.

Whitfield, P. 1998, *New Found Lands: Maps in the History of Exploration*, Routledge, New York.

Wilkinson, M., Dr R. Marika and N. M. Williams 2009, 'This place already has a name', in *Aboriginal Placenames: Naming and Re-naming the Australian Landscape*, H. Koch and L. Hercus (eds), Aboriginal History Monograph 19, ANU E Press and Aboriginal History Incorporated, Canberra: 403–462.

Yazzie, R. 2000, 'Indigenous Peoples and Postcolonial Colonialism', in *Reclaiming Indigenous Voice and Vision*, M. Battiste (ed.), UBC Press, Vancouver – Toronto: 39–49.

19. Please adjust your bearings...

Huia Pacey

1. Preface

Changes to the appellations (names) of some Māori land blocks are occurring due to the Māori Freehold Land Registrations Project being undertaken by the Māori Land Court as part of the requirements within section 123 and 124 of the 1993 Te Ture Whenua Māori Act.[1] Many of the original titles of ownership for Māori land blocks in Te Waipounamu Māori Land Court district (South and Stewart Islands and Chathams group of islands of New Zealand) were not constituted from Māori Land Court Orders. They were derived as part of the Reserves set aside at time of sale in the mid 1800s, or from the provisions of the 1906 SILNA (South Island Landless Natives Act) legislation. Consequently, the legal appellation for most of these land blocks were as set down in Crown Grants.

Being derived from a Crown Grant means the appellations of these land blocks are based on notional survey district boundaries, e.g. Section x, Block x, ABC Survey District. This nomenclature was instituted in 1876, however the Native Land Court (subsequently named the Māori Land Court) did not always follow this structure within their records. The mixture of Māori and settler placenames within Land Court appellations appears to have been taken from the traditional or local placenames promulgated in original Gazette notices of inquiry into land ownership.

As the land registration project proceeds, changing the name of land blocks to that scripted on a Crown Grant could create confusion for some Māori land owners. For example: there are 118 Māori Freehold Land Titles in the Gore Survey District. The Court/local name for Big Bay Section 27 will be changed to the legal appellation of Section 27, Block VII, Gore Survey District. Okoha VIII, Section 4 is also within the Survey District and its traditional name will be submerged within the system when it changes to Section 4, Block VIII, Gore Survey District. For many owners, potentially the most confusing factor is that the Gore Survey District is in Marlborough, the upper South Island: whereas the town named "Gore" is in Southland, the lower part of the island. It is no stretch

---

1 Section 123 of the Te Ture Whenua Māori Act 1993 requires every Order of the Māori Land Court to be registered in the Land Titles Office and section 124 provides for registration of unsurveyed blocks of Māori land.

of the imagination to envisage a land owner, having known their land block as "Big Bay" or "Okoha", being confused at what appears to be an apparent relocation of landshares from one end of the island to the other.

Additionally, the 'old' name for the land block will be assigned to the 'alternative' name field within the Court's database, which will be problematic for those who search the online database, because they cannot search using the "alternative name" facility. Furthermore, as the database system only allows one alternative name to be recorded at this time, there may well be confusion if the appellation has been changed more than once during its history within the Court's system.

Applying the legal appellation to a land block may simply be an administrative process driven by legislation: the land's status will be recorded as Māori Freehold Land and safeguarded against inappropriate alienation; Māori Freehold Land ownership records will be accurate, up to date and correlated in two parallel registers; a State guaranteed title to land will be embedded within the Land Registry's ensuing Computer Freehold Register title for Māori land (not implying that Māori Land Court title is any less legal), and all unsurveyed Māori Land will have approved surveys conducted prior to registration with the Land Registry Office.

While the learning curve for Māori land owners may be a short one, as owners come to grips with the 'new', legal name for their land, there is an interesting cultural implication to consider when assessing the outcomes of this project: whether changing the name of land to one superimposed by a settler government which usurped Māori control over their landscape is acceptable to a culture that relies on placenames as an integral part of their identity?

To provide context for this implication, it is perhaps appropriate to traverse how Māori view placenames and how Crown Grant definitions of land parcels were instituted before exploring what changes are occurring in the contemporary placename landscape.

2. Connections to place

In many indigenous cultures, transmission of cultural spatial elements occur during the oral transmission of stories and history, dance and other elements that inform and reinforce cultural heritage. Accordingly, the rich heritage of a people's history, boundaries, landmarks, harvesting and nursery sites, resource rights and use, healing centres, etc. are preserved and handed down to successive generations devoid of paper placemarkers. These relationships are preserved through korero (stories/history) and are often identified through the expressions of whakatauki (relationships/proverbs).

Ko Putauaki te maunga (Putauaki is the mountain)

Ko Tarawera te awa (Tarawera is the river)

Ko Tuwharetoa te tangata (Tuwharetoa is the man)

Ko Tuwharetoa te iwi (Tuwharetoa is the tribe)

Thus the relationship of Putauaki the mountain, Tarawera the river and Tuwharetoa the iwi are linked through the mana (authority/power) of Tuwharetoa i te Aupouri, the eponymous ancestor of the Ngati Tuwharetoa tribe who lived within sight of his maunga Putauaki, next to his awa Tarawera, who died of old age near the foothills of Putauaki and was subsequently buried within a few miles of his maunga.

The whakatauki reaffirms the mana of Tuwharetoa i te Aupouri over the maunga and the awa and the rohe (tribal domain), providing pivotal Pou (placemarkers) for the identity of nga uri o Tuwharetoa (the descendants of Tuwharetoa) wherever they venture. Whakatauki such as these have linked people, places, events and history for generations.

Whakatauki are only one method of recollecting and reinforcing tribal korero. Cultural cartography in the forms of Waiata (song), Haka (dance form of challenge), Poi (dance form with string balls), Oriori (lullaby chant), Moteatea (lament) and Tauparapara (chant) to name a few, also commemorate places, people and events that have contributed to the rich tapestry of tahuhu korero o nga iwi (ancient history of the tribes). Visual representations of korero are manifested in many media. Whakaiiro (carvings), tukutuku (weaving panels), pou (carved pillar), moko (traditional tattoo) and raranga (weaving) have been used for those same generations as a means to celebrate, cement and visualise their link to their tupuna (ancestors) and their turangawaewae (place to stand, home).

This relationship is also embedded within placenames bestowed on the whenua (land) through a traditional practice called Taunaha whenua or naming the land.

3. Placenames

Metaphoric placenames that commemorate cosmology and ancestral exploits provide a vibrant and enduring connection to an ancient cultural landscape. The exploits of the tipua (demigod) Maui Tikitiki a Taranga, are widespread amongst Pacific cultures including Māori.

The name for the North Island (Te Ika a Maui or the fish of Maui) commemorates Maui's mighty feat in fishing up the North Island whilst out fishing with his brothers. Te Upoko o Te Ika (Wellington, the head of the fish); Te Kauae o Te Ika (Southern Hawkes Bay, the jawbone of the fish) and Te Hiku o Te Ika (Northland, the tail of the fish) provide spatial description to the shape of the island.

The South Island is commonly known as Te Waipounamu.[2] However various tribal korero also record it as being the canoe from which Maui fished up the island – Te Waka a Maui or the canoe of Maui. Other korero says the waka predates Maui and should be attributed to Aoraki, half brother of the early gods. Te Tau Ihu o Te Waka (Marlborough/Northern portion of the South Island, the prow of the canoe); Te Taumaunu o Te Waka a Maui (Kaikoura, the thwart of the canoe) and Te Punga o te Waka (Rakiura/Stewart Island, the anchor of the canoe) enclose the southern islands.[3]

Rekohu (Wharekauri/Chatham Islands), the islands lying some six days canoe travel to the east of Te Ika a Maui and Te Waipounamu, completes the main islands that Māori have occupied for centuries.

Throughout those centuries a multitude of descriptive placenames were bestowed on the landscape within the islands. Perhaps the most descriptive placename is the iconic "Taumata whaka tangi hanga koauau o Tamatea turi pukakapi ki maunga horo nuku poka i whenua ki tana tahu" which translates as the 'place (hill) where Tamatea, the man with the big knees, who slid, climbed and swallowed mountains, known as land-eater, played his flute' (for his recently deceased brother). The shortened form of "Taumata" is used in everyday conversation; however, formal occasions demand the full placename be used.

Placenames described and located occupation and resource use and phenomena of both biophysical and metaphysical origin. These location markers were also embedded within traditional korero that recorded phenomena which contemporary scientists have recently (by comparison) come to terms with. An example is the legend of Ngatoroirangi and the coming of geothermal activity to the North Island.

This (very) abbreviated korero describes the travels of the tohunga Ngatoroirangi (expert navigator and priest of Te Arawa, an early migrant canoe). On one journey he and his companion Aruhoe were ascending the mountain Tongariro. During their ascent they were overcome with cold and Ngatoroirangi called on the aid of his two sisters in Hawaiki (the ancestral home of Māori).

---

2 Both "Aehino Mouwe" and "Tovy poinammu" (Te Ika a Maui and Te Waipounamu respectively) were placenames given to Cook during his visit in 1770.
3 The name "Aotearoa" designating the country as a whole, is itself considered to be a late 19th century invention. However, it is now the accepted 'Māori' placename for the islands.

Kuiwai and Haungaroa heard his prayers and plunged into the sea bringing fire to his aid. They surfaced at Whakaari, then Okakaru, Te Rotorua nui a Kahumatamomoe, Tarawera, Orakei Korako, and finally Tongariro where their brother lay near death.

The heat revived Ngatoroirangi although by that time his companion Aruhoe had died. Aruhoe is commemorated within the name, Ngaruhoe, the nearest mountain to Tongariro.

This oral map describes the interconnection of the subsurface geothermal resource of the major geothermal belt that is found in the North Island.[4] The korero illustrates a relationship between space, place and resource which was examined, analysed and embedded within a cultural landscape well before modern technology was developed. Undeniably, the korero proves an intimate knowledge of place, illuminating the sophisticated cerebral cartography to be found within Māori oral maps prior to european exploration and 'discovery'.

4. 'Discovery'

Similar to other indigenous experience, the colonial practice of supplanting indigenous placenames with ones commemorating European 'discovery' affected the cultural landscape of Māori. The 17th century explorer Abel Tasman first mistakenly named the country, "Staten Landt" when he sighted the west coast of the South Island in December 1642. His geographical error was quickly realised and by 1645 the landmass he had sighted was referred to variously as "Zealandia", "Zealandia Nova" and "Nieuw Zeeland".

Captain James Cook would add to this when he journeyed throughout Pacifica over 100 years later to record the transit of Venus. During his circumnavigation of New Zealand, he conferred various mountains, bays and points of land with names that commemorated expedition experiences and important political figures in England. For example, Te Kuri a Paoa was renamed Young Nicks Head to commemorate the first sighting of land by the expedition as well as the name of the young crewman who first sighted it. Taranaki – the ancestral mountain for eight hapu of the Taranaki region – was named Mount Egmont after the First Lord of the Admiralty (the Earl of Egmont), who promoted Cook's first voyage. Similarly, Putauaki – ancestral mountain of Ngati Tuwharetoa – was named Mount Edgecumbe after John Edgecumbe, Cook's Sergeant of Marines. Edgecumbe would also have his name inscribed at Edgecumbe Point in the Queen Charlotte Sounds (Morris 1900). Totaranui, or The Queen Charlotte Sounds,

---

4 There are several versions of this korero as well as a number of other places that Kuiwai and Haungaroa are attributed as having surfaced at – however in this paper I have recounted the korero that I am familiar with.

was named after the wife of King George the Third while Endeavour Inlet was named after the ship Cook commanded on his first visit – the *Endeavour*. Cook himself was later commemorated during the 1851 *Archeron* survey when Aoraki – ancestral mountain of the Ngati Mamoe, Waitaha and Kai Tahu was given the name Mount Cook.

Dutch and English names would not be the only names superimposed on the landscape of Aotearoa. During his 1827 exploration the French explorer, Dumont d'Urville, named Croisilles Bay after his mother and "Passe des Francais" or French Pass as it is known today. D'Urville himself was commemorated by his officers who named an island after their captain, supplanting the original name Te Rangitoto ki te Tonga.

As imperial exploration occurred throughout the 19th century, expeditions continued the custom of superimposing names. In 1834 Captain Lambert of the HMS *Alligator* named Port Gore after the Vice Admiral and Commander-in-Chief in the East Indies, Sir John Gore (Marshall 1836: 151; McNab 1913: Ch. 7);[5] Port Hardy was named after Sir Thomas Hardy, Nelson's flag captain at Trafalgar (Marshall 1836: 154; Allan 1965: 27), and in 1838, Pelorus Sound was named after the HMS *Pelorus*, which was conducting an exploration mission for the New Zealand Company (McNab 1913: 224–225).

The actions of replacing indigenous placenames with those transplanted from other landscapes did not always sit well with some early explorers. Marshall, the surgeon on board the HMS *Alligator* wrote,

> 20th. --Weighed, and made sail from PORT HARDY, so called for the first time out of respect to the gallant Sir Thomas Hardy, Nelson's flag captain at Trafalgar, whose services and public character well entitle him to the honour of giving an English name to one of the finest harbours in the Southern Hemisphere; although the propriety of giving arbitrary names at all to places not belonging to us, and names, too, having no manner of connection whatever with the character or circumstances of the places they are designed to represent, may be doubted...
>
> ...the native names of places are in some instances abandoned, and the names employed by their visitors preferred; though the former were in all, or almost all, instances, names descriptive of things; and the latter are, as frequently, mere sounds without any corresponding sense. (Marshall 1836: 154–155)

Marshall's view is in all likelihood a minority one. His opinion is firmly contrasted with that of Dr Hinds, the Dean of Carlisle and contemporary of

---

5   See also http://www.teara.govt.nz/european place names.

Edward Gibbon Wakefield, an avid supporter of colonisation and principal of the New Zealand Company (the venture company responsible for the first wave of colonial settlement in New Zealand). Wakefield concurred wholeheartedly with Hind's view that, "Names of places, too, should be changed; they make part of the moral atmosphere of a country" (Wakefield 2001 [1849]: 39).

The practice of transplanting placenames continued as explorers charted the New Zealand landscape which was in the process of becoming a British colony. When the Treaty of Waitangi was signed in 1840, Māori still asserted firm control over their landscape. The landscape reverberated with traditional Māori placenames with a light sprinkling of English, Dutch or French names – and even hybrid placenames like Cape Koamaru, originally Operuahua, in the Marlborough District.

After the Treaty of Waitangi was signed in 1840, successive waves of colonial immigrants affected the landscape on a grander scale than early colonial explorers. However, as authors and manufacturers of paper documents that delineated and chronicled land space, surveyors would play a key role in actually redefining that landscape.

5. Surveying in the 19th century

Surveying expeditions for the first 40 years after the Treaty was signed were an ad hoc adventure for both skilled and poorly trained men (see for example Easdale 1988 and Byrnes 2001). Exploration for potential settlement sites was sporadic, mainly reconnaissance in nature, and were badly resourced as land speculators, settlers and provincial governments struggled to establish the new colony. Exploration treks through the dense rugged bush of early colonial New Zealand, inevitably required months of travel: often following Māori pathways and frequently reliant on Māori hospitality. An essential member of any scouting party was a Māori guide who eased the surveyors' passage through the landscape by not only showing them the land but also showing them how to live off the land.

From the early 1850s onwards, official survey instructions were to ascertain and map Māori names of boundaries or natural features. The instructions were not always followed explicitly. During exploration treks, surveyors noted and mapped traditional placenames or conferred their own choices. They also had places named after them, such as the Lewis Pass, named by Henry Lewis and Christopher Maling and also Arthurs Pass which was named after Arthur Dobson, the first european surveyor to traverse it. Dobson himself was possibly ambivalent about the Pass being named after him as he took the view that he needed to "ascertain as accurately as possible the native names of all the natural features of the country" (Dobson 1930: 59). Dobson was not the only early surveyor who declined to give English names to points of interest they encountered on their travels. Heaphy and Brunner, two early explorers of New Zealand, were noted as having declined to give English names to landmarks on their first journey (Host 2006: 57). Possibly, this stance was only due to compliance with their instructions as Heaphy felt the Māori language was not particularly worthy of conserving. He wrote, "as regards the New Zealand language being lost by the introduction of another, it would be a benefit rather than an injury, as … the substitution of a copious and powerful language [English] for a meagre and inexpressive one [Māori] is to every nation a desideratum." (Heaphy 1968 [1842]: 54–55).

Like Dobson, both men had places named after them. Te Kotuku Whakaoka (the diving Kotuku) was named Lake Brunner as Brunner had been the first european to visit the site. A major expedition pathway through dense bush navigated by Heaphy, Brunner and their guides Kehu and Etau (and now classified as one of New Zealand's top ten walking tracks) was named the Heaphy Track.

Surveyors also used their own placenaming notions when completing their commissions. Edward Jollie's 1850 plan of the new city of Christchurch (Otautahi) illustrates a colonist desire to transplant a feel of his 'English homeland' in an attempt to normalise their vastly different surroundings.

> As soon as I completed the map I took it to Thomas, who, putting on his gold spectacles and opening his 'Peerage' would read out a bishop's name to hear if it sound well and if I agreed with him that it did, I put the name to one of the streets requiring baptism. Lyttelton being the first-born town got the best names for its streets. Sumner being next had the next best and Christchurch being the youngest had to be content with chiefly Irish and Colonial Bishoprics. (Jollie, as quoted in Holm 2005: 37)

The mixed regard that surveyors had for original Māori placenames continued as they measured and inscribed the landscape. As instructed, many survey maps recorded both Māori and colonial placenames and also dual placenames (with the Māori name now bracketed denoting an 'other' status). The product of survey work, a paper document, would ultimately provide the means by which many Māori placenames were usurped and Māori land alienated.

6. A changing landscape

Throughout a period of change in power relations between Māori and Pakeha colonisers, ad hoc survey systems produced discrepancies in survey plans.

Māori land had been surveyed by "a class of surveyors who are said to have been very imperfectly acquainted with their profession" who produced surveys that were found to be "fatal to accuracy and system".[6]

A surveyors grid was established which helped codify and simplify the settlers new world. The new nomenclature defined landparcels as Section x, Block x, ABC Survey Districts. The notional grid standardised land appellations for the entire country with the intention that a parcel of land anywhere in New Zealand could be identified by its appellation. The grid confirmed the intrinsic epistemological difference in how Māori and europeans viewed land; one as a living landscape, the other as a commodity.

Separate land registries were established that recorded land ownership rights differently. The Native Land Court determined ownership of Māori land through the mechanism of land court hearings. Claimants to Māori land defined tribal/hapu boundaries using traditional placenames and defended them by referencing their longstanding association with the land. Appellations for lands in the North Island typically had Māori locational placenames as land block titles. Due to derivation of title being from Crown Grants, land appellations in the Southern Islands had three categories – the traditional, the settler and the Crown Grant. The first two were in general use and the third sequestered location and land identity to a surveyors grid. Both Māori and non-Māori placenames were eventually used for landblock names.

The decimation of Māori cultural and land rights continued throughout the latter part of the 19th century up to the 1970s when a cultural revitalisation period prompted significant social change. The Waitangi Tribunal was established; the Kohanga Reo movement commenced; Māori language became an official language and the Te Ture Whenua Māori Act was enacted. In many respects the legislation and social change that occurred through the 1970s and 1980s emphasised the Māori philosophy that both land and language are taonga tuku iho. The link between land and language is also reinforced through dual placenames.

Dual placenames are slowly re-embedding traditional placenames onto the landscape. More than 140 dual placenames are now recorded in the placenames database held by the New Zealand Geographic Board. Many of these have been put in place by post treaty settlements. The Ngai Tahu Act added a proactive function to the work of the New Zealand Geographic Board wherein the Board was required to encourage use of original Māori placenames on official maps. The reimplanting of traditional names through mechanisms such as dual placenames confirms relationship to place and identity is as important for Māori today as it was prior to colonisation.

---

6   'The state of surveys in New Zealand', AJHR, 1875, H-1, pp. 6, 18.

There have been no apparent local community reactions to replacing or changing placenames that result from post-treaty settlement mechanisms, however, some reaction has been engendered by the replacement of locational placenames for some Māori landblocks. The Māori Freehold Land Registration project has been established to satisfy legislative requirement to register all Māori Land Court orders with the Land Transfer Office (LINZ). The legal appellations of the landblocks will mirror the description of the title that created the block, which in most cases for the North Island will be the Māori Land Court partition order. The appellations for the Southern Islands will be different as they were predominantly derived from Crown Grants.

The landblocks within the Gore Survey District, which represent just over 15 per cent of the landblocks within the Te Waipounamu Māori Land Court district, will lose traditional and historic locational placenames to one superimposed by a surveyors grid block.

Table 1: Gore Survey District appellations.

Traditional	Current historic appellations	Crown Grant legal appellation
Parerangi	"Big Bay"	Section x, Block VII, Gore Survey District
Anakoha, Okoha	"Okoha"	Section x, Block VIII, Gore Survey District
Te Kurakura	"Edgecombe"	Section x, Block X, Gore Survey District
Punaruawhiti	"Endeavour Inlet"	Section x, Block XI, Gore Survey District
Punaruawhiti	"Endeavour Inlet Queen Charlotte Sound"	Section x, Block VI, Gore Survey District
Kakahau, Anamahanga	"Port Gore (Okoha Bay)"	Section x, Block XII, Gore Survey District
Oamaru	"Oamaru"	Section x, Block XXII, Gore Survey District

Source: Compiled by the author.

This wholesale replacement of locational references to that of a Survey District will more than likely prompt reactions from landowners. As mentioned in the preface, Port Gore (probable derivation of the Survey District name) was named after an Imperial Commander in Chief, Colonel John Gore. It is also located in the Marlborough region (the northern district in the South Island). The town of Gore is located in Southland, was originally known as Longford, and was named after Sir Thomas Gore-Browne in 1882.[7] Aside from the loss of locational reference to their land, what might prove more disturbing for landowners, is that the Survey District name not only commemorates a figurehead of imperialism who never

---

7 http://goredc.govt.nz/sites/default/files/documents/201204_settling_in.pdf.

stepped foot on the land, but chillingly resonates to the name of the man whose actions precipitated the outbreak of the devastating war in 1860 which led to massive Māori land confiscations and debilitating loss of Māori sovereignty.

7. Adjusting your bearings

The theme of this discussion has been placenames: their importance to Māori identity and how the cultural landscape of Māori was reoriented over decades of colonisation. The revitalisation of Māori culture has since shifted that orientation towards positive social and cultural development.

Cultural identity is being strengthened through initiatives such as dual placenames that re-embed traditional placenames which reconnect fundamental relationships with tipuna and turangawaewae; through legislative changes which have provided positive platforms of engagement (the Foreshore Seabed legislation a profound exception); through focussed educational programmes that have steadily increased the numbers of Māori participating at higher levels of academic and cultural learning; through post settlement development mechanisms; through unprecedented levels of participation in local, regional and national affairs, and through innovative language and culture programmes disseminated through all manner of communication media.

Given the significant signposts that these initiatives reveal – that Māori continue to regard land and language as intrinsic components of Māori cultural identity – the replacement of locational placenames for Māori landblocks does raise some questions.

Questions such as: does the submerging of language as an incidental consequence of a project with beneficial intent, diminish in any way the gains of the last 40 years to restore the relationship between place, identity and culture? Or, could the replacement of land appellations to one that represents a colonial tool motivated entirely for the commodification of land (and all the associated connotations of usurping Māori sovereignty), actually be a backwards step?

Perhaps not. Perhaps it is just an incidental consequence of a beneficial project; just a low-key, administrative process that achieves a mutually acceptable alignment of records.

A potential pathway to shift the orientation of place [land] names back to one which reinforces Māori aspirations does exist, although it has not been tested at this time. Section 125A of the Te Ture Whenua Māori Act enables landowners to apply to the Court to change the appellation of their landblock, however, no applications have been made, yet. The regulatory requirements to be satisfied before the application is submitted to the Court are also quite complex. In view of the fact that the project is handling a big workload as the two original institutions interlock their records, it is unknown whether communication strategies have even been considered necessary as yet. Perhaps the Project will simply wait to get reactions, and if they do, decide what response measures, if any, they will implement.

In the preface, I asked the question whether changing the name of land to one superimposed by a settler government which usurped Māori control over their landscape is acceptable to a culture that relies on placenames as an integral part of their identity?

It is unclear how many owners in the 26,000 odd blocks of Māori land are concerned about the name changes. Perhaps there will only be a few owners who will take note of the change. The majority may well be content with it. Perhaps as long as owners know what name the land has been given; and they can find the landblock in the records; and they recognise their landblock in the Court notices, they will accept it. However, for a culture that relies on placenames as an integral part of identity and has fought hard to reimplant them into the New Zealand landscape while revitalising their culture: it will be ironic if response is muted to the superimposing of a colonial surveyors grid name on remnants of ancestral land.

The Māori Freehold Land Registration Project is a work in progress. As such, there is no definitive answer to any of the issues raised or questions posed within this document. It is difficult to draw conclusions at this time since there has been no research or statistics reported on how many blocks will be affected by name changes or what range of responses have been engendered by the changes. Whether there is passive acceptance to this change or a rash of applications to change appellations is speculative at this stage. However, with tongue firmly held in cheek, an appropriate (and final) comment is that we watch this 'place' with interest.

8. Postscript, September 2013

Since writing this paper in 2007 the main tranche of Māori Freehold Land registration work for the Māori Land Court has been completed; the legal appellations now appear in the Māori Land Court records and their formal Court proceedings as well as the general land registry held by Land Information New Zealand: and the response to change in traditional/historic and now legal appellations for landblocks appears to be a pragmatic one by both owners and the Māori Land Court. Searches for land block information can be based on both historic and legal appellations. Anecdotal information suggests a uniform response from Māori Land Court staff to helpfully locate the appropriate land parcel and the appropriate appellations for future reference. The complexities of legal and technical changes to traditional land names appear to have been accepted with (at the most) slight agitation when first confronted with the change. Given that land appellations have undergone change for nearly 150 years, and Māori have proven how resilient they are in face of those changes, perhaps their connection to place haven't been affected by the change in placenames; or perhaps it is just too early to tell.

References

Allan, R.M. 1965, *Nelson, a History of Early Settlement*, A.H. & A.W. Reed, Wellington.

Byrnes, G. 2001, *Boundary Markers, Land Surveying and the Colonisation of New Zealand*, Bridget Williams Books, Wellington.

Dobson, A. 1930, *Reminiscences of Arthur Dudley Dobson engineer* (2nd ed), Whitcombe and Tombs Limited, Wellington.

Easdale, N. 1988, *Kairuri the Measurer of Land, the Life of the 19th Century Surveyor Pictured in his Art and Writings*, Highgate/Price Milburn Limited, Petone.

Heaphy, C. 1968 [1842], *Narrative of a Residence in Various Parts of New Zealand. Together with a Description of the Present State of the Company's Settlements*, Hocken Library Facsimile No 7, Hocken Library, University of Otago, Dunedin [Smith, Elder and Co, London].

Holm, J. 2005, *Caught Mapping, the Life and Times of New Zealand's Early Surveyors*, Hazard Press Limited, Christchurch.

Host, E. 2006, *Thomas Brunner, his Life and Great Journeys*, Vivienne Nelson (ed.), Nikau Press, Nelson.

McNab, R. 1913, *The Old Whaling days: a history of Southern New Zealand from 1830 to 1840*, Whitcombe and Tombs, Wellington. Accessed from http://www.nzetc.org/tm/scholarly.

Marshall, W.B. 1836, *A personal narrative of two visits to New Zealand in His Majestry's Ship Alligator A.D. 1834*, James Nisbet and Co., London. Accessed from http://www.enzb.auckland.ac.nz.

Morris, E.E. 1900, 'On the Tracks of Captain Cook', *Transactions and Proceedings of the Royal Society of New Zealand* 33. Accessed from http://rsnz.natlib.govt.nz/volume/rsnz_33.html.

'The state of the surveys in New Zealand', *Appendix to the Journals of the House of Representatives (AJHR)*, 1875, H-1, pp. 6, 18.

Wakefield, E.G. (ed.) 2001 [1849], *A view of the art of colonization, with present reference to the British Empire; in letters between a Statesman and a Colonist*, Batoche Books, Kitchener [John W Parker, London]. Accessed from http://socserv.mcmaster.ca/econ/ugcm.

20. Accommodating the Inuit majority: Traditional placenames in Nunavut today

Lynn Peplinski

Inuit Heritage Trust, Nunavut

For 4,000 years, Inuit and their predecessors have combed the almost 2 million square kilometres of the northern Canadian landscape, now known to the world as Nunavut, "Our Land". Evidence of extensive Inuit land use and occupancy is present in the more than 8,000 placenames that, lamentably, have yet to appear on official maps. While recognition of the Inuit home land came in 1993 with the signing of the Nunavut Land Claims Agreement, maps of the Arctic continue to reflect centuries of European exploration and discovery. The Inuit Heritage Trust has been documenting Inuit traditional placenames and has submitted close to 5,000 placenames to the Government of Nunavut to make them official since 2005, and estimate that more than 3,000 still need to be verified and processed. This paper grew out of a meeting with members of the Geographic Names Board of Canada who were assembled in Yellowknife, Northwest Territories in August 2007. Here, the author spoke with provincial and territorial representatives from across Canada about issues relating to aboriginal placenaming policies with particular attention to the use of non-aboriginal generics. Given that the Canadian Government's Principles and Procedures for Geographical Naming state that first priority shall be given to names with long-standing local usage by the general public, and Inuit comprise 85 per cent of the population in Nunavut, the time for Inuit names to appear on Canada's maps is overdue.

Twenty years after the signing of the Nunavut Land Claims Agreement, thousands of traditional placenames have been documented and submitted to the Government of Nunavut (GN) but have yet to appear on Canada's official maps. Traditional placenames clearly demonstrate the extent of Inuit land use and occupancy of the vast northern land that is Nunavut. Given the enduring presence of Inuit living in Nunavut, and the steady domestic and international interest in the potential of a northwest passage in Canada's north, there are many reasons why Inuit traditional placenames should see the light of day.

While Canada is officially a bilingual nation with both English and French enjoying equal status, only 23 per cent of the population considers French as their mother tongue, and an overwhelming majority of francophones (18.5 per cent) are concentrated in one province, the province of Quebec.[1]

In Nunavut, a different version of bilingualism reigns with Inuktitut dominating French. Geographically isolated from the rest of Canada – its remoteness due to distance from and the lack of road infrastructure linking it to the rest of Canada, Nunavut has been home to Inuit and their predecessors for the past 4,000 years. Today, the territory boasts a population of about 32,000, 85 per cent of whom are Inuit, settled in 23 communities.[2] There are arguably two Inuit languages in Nunavut. Inuktitut is spoken in all but two communities, where Inuinnaqtun is spoken. Each community is made up of speakers of one or more dialects depending upon where the family groups' ancestors lived on the land prior to moving into established communities around 50 years ago. There can be many dialects present in one community, again depending on where individual families resided on the land prior to moving into established settlements.

The year 2013 marks the 20th anniversary of the signing of the largest land claim in Canadian history, the Nunavut Land Claims Agreement (NLCA). Nunavut, formerly part of the Northwest Territories, covers just less than 2 million square kilometres occupying one fifth of Canada's land mass.

Created under the NLCA, the Inuit Heritage Trust exists to support an Inuit voice on issues relating to heritage including archaeology and placenames. With regards to traditional placenames, the Inuit Heritage Trust (IHT) organisation has two main goals:

1. The distribution, in communities, of traditional placenames knowledge on topographic, thematic maps.

2. Ensuring the traditional names are made official. This is also a land claim obligation for IHT (NLCA, Article 33 Part 9).

IHT's policy regarding naming features on maps is to capture the most appropriate dialect for the place where possible. That is, the dialects of descendants of family groups tied to specific geographical areas receive priority. Names for the same features, in other dialects may appear in the legend of the map. This effort is also explicitly noted on the individual map sheets produced by IHT.

---

1 Statistics Canada, 'Mother Tongue, Percentage Distribution for Both Sexes, for Canada, Provinces and Territories – 20% Sample Data', http://www12.statcan.ca/english/census01/products/highlight/LanguageComposition/Page.cfm?Lang=E&Geo=PR&View=1a&Code=0&Table=2a&StartRec=1&Sort=2&B1=Distribution&B2=Both (accessed 2 August 2007).
2 Statistics Canada, 'Number and distribution of the population reporting an Aboriginal identity and percentage of Aboriginal people in the population, Canada, provinces and territories, 2011', http://www12.statcan.gc.ca/nhs-enm/2011/as-sa/99-011-x/2011001/tbl/tbl02-eng.cfm. (accessed 9 September 2013).

Greenland, whose capital city of Nuuk is just two hours by air charter east of Iqaluit, Nunavut's capital city, has approached the dialect issue differently. Whereas in Nunavut, efforts are made to respect and record placenames in local dialects, in Greenland, the official language in all documentation including placenames is the Nuuk dialect of Inuktitut (language of the Inuit, also referred to as Greenlandic). Individuals in small communities are encouraged to speak their own dialects and maintain their own traditional placenames, but all written documentation, including placenames on maps, is in the Nuuk dialect. Also in Greenland, all names are written in roman orthography, a result of the Inuit language there having benefited from the written word more than 100 years earlier than its Canadian cousins. For these and other reasons, Greenlanders enjoy maps with their traditional Inuit names entirely in Greenlandic.[3] Also worth pointing out is the disfavour with which Inuktitut names on maps are viewed by some non-Inuit. In a personal email from a staff person in a Danish Geodata Agency, Greenlandic maps were described as a "path of thorns for international users".[4] Not everyone is impressed by the move to finally legitimise traditional indigenous names by putting them onto maps.

When compared with other indigenous populations in the world, Inuit of the eastern Arctic enjoy one of the highest percentages of native-language speakers: 64 per cent of the population in Nunavut can converse in Inuktitut or Inuinnaqtun.[5] In the central and eastern arctic, the preferred orthography is still syllabics. This writing system was introduced by missionaries in the late 1800s to a people that had heretofore no written language. In a personal communication Kenn Harper, a local author and historian, recounted that when syllabics were introduced in the eastern arctic, people could learn the basic system in a couple of hours and then were expected to teach it to someone else. In this way the early system of syllabics swept through the eastern arctic. In a very short time after the introduction of syllabics, missionaries made Inuktitut reading materials available to Inuit in their own language.[6]

Though most young *Nunavummiut* (residents of Nunavut) in schools today learn English and use roman orthography, they also learn to write Inuktitut in syllabics. There is considerable debate about the advisability of maintaining two distinct writing systems, with some favouring abandoning syllabics for roman orthography; however, syllabics still appear to have strong support. In IHT's experience, Inuit in communities prefer to read Inuktitut placenames on

---

3 Pers. comm. with Carl Christian Olsen, Director Greenland Language Secretariat and Chair, Greenland Place Names Authority.
4 Private correspondence by email with an individual from the Danish Geodata Agency, 2007.
5 Statistics Canada, 'Aboriginal people and language', http://www12.statcan.gc.ca/nhs-enm/2011/as-sa/99-011-x/99-011-x2011003_1-eng.cfm (accessed 13 December 2013).
6 Kenn Harper, author, historian and entrepreneur is a long-time resident of Iqaluit. He has researched and continues to write extensively about Inuit history, including weekly articles in the Nunatsiaq News.

paper maps or in Google Earth, in syllabics. Thus the Inuit Heritage Trust is committed to producing maps with traditional placenames using syllabics. The Canadian Government, however, when it publishes maps for the wider public with the newly adopted traditional names, will transcribe the names in roman orthography. The volume of names, and the length of the names themselves may be problematic for government cartographers on a practical level. The syllabics characters combine consonant/vowel sounds (i, pi, ti, ki gi represented as syllabics) thus taking up less space on the map. A practical solution may be to limit the number of names on the maps, a standard practice in cartography but an unsatisfactory one for northern travellers. Typically the scale of a map dictates the amount of information that can be included. More placenames may be expected to be found on maps at larger scales such as 1:50,000 (of which there are 16 in an area covered by a 1:250,000 map). However, in IHT's experience, people prefer to see *all* the placenames information on 1:250,000 scale maps, with none omitted for the sake of a clean, uncluttered map. Given the vast distances hunters may cover in a day of travel by boat or snow machine, one reference map, rather than more than a dozen, is far more practical.

Draft topographic maps produced by IHT may contain hundreds of traditional placenames. One map (1:250,000) in particular, for an area of Cumberland Sound near Pangnirtung contains over 400 traditional placenames – a daunting challenge for the cartographer.[7] If and when Inuit traditional placenames become official, will the Canadian Government be able to demonstrate them satisfactorily on maps? Unfortunately, IHT only has resources enough to produce a small selection of maps that are shared with communities. Though at the federal level there is currently a small group of individuals in the Mapping Information Branch that has been trying to promote interest in a program to produce "Canadian Arctic Prototype Maps – Customized, Multilingual, Topographic", they have been unsuccessful due to reduced budgets.[8]

Concern exists that if not added to current maps, traditional names will become a relic of a way of life only 50 years ago – a way of life which has been rapidly and even traumatically replaced by modernity. However, the land has not changed and neither has the need to know and understand the land, if not for one's absolute survival, then for Inuit to retain a sense of themselves and their culture. Traditional placenames allow today's Inuit to maintain an appreciation and an intimate connection to the land, similar to that of their predecessors. By way of

---

7 Map 26J is the map with the greatest number of traditional, but still unofficial placenames (as of 09/2013) in Nunavut. This map was made by the Canada-Nunavut Geoscience Office in partnership with IHT and may be accessed online at (with instructions): http://geoscan.ess.nrcan.gc.ca/cgibin/starfinder/0?path=geoscan.fl &id=fastlink&pass=&search=R%3D288016&format=FLFULL   Click on GeoPub: Free download (zip 42577 kB) near the top of the page; page 2) choose 'Download this publication'; page 3) enter email and Accept Agreement; page 4) right click on the browser link and do 'Save Target A'.

8 Pers. comm. with Eva Siekierska of the Mapping Information Branch, Earth Sciences Sector, National Resources Canada.

example, in the summer of 2007, a group of hunters attempted to trap beluga whales in an inlet on the descending tide by throwing rocks into the water to keep the belugas in, trapping them behind a sand bar. The inlet, *Millorialik*, "where you throw something", is named for this activity. Despite the hunters' efforts, the beluga managed to escape. The hunters left the area disappointed but with a renewed sense of the challenge experienced by their predecessors to survive on the land.[9] Formerly for Inuit, the animals meant everything: food, shelter, tools, transportation. Besides a few wild roots and berries, there was no other option for sustaining life in this harsh northern country. Though modernity has meant a move to settlements, heated homes and the availability of store-bought food, hunting remains a necessary cultural activity to put food on the table. A study exploring the issue of food security in Nunavut found that relying exclusively on market food is an unaffordable option for many families (Chan et al. 2006: 416–431). Traditional placenames not only offer insight into past land use but practical information for the modern hunter.

Nunavut is still a relatively new territory and the population small. There are fewer than a handful of individuals working on placenames issues on a regular basis. Therefore, progress to make traditional placenames official is slow. In 2009, IHT submitted 11 maps to the Government of Nunavut containing approximately 900 traditional placenames. Two of these maps (with a total of 290 names) have gone through the GN system and may be official as of 2014. Since 2011 an additional 4,000 were submitted to the GN to be made official. There still remain thousands of names that need to find their way onto official maps.

1. Generics

The issue of generics and how these are handled across jurisdictions varies. There are a relative few traditional placenames currently dotting Nunavut's maps, the ones placed there when the territory was part of the Northwest Territories and prior to a made-in-Nunavut Toponymy Policy. However, all of these names are accompanied by English generics. For example, Qikiqtarjuaq Island and Tasiujarjuaq Lake are both very common names meaning Big (*-juaq*) Island (*Qikiq-*) and Big (*-juaq*) Lake (*Tasi-*), making the added English "Lake" or "Island" generics redundant. Examples of this tautology are also very common for maps in northern Quebec.

The province of Quebec, located south of Nunavut has more than 7 million inhabitants with more than 80 per cent claiming French as their first language.[10]

---

9   My colleague at the Inuit Heritage Trust, Sheila Oolayou, spoke directly with hunters from the group, 2007.
10 Statistics Canada, 'Table 11', http://www12.statcan.ca/census-recensement/2006/as-sa/97-555/table/t11-eng.cfm (accessed 20 July 2007).

However, the northern third of the province, a region known as Nunavik, is sparsely populated with about 10,000 Inuit living in 14 communities scattered along the coast. Here Inuktitut is the first language of over 90 per cent of the Inuit population according to the Avataq Cultural Institute.[11] In everyday communications, therefore, English and French take a back seat to Inuktitut in the lives of the people who have lived in this northern land for centuries. In a sense, Nunavik is a nation within a nation, geographically isolated from the more densely populated part of the province, as Quebec is also a unique nation within the larger Canada because of its culture, language and set of laws (Sheppard 2006).

In Canada, Inuit distinguish themselves from other First Nations groups. That is, Inuit do not fall under the general umbrella of First Nations; they remain their own distinct group. In Quebec, as in most of the provinces and territories in Canada, aboriginal (First Nations peoples including Inuit) make up 8.1 per cent of the province's population, with some First Nations living on reserves, some not.[12]

On the Nunavik (Quebec) maps much effort was undertaken to document almost 8,000 traditional Inuit names which were eventually published in an Avataq Cultural Institute gazetteer in 1987.[13] However, those traditional names were altered by the Commission Toponymique du Quebec when they were made official, by the addition of French generics. With regards to generics, the Quebec Toponymy Policy (adopted in 1987 and revised in 1990) states that:

> Aboriginal place names that contain a generic (attached to or separate from the specific) in their language of origin are assigned a generic in French when they are officialized. This French generic represents the best possible translation of the Aboriginal term.
>
> The separate Aboriginal generic is not included in the official name, unless it constitutes the sole element of the original place name. To counter the often negative reaction to the Aboriginal place names that are considered too long and difficult to pronounce or remember, the Commission may officialize shortened versions of inventoried names provided their meaning is not lost as a result.

---

11 Avataq Cultural Institute, 'Inuktitut Language Program', http://www.avataq.qc.ca/programs/language_en.cfm (accessed 20 July 2007).
12 Statistics Canada, 'Aboriginal peoples of Canada: A demographic profile', Statistics Canada 2001 Census: analysis series, http://www12.statcan.ca/english/census01/Products/Analytic/companion/abor/pdf/96F0030XIE2001007.pdf (accessed 15 July 2007). Page 23.
13 Avataq Cultural Institute, 'Nunatop: Inuit place names', http://www.avataq.qc.ca/en/Institute/Departments/Research-Library-and-Archives/Place-names/Nunatop-Inuit-place-names. (accessed 9 September 2013).

When an Aboriginal place name does not include a generic in its original form, the Commission, in officializing the name, will add a French generic if and when this type of place name is usually expressed with a generic in French.[14]

One could argue that adding French generics makes placenames more accessible to the "whole" Quebec community. However, the "whole" by large majority, in this particular region of Quebec consider Inuktitut to be their first language. The added French generic effectively changes the name. Also, if you are a native speaker the name/generic combination becomes almost farcical because of the tautology.

Given the geographical isolation of many Inuit communities from the more densely populated parts of Canada and the intense role the land plays in everyone's lives, in addition to the language reality, Inuit and the wider public may be better served by the publication of a glossary of Inuktitut placenames. Such a glossary would provide insight into the language and the world view present in the traditional naming system of Inuit in northern Canada rather than adding a generic to satisfy the French/English speaking minority.

Kearns and Berg (2002) discuss the issue of placenames as a form of resistance and contend that resistance to naming can occur on at least two levels: the creation and deployment of alternate names and the use of alternative pronunciations for established names. By its policy to replace aboriginal placename generics with French ones, or to add generics to aboriginal names, is the Quebec Government, through its Toponymy Policy, resisting efforts by Inuit wishing their own names to be legitimised? This exercise has its roots in Quebec's *Charter of the French Language*, safeguarding French, in Quebec, as the dominant language.

Quebec is an interesting case because it is the largest province in Canada in area (the three northern territories do not count as provinces) and the second largest in population. As a primarily French-speaking province, Quebec has fought long and hard against the cultural domination of the English majority in Canada. By introducing *Bill 101*, the *Charter of the French Language*, the government has sought to protect the language and to ensure the province's status and future as a French-speaking nation. All signage, commercial advertising, street signs and services, as well as placenames generics, are in French. As has been noted though, fully a third of Quebec's land mass is understood to be Inuit territory, where a version of a self rule accord looms. Criticism of Quebec's *Charter of the French Language* has been widespread, considered by some to be an infringement on their rights and freedom to work, be educated or read or post signage in their

---

14 Commission de Toponymie Québec, 'Politiques de la Commission de toponymie (1990)', http://www.toponymie.gouv.qc.ca/ct/toponymie_expliquee/politiques_topo.html (accessed 20 May 2007).

language of choice, most often English. However, 30 years after its introduction *Bill 101* has been reported as being relatively well accepted in the province (Bauch 2007).

According to Danielle Turcotte, Director, Commission de toponymie, the Quebec Government is currently seeking a way to publish on the web both the official placenames as well as the unofficial aboriginal placenames in a way that will underline the official status of names while also providing visibility for the purposes of conservation of the aboriginal placenames in the memories of aboriginal communities.[15]

For Nunavummiut to insist on their traditional names becoming official is a logical, natural follow up to the Nunavut Land Claims Agreement. Kearns and Berg (2002) also note that:

> Place names are publicly pronounced, [and] there is thus scope to not only *identify* a point on the map, but also to *make* a point through (metaphorically) mapping out one's politics of place in speech. (Kearns and Berg 2002: 287)

Indeed, the Nunavut Land Claims Agreement is the largest in Canadian history. Nunavut is not Nunavut Territory, it is Nunavut (without the added generic); translated as Our Land, the name is a significant statement when one locates this massive territory on a map. Accordingly, all traditional placenames are expected to be accepted as is, without the addition of English generics. There is an exception to this rule, however. The Geographic Names Board of Canada maintains a list of names of pan-Canadian significance. The names on this list of prominent geographical features are to appear in all official documentation with English and French names only. This may not be hugely problematic given that many of the more prominent geographical features identified as having pan-Canadian significance do not have traditional names. For example, Inuit tended not to name large features that extended for hundreds of kilometres (Frobisher Bay or the whole of Cumberland Sound or Baffin Island). There are exceptions however, as in the case of seven First Nations groups in the Northwest Territories, each traditionally having their own name to the Mackenzie River, a significant river in Canada's north-west.[16]

As noted earlier in this chapter, a staff member from the Danish Geodata Agency referred to Greenlandic placenames as a path of thorns. While Greenlandic names on maps and charts may be difficult to pronounce, so are many foreign names to the uninitiated anywhere. However, those Greenlandic names are also a pronouncement; they make a strong statement about the Inuit presence on the

---

15 Pers. comm. with Danielle Turcotte, Commission de toponymie du Quebec, by email, 2007.
16 Pers. comm. with Tom Andrews, Government of the Northwest Territories, Cultural Places Program, 2007.

islands and in the fiords of *Kalallit Nunaat* (Greenland). Also worth pointing out is that English or French or Danish names, as in the Greenland example, are equally difficult for native Inuktitut speakers to pronounce. Despite the fact that there are maps with official English toponyms in Nunavut, Inuit continue to refer to places on the land using traditional Inuktitut names, which to them, are far more informative, and easier to pronounce in their own language. Finally, as stated in the Canadian Government's Principles and Procedures for Geographical Naming 2011, Principle 2:

> First priority shall be given to names with long-standing local usage by the general public. Unless there are good reasons to the contrary, this principle should prevail.

Consider the following passage by Canadian author Peter Steele, in his book, *The Man who Mapped the Arctic*:

> The chaps in this narrative were much exercised about maps. Mapping was why they were there. The indigenous peoples appear to have given few names to prominent geographical features, certainly not the plethora that sprang from visits by Europeans. Franklin, Back, and other explorers could, and did, walk in and map a continent. Then by way of recognizing their patrons and sponsors these first "white men" sprinkled the maps they drew with the names of luminaries, major and minor, who are now recorded in perpetuity to the total denial of the native culture. (Steele 2003: xx)

(As a northerner himself, Steele apparently had little awareness of the extent of traditional aboriginal placenames that existed prior to these "others" entering the scene.)

The type and scale of features named on maps gives insight into many aspects of the Inuit presence on the land. The explorers and other adventurers who bestowed their names on the coastal areas often did so from the decks of their relatively large ships. With these they also travelled faster than did Inuit in their small *qajait* (kayaks) in summer or fall, or by dog team or on foot in winter. There are many examples where names of large inlets and other bodies of water do not have Inuktitut counterparts to the "colonial" ones on the maps. However, the more discrete features within those larger bodies do have traditional names. For example, only the end of Frobisher Bay is named *Tasiujarjuaq* (like a big lake); the name represents almost a third of the whole named bay that is hemmed in by islands, but not the whole bay.

A working paper prepared for a 2004 meeting of the United Nations Group of Experts on Geographical Names describing Canadian activities with respect to indigenous names shows an evolution in the practice of accepting indigenous names into official nomenclature.[17] In this paper, O'Brien notes that at one time names that were deemed cumbersome and unpronounceable were shortened or rejected and that, in recent years, the provincial and territorial names boards have been more open to the approval of names with long specifics. Both examples of long names (one had 31 letters) still had English and French generics attached to them. However, the author does note further in the document that geographical names usually include both a specific and a generic and that the generic term will be in English, French, or in an aboriginal language.

Beyond Quebec, a look at the treatment of generics and placenames in other Canadian provinces and territories and the United States follows.

2. Moving from west to east across Canada[18]

Janet Mason, Provincial Toponymist in British Columbia (BC), related that as part of the Nisga'a Treaty signed in 1999, 40 traditional placenames were adopted into legislation. However, despite there being intensive native language programs in schools since this time, these names, entirely in the Nisga'a language, are not in local use, suggesting a disconnect between the older and younger generations. British Columbia's Toponymy Policy, available on the internet, states that placenames will be accepted in a single language form; however, despite this statement, aboriginal names with English generics are accepted if this is how the names are used locally.[19] Mason, emphasised that, in her opinion, maps are not a tool for language retention. This comment contrasts with the Nunavut experience where, in the Inuit Heritage Trust's experience, maps with Inuktitut placenames (as opposed to the more widely available topographic maps with primarily English-only toponyms) are actively sought by hunters who tend to communicate with each other over short wave radio in Inuktitut while "on the land".

In Alberta, local use dictates the form of the name confirming that English generics are not automatically added as a matter of course.[20]

---

17   United Nations Group of Experts on Geographical Names, 'Standardization in Multilingual Area; Some Canadian Activities with Respect to Indigenous Names', Twenty-second Session New York, 20–29 April 2001. Working Paper No.15 (A) Item 18 of the Provisional Agenda, http://unstats.un.org/unsd/geoinfo/UNGEGN/docs/22-GEGN-Docs/wp/gegn22wp15a.pdf.
18   I attended a Geographic Names Board of Canada meeting in Yellowknife, Northwest Territories in August 2007 where I was able to ask provincial and territorial representatives about issues relating to the treatment of generics in their jurisdictions.
19   Geographical Names Office, 'British Columbia's Geographical Naming Principles: Geographical Naming Policy and Procedures', http://geobc.gov.bc.ca/bcnames/files/GeogNamingPolicy.pdf.
20   Geographical Names Manual. Government of Alberta Historic Resources Management Geographical Names Program. See pages 12–12 for Principle 5(B) Names in Languages other than English and Principle6 (B) Form and Character of Aboriginal Names. http://culture.alberta.ca/heritage/resourcemanagement/archaeologyhistory/geographical/pdf/2012/alberta_geographical_names_manual_12.pdf.

Alberta's example is unlike its neighbour to the east, Saskatchewan, which though it describes itself as "aligned with the Geographic Names Board of Canada", has a similar policy to that of Quebec. That is, the English generic is always attached to the aboriginal name. If a generic is integral to the name, an English generic would be added. If the generic is separate from the specific, the aboriginal generic might be dropped. Here, the provincial names authority indicated that there is interest in capturing the aboriginal names and their meanings but these would appear in a database and not in the official road signs or other documentation.

Manitoba's policy is similar to that of Saskatchewan and Quebec in that placenames always are given an English generic. One exception was noted — that of a populated place known by the aboriginal name "Manitou" with no generic. Incidentally, Manitoba is also a province with an outspoken French-speaking minority.

Ontario, the most populous province, home to almost 40 per cent of the Canadian population has a relatively small First Nations population (less than 2 per cent of the total population).[21]

Ontario accepts aboriginal generics, as in the case of a recent aboriginal name that was approved in Ontario: *Miskwaa Ziibi* where the entity type is listed as River, and the generic in the name itself "*Ziibi*" means "River". Therefore the name – *Miskwaa Ziibi* – stands on its own without an English or French generic in the name itself.[22]

The Nova Scotia placenames policy stipulates that names should be adopted in a single language form; this includes a provision allowing the generic term to be recorded in an aboriginal language.[23]

New Brunswick, in many ways, is just getting started with its Toponymy Office. As in some of the other provinces names changes are not encouraged. However, First Nation peoples on reserves in the province may apply to the federal department of Indian and Northern Affairs with a proposal for a new name, a process in place in all the provinces. New placenames proposals with demonstrated support and little or no conflict have a better chance of being accepted.

In Newfoundland, the Geographical Names Board Act, states that the Inuit Central Government is the final authority on the spelling and pronunciation of

---

21 Pers. comm. with Carl Christian Olsen, Director Greenland Language Secretariat and Chair, Greenland Place Names Authority.
22 Ontario Geographic Names Board, 'Principles of Geographic Naming', http://www.mnr.gov.on.ca/stdprodconsume/groups/lr/@mnr/@geographicnames/documents/document/stel02_207469.pdf.
23 Nova Scotia Government, 'The Naming Process: Guiding Principles', https://www.gov.ns.ca/snsmr/placenames/namingprocess.asp (accessed 31 August 2007).

Inuktitut placenames in the province. The Inuit of Nunatsiavut, a land claim settlement area within the province of Newfoundland and Labrador, number about 5,500 persons. The actual area covered in the Labrador Inuit Land Claims Agreement, consists of 28,000 square miles (72,520 km²) of land in Labrador and 17,000 square miles (44,030 km²) of sea. Labrador Inuit do not own this land, but have special rights related to traditional land use.

With regards to placenames, the Nunatsiavut Land Claim Agreement[24] states that the Nunatsiavut Government will have the exclusive right to establish official placenames in Labrador Inuit Lands, subject to approval by the responsible provincial minister. The Government of Newfoundland and Labrador must consult the Nunatsiavut Government on any proposed placenames in the Settlement Area outside Labrador Inuit Lands.[25]

In the Yukon, one of Canada's three northern territories, aboriginal names stand on their own. There are special challenges here as there may be as many as four First Nations groups that claim a particular area and therefore a feature might have four aboriginal names, with the addition perhaps of a fifth non-aboriginal name. The Yukon Government has a unique format to handle some of the overlapping First Nations names through a Land Claims Umbrella Final Agreement (UFA) in which Alternate Placenames are recognised by Canada, but do not show up on maps and road signs. Worthy of note is that as of 2003, the official name of Yukon Territory was changed to Yukon, dropping the generic.

The situation in the Northwest Territories is similar to that of the Yukon but here the Government of the Northwest Territories insists that as many as seven aboriginal names for one feature, the Mackenzie River is a prime example, be accepted and that Ottawa (the seat of the federal government) must figure out a way to make this work. This act is also in conflict with a United Nations principle of univocity, one name for one place. A First Nations leader, guest at a Geographic Names Board of Canada meeting in Yellowknife in August 2007, also expressed that, in naming, the contributions of white pioneers in Canada's north should not be forgotten. He noted that the traditional names must appear but the other non-traditional names are also an important part of history.

In terms of trends in toponymy in Canada, a working group of the Geographical Names Board of Canada presented a report on Proposed Delineation Guidelines at its annual members meeting in August 2007. In this report they noted how toponymic and topologic perspectives do not necessarily agree and that an important distinction must be made between the application of a geographical

---

24 Government of Newfoundland and Labrador, 'Nunatsiavut Land Claims Agreement' http://www.laa.gov.nl.ca/laa/claimsaip/Aipchp16.htm (accessed 2 August 2007).
25 Nunatsiavut Government, 'Highlights of the Labrador Inuit Land Claims Agreement', http://www.nunatsiavut.com/en/lilca_highlights.php (accessed 2 August 2007).

name based on local usage and the physical extent of a feature. The example given is of a hydrologist defining a river based on its physical measurements of its source, length and flow. Local citizens, however, may apply the name to only a portion of this physical feature. These Delineation Guidelines will be of assistance to the Inuit Heritage Trust as we struggle to translate the Inuit concept of a named place to an "acceptable" generic in English when there is not a perfect fit between language, cultures and world views. When we submit placenames to the Government for them to be made official, we normally also submit an electronic map with shape files with named areas delineated. These new Delineation Guidelines reflect the reality that we are working in.

Finally, a glance in the direction of the Principles, Policies, and Procedures: Domestic Geographic Names (2003) for the United States as a whole (as opposed to state by state).

The United States Board on Geographic Names (USBGN) does not encourage changes in official geographic names. However, the USBGN supports the expert documentation of geographic names derived from Native American languages. The USBGN recommends the use of generic terms with names derived from Native American languages that are easily understood by the general public and are common to the areas in which the names are applied. This policy applies even though the Native American names may already contain generic elements. This being said, Louis Yost of the USBGN did express that the Board will consider applications with no generics. Though it highly recommends English generics, the USBGN has been asked by native groups to consider names as they are used locally.[26]

3. Summarising approaches to generics with aboriginal placenames in Canada

The position of the national authority, the Geographic Names Board of Canada is that placenames generics can be in English, French or in an aboriginal language. However, the provinces and territories have the authority for naming decisions within their jurisdictions and the GNBC follows the lead of these jurisdictions. In provinces and territories where there is either a large and/or outspoken First Nations or Inuit presence, naming authorities are accepting traditional placenames as they are used locally, without English or French generics, into

---

26   As noted in footnote *xiv*. Also United States Board on Geographic Names, http://geonames.usgs.gov/pppdgn.html#3-J.

official nomenclature. Three exceptions are Manitoba, Saskatchewan and Quebec, though these three appear to be willing to accord visibility to the aboriginal names without going all the way to accepting the names as official.

Quebec has been making efforts to grant visibility to aboriginal placenames in their original forms for the benefit of aboriginal communities. At a meeting of the Geographic Names Board of Canada (GNBC) in August 2007, the Director of the Quebec Commission de toponymie, in a teleconference, mentioned to the assembled group that her office had a received a proposal for 900 aboriginal placenames. She wondered openly if anyone else in the country was dealing with similar volumes of names changes and new names. In fact Nunavut is leading the country with proposals for thousands of placenames to be made official.

In the rest of the country, and particularly where First Nations and Inuit populations are in the majority, such as in the territories north of the 60th parallel, the trend is towards reverting to aboriginal placenames and ensuring that the integrity of these names is not marred by the addition of English and French generics and that the names stand as they are in use by local populations.

References

Avataq Cultural Institute, 'Inuktitut Language Program' http://www.avataq.qc.ca/programs/language_en.cfm (accessed 20 July 2007).

—, 'Nunatop: Inuit place names', http://www.avataq.qc.ca/en/Institute/Departments/Research-Library-and-Archives/Place-names/Nunatop-Inuit-place-names (accessed 9 September 2013).

Bauch, H. 2007, *Language law widely accepted after 30 years: Quebec's Bill 101 engendered new era of social peace.* http://www.canada.com (accessed 26 August 2007).

Chan, H.M., K. Fediuk, S. Hamilton, L. Rostas, A. Caughey, H. Kuhnlein, G. Egeland and E. Loring 2006, 'Food security in Nunavut, Canada: barriers and recommendations', *International Journal of Circumpolar Health* 65(5): 416–431.

Commission de Toponymie Québec, 'Politiques de la Commission de toponymie (1990)', http://www.toponymie.gouv.qc.ca/ct/toponymie_expliquee/politiques_topo.html (accessed 20 May 2007).

Department of Culture, Language, Elders and Youth, Government of Nunavut, http://www.gov.nu.ca/cley/ (accessed 15 August 2007).

Geographical Names Office, 'British Columbia's Geographical Naming Principles: Geographical Naming Policy and Procedures', http://geobc.gov.bc.ca/bcnames/files/GeogNamingPolicy.pdf.

Government of Manitoba, 'Manitoba Geographical Names Program', http://www.gov.mb.ca/conservation/geomatics/geo_names/index.html.

Government of Newfoundland and Labrador, 'Labrador Inuit Land Claims Agreement in Principle,Chapter 16: Place Names', http://www.laa.gov.nl.ca/laa/claimsaip/Aipchp16.htm (accessed 2 August 2007).

Kearns, R.A. and L.D. Berg 2002, 'Proclaiming place: towards a geography of place name pronunciation', *Social and Cultural Geography* 3(3): 283-302.

Nova Scotia Government, 'The Naming Process: Guiding Principles', https://www.gov.ns.ca/snsmr/placenames/namingprocess.asp (accessed 31 August 2007).

Nunatsiavut Government, 'Highlights of the Labrador Inuit Land Claims Agreement', http://www.nunatsiavut.com/en/lilca_highlights.php (accessed 2 August 2007).

Ontario Geographic Names Board, 'Principles of Geographic Naming', http://www.mnr.gov.on.ca/stdprodconsume/groups/lr/@mnr/@geographicnames/documents/document/stel02_207469.pdf.

Sheppard, R. 2006, 'Quebec nationalism, a long history', CBC News, http://www.cbc.ca/news/background/parliament39/quebecnation-history.html (accessed 31 August 2007).

Statistics Canada, 'Aboriginal people and language', http://www12.statcan.gc.ca/nhs-enm/2011/as-sa/99-011-x/99-011-x2011003_1-eng.cfm (accessed 13 December 2013).

—, 'Aboriginal peoples of Canada: A demographic profile: 2001 Census: analysis series', January 2003, http://www12.statcan.ca/english/census01/Products/Analytic/companion/abor/pdf/96F0030XIE2001007.pdf (accessed 15 July 2007).

—, 'Mother Tongue, Percentage Distribution for Both Sexes, for Canada, Provinces and Territories – 20% Sample Data', http://www12.statcan.ca/english/census01/products/highlight/LanguageComposition/Page.cfm?Lang=E&Geo=PR&View=1a&Code=0&Table=2a&StartRec=1&Sort=2&B1=Distribution&B2=Both (accessed 2 August 2007).

—, 'Number and distribution of the population reporting an Aboriginal identity and percentage of Aboriginal people in the population, Canada, provinces and territories, 2011', http://www12.statcan.gc.ca/nhs-enm/2011/as-sa/99-011-x/2011001/tbl/tbl02-eng.cfm. (accessed 9 September 2013).

—, 'Table 11', http://www12.statcan.ca/census-recensement/2006/as-sa/97-555/table/t11-eng.cfm (accessed 20 July 2007).

Steele, P. 2003, *The Man Who Mapped the Arctic: The Intrepid Life of George Back, Franklin's Lieutenant*. Raincoast Books, Vancouver, British Columbia.

United Nations Group of Experts on Geographical Names, 'Standardization in Multilingual Area; Some Canadian Activities with Respect to Indigenous Names', Twenty-second Session New York, 20–29 April 2001. Working Paper No.15 (A) Item 18 of the Provisional Agenda, http://unstats.un.org/unsd/geoinfo/UNGEGN/docs/22-GEGN-Docs/wp/gegn22wp15a.pdf (accessed 3 June 2007).

United States Board on Geographic Names, 'Policy X: Names of Native American Origin from United States Geological Survey: Principles, Policies, and Procedures: Domestic Geographic Names', Geographic Names Information System website, Online Edition (revised), 2003, http://geonames.usgs.gov/pppdgn.html#3-J (accessed 3 June 2007).

21. Khoisan indigenous toponymic identity in South Africa

Peter E. Raper
University of the Free State, South Africa

1. Introduction

According to Webster's Dictionary (Gove 1961: 1151) 'indigenous' means 'not introduced directly or indirectly according to historical record or scientific analysis into a particular land or region or environment from the outside'. In terms of this definition the Bushmen (also called San) and Hottentots (also called Khoikhoi) are the true indigenous inhabitants of Southern Africa. These people, collectively known as the Khoisan, occupied vast areas of the African sub-continent, from the Zambezi Valley to the Cape (Lee and DeVore 1976: 5), for thousands of years (Mazel 1989: 12), and left behind a rich legacy of placenames. However, the Khoisan peoples were pre-literate, and their languages and the names they bestowed were unrecorded until the seventeenth century.

The African or 'Bantu' peoples migrated southwards in small groups or clans from the Great Lakes regions of Equatorial Africa (Krige 1975: 595–596), reaching the present KwaZulu-Natal between 1,500 and 2,000 years ago (Maggs 1989: 29; Mazel 1989: 13) and settling especially in the northern, eastern and south-eastern parts of the sub-continent.

From the late fifteenth century, Portuguese navigators sailed around the coast of Africa, and in 1652 the Dutch established a refreshment station at the Cape of Good Hope, leading to permanent settlement. They were followed by French, British, German and other peoples from Europe and Asia. Each wave of migrants adopted existing placenames, adapting them phonologically and later orthographically, translating some names fully or partially, and bestowing new names in their own language. Of course, when languages come into contact, mutual influence takes place, with sounds and words being 'borrowed' by each group of speakers.

In the course of time, and particularly during the past few centuries, many of the Khoikhoi and San cultures, and the languages spoken by these people, have to a large extent become extinct, and others are in the process of becoming so (Traill 1978: 147). Although many Khoikhoi placenames have survived, albeit in adapted form (Nienaber and Raper 1977; 1980), relatively few San placenames were considered to have survived (Pettman 1931: 13–17). Current research indicates, however, that a large number of San placenames have indeed survived, albeit adapted or transformed into the phonological and orthographic systems of Khoikhoi, African (Bantu) and European languages.

The present paper concentrates on placenames that are regarded as originating in European or African languages, but are in fact of Bushman or San origin.

From their placenames a great deal can be deduced about the identity of the San, and the things that make their placenames unique, e.g. the click sounds and various other aspects of their language. Some San words that are used as components of placenames reflect their environment, describing natural features and the character of their surroundings, and referring to animals and plants so essential to their survival, to the cosmetic and aesthetic use of natural pigments, and perhaps even to their deity. Many of these things have been recorded by anthropologists, linguists, Khoisanologists and others. But from a study of the vast corpus of placenames, many new facts may emerge, and above all, the original San placenames may be reconstructed by reversing the processes of adaptation, and recognised as the original indigenous toponyms of South Africa.

2. Determining San influence

The key to determining San influence on placenames hinges on the lexical meaning of the names, that meaning that first gave rise to the name, that was in the minds of the people who first gave and used the name (Sedgefield 1969: 1, 3). Nicolaisen (1976: 30) points out that the primary aim of onomastic research is to determine this meaning, so that 'something which is now opaque might be made transparent again. ... Without this maxim there would be no point in, and therefore no scholarly discipline of, the study of names'. This lexical meaning has, in the case of many San names and their adaptations into other languages, been preserved, through oral tradition and subsequent graphic recording. It is through comparing the preserved meanings with similar known San words that influence may be demonstrated.

The African (Bantu) languages and the Khoisan languages are not believed to be descended from a common ancestor and are thus not related to each other. When the term 'cognate' is used for words from these different languages, it is used in the sense of the definition given by Webster's Dictionary, namely 'related in a manner that involves borrowing rather than descent from or as well as descent from an ancestral language' (Gove 1961: 440).

In order to appreciate the processes of adaptation that led to the present state of San names disguised as African-language names, note may be taken of some grammatical aspects of African and San languages.

3. African languages

African language names, like all nouns, consist of a stem and a prefix, and frequently also a suffix. The stem conveys the lexical meaning of the word, while the prefix indicates number (singular or plural), concord (which set of concordial agreement should be employed for agreement with other parts of speech in a sentence), and so forth (Koopman 2002: 267). Removing the prefix reveals the stem of a noun, and it is under this stem that the word is entered in dictionaries (Doke and Vilakazi 2005: xviii).

The Constitution of the Republic of South Africa (1996: 4) lists the official African languages as 'Sepedi, Sesotho, Setswana, siSwati, Tshivenda, Xitsonga, isiNdebele, isiXhosa and isiZulu', thus incorporating in the names of the languages the prefixes in each of the languages concerned. In academic and popular usage, however, non-mother tongue speakers generally employ the terms 'Zulu', 'Xhosa', 'Swazi' and so forth when referring to these languages and to the speakers concerned, terms that have also gained currency outside South Africa (Van Wyk 1993: 108). In the present paper the latter academic usage will be followed.

Several African languages, e.g. Sotho, Swazi, Xhosa and Zulu, have click sounds that are derived from the Khoisan languages. These are the dental click, written as *c*; the lateral click, written as *x*, and the palato-alveolar click, written as *q*. Whereas more than 70 per cent San words start with a click, comparatively few names in Nguni and Sotho languages do, and in some other languages not at all. The clicks originally occurring in San names and other words can thus be assumed to have been adapted to the African-language sound organically closest to the click.

In some African languages, e.g. Zulu, the juxtaposition of vowels is impermissible, and when words (and names) from other languages are taken over into such languages, the two vowels are contracted into one, or coalesced, or the first vowel is changed into the corresponding semi-vowel, or a consonant is inserted between the vowels, and so forth. Zulu, for example, does not permit the juxtaposition of certain consonants, for which reason *Pretoria* is adapted as *ePitoli*, *Vryheid* as *eFilidi*, etc. Also, African-language words must end in a vowel, except in the case of a syllabic *m*.

African names frequently display the structure generic + specific, e.g. *Thabazimbi*, from *intaba* 'mountain', *insimbi* 'iron'; but some demonstrate the structure specific + generic, e.g. *Nhlazatshe*, from *-luhlaza* 'green', *itshe* 'stone'.

4. San languages

The San languages are characterised by click or suction consonants. These have been standardised in writing as:

(a) /, the dental or alveolar fricative click, pronounced by placing the tip of the tongue against the upper front teeth or alveolar ridge and withdrawing it rapidly;

(b) //, the lateral click, pronounced by placing the upper part of the tongue-tip against the alveolar ridge, with the tongue far back against the velum and the sides of the tongue against the upper side teeth, and withdrawing one side of the tongue from the upper teeth;

(c) !, the cerebral or palato-alveolar click, pronounced with the tongue-tip placed firmly on the point of division between palate and alveolar ridge, the back of the tongue placed against the velum and the sides of the tongue against the side upper gums, and releasing the tongue-tip sharply downwards, the resulting click resembling the sound of a cork being drawn from a bottle;

(d) ≠, the alveolar click, formerly called the palatal click, pronounced with the upper part of the tongue behind the tip pressed firmly against the gum-ridge behind the central upper teeth, the back of the tongue raised to touch the velum, and the sides of the tongue raised to complete the space of rarefaction between velum and alveolar ridge, and bringing the front of the tongue sharply down, the resulting click resembling the sound made by a child when tasting something sweet;

(e) the bilabial click, or lip click, usually represented in writing as a circle with a dot in the middle, but in this paper represented as Θ; and

(f) the retroflex click, variously represented in writing as !! or /// (Bleek 1929: i; Bleek 1956: 640; Rust 1960: viii; Traill 1978: 137–138).

In all these clicks there is double closure: the back of the tongue is pressed against the velum and the sides of the tongue also touch the roof of the mouth, to create a space of rarefaction; as that is the same for all except the lip click, and is done quite unconsciously, I do not particularly name it in describing each click (Bleek 1929: 13).

The San clicks are not pronounced in isolation. Each of the clicks is pronounced with distinctive releases, accompaniments or *effluxes*, e.g. aspirated, ejected, fricative, glottal, nasal, preglottal, prevoiced, voiced, etc. The voiced efflux is indicated as in /gã, the nasal efflux as in /na, the fricative efflux as in /xã, the aspirated efflux as in /ha, and so forth. These effluxes yield between 20 and 85 distinct click segments for different languages, and some of them combine on a single click, 'yielding a system that is staggering in its phonetic complexity' (Traill 1978: 138).

In addition to the clicks, the San languages have many other complexities of pronunciation involving both consonants and vowels. 'The vowels of these languages are notable for their complex colourings, including plain, nasalised, breathy and pressed vowel colourings. These combine with each other to produce up to seven vowel colours for each of the five vowels.' (Traill 1978: 139). In this paper the symbol ɛ is used to indicate a pressed vowel.

The San languages are tone languages. 'That means roughly that different words may have identical vowels and consonants but be distinguished by their tone alone.' (Traill 1978: 139). However, no attempt will be made in this paper to seek correspondences between San and African-language tones, since 'too many variables enter into the interpretation of the absolute pitch of the syllables of the words recorded on any particular day, and this makes it impossible to give such absolute pitch any accurate systematic phonetic or phonological interpretation.' (Doke and Vilakazi 2005: i), and 'Although tone has always been a useful tool when doubtful cases ... are to be distinguished from one another, it has very little value when it comes to place names, since tone can for reasons which are obvious, not be indicated on place names in gazetteers, atlases, etc.' (Louwrens 1994: 6). Furthermore, indigenous San placenames are ancient, and in their adaptation into African and other languages, the original tone structure may well also have undergone changes to fit the systems of the receiver languages. An investigation into the tones used by speakers of the receiver language today can reveal no more than the tones used in the adapted name or component, which may in some cases be a folk-etymological misinterpretation.

On the basis of the number and distribution of clicks, similarities in the roots of words, and other grammatical similarities, Bleek (1929; 1956) divided the San languages into three groups, namely the Southern, Central and Northern Groups, and allocated the symbols S1, S2, S2a, N1, N1a, N2, N3, C1, C1a, etc. to them to facilitate reference to them. In the present investigation the name of the language referred to is given, together with the appropriate symbol in parentheses, e.g. /Xam (S1), Hadza (C3), Kung (N2).

5. Adapted San placenames

As stated previously, the lexical meanings of many placenames have been preserved and recorded, and these meanings provide the key to ascertaining San origins of African-language placenames. Four onomastic techniques are employed in determining the San elements comprising the name:

(a) If a meaning has been recorded for the African-language name, that meaning is tested linguistically against recorded San words with the same meaning to determine possible semantic correspondence;

(b) where both an indigenous and European name occur for a feature, the possibility is examined of corresponding meanings that may indicate translation;

(c) topographic congruity, the occurrence of toponyms from different languages in close spatial proximity, may reveal transference and translation;

(d) topographical, geographical, geological, botanical or other evidence in the region or vicinity where the name occurs may give an indication of the meaning for the name, since these may have triggered the name or been the toponymic motive.

In all instances cognisance is taken of the possibility of folk etymological explanations.

6. Given or recorded meanings

In the following instances, the underlying San component(s) can be determined by comparison with the recorded meaning of the names.

The name *Tshokwana* is cognate with Hadza (C3) *ts'okwana* 'giraffe' (Bleek 1956: 219), the only phonological difference being the replacement of the San alveolar affricative plus glottal stop *ts'* by the Sotho lateral affricative *tsh*.

The river-name *eMpunzini* is said to be derived from the Zulu word *impunzi*, 'duiker' (Koopman 2002: 129). The component *mpun* of the word *impunzi* is cognate with Sesarwa (S5) *Θpyn* 'duiker buck' (Bleek 1929: 35). The stem of this word is thought to be *phunzi*, 'common grey duiker buck' (Doke and Vilakazi 2005: 678), but the voiced bilabial consonant *m* of the component *im-* is a replacement of the bilabial click Θ, the cluster Θ*p* thus corresponding to the Zulu nasal bilabial consonant *m* plus ejective bilabial *p* in the cluster *mp*, while San *y* in the word Θ*pyn*, pronounced like *u* in French 'du', occurs as the Zulu high back vowel *u*.

Madzivhanani is the name of a settlement, said to be of Venda origin and to mean 'where lakes are found', from *madzivha* 'lakes' (South African Geographical Names Council Agenda for 20 March 2002). Removal of the plural prefix *ma-* reveals the stem *dzivha* 'lake', cognate with Hie (C1) *džiba* 'lake, pool' (Bleek 1956: 33). The component *nani* is perhaps a Venda locative suffix.

uKhahlamba is the Zulu name for the Drakensberg Mountains (Koopman 2002: 155). This name is derived from the noun *khahlamba* (*u(lu)kahlamba*), meaning 'Broken mountain range' (Doke and Vilakazi 2005: 374). Other written forms of the name include *Quahlamba*, *Quatlamba*, *Kwahlamba* and *Kwathlamba*, all being attempts at rendering in writing the pronunciation of the name, indicating that the component *Kha* is a coalesced form of *Qua*, *Kwa*. This component is cognate with /Xam (S1) *!kwa*, Kung (N2) _*!kwa* 'to break' (Bleek 1929: 24). The underscore before the click denotes a low tone in the pronunciation of the word. The component *hlamba* is cognate with the /Xam (S1) word *//khami* 'chain of mountains' (Bleek 1956: 573). The *hl* of *hlamba* is the unvoiced alveolar lateral fricative corresponding to the unvoiced lateral fricative click *//*; the voiced bilabial consonant *m* is perhaps a relic of a masculine singular ending later occurring as *b*.

Umtongata is the spelling given by Gardiner (1966 [1836]: 182) for the river name also encountered as *Umtongate*, *Thongathi*, *uThongathi*, *Tongati*, etc., and as *Tongaat* for the town. Stayt (1971) gives as one possibility the meaning of 'The Twisting River'. The component *Um* is the Zulu prefix; the component *tonga* is perhaps cognate with Kung (N2) *tuŋ-a*, *tuŋ'a* 'turn' (Bleek 1956: 241, 766), San *u* variously heard as *u* (back close) or *o* (back half-close) (Bleek 1956: 246). The final component of the name, *-ta* or *-ti*, is a fluvial generic term, *ta* perhaps cognate with /Xam (S1) /*k'a* 'river' (Bleek 1929: 70); *ti* perhaps with /Auni (S4) *≠ei* 'river' (Bleek 1956: 643), the unvoiced alveolar plosive consonant *t* corresponding to the alveolar click / in the first case and with the alveolar plosive click ≠ in the second, in which the vowel cluster *ei* is coalesced to the syllable peak *i*.

7. Allonyms

Many places, towns as well as natural features, have both African and European names. Of the former, some are demonstrably of San origin.

Mangaung, the Southern Sotho name for *Bloemfontein*, means 'place of cheetahs', *Acinonyx jubatus*, from *mangau*, the plural of the Class 6 noun of which the stem is *ngau* 'cheetah', cognate with the Hie (C1) word *khao* 'cheetah' (Bleek 1956: 88), the Sotho voiced velar nasal compound *ng* replacing the San aspirated velar consonant *kh*, the San back close vowel phoneme *u* variously heard as back close *u* or back half close *o* (Bleek 1956: 246). The addition of the Sotho locative suffix *-ng* completes the adaptation to *Mangaung* (Louwrens 1994: 25).

Mašišing is the Sotho name for Lydenburg (Louwrens 1994: 9, 25), derived from the Class 6 noun *mašiši* 'tambookie grass' (Louwrens 1994: 10) plus the Sotho locative suffix *-ng*. The component *šiši* is cognate with the Auen (N1) word *//e:si* 'grass' (Bleek 1956: 519), the San lateral fricative click *//* replaced by the unvoiced fricative *š* in the first syllable, the San unvoiced alveolar fricative *s* by the unvoiced prepalatal fricative *š* in the second syllable.

8. Translations

In some instances European allonyms seem to be translations of San placenames, or at least to have the same meaning.

The Dutch name *Baviaans Rivier* means 'baboon river'. The Xhosa name for this river is *iNcwama* (Skead 2001: 54–55), derived from *ingcwam*, a dialectal word for 'baboon' (Pahl in Skead 2001: 54). A /Auni (S4) word for 'baboon' is *//nwaaŋ* (Bleek 1956: 623), cognate with the Xhosa root *ngcwam*, the San lateral click with voiced release *//n* approximated by the Xhosa voiced form of the dental click preceded by the nasal, *ngc*, the San nasal *ŋ* often taking the form *m* (Bleek 1956: 131). An alternative version of the Xhosa name is *i-Quamma* (Skead 2001: 54–55), the stem *quam* also cognate with *//nwaaŋ*, the San lateral click *//*, also called the retroflex fricative click, 'made by spreading the tip of the tongue across the palate and drawing it gently backwards' (Bleek 1929: 13), correlating with the Xhosa palato-alveolar click *q*. It is therefore clear that the Dutch name Baviaans Rivier translates the San word *//nwaaŋ* 'baboon', preserved in the adapted Xhosa name *iNcwama* and *i-Quamma*.

Cainsheneuj was recorded in 1777 by Colonel Robert Jacob Gordon as the Khoikhoi name for *Grootvadersbos*, and said to mean 'blind-fly forest', the component *cainshe* considered to be similar to Nama /*geina*, /*gena* 'blind-fly' (Nienaber and Raper 1977: 269), the component *neuj* 'forest' cognate with the element *ney* in the name *Coerney* 'narrow forest' (Raper 2004: 45). 'Grootvadersbos' literally means 'grandfather's bush'. The Batwa (S3) word for 'grandfather' is *!xeinja* (Bleek 1956: 490), which is similar in sound to *cainshe*, while the component *neuj* is like Kung (N2) /*ku⁻i* 'bush' (Bleek 1956: 324, 701), the alveolar nasal *n* approximating to the alveolar click /.

For the *Cowie River* that joins the Koonap at Adelaide, the Xhosa name *iQoyi* seems to be used consistently, i.e. with the palato-alveolar click Q. Earlier variants of the name include *Kowie* (1809), *Qohi* (1860), *Kowie* (1856)] and *iQoyi*

(1915) (Skead 2001: 663–664). The Dutch name *Kromme*, meaning 'crooked', appears as an alternative to *Kowie* on Arrowsmith's map of 1835 (Skead 2001: 663–664). The winding course of the river was the reason for the name in Dutch, and may well also have been the toponymic trigger for the name in San. A Kung (N2) word for 'crooked, bent' is ⁻//*kubbi* (Bleek 1956: 591), which is phonologically similar to *Kowie* and variants, the San click with velar efflux //k approximated by the velar plosive *K*, the San vowel phoneme *u* variously heard as back close *u* or as back half-close *o* (Bleek 1956: 246); the bilabial vowel *b* in the second syllable frequently changing into *w* (Bleek 1956: 13). *iQoyi* is the Xhosa adaptation, the *i*- being a locative prefix.

eMnqwala is the Xhosa name for the *Waterkloof River* that enters the Koonap at Adelaide (Skead 2001: 418). An older form of the name, recorded in 1851, is *Gwala*. *Waterkloof* is Afrikaans for 'water ravine', thus a translation of an older San name similar to *Gwala* of which *eMnqala* is the Xhosa adaptation. The component *eM* is the Xhosa prefix; the component *nqwa* is cognate with /Xam (S1) *!khwa:*, *!kwa:* 'water' (Bleek 1956: 431, 457), the voiced velar plosive consonant *G* of the component *Gwa* and the nasal form of the palato-alveolar click *nq* reflecting the ejective preceded by the palato-alveolar click, *!k*. The component *(a)la* of the name is perhaps cognate with San /*ara* 'kloof', 'ravine' (Bleek 1956: 729), the voiced alveolar consonant *l* regularly replacing the voiced alveolar *r* . The component *la* may also be a fluvial generic term that occurs in river names such as *Palala*, *Tugela*, *Pongola* and so forth.

Mzinyathi, a Zulu river-name, is generally accepted as meaning 'home of the buffalo, buffalo village' (Botha 1977: 170), derived from *umuzi* 'home, village', and *inyathi* 'buffalo' (Doke and Vilakazi 2005: 895). However, Doke and Vilakazi inform us that this is the Zulu name for '*BloodRiver* in North-west Natal' (Doke and Vilakazi 2005: 895). As frequently proves to be the case, *Blood River* is synonymous with an original San name of which *Mzinyathi* is a folk etymological adaptation. The component *(U)m* is the Zulu prefix; the component *zin* is cognate with Auen (N1) /*iŋ* 'blood' (Bleek 1956: 292), the Zulu voiced alveolar fricative consonant *z* corresponding to the San alveolar fricative click /, the nasals *n* and *ŋ* often interchanging (Bleek 1956: 140). The component *nyati*, where the *ny* is perhaps a click replacement, is cognate with the San word *ati* 'water' (Bleek 1956: 769), although the *y* may well be a glide between /*iŋ* 'blood' and *ati* 'water'. Thus /*iŋati* > *zinyati* > *(uM)zinyathi*.

Mzinyathi is also the Zulu name for the stream known in Afrikaans as the *Wakkerstroom*, and for the town of the same name (Raper 2004: 399). In this case there is reason to suspect a San origin for the Zulu name. *Wakkerstroom* means 'lively stream', literally 'awake stream', *wakker* being Dutch and Afrikaans for 'to be awake'. A Batwa (S3) word for 'to be awake' is /*he:nja* (Bleek 1956: 287), which corresponds phonologically to the component *zinya* of the name *(uM) zinyati*, the voiced alveolar fricative *z* approximating to the alveolar fricative click / (Bleek 1929: 13), the front close vowel *i* interchanging with the front half-close vowel *e* (Bleek 1956: 66). *uM* is the Zulu prefix and *ti* an adaptation of a fluvial generic term, e.g. /Auni (S4) ≠*ei* 'river' (Bleek 1956: 643), or the //ŋ !ke (S2) word /*k'ẽi* 'river' (Bleek 1929: 70), the alveolar click ≠ and / both approximating to the alveolar plosive consonant *t*, the vowel cluster *ei* coalesced to *i* in order to obviate the juxtaposition of two vowels that would violate the Zulu canon.

Tlokwe, the Tswana or Northern Sotho name for the *Mooi River*, is a name proposed as a replacement for the town name Potchefstroom. The component *kwe* is cognate with the Hie (C1) word *kwe* 'river' (Bleek 1929: 70), suggesting the possibility of the component *Tlo* being an adaptation of a San word meaning 'pretty', of which *Mooi* is the Afrikaans translation. Louwrens (1994: 7) points out that the eastern Sotho dialects are renowned for displaying dental sounds (e.g. *th* and *t*) for lateral sounds (e.g. *hl*, *tl*, *tlh*) in the standard language. The component *Tlo* may thus be cognate with the Naron (C2) word *tõe*, *tõi* 'pretty' (Bleek 1956: 207), *Tlokwe* thus meaning 'pretty river', Afrikaans *Mooirivier*.

uThukela is said to be the correct Zulu spelling for the name of the *Tugela River*. This name has been explained as 'the frightening one, the fearsome one' (Botha 1977: 206), derived from the ideophone *thuka* 'of fright, startling; of sudden fear' (Doke and Vilakazi 2005: 804). The earliest recorded form of the name was *Tugala* (Gardiner 1966 [1836]: 30, 69, 312, 372; Owen 1836: (Cory 1926: 271)), thus with an *a* after the velar *g*. An early name for the Tugela was *Fisher's River* (Botha 1977: 207; Hermann 1936: 56; Skead 1973: 230). The river also bore the Portuguese name *Rio da Pescaria*, 'river of fishers', and the headland at its mouth now the *Tugela Bluff* bore the Portuguese name of *Ponta da Pescaria*, recorded as such by Perestrelo in 1675 (Da Costa 1939: 85). The name *Tugela*, or *Tugala*, is thought to have the same meaning as *Rio da Pescaria* and *Fishers River*. The stem of the name has been recorded as *Tu*, *To*, *'Tu*, *Toe*, etc., cognate with //Khau (S2b) *tho:e:* 'fish' (Bleek 1956: 200). The second component of the name, recorded as *ga*, *ge*, *gee* and *ke*, may be cognate with /Xam (S1) !*k'e*, !*'e*, !*ke*, !*e* 'people, men' (Bleek 1929: 56; 1956: 373), and the final component, *la*, a fluvial generic as in *Pongola*, *Palala*, etc.

The town name *Lephalale*, taken from that of the *Palala River*, is said to be derived from the Tswana and Pedi verb -*falala* 'overflow' (Louwrens 1994: 23). However, Louwrens's statement that 'The resulting deverbative can ... not be translated in a sensible way' (Louwrens 1994: 23), and the seemingly anomalous spellings of the verb *falala* and its development from verb to noun as *(le)phalala*, prompt the suspicion that the explanation of the name given above may have been suggested by the similarity in sound of the river-name to the verb *falala*. A variant name for the Palala River is *Rhooebok R.* (Skead 1973: 175). *Rhooebok* is a misspelling of 'rooibok', Afrikaans for 'redbuck, impala antelope' (Kritzinger 1954: 403). The component *Le-* in the variant *Lephalala* is the Sotho class 5 prefix (Louwrens 1994: 22), the stem of the name being *phala, pala*. As is frequently the case when a feature has both a European and an indigenous name, they have the same meaning, the root *pala* being cognate with the Hukwe (C2b) word *pala* 'rooibok' (Bleek 1956: 156). The suffix *-la* of the name is thought to be an adapted generic term meaning 'river' that also occurs in river-names like *Tugela, Pongola*, and the like.

9. Topographical congruence

In a number of cases topographical congruity provides the explanation for the origin or meaning of a name. In other words, where given meanings are suspect or unsatisfactory, or no meaning can be found, the name of a feature close to the one in question, part of the same toponymic configuration, may provide the key in the form of a translation.

eAdo, also recorded as *eNqado*, is the Xhosa form of *Addo*, the name of the famous elephant park. Earlier recorded Khoisan forms include *Kadouw* (1820), *Ado* (1832), *K`adouw* (1833) and *Kadouw* (1843), in each case written with one intervocalic *-d-*, as opposed to the two in the form recorded by Thompson 1827 as *Addo*, by Hall (map 1856) in the name *Kaddobush*, etc. Nienaber and Raper (1977: 170) suggested the meaning of 'Euphorbia pass', from Khoikhoi *!Ga* 'poison'. Arguments against this explanation are that the Khoikhoi word for 'poison' is consistently written with a *g*, while the placename has never been recorded with a *g*; and that 'Euphorbia' and 'poison' are not synonymous. Skead (pers. comm. in letter 22 June 2005) states that the Addo Valley consists of flat ground between low, widely-separated scarps, and that *Soutkloof* is the only kloof or pass in the valley. This pass carries the main roads through the otherwise steep escarpment, and would also have been the route traversed by wagoners in olden times. Besides correlating well with Addo topographically, the linguistic congruence between the two names is convincing. The name *Soutkloof* is Dutch (and Afrikaans) for 'salt ravine'. A Khoisan word for 'salt' is *kxa* (1689) (Nienaber 1963: 464), cognate with Sesarwa (S5) *!xa:ne* 'salt' (Bleek 1929: 71). The unvoiced velar fricative *x* being represented in the written records by the apostrophe ` shows *kxa* to correspond to the element *K'a-* of *K'adouw*, devalarised as *Addo*, while for 'ravine' or 'kloof' the word *dau* was recorded in 1689 (Nienaber 1963: 342), which correlates with the element *do* of *Addo* (Nienaber and Raper 1977: 169). *Soutkloof* is a translation of *Addo*, 'salt ravine' or 'salt pass'.

The name *Cango*, also encountered in the form *Kango*, from which the famous *Cango Caves* take their name, is said to mean 'wet mountain'. The component *Ka(n)* is cognate with /Xam (S1) /ka:ˁ, //ka: 'to be wet' (Bleek 1956: 294), the component *(n)go* with /Auni (S4) !gou, !kau, Hie (C1) !gau 'mountain, hill' (Bleek 1956: 387). One wonders whether a more directly descriptive aspect could have led to the name of this mountain. The region known as the *Kango* or *Cango* is on the southern slopes of the *Swartberg*, and probably took its name from the mountain itself. *Swartberg* is Afrikaans for 'black mountain' (Raper 2004: 360). A San word for 'black' is /k"a:a, (Bleek 1956: 698), which is phonologically compatible with the component *Ka(n)* of the name *Kango*, the component *(n)go* with /Auni (S4) !gou, !kau, Hie (C1) !gau 'mountain, hill' (Bleek 1956: 387), as shown above, so that *Swartberg* is perhaps a translation of the San name, or at least synonymous.

eNtabazwe is the Zulu name for *Harrismith*, said to be derived from *intaba* 'mountain' + *izwe* 'country', and to refer to mountainous country (Koopman 2002: 124). Considering such an explanation to lack distinguishing valence, an alternative explanation, based on topographic contiguity, was sought. To the east and north-east of Harrismith is a large mountain with the Afrikaans name *Platberg* (Walton 1984: 151), meaning 'flat mountain'. The Zulu name of that mountain is *eNtabazwe*. It is believed that Harrismith took its Zulu name from the mountain, and that *eNtabazwe* is an adaptation of a San name meaning 'flat mountain'. The component *ntaba* is cognate with Naron (C2) /ka:ba 'flat' (Bleek 1929: 39), the alveolar plosive consonant after homorganic nasal *nt* of *ntaba* approximating to the San alveolar click with ejected efflux /k of /ka:ba; the component *zwe* cognate with Batwa (S3) *zhe* [3e] 'stone'.

iKhalana, also encountered as *Kalana*, is the Xhosa name for the *Little Thomas River* (Skead 2001: 221). Pahl (1982 in Skead 2001: 221) derives the name from the word *ikhalana*, 'small aloes, e.g. Aloe tenuior'. The presence of small aloes along the river seems to have been the reason for its name in Xhosa, and may well also have been the reason for its name in San. A Naron (C2) word for 'aloe' is ≠*umme* (Bleek 1956: 676). Recognising that the San alveolar or dental click ≠ is frequently replaced in the adaptation process by the dental or alveolar consonant *t*, and considering the variability in pronunciation of *u* and *o* (Bleek 1956: 246), it is possible to see that the San word ≠*umme* 'aloe' has been interpreted folk etymologically as *Thomas*.

Modimolle is the Northern Sotho name that replaced the town name *Nylstroom*. *Modimolle* is primarily the name for *Kranskop*, a hill to the north-east of the town. The name 'Kranskop' means 'cliff hillock', from Afrikaans *krans* 'cliff', *kop* 'hillock'. The component *Mo-* of the name *Modimolle* is the Sotho Class 1 prefix (Louwrens 1994: 17), the component *dimo* cognate with the Hie (C1) word *njimo* 'high' (Bleek 1956: 147). The component *olle* is an adaptation of the

Hadza (C3) word //ulle 'hill' (Bleek 1956: 628), the lateral click dropped in the adaptation process, the vowels *o* and *u* variable (Bleek 1956: 246). *Modimolle* is thus an adaptation of the San name meaning 'high hill', descriptive of the feature later known as *Kranskop*.

Kurrichane was the name of the early nineteenth-century capital of the Bahurutshe, situated north-east of Zeerust, on the slopes of the present Enselsberg. There is a topographic correlation between Kurrichane and the pass where it was situated, *Witpoortjie*, formerly bearing the Dutch name *Wit Poortje*. The latter name means 'little white pass', *Wit* meaning 'white', *poort* being defined as 'gate, gateway; narrow pass between precipitous mountains'. A linguistic correlation between the names *Kurrichane* and *Witpoortjie* is demonstrable. The component *Kurri* of the name *Kurrichane* is cognate with the /Nu//en (S6) word !kari 'white' (Bleek 1929: 91), while the component *chane* is cognate with the /Auni (S4) word !ane 'path' (Bleek 1929: 64). In the former case the alveo-palatal click ! has not been retained in the Tswana adaptation; in the latter the San palato-alveolar click ! has been replaced by the sound represented as *ch*.

10. 'Corrections'

Attempts are sometimes made to correct placenames, to bring them in line with the most recent orthographic rules, or to give 'meaning' to names the meanings of which are unknown or uncertain.

For example, *Pudimoe,* the name of a town, was changed to *Pudumong*, said to mean 'place of the black wildebeest', from Tswana *pudomô* 'black wildebeest' (*Connochaetes gnou*) plus the locative suffix *ng* (Raper 2004: 313). It seems, however, that *Pudimoe* was the correct rendering of an original San name meaning 'goat spring', *pudi* being Hie (C1) for 'goat' (Bleek 1929: 43), *moe* cognate with Hie (C1) *moe*, (Bleek 1956: 137), Khoikhoi *mũ*, 'eye, spring, fountain' (Nienaber 1963: 408). *Pudumong* thus seems to be based on an attempt at seeking a Tswana explanation for the San name *Pudimoe*, with the addition of the Tswana locative suffix *-ng*, and the 'correction' seems to be unjustified.

In an attempt at 'correcting' the name *Kurrichane*, and in the belief that early recorders were incapable of correctly hearing and interpreting Tswana words and names, Boeyens and Cole (1995: 21; 2005: 32) state that *Kurrichane*, the name of the early nineteenth-century capital of the Bahurutshe, is a corruption of *Kaditshwêne*, 'most probably derived by ellipsis from the idiomatic expression "Ga se ka ditshwêne" (What an incredible number of baboons!)' However, the form *Kaditshwêne* first appeared in an article published in 1937 (Boeyens and Cole 1995: 11), and could thus not have been the original form of the name, being coined one hundred and seventeen years later after *Kurrichane* was recorded. *Kaditshwêne* therefore seems to be an attempt at rendering in modern Tswana orthography the San name adapted as Bahurutshe *Kurrichane*.

At the 14th Congress of the Names Society of Southern Africa, held at the Ithala Game Reserve in November 2006, Professor Noleen Turner announced that Zulu placenames were systematically being corrected to bring them in line with the latest Zulu orthography. At the time I appealed for the information on the previous renderings of the names to be preserved in view of current research indicting that many Zulu placenames are in fact adaptations of Bushman names, and the more they are 'corrected', the more the indigenous toponymic identity of the San is obliterated.

11. Conclusion

A large number of placenames from San languages have been adapted into Sotho, Swazi, Tswana, Venda, Xhosa, Zulu and other African languages. In the process the placenames bestowed by the San have been obliterated or at least rendered unrecognisable, and the toponymic indigenous identity of the San has been disguised and obliterated. The San languages are not official, and there are few officially approved San placenames.

In terms of the South African Geographical Names Council Act (Act No. 118 of 2002), one of the functions of this Council is 'the transformation and standardization of geographical names'. By 'transformation' is meant replacing names of 'European' origin with one from African languages. Thus *Ellisras* was changed to *Lephalale*, *Nylstroom* to *Modimolle*, *Messina* to *Musina*, *Pietersburg* to *Polokwane*, and so forth (South African Geographical Names Council Agenda 20 March 2002). Several of these names, however, attest to a San identity.

The Constitution of the Republic of South Africa (1996: 4) states that, 'Recognising the historically diminished use and status of the indigenous languages of our people, the State must take practical and positive measures to elevate the status and advance the use of these languages', and that the 'Pan South African Language Board must promote and create conditions for the development and use of ... the Khoi, Nama and San languages'.

In accordance with the stipulations of the Constitution, and in pursuance of United Nations resolutions urging the recognition of the national identity of indigenous minority groups, it may be advisable to give greater recognition to San origins of placenames.

The present paper is based on a research project that is still in its infancy. New findings have thrown light on the relationship between prefixes and word stems in the African languages, on that between generic terms and suffixes, on the morphological structure of placenames, and so forth. However, the full ramifications of this research can only be guessed at. Indications are that discoveries will be made on the relationship between the various San languages and their classification, on the influence of San languages on African language dialects, and so forth, as well as on aspects relating to the cultural and social heritage of the San.

References

Andrews, T.E. 1991, *Indigenous Place Names Past and Present: Natal, Zululand, Swaziland*, Private Publication, Pretoria.

Bleek, D.F. 1929, *Comparative Vocabularies of Bushman Languages*, University Press, Cambridge.

— 1956, *A Bushman Dictionary*, American Oriental Society, New Haven, Conn.

Bleek, W.H.I. 1862, *A Comparative Grammar of South African Languages*, Trübner & Co., London.

Bornman, H. 1993, *A Dictionary of siSwati Place Names*, Country Life, Nelspruit, South Africa.

Botha, T.J.R. 1977, *Watername in Natal*, Raad vir Geesteswetenskaplike Navorsing, Pretoria.

Boeyens, J.C.A. and D.T. Cole, 1995, 'Kaditshwene: what's in a name?', *Nomina Africana* 9(1): 1–40.

— 2005, 'Whence Tswenyane? The etymology of an age-old Tswana place name in the Marico', *Nomina Africana* 19(1): 31–65.

Constitution of the Republic of South Africa, 1996, Government Printer, Pretoria

Cory, Sir G.E. (ed.) 1926, *The Diary of the Rev. Francis Owen, M.A., Missionary with Dingaan in 1837–38*, Van Riebeeck Society, Cape Town.

Da Costa, A. F. (ed.) 1939, *Roteiro of the South and South-East Africa, from the Cape of Good Hope to Cape Corrientes (1576) by Manuel de Mesquita Perestrelo*. Republica Portuguesa Ministério das Colónias, Lisboã.

Doke, C.M. and B.W. Vilakazi (comp.) 2005, *Zulu-English Dictionary*, Witwatersrand University Press, Johannesburg.

Duminy, A. and B. Guest (eds) 1989, *Natal and Zululand from Earliest Times to 1910: A New History*, University of Natal Press and Shuter and Shooter, Pietermaritzburg.

Gardiner, A.F. 1966 [1836], *Narrative of a Journey to the Zoolu Country in South Africa*, [William Crofts, London], Facsimile reprint, Struik, Cape Town.

Gove, P. B. (ed.) 1961, *Webster's Third New International Dictionary of the English Language Unabridged*, G. Bell and Sons, London; G. & C. Merriam, Springfield, Mass.

Hattingh, P.S., N. Kadmon, P.E. Raper, and I. Booysen (eds) 1993, *United Nations Group of Experts on Geographical Names Training Course in Toponymy for Southern Africa*, University of Pretoria, Pretoria.

Hermann, L. (ed.) 1936, 1937, *Travels and Adventures in Eastern Africa* by Nathaniel Isaacs, 2 volumes, Van Riebeeck Society, Cape Town.

Jenkins, T. and P. V. Tobias 1977, 'Nomenclature of population groups in Southern Africa', *African Studies* 36: 49–55.

Koopman, A. 1983, 'Zulu place-names in the Drakensberg', in *GS Nienaber – 'n Huldeblyk*, A.J.L. Sinclair (ed.), University of the Western Cape, Bellville: 297–306.

— 2002, *Zulu Names*, University of Natal Press, Pietermaritzburg.

Krige, E. J. 1975, 'Zulu', in *Standard Encyclopaedia of Southern Africa*, D.J. Potgieter et al. (eds), vol. 11, Nasou, Cape Town: 595–601.

Kritzinger, M.S.B. (ed.) 1954, *Groot Woordeboek Afrikaans-Engels, Engels-Afrikaans*, Van Schaik, Pretoria.

Lee, R. B. and I. DeVore (eds) 1976, *Kalahari Hunter-Gatherers: Studies of the !Kung San and their Neighbours*, Harvard University Press, Cambridge, Mass.

Lubbe, H.J. (ed.) 2007, *Kritiese Aspekte van Naamsverandering/ Critical Aspects of Name Changing*, Acta Academica Supplementum 2007(1).

Louwrens, L.J. 1994, 'A linguistic analysis of Sotho geographical names', *Nomina Africana* 8(1): 1–42.

Maggs, T. 1989, 'The Iron Age farming communities', in *Natal and Zululand from Earliest Times to 1910: A New History*, Andrew Duminy and Bill Guest (eds), University of Natal Press and Shuter and Shooter, Pietermaritzburg: 28–48.

Mawer, A and F.M. Stenton (eds) 1969, *Introduction to the Survey of English Place-names*, University Press, Cambridge.

Mazel, A. 1989, 'The Stone Age peoples of Natal', in *Natal and Zululand from Earliest Times to 1910: A New History*, Andrew Duminy and Bill Guest (eds), University of Natal Press and Shuter and Shooter, Pietermaritzburg: 1–27.

Nicolaisen, W.F.H. 1976, *Scottish Place Names*, BJ Batsford, London.

Nienaber, G.S. 1963, *Hottentots*, Van Schaik, Pretoria.

Nienaber, G.S. and P.E. Raper 1977, 1980, *Toponymica Hottentotica*, 3 volumes, Raad vir Geesteswetenskaplike Navorsing, Pretoria.

Pahl, H. 2001, Correspondence incorporated in Skead, C.J. 2001, *Pilot Gazetteer of Xhosa Placenames*, Port Elizabeth Museum, Port Elizabeth.

Perestrelo, M. de Mesquita 1576, *Roteiro of the South and South-East Africa, from the Cape of Good Hope to Cape Corrientes (1576)*, annotated by A. Fontoura da Costa, Ministério das Colónias, Lisboa, 1939.

Pettman, C. 1931, *South African Place Names Past and Present*, Daily Representative, Queenstown.

Potgieter, D.J. (ed) 1975, *Standard Encyclopaedia of Southern Africa*, Nasou, Cape Town.

Raper, Peter E. 2004, *New Dictionary of South African Place Names*, Jonathan Ball, Johannesburg and Cape Town.

— 2007, 'Transformation of place-names in South Africa', in *Kritiese Aspekte van Naamsverandering/ Critical Aspects of Name Changing*, H.J. Lubbe (ed.), *Acta Academica Supplementum 1*: 110–138.

Rust, Fr 1960, *Deutsch-Nama Wörterbuch*, Rheinischen Mission in Südwestafrika, Windhoek.

Sedgefield, W.J. 1969, 'Methods of place-name study', in *Introduction to the Survey of English Place-names*, A. Mawer and F.M. Stenton (eds), University Press, Cambridge: 1–14.

Skead, C.J. 1973, *Zoo-Historical Gazetteer*, Cape Provincial Museums, Grahamstown.

— 2001, *Pilot Gazetteer of Xhosa Placenames*, Port Elizabeth Museum, Port Elizabeth.

Stayt, D. 1971, *Where on Earth? Place-names of Natal and Zululand*, The Daily News, Durban.

Thompson, G. 1927, *Travels and Adventures in Southern Africa*, Henry Colburn, London.

Tobias, P.V. (ed.) 1978, *The Bushmen*, Human and Rousseau, Cape Town.

Traill, A. 1978, 'The languages of the Bushmen', in *The Bushmen*, P.V. Tobias (ed.), Human and Rousseau, Cape Town: 137–147.

United States Board on Geographic Names 1992, *Gazetteer of South Africa*, 2nd ed., 4 volumes, Defense Mapping Agency, Washington, DC.

Van Wyk, E.B. 1993, 'The standardization of African languages', in *United Nations Group of Experts on Geographical Names Training Course in Toponymy for Southern Africa*, P.S. Hattingh, N. Kadmon, P.E. Raper, and I. Booysen (eds), University of Pretoria, Pretoria: 105–115.

Walton, C. (ed) 1984, *Reader's Digest Atlas of Southern Africa*, Reader's Digest Association, Cape Town.

www.ingramcontent.com/pod-product-compliance
Lightning Source LLC
Chambersburg PA
CBHW040934240426
43670CB00033B/2973